THE BIGGEST
FILM BIOGRAPHER
IN THE WORLD

Delancey Street Press
1133 Venice Blvd, Los Angeles, CA 90015
www.delanceystreetpress.com

Copyright © 2025 George Porcari

All rights reserved. No part of this book may be reproduced, stored in a retrieval system, or transmitted in any form or by any means without the prior written permission of copyright owner(s) and the above publisher of this book, except in the case of brief quotations embodied in critical articles or reviews.

Library of Congress Control Number 2019947992
ISBN 978-1-937357-84-9
Printed in the United States of America

Typeset in ABC Prophet

DESIGN AND ART DIRECTION BY JESSICA D'ELENA-TWEED

THE BIGGEST
FILM BIOGRAPHER
IN THE WORLD

THE FILMS OF KEN RUSSELL

GEORGE
PORCARI

Dedicated to
my family,
past, present
and future.

Contents

Introduction	**11**
1. The Exuberance of Influence	
2. Notes on the Text	
Three Short Films	**37**
The BBC 1 *Monitor and Omnibus*	**43**
The BBC 2 *Pop Goes the Easel*	**91**
The BBC 3 *Dante's Inferno: The Private Life of Dante Gabriel Rossetti, Poet and Painter*	**113**
The BBC 4 *Song of Summer*	**137**
Independence 1: From *French Dressing* to *Savage Messiah*	**151**

Independence 2: Russell and D.H. Lawrence	**175**
Independence 3: *The Devils*	**201**
Independence 4: *Mahler*	**223**
Independence 5: *Tommy*	**241**
Independence 6: *Gothic*	**261**
Hollywood Detour: Neo-Musicals, Neo-Noir, Neo-Horror and Neo-Realism	**273**
British Television Redux & Home Video	**319**
Index and Filmography	**408**

Passion paralyzes good taste.

SUSAN SONTAG
Journals and Notebooks, 1947-1963

Earth and sex
are in us –
outside there are
only stars.

JEAN-LUC GODARD
Hail Mary

Stéphane Mallarmé, the nineteenth century poet, described the process of adjusting to the world as 'a child abdicating his ecstasy.' I think it could be said that Ken Russell never abdicated his ecstasy.

ELIZE RUSSELL
Ken Russell: The Boy Behind the Man

An Exuberance of Influence

By the time Ken Russell arrived at the doorstep of the BBC in London in November of 1958 looking for work as a film director he was 32 years old, married with one child and another soon on the way - his job history was sketchy, his background was working class, and he had spent time in two of the British armed forces, the Merchant Navy and the Royal Air Force. Russell had made three short films that were his portfolio that got him in the door that day for a coveted job opening in the weekly series *Monitor*, the first regular arts program in England. At the time Russell was married to Shirley Ann a costume designer whom he had met in art school while he ostensibly worked as a photographer, teacher, and selling art in a gallery. They lived in South-East London in near poverty and with a growing family to feed the pressure was on to secure any steady employment. But what the BBC promised was not just any job but the prospect of joining a crew of directors for a highly prestigious and respected television show with wide viewership. Two of those BBC directors, Tony Richardson and John Schlesinger, were moving into feature films so the job was also seen as a springboard for eventual work in the film industry. Russell knew that his short films that got him the audition that day were very different from both the work being done by his peers in London, pushing for a confrontational moral realism, and from the older established generation that made genre films attuned to Hollywood's rule book. Russell's work was operating in a different universe of influences and confluences. In short, his job prospects looked like a long shot and there was good reason to be nervous.

Russell was born and raised in Southampton, Hampshire, then a sleepy port town, both close and very far from London – there is a ferry in the town (featured in his film *Road to Mandalay*) that takes you to the Isle of Wight. Russell's father, a shoe shop owner, was distant, irascible, and prone to sudden violent rages so he spent a lot of time at the local cinema with his mother who was mentally ill. He remembers being impressed by Fritz Lang's romantic fantasy *Die Nibelungen* (1924) and *Metropolis* (1927), but unsatisfied with the local theaters when he was a boy he took up projecting films in his parents' home. Russell: "As soon as I could walk I was seeing *Old Mother Riley* and *Flash Gordon* twice a week at the Picture House. My childhood companions were Felix the Cat and Betty Boop. I grew up cranking a *Pathescope Ace* projector throwing images of Harold Lloyd and Charlie Chaplin onto the dining-room wall. At the age of twelve I got hold of an old 35-mm projector and a trunkful of highly inflammable films and nearly burnt the house down. All further shows took place in the garage where a horn gramophone added luster to the silent films."[1] Russell points out how people, including his parents, went to see Lang's German films while they were at war with Germany and he even used the small amounts of money that he collected (to enter his garage) for the local war fund – but as Russell said: "art has no borders."[2] Elize Russell (Ken's fourth wife): "Essential to understanding Ken's work is that WWII and the subsequent Southampton Blitz of 1940 changed Ken's life when he was twelve. A munitions factory down the road made his neighborhood particularly vulnerable. The Luftwaffe made 57 attacks on the city. The water supply was ruined and fires were left to burn themselves out. The Conker tree in the back garden became his refuge and stage set and had been from an early age."[3]

Russell's only tragedy at this early stage, that left a lifelong trauma that he never got over, was the death of his beloved, "sunny and brave" cousin Marian, whose "presence in his life from birth to age thirteen was a source of unconditional love and joy."[4] In an interview shortly before he died Russell summed it up: "Marian's death is the one thing I have never reconciled. She was playing alone on the beach age thirteen and for some unknown reason ignored the warning signs and climbed a fence into a forbidden zone. A buried landmine went off and she was instantly killed. Her father, uncle Jack, immediately came over to tell us. For me, a light went out."[5]

Russell admitted the reason for joining the Merchant Navy was primarily so he wouldn't have to join his father's shoe shop. Another reason was because he fancied the films of Dorothy Lamour, a specialist in "sarong films," who had made him long fantasize about beautiful women in the South Seas.⁶ It makes a great deal of sense that films would have triggered his fantasy life to the extent that he would join the Navy - undoubtedly Ms. Lamour inspired many such acts of recklessness. Russell was discharged from the Navy for mental health reasons – labeled then "anxiety disorder." It was while convalescing that on the radio he heard Tchaikovsky's Piano Concerto No.1. Elize Russell: "As soon as Ken was captivated by classical composers, he was on his way. He knew his place. Images poured forth to accompany the music. His internal dialogue, flattened by nervous exhaustion was reinvigorated by music. His depression was vanquished."⁷ Russell was forced to shift to the Royal Air Force, to finish his tour of duty, but clearly the services were not for him.

His first ambition was to be a ballet dancer starting at the age of 20 – something he pursued for five years with some grudging success. He joined the Norsk Ballet Company under the tutelage of the Russian maestro Konstantin Sergeyev. He performed as the Toymaker in *Coppélia* and in *Swan Lake* and toured England with the chorus of *Annie Get Your Gun*. He then got a job at a gallery selling art but found he wasn't good at it. In his off hours he wandered the streets taking pictures with his Rolleicord camera doing street photography but also asking friends to pose, creating tableaus reminiscent of fashion work but with a gothic flair. As to be expected he was a fanatical filmgoer, but also a model train enthusiast, and, after discovering classical music he obsessively collected records, spending long hours listening to music. Aside from most of the British productions and the Hollywood films from the 1930's/1940's that were distributed in England, Russell also saw many newsreels, cartoons, coming attractions, and even silent films that were shown regularly in cinemas then. This conjunction of many different types of films being show on the same evening – then standard fare – arguably influenced his collage aesthetic.

There were no films schools then – The National Film School would not be founded until 1971, a year after Russell left the BBC - so after his adventures in the armed services Russell attended the South-West Essex School of Art, in Walthamstow where he studied photography, and where he met his first wife who was studying fashion design. By 1954 he was a practicing photographer working mostly for *Illustrated*, *Picture Post* (the British version of *Life* magazine), and the Sunday supplement section of various newspapers that always heavily featured photography – they were syndicated through Pictorial Press, an agency that got photographers work. These magazines – considered at the time disposable like newspapers - actually made it possible for a photographer to earn at least a modest living that he or she might supplement by part-time teaching, as did Russell. The demand for pictures was so high it gave opportunities not only to untried photographers like Russell but also to many women who wanted to get into the industry such as Jane Bown, the brilliant portraitist, who worked regularly for *The Guardian* and Penny Tweedie who worked in photojournalism for the magazine *Shelter*. It is not unusual for film directors to start out as photographers – Stanley Kubrick, Agnés Varda, and Chris Marker all began their careers similarly around the same time.

Russell photographed exposes on Teddy Girls and other current trends in popular culture on a regular basis but by the late fifties and early sixties television was beginning to make it obvious that the days of the picture magazines were numbered – everyone was scrambling including Russell. This is how the photo historian Martin Harrison described Russell's photos from the mid 1950's: "Russell was a one-off, a transitional figure whose work anticipated elements of the new photojournalism, although his most original photographs involved elaborate, theatrical scenarios that presage his film direction."[8] True to form during Russell's years as a professional photographer he used his talents to photograph everything from bicycle races to naked female models for *Men Only Magazine*. But Russell's passion was always directed toward the myth-making element of cinema, not the descriptive qualities of photojournalism or erotic photography. But from his work he was able to support a family and finance his short films. Russell, despite his self-deprecating sense of education, was self-taught about the arts, music and cinema. Russell: "When I'd tired of a Hollywood diet, I developed a more cosmopolitan palette and sampled the great chefs of Europe and Russia – Cocteau, Renoir, Vigo, Murnau, Pabst and Eisenstein. I lived and breathed films. I even dreamed film and wrote down the scenarios at breakfast. I lived in the dark."[9]

HUW WHELDON AND THE BBC
In 1959 Russell joined the *Monitor* team at the BBC helmed by Huw Wheldon who had been impressed by Russell's short *Amelia and the Angel* (1958) and decided to give him a shot. Of course as was common then there was an interview first at the local pub, in this case the Red Lion Pub on Ealing Green across the street from the BBC's Studios. Russell:

"I waved my wife goodbye and walked off into the winter mist feeling nervous and insecure. My whole future rested on this meeting. If Wheldon didn't like my style of filmmaking, who would? It was hopelessly unfashionable, the very antithesis of the "free cinema" championed by the British Film Institute...It was sink or swim. We lived in a haunted Regency house in South London that we couldn't afford to heat. We sat about in overcoats and lived on cod pie ...on the train from South Norwood to Victoria I wondered how I'd conduct myself during the interview. By nature I was shy and modest, not the best possible credentials for a career in the tough world of TV...I wondered what on earth I'd say if Wheldon asked me why I wanted to make films, as I felt sure he would. He'd probably scoff if I said films were my very life...I dragged my feet across the Common and found a quiet corner in the Red Lion where I sipped a pint of beer and kept by eyes peeled for him. What little I knew of Wheldon I'd picked up from reviews and opinions in the papers. He was about forty-five and an ex Welsh Guardsman with beetling brows, a charming but penetrating manner and a roguish face that lent itself to caricature. I'd once seen him depicted as Punch lambasting Judy (labeled "The Arts") with a big stick. Now it was my turn. I couldn't face him...I panicked, got up and knocked over my glass. What a fool! I caught his eye and gave a weak grin. "Russell?" Guilty, I nodded. He ordered another beer for me and shouted "Cheese sandwich?" The ice was broken, now all I had to do was fall through...At home, over a bottle of wine and what was to be our last fish pie ever I wondered aloud how on earth I'd landed such a plumb job after such an appalling interview. Shirley had the answer: He must have liked your films, muggings."[10]

Russell's decade long span of work at the BBC (1959-1970) constitutes one of the major bodies of cinematic work in the 20th century. The films (10 to 90 minutes) were first made for the series *Monitor* (1958-1965) and then for *Omnibus* (1966-1970). A list of some titles gives a hint of their depth and range: *Bartok* (1964), *The Dotty World of James Lloyd* (1964), *Scottish Painters* (1959), *Prokofiev: Portrait of a Soviet Composer* (1961), *Journey Into a Lost World: Mary McCarthy* (1960), *The Strange World of Hieronymus Bosch* (1960), *Shelagh Delaney's Salford* (1960), *Lotte Lenya Sings Kurt Weil,* (1961), *Daumier: a Double Life* (1961).

It was a dizzying pace — 36 films in 11 years (1959-1970) — made in conjunction with the work of the New-Wave movements that were worldwide phenomena but whose

shifting center of gravity was Paris – both in opposition to Hollywood and very much in tune with its history, that was seen as a playground to explore. Russell's films from that second Renaissance known as "the sixties" belongs alongside that body of work but is fundamentally, peculiarly British. Russell, ever the fox in his multifaceted approach, parodying many film styles in his body of work (as did Godard), including his funny and moving variant on the French New-Wave, *Don't Shoot the Composer* (1966). Russell assumed, like the young filmmakers in Paris, that all film styles were there to be *used*. Their approach was akin to Gustav Mahler's in that they wanted to get the whole world into their work and if the end result seemed somewhat raw, dense, contradictory, inchoate, juvenile, confused or disparate– this was a price well worth paying for the end result - this book is about that result and how Russell got there.

Ken Russell's career at *Monitor* started with *John Betjeman: A Poet in London*, a 12 minute black and white documentary on the little known contemporary English poet. Russell's first film that dealt with music, a subject that would preoccupy him for the rest of his life, was *Gordon Jacob* (1959), a film that profiled the obscure English composer, teacher, and music historian. The first longer and more substantial film in his *Monitor* series was *Prokofiev: Portrait of a Soviet Composer* (1961) - this is the film that Russell considered his first real biography and where he found his voice. Between early 1959 and late 1962 when he first achieved worldwide recognition with the groundbreaking *Elgar* Russell made 21 short documentaries in the most prolific period of his career.

Monitor was a Huw Wheldon production - he had conceived it, hired all of the creative talent that made it work, and wrote and delivered his own voiceover narration for almost all of the programs regardless of who wrote or directed. It was a popular show, coming on at Sunday evenings at 9:30PM – an adult time slot - being one of the few things on the BBC that was challenging and unusual. Russell:

> "Huw went on liking my films for many years, some more than others, but whatever his personal feelings he always helped polish my rough diamonds till they glittered. And when I disappointed him with a paste job, he worked even harder to make it shine – shaping and reshaping, cutting and chipping away until it was ready for his sparkling commentary. To start with I just used to sit next to him over a

> Moviola simply supplying the facts, but bit by bit he began dragging words, phrases, even sentences out of me which I never thought I possessed. It was painful. All the other directors in the program had university degrees. I knew how to navigate and tie a double sheep's bend, and I knew a bit about the arts and that was all. But my education proper began at the age of thirty-two with Huw Wheldon."

In the early stages it took Russell time to reach maturity as an artist but he caught up fast. He was fortunate in having Wheldon as his producer, who would prove to be an ideal mentor. Wheldon was down-to-earth to a fault, knew his film history inside and out, was open minded, intelligent, and had a sense of humor. For an unschooled maverick filmmaker from the wrong side of the tracks like Russell, who was trying to find his way, Wheldon was the right teacher at the right time. Russell returned the favor years later, dedicating his autobiography, *A British Picture* (1989), "With thanks to Huw Wheldon." He knew that without Wheldon there would have been no "Ken Russell, film director."

For Wheldon the new documentaries for the BBC, using black and white 35mm film, were to be free of the stodginess and talking heads that were a regular feature of programming in the post-war era. By then these conventions were beginning to look old fashioned and contrived, and the new work, as envisioned by the team, would be more dynamic, using lighter, more flexible equipment, and quick cutting, common to Cinéma Vérité, and the New Wave films coming from France. In short, they would be "modern" biographies of major artists, writers, and composers, concentrating on British lives but not limited to them. There was to be a voice over narration that was explicitly an authorial voice, as was typical of documentaries then and now, and there was to be use of historical material made available through the vast BBC archives.

For some people at the BBC, such as Wheldon, Russell was a welcome breath of fresh air, someone who was set to revitalize its mission and its brand, while bringing in younger viewers, along with college educated professionals looking for more adventurous fare. This was exactly the audience the BBC was after. But for others Russell was a provocateur, a loose cannon who would, sooner or later, get himself and the BBC into trouble. This is precisely what happened in 1970 but by then Russell was already an established filmmaker who needn't look back but forward to some of his best work.

THE ENGINEERS

It is worth remembering that the major power brokers in the early days of television, both in England and elsewhere, were not exclusively the producers, writers or directors, but the engineers. The technology was in its infancy and very complicated, demanding, and finicky. Engineers liked a lot of light so everything would be clear and visible – so much light that very often makeup had to be applied to both men and women so their features would not completely wash out. They preferred low contrast 35mm film that would provide a wide variety of grays but no deep blacks that sometimes took on the quality of objects on-screen, even if they were shadows, or pure whites that tended to at times create a flash effect. They even turned the knob on the controls during broadcasting to tone down the contrast further. By the 1960's directors such as John Schlesinger, Lindsay Anderson and, of course, Russell, were challenging the authority of engineers in search of a more cinematic approach. Russell liked high contrast and at times, as in *Dante's Inferno*, pushed it in the lab. He also liked to be present during screenings of his work at the master controls of the BBC to make sure those engineers did not turn the contrast knob down. When one engineer actually dared to do so in his presence Russell slapped the man's hand.[11] Power was clearly shifting to the director, something that was also happening in feature filmmaking, particularly in Europe where the director was seen not only as the ultimate authority during the shoot but the final "author" even if there were writers, cinematographers, designers and actors whose input was essential.

Usually there were a few short documentary segments that filled that one hour slot for *Monitor*, but in rare times there would be one film that would take up the entire segment. These coveted longer works were reserved for veteran filmmakers like John Schlesinger, who had, independently, made the short film *Terminus* (1961), one of the landmark films of the Free Cinema movement as actors mixed freely with travelers in Waterloo Station in London providing a cultural portrait of the city in an important transitional moment. Schlesinger followed this up with *A Kind of Loving* (1962), one of the feature films from the Kitchen Sink School that actually enjoyed international success, jump-starting his career as a feature filmmaker. Unfortunately Schlesinger would not follow up this beautiful, sensitive, hybrid of reality and fiction that he had mastered, preferring to move to Hollywood to make genre films. Schlesinger's departure from *Monitor* left an opening for one of the in-house directors to make longer, more ambitious films with bigger budgets – this spot was filled by Russell.

In Russell's tenure at the BBC some of the subjects were chosen by him and he wrote the script such as *Elgar* and *A House in Bayswater* while others were projects with scripts ready to go that were handed to him, such as *Scottish Painters* and *The Strange World of Hieronymus Bosch*. Wheldon left Russell alone during the shoot but supervised all aspects of post-production and wrote his own introduction and narration to each film that he would deliver directly facing the camera or in voiceover. The *Monitor* documentaries typically featured one artist, poet, composer or writer but there were some that featured a theme. Some examples of Russell's early thematic work: *From Spain to Streatham* (1959) looked at the guitar craze sweeping England in the wake of the success of Spanish guitar music, made popular by Andrés Segovia, and the success of the Skiffle movement in England, that greatly influenced the Beatles and other bands then coming up. *The Light Fantastic* (1960) looked at traditional and modern dance forms sharing the spotlight in theaters around London.

Arguably the most unusual thematic film for the BBC that Russell made was *Lonely Shore* (1962), scripted by archeologist Jacquetta Jawkes. The 16 minute film is a post apocalyptic science fiction faux documentary that imagines a team of alien archaeologists visiting Earth and sifting through the artifacts and rubble that have washed ashore on a deserted beach. One of the things they find is Van Gogh's *Sunflowers* partially destroyed by the sea that gives us good idea of the level of destruction that has taken place as the painting becomes a synecdoche for a nuclear war that has already taken place, but it also shows the importance of art in Russell's world view as the emotional impact of human destruction is delivered in the form of a painting. *Lonely Shore* is the closest that Russell ever came to making a Surrealist film – a strong influence that always found its way into his work although more often than not with a strong sense of British self-deprecating irony that took the air out of any pretensions.

FREE CINEMA AND KITCHEN SINK
Russell, despite his misgivings, in the early stages of his work was heavily influenced by The Free Cinema and Kitchen Sink movements, that in 1959 were in full swing, mixing documentary and staged scenes to the point it was impossible to tell where one began and the other ended. With Free Cinema actors who had been given a character and a situation intermixed with people in social situations that were real and the actors then improvised freely. These short films were often shot silent and then recordings were made on site so the image and the sound might very well be from the same place

but did not match exactly with the image. Free Cinema films invariably had little or no budget, no screenplay, were shot on 16mm, using small crews often consisting of the director and the cinematographer. The feel and texture of reality were more important that the technical finesse of professional standards, that were consciously avoided, that is, no attempt was made to mimic them using basic equipment. The amateur aspect was emphasized rather than concealed – an aspect of filmmaking that Russell always treasured. While influenced by Neorealism these films went much further, as the Italian work was still tied to elements of melodrama, conventional establishing shots, and traditional musical cues. With films like Tony Richardson's *Mama Don't Allow* (1956), and Karel Reisz's *We Are the Lambeth Boys* (1959) British cinema dove into the deep end of the New-Wave moments across the globe mixing avant-garde cinema, Neorealism, and the close observation of ethnographic films.

Kitchen Sink Films got that sobriquet due to the fact that dirty kitchen sinks piled high with dishes had not been seen before in the genteel and fantasy laden post-war films from England and the US – what the Italians derisively called "white telephone films." But suddenly with the Kitchen Sink Films those clogged and filthy sinks were front and center, and people took notice. Kitchen Sink films were typically done with traditional crews of about six people, 35mm film, a screenplay, and professional actors often taken from the stage. The writers who provided the screenplays for Kitchen Sink works were part of the "angry young man" movement in the theater in England led by John Osborne and his now classic play *Look Back in Anger* (1956). Their work was motivated by a desire to eradicate the staid, polite, traditions of British novels, theater and cinema by introducing a harsh realism, so people spoke – or in some cases remained painfully silent – as they did in real life, using slang, obscene language, non-sequiturs, and vulgar double meanings. The writers used actual contemporary neighborhoods rather than fictional locations, speech rather than rhetoric, and episodes rather than stories. Kitchen Sink and the "angry young man" movements were principled and belligerent – like their counterparts in painting (Abstract Expressionism) and philosophy (existentialism) there were elements of frustration, anger and despair that were exposed as open wounds – all seen as part of the life-struggle in the face of oblivion. Russell was open to this approach and, particularly in his early work, contributed to the aesthetic pluralism that flowered in the sixties and came into its own.

But as the sixties wound down, taking many casualties along the way - as creatively explosive periods are prone to doing – Kitchen Sink fell from favor and also moved into color, expanding its borders to include fantasy and the musical, in films such as *All the Right Noises* (1971), *Quadrophenia* (1979), *Hard Labor* (1973), and *Oh Lucky Man* (1973) among others, in effect shifting to a more streetwise, New-Wave approach also common to the New Hollywood. It is exactly in this period that Russell moved into independence as a filmmaker, becoming in one sense, a gun for hire, always on the prowl for work.

KALEIDOSCOPIC NON-LINEAR NARRATIVES

Russell's cinema was always a place of contradictions – he described his films from the 1960's as "kaleidoscopic biopics"[12] and it is this "kaleidoscopic" or collage aspect that made the works fresh and modern. Needing to squeeze a great deal of information into short films he compressed the material saturating every shot with multiple meanings, even if these contradicted themselves. In his work of the sixties Russell would establish the form of the film based on the subject rather than have a preconceived format or concept. As Russell put it, "the form of the film would be dictated by the biographical subject."[13] For example, *Elgar* would be romantic, reserved, elegiac, melancholic, and heavily feature the landscape of the English Midlands, whereas *Shelagh Delaney's Salford* was fast paced, and done in the style of Kitchen-Sink using everyday sounds for punctuation rather than music. Delaney, despite her youth, was one of Kitchen Sink's most honored members with her successful play (eventually made into a film by Tony Richardson) *A Taste of Honey* (1961). Most documentaries, then and now, are primarily concept-driven and the subjects are slotted into pre-existing templates – this is why Russell's work seemed unusual from the get-go because what he wanted was an improvisation with his subject more akin to jazz than to the rules of documentary narrative.

The strange thing about improvisation (in jazz or elsewhere) is that mistakes are not only allowed but welcome - the reason is that they open up new areas to explore that were hitherto not considered that are often more interesting or profound than the original idea. Herbie Hancock, the jazz pianist, recalls playing live with Miles Davis in the 1960's and, during a particularly difficult passage, making a mistake that was very obvious and embarrassing – Davis simply used the "mistake" to go in that direction, treating it like an open door rather than a pothole on the road that best be avoided.[14] Of course there

was no way to know what was on the other side of the door that Hancock had opened but Davis was game – he simply said (with his playing) "let's explore this." Russell was exploring as well and so the subjects, particularly if they were living artists, such as Shelagh Delaney, Georges Delerue, or Pauline Boty consequently had a great deal of input into the form of the film as they improvised with Russell and the team to create the film as they went along, but always having a strong script as a base or foundation.

As the sixties rolled on Russell learned fast and was soon ahead of the game – in his work the hard realities of the life and the brutal history and politics of the period are often expressed in Kitchen Sink style, while, in the same film, the personal connections, or love story aspect, were depicted as a drama that is pushed to hysterical levels normally seen only in Restoration plays, that is, they are bursting with fury, sarcasm, a theatrical sexuality, and dark, morbid cruelties. Of course this was all offset by a crucial element in all of the BBC work: the calm, reasonable, British male voiceover that explained the situation and the historical circumstances, often completely contradicting the characters, or interrupting them to show photographs and paintings of the period to put things in perspective. In that sense Russell's work was an exemplary version of corporeal cinema, that is, films that deal with tangible physical realities – even prosaic or crude ones – in a direct, sometimes brutal manner. While corporeal cinema offers a wide range – from The Marx Brothers to Michelangelo Antonioni - corporeal cinema also stands at the opposite end of what Paul Schrader called the "transcendental style" in film exemplified (for him) with the work of Ozu, Bresson and Dreyer.

Russell also took advantage of the vast photo and film documentary archives available at the BBC and incorporated it regularly into his films – since much of this work was silent he would edit to music cues that would often go on for some time. Russell then orchestrated all of these varying styles – documentary, fake documentary, comedy, found footage, theatrical set-pieces, improvised scenes, tableaus, photographs, into a cohesive collage, held together by the interplay, or the tension, between the subject and the constantly shifting narrative. The films, in effect, were polyphonic, that is, they existed on several layers at once like a palimpsest.

This layered, non-linear narrative that Russell constructed would be a major contribution to the film arts. What made Russell such a great filmmaker is that he did not suppress any

of these very contradictory qualities found in his work or try to bring them into line, but simply assumed that they could all share the same crowded set at the same time in the same film – *anything* was game but mindless good taste. In that respect at least he was closer to Benny Hill (a childhood neighbor in Southampton) than to David Lean. Lean's epic cinema was breathtakingly handsome and solid but messy reality, with its absurdities, inscrutable mysteries, loose ends, and nonsense - was nowhere to be found. Benny Hill's outrageous television work put them all back into the public consciousness with his spirited reinvention of vaudeville and music hall for the TV era. A life included the whole of human experience and Russell orchestrated the mélange like a mad conductor on set - and then a second time in the editing room, finessing the finer points creating "auteurist biopics" (Brian Hoyle) that he would elaborate and expand upon over the course of his long career.

The primary lesson that Russell learned from his early days when he had only 12 minutes to make a film was to condense his work to the point of abstraction and Russell was well aware of the trajectory he was pushing toward, that is, the dissolution of narrative itself. The radical condensation of content in Russell's work was similar in some ways to that found in a trailer, that is, a one or two minute film that is usually plot-less and leaves a lot of open questions and suggestive dangling clues that beg for answers. This "film trailer aesthetic" was something Russell used as an early influence and eventually turned into a *method*. Russell:

> "People are saying to me your films are too concentrated. Well, that's the way they are, and that's the way they're going to be. I think the one thing that Godard did that was any good was to scrap continuity in Breathless. That was a great leap forward. Hollywood films all seem so slow and tedious and boring to me. I think they are the death of film. Film wants to get more concentrated than ever. We're just on the borders of trying to get towards what it can be. I think it's got to get so concentrated that in the end you don't know what it's about. It's gone right within you, and you've got something out of it but you're not quite sure what. That's what I'm interested in doing."[15]

The great advantage of this concentrated abstraction is that the images can, to some extent, enter into the consciousness of his subjects in a way not available to conventional

narrative that is bound to exposition. To Russell's credit he not only did that on a regular basis but he expanded upon it over time throughout the 1960's. By the end of that period people very often didn't know "what it was about" but it had gone right within them.

THE 1960's: COUNTER CULTURE
The works that Russell made for the BBC in the 1960's chart his artistic maturity but they are inconceivable without the cultural and counter-cultural input from various fronts that were a constant throughout the 1960's. Many people who were fortunate enough to live through this second Renaissance explain that it was as if one were being constantly bombarded not only by great new music, films and books, as one would expect, but also by graphics, textile design, television, fashion, photography, shop displays, and advertising. This brilliant work seemed to be coming from all directions at once – it was a confusing, overwhelming, and energizing period. Throughout the 1960's there was an impatience with belles-lettres, and the sclerotic canons of high-art, classical music, and studio films, coinciding with a greater personal and political engagement, an invasion of informality, experimentation, and improvisation. Narrative films, for once, shared the stage with non-narrative works and culture and counter culture played their tunes in the same park creating a cacophony that drove some people crazy.

This was a cinematic era that coincided with the slow death of the old studio system, before it arose from the dead – a zombie dream factory. Hollywood rose up again in the 1970's with strong independent films – referred to as the New Hollywood – such as *Mean Streets, Wanda, Five Easy Pieces,* and *A Woman Under the Influence*; but it was also a return to spectacle (*Jaws*), melodrama (*Rocky*), adventure (*Indiana Jones*), and serialization (*Star Wars*). Eventually the genres used by "the industry," as the locals call it, became the template of a new entertainment industrial complex, based in Los Angeles, that ruled the world – even the independent New Hollywood maestros eventually buckled under and joined the winning team, making extravaganzas for mass audiences (Scorsese's *The Aviator*, Coppola's *The Cotton Club*, Hellman's *Silent Night, Deadly Night 3*, Rafelson's *Black Widow*). This was the rough and dangerous terrain that Russell entered as he shifted from the BBC to feature films.

Interestingly, something similar happened to the Fine Arts, that is, like Hollywood it began its slow, painful death spiral in the 1970's as Pop Art, minimalism and conceptual art entered the prescribed narratives outlined by institutions and the "free market."

Once Fine Art hit the ground its various pieces – a zombie arts – wandered the landscape looking for a home. If Fine Art found the anodyne Gallery/Museum to be a safe refuge, art itself seemed to do just fine: Sometimes people called it "photojournalism," "graffiti," "advertising," or "movies" and at others it was "graphic design," or "illustration;" a few times (granted very few) art even happened under the guise of "television." Russell figures in this last category along with a handful of writer/directors that worked regularly for British television such as Jonathan Miller (who adapted Plato and Mozart operas for the modern era), Alun Owen (who wrote *A Hard Day's Night*), Jane Arden (who made feminist avant-garde films), Jack Bond (who made avant-garde documentaries and music videos), Nigel Kneale (the Rod Serling of England), Dennis Potter (who combined musicals with historical analysis), Peter Cook and Dudley Moore (who re-invented sketch humor as a form of anarchic criticism), along with the Python gang (that re-iterated that criticism but added Dadaist absurdity). These people rewrote the history of the TV medium, taking it to the level of an art form on a par with the auteur cinema of the period.

THE STUDIO FILM: LE CINEMA DE PAPA
What these television artists were seeking to do was to overthrow, in one way or another, the conventional studio style of making films. Sergei Eisenstein explained in his essay on Charles Dickens that the basic traditional story arcs used in studio films came from the 19th century European novel; but in this reformatting to cinema the studios astutely (from a financial perspective) left out the social critiques (Zola, Flaubert), the questions of sex and class (Austen, the Bronte's) and the sometimes elliptical or episodic narrative digressions (Sterne, Stendhal) found in 19th European narratives. In effect the work of many writers (Joyce, Woolf, Dos Passos, Cummings) were more adventurous, and in some cases more *cinematic* than the feature films made by the studios that relied on easy-to-read narrative arcs and emotional cues, along with recognizable stock character types.

Most conventional films had 90 minutes to tell a story coherently to a mass audience who were in many cases uneducated and had never read a novel or seen a play – film structure was at the service of the story. The studio film became expert at a particular kind of entertainment that serviced or managed the psychological anxieties of a growing middle-class. These templates did not so much dissipate fears but (to quote Paul Virilio) "administrated" them. The fundamental framework of conventional narratives or stories is that life makes sense – while it might at times be confusing, painful, or even incomprehensible at the end it will resolve itself and we will reach an understanding. The fundamental framework of collage or countercultural narratives from the 1960's – from Antonioni to Robbe-Grillet and from Duras to Godard – is that reality doesn't care about your need to know, your narrative, or your framework – the mysteries of fundamental reality are located elsewhere and beyond the scope of reason or any narrative that might try to explain it, classify it, or categorize it – our very DNA just isn't up to it. To even speak about reality coherently required a poetics that must (by design or by default) leave narrative behind. The radical counter-cultural work of the sixties saw an opening for a new kind of more abstract work that had a point-of-view that was critical, off-center, contradictory, political, absurdist, self-referential, and anti authoritarian, often venturing into uncharted waters.

While there were exceptions to the mediocrity of studio films made in England, such as *Brief Encounter* (1945) and *A Matter of Life and Death* (1946) the great majority of films made by the British studios in the post-war era were hackneyed, cliché ridden, and lacked a sense of real time and place. It is this studio work that Francoise Truffaut in 1954, with his then youthful bravado and sarcasm, called "le cinema de papa."[16] Russell was something of an expert on British cinema, eventually writing a fine book about its history, *Fire Over England: The British Cinema Comes Under Friendly Fire* (1993). Here is Russell describing these studio works from his youth and succinctly identifying the problem: "There were the Ealing Film Studios where all those overrated comedies that give such a bogus view of British life were churned out – and studios like Riverside and Hammersmith where upper-class musicals like *Spring in Park Lane* and *Maytime in Mayfair* were artificially inseminated into being."[17] "Whether the location was Lavender Hill, Kentish Town, Pimlico or Mayfair, it was usually the same set revamped on the back lot. The characters were interchangeable. Most of those films were weak situation comedies in search of an identity."[18] Russell here very astutely pinpoints the problem – not a lack of craft or acting talent, that in England were in abundance, but of identity – this mirrored Truffaut's criticism of French cinema in the same period.

A FIELD

The French New Wave was at the forefront of the new counter-cultural cinema replacing continuity editing, narrative logic, and linear time progression with a *field*. In this new domain the filmmaker could try out various ideas, and use different styles and forms playing them off as in counterpoint – she could jump time periods, genres, or points-of-view at any point. In this new atmosphere images and narrative shifted easily from quietly observational to artfully staged - it was simultaneously Brechtian and intimate, ironic and heart-on-sleeve, plotted and fragmentary in style. Stories (in the plural sense) could move between humor, horror, absurdity and visceral truth telling, as easily as shifting gears in a car. This aesthetic was then grounded in an impassioned realism that often mimicked the documentary, italicizing the present moment, regardless of the genre(s) being deployed – Godard famously said that he shot *À Bout de Souffle* in the style of a documentary about a gangster film but using the Parisian landscape in the Spring of 1959 like a painter.[19] But while the masters of the New-Wave were deeply influenced in their collage aesthetic by modernist novels (except perhaps for Eric Rohmer who went his own way with Goethe's *Elective Affinities,* Flaubert's *A Simple Heart* and *Sentimental Education,* and Maupassant's richly moral panorama of Paris). Russell was more in tune with modernist and populist cinema, television, painting and photography.

KEN FRANKENSTEIN

At the BBC Russell's ability to make the work that he wanted to took a span of years – at first he "was not allowed to show them (the main subjects) as we had to show just photographs. It was a very purist documentary. One had all the boredom of two decades of English documentary behind one to shake."[20] As Russell pushed for more freedom to create the work he envisioned, putting fiction and documentary on the same plane so they could be orchestrated in counterpoint, Wheldon pushed back. The struggle between them reaches the comical with *Prokofiev: Portrait of a Soviet Composer*. Russell:

> "There was no film in existence on Prokofiev so I built up a picture of his life from Soviet propaganda films and old Russian newsreels. I also had still photographs of the composer but I wanted him in motion. Huw heard about it and there was a confrontation. 'I gather we're planning to get out the dressing-up basket again?' This time I've got better actors, I said. 'Assuming that you have, how do you propose to integrate them with all of this old archive material?' By degrading the material I shoot myself so that it looks as grainy and contrasty as the real thing, I said. Wheldon replied: 'That's immoral! You're deliberately setting out to deceive the public. I'm going go to forbid you to have an actor impersonating Prokofiev and pass him off as the real man!'"[21]

Russell then asked if he might shoot the hands of the composer playing the piano, or his reflection in a pond? "So long as it's a murky pond and the water is rippling' he said. In the event, I was allowed to show the feet and the back of his head as well. These shots, combined with genuine photographs convinced many of the audience that they had actually seen the man himself. In reality he was a collection of bits and pieces – a pianist's hands, an actor's back, a friend's feet: Ken Frankenstein had made his first monster."[22]

This "monster" *Prokofiev: Portrait of a Soviet Composer* (1961) is the first film where Russell finds his own voice and where he shifts, ever so slightly, from making documentary films into the realm of collage and the essay film, which we will expand on shortly; but it would be in *Elgar* where he would reinvent the biographical film in a more direct, systematic way and get his first taste of international recognition. Russell was not alone in re-inventing staid genres – as often happens inventions are in the air and many people get the idea at the same time, particularly in the 1960's when genre films were fundamentally re-invented by filmmakers who abandoned the studio system: From the reinvention of the romantic adventure film in Antonioni's *L'Avventura* (1960) to the biblical epic in Pasolini's *The Gospel According to St. Matthew* (1964), from the musical in Demy's *Young Girls of Rochefort* (1967) to the melodrama in Varda's *Le Bonheur* (1965), from the western in Jodorowski's *El Topo* (1970) to the documentary in Fellini's *A Director's Notebook* (1969), and from film noir in Truffaut's *Shoot the Piano Player* (1960) to the science fiction film in Godard's *Alphaville* (1965), the era was rife with masterpieces – hence the term second Renaissance. Any Renaissance, by its very nature, is bound to be unique, fragile, wondrous, explosive, and short-lived. If one is fortunate enough to have lived through such a historical period one understands its contingencies, vulnerabilities and its overwhelming emotional power that leaves one dazed and often confused.

THE ESSAY AND COLLAGE FILM
Elgar (1962) ventures into the essay and the collage film, which is why it was so revolutionary – formats that Russell would develop and master over the next decade. The first essay film is arguably Chris Marker's *Letter From Siberia* (1957). There had been travelogue films to distant lands (distant to Europeans) and there had been ethnographic films, but Marker's work goes in a different direction while he clearly avails himself of both genres, treating them as a *style*. The form is simple: a voiceover reads letters from

Siberia in French to a friend, presumably back at home in France, describing the place while we see 16mm color footage of Siberia shot in 1957 by Marker. The letter being read is at times prosaic, at times poetic, and at others personal – sometimes it corresponds to the image and at others it does not – it is highly individualized, no attempt is made to give an "objective" tone to the voiceover as was (and is) usually the case with documentaries. In effect the letter becomes the equal of the images but is not bound to them – the result is more a poem about Siberia than a documentary. Andre Bazin, the critic for *Cahier du Cinema* at the time of its release wrote a review: "*Letter From Siberia* is like absolutely nothing that we have ever seen before in films with a documentary basis. It is an essay on the reality of Siberia past and present in the form of a filmed report. The important word is 'essay,' understood in the same sense that it has in literature."[23] Henceforth there would now be something called the "essay film" that Marker would turn to repeatedly in his work, making variations on it, some simple and amusing (*Perched Cats*) and others highly complex and multi-layered (*Sans Soleil*). In short, the straight documentary always points outward while the essay film points outward and inward at the same time – something only possible in poetry.

Aside from the essay film with *Elgar* Russell also ventured into collage films, one of the main strands of avant-garde cinema from Joseph Cornell's *Rose Hobart* (1936) to Mary Mencken's *Go! Go! Go!* (1964). A collage film is a created by juxtaposing found and/or original footage from disparate sources – treating it as raw material - such as newsreels, home movies, educational films, Hollywood spectacles, etc. and creating a new, often plot-less, often humorous, work based around a theme. Mediums are never passive and always bring baggage with them - collage film is no different, being a series of fragmentary forms on a "ground" made not from paper or canvas but from time. In collage there is no whole, no completion, no totality as there is in classical art, there are only provisional *fragments* therefore we never have a complete picture of the world – collage exists in a state of transit, in a state of *immanence*.

Collage is the fundamentally anti-classical form that Russell would develop, and *integrate* into the classical narrative documentary film, with *Elgar* in 1962 – that is why the film was radical. This is in many ways analogous to Godard's integration of the jump cut into feature films with *À Bout de Souffle*. Where we find justification for using the term collage is Russell's use of found footage from the BBC archives, particularly *Elgar's* 11 minute sequence that at times uses ships sailing, or zeppelins flying over London, or pedestrians getting on a bus, that are not in any sense illustrating either Elgar's biography or his music – but they are very much in *dialog* with both thereby creating a film poetics most often called collage. In a collage film the various genres being deployed are not simply there to shock or to amuse (although they might do both) but they are in dialogue with each other – riffing on each other without the need for traditional narrative, existing in a state of inter-textual awareness. There is a great fraternity or community of metaphors in play, and that is why the poetics of collage have no need of narrative as such – it can generate different readings and different meanings without ever reaching a conclusion, like a work of art. In Russell's work the narrative flow occasionally gives way to extended lyrical meditations set to music, that is, the narrative drama, the "prose," gives way to "poetry." It is then up to the viewer to decide on the strict meaning the work might have since, due to the sheer density of material, the films are open to various interpretations.

BBC: THE END OF THE LINE

Russell's tenure at the BBC ended on a high note in 1970 with his first color film, a one hour biography on the life of Richard Strauss, *Dance of the Seven Veils: a Comic Strip in 7 Episodes on the Life of Richard Strauss (1864-1949)*. The film was, as the title makes explicit, a cartoonish, over the top, highly personal interpretation of Strauss' life and work. Unfortunately the Strauss family was horrified by the film and refused to let the music be used, going so far as to sue the producers, knowing that without the music the film could not be shown. The matter went to the courts where it was decided to shelve the work for fifty years. Russell's contract for the BBC was allowed to quietly expire. This was the beginning of Russell's reputation as an enfant-terrible – a situation that he enjoyed as it gave him a wider audience, providing Russell with an immediately recognizable style, akin to Fellini or Bergman; but the tag was a double-edged sword as producers and money people were shy around a director whose work could be so controversial that it was actually withdrawn for half a century. The BBC could easily withstand the financial loss but other producers might think twice, and he was always fighting and using up creative energy to get funding that would at times be pulled out at the last minute when the producers discovered Russell's "terrible" past.

Russell's post BBC work would sometimes degenerate into bombastic caricature, as in *Lisztomania*, a biography of Franz Liszt, or *The Boy Friend*, a pastiche of Busby Berkeley musicals, that were certainly humorous and visually imaginative – Russell was never lazy

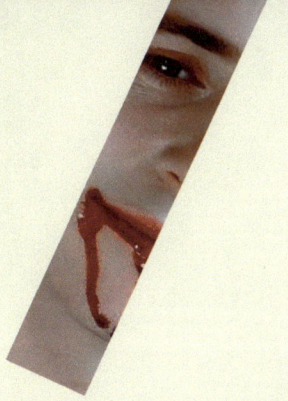

even with work he was doing only for money - but many of the later works lacked the depth of the writing found in the films from his days at the BBC. As the work went further into pastiche and parody, with films like *Crimes of Passion,* they also lost the thread of the corporeal element that had made those works of his BBC period so unusual, breathtaking, and radical. It was almost as if the overwrought and self-conscious nudity of his later work were a form of compensation for that missing corporeal element — but once it left it simply never came back.

While the latter films certainly had an abundance of visual fireworks and assertive confidence the early BBC work had something more important, namely, doubt. Each of the *Monitor/Omnibus* works is as study in ambivalence, in uncertainty. They *modestly* subverted their own certainties leaving room for ambiguity — the films could breathe on their own and seemed to create their own world that questioned our reality. In this respect they belonged to the rich tradition of European literature (*The Castle, Death on Credit, The Erasers, The Book of Laughter and Forgetting, Austerlitz*) and cinema (*The Rules of the Game, La Notte, The Other Side of the Underneath, Herostratus, The Night Porter*) that upset dogmas and questioned fixed positions — in such works everyone has their reasons, their histories, their inscrutable psychic dramas, and their worldview.

Another crucial missing element in Russell's work that was sorely missed after his tenure at the BBC was the inclusion of archival documentary films — material that he would often mimic with fake documentary footage and then integrate into the editing process creating a seamless whole. This aspect made the films original and emotionally involving, transforming the way we think of documentaries or the presentation of "reality" on screen by bringing the collage aspect to the foreground. Other directors came after Russell to this collage aesthetic (Pasolini, Tarkovsky, Fellini, Godard) but they explored and exploited it more thoroughly and with greater consistency. The BBC works audaciously plundered the art of the past, deploying an immersive, poetic, non-linear narrative, what Russell called a "kaleidoscopic condensation" that seems to have gone missing in his later films, replaced by pastiche, ironic asides, and naughty jokes.

But Russell was not short of ideas and he continued to make films that he financed himself, and shot on video, such as *The Fall of the Louse of Usher* (2002) based on Poe's short story but changing "House" to "Louse" in a typically broad gesture of comic anarchy. The later films incorporated music and droll comedy, emphasizing the artificiality

of the sets and costumes, and exaggerating the absurdities of the horror, ever present in his work. In these final films he also kept a more insistent, mordant eye on the absurdity of the human condition and the brevity of life. He died at the age of 84 in 2011 from a heart attack in Lymingnton, England a port town in the Hampshire area close to where he was born; true to form, he was in pre-production for a revenge film to be titled *Kings X* as well as an adaptation of *Alice in Wonderland*.

Whatever the shortcomings of his later work in Russell's best films there was what we might call, with apologies to Harold Bloom, an *exuberance of influence* that delighted audiences because it challenged them to understand places, times, and people that were as complex, intriguing and curious as themselves – it put their own era into some perspective. From the vantage point of the early millennium Russell's best work looks more modern, more engaging, more intelligent, and more *alive* than anything in contemporary media or cinema. Those films are teeming with a sense of immediacy and vitality and, in spite of the didacticism inherent in the initial project, at least as it was originally conceived by the BBC, there is still much that we can learn from them.

A TRAVELING PREACHER

In an interview from 2008, looking back on his long career, Russell suggested a motivation for his early passionate work, and that was his desire to get the word out about artists and composers that he loved and that had changed his own life for the better. Russell early on realized that certain great works that one comes into contact with, regardless of their original place and time, regardless of their intentions, do not simply entertain, educate, or amuse, (all fine things) but they re-wire your brain. The scope of what you can see or hear, or understand, expands, and you are, in effect, a different person after seeing certain paintings, reading certain books, or listening to certain music – you tap into a collective source of creativity and understanding that transcends rational discourse, in a sense bypassing the academic aspect of art, music or cinema. But for this process to happen the viewer needs to cooperate, needs to want to go beyond herself – to self-transcend in a sense - and to see that project as the adventure of a lifetime.

Of course for each person the works that will cause this epiphany are different. Russell was always more attracted to Romantic (with a capital "R") artists and composers. He was always more keen on Ralph Vaughan Williams and Arnold Bax, two unrepentant

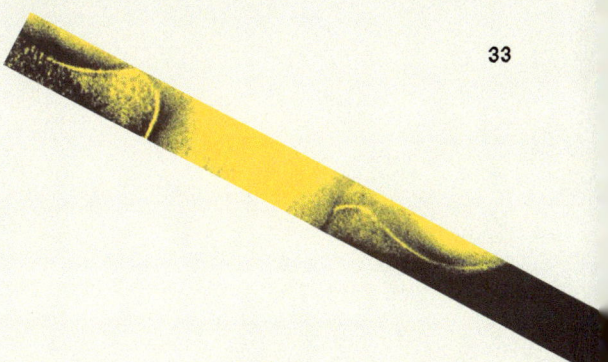

20th-century British Romantics that he devoted films to, than on Arnold Schoenberg and Karlheinz Stockhausen (a contemporary of Russell's), two unrepentant modernists. But he understood that you don't choose your artistic loves, but rather, in a sense, they choose you – you find each other in the eternity of time and hold on for dear life – and then you enter into a relationship that changes over time (as relationships are wont to do). This lifelong love affair, with its many ups and downs, breakups and reconciliations, leads to forming links to other artists, composers, writers and filmmakers, in a series of ever expanding relations, eventually forming a family of sorts. This fragile chain of being can also be a path or clearing - a measure of our humanity. To his credit Russell was also not averse to modern classical music and made a sympathetic portrait of Bela Bartok, as part of his BBC work. He was willing to listen but he had by the 1960's already formed his "family."

For Russell, in effect, works of art (like religion) can save you, that is, they can show you a portion of yourself that you would not have discovered otherwise – thereby saving you from remaining unfulfilled, incomplete and without a cultural family from which to draw on when one is suffering, searching, or simply looking for a light in the dark. While your biological family may be problematic, or worse, the family you carry with you, of the work you love, is always there when things get bleak. Great works can also prevent you from falling for the fake work of art or the fake piece of music, of which there are too many examples to name – once you are onto the real thing the fakes are visible miles off, even if they have the money men behind them pushing them down your throat. Great works automatically upgrade your bullshit detector, and regulate it to keep up with ever new spectacles, ever younger art stars, and ever more glittering prizes.

Russell provided general audiences, who ordinarily might not ever go to a museum or a concert hall (and might perhaps even laugh at the idea) with a window into the world of serious artists and composers. When it comes to art the masses of people are always playing someone else's game, never their own – one needs an entry point and Russell provided just that on a regular basis for thousands of people. He was always being stopped on the street, or in bars and restaurants, as people wanted to thank him for having given them the gift of this magic world of art and music; he realized after a time that he had transformed many lives for the better and, surprisingly, this surprised him. It shouldn't have, as this is a world that under normal circumstances they might never have encountered. In the final moments of the interview from 2008 Russell comes to realize

that, despite at some point loosing his Catholicism, he was something of a "traveling preacher." Not for religious orthodoxy certainly or even spiritual transcendence, but a "preacher" for the music and the art that he loved – an art that, in essence, made him Ken Russell.[24]

NOTES ON THE TEXT

My first exposure to Russell's work was thanks to Public Television in Los Angeles that broadcast his films in the late 1960's and early 1970's – *Dante's Inferno* and *Song of Summer* took hold of my imagination when I was a teenager and never let go. I absorbed all of Russell's subsequent work as it was released. This book began as an essay titled *The Biggest Film Biographer in the World: the Films of Ken Russell for the BBC* published by *CineAction* magazine in 2010. At the time of that initial publication I realized it needed to be a book but I was working as Acquisitions Librarian at an art college in Pasadena and so the writing was slow. After I retired in 2017 I dedicated myself to publishing a selection of essays on photography and film titled *One Second to Live: Photography, Film and the Corporeal in an Age of Extremes* (2023). After my part in that project was finished in 2021 I devoted myself full time to the Russell book, but even at this late date there were some films by him that I had not seen due to unavailability and there were others that were only available as very mediocre prints on YouTube, but I soldiered on.

The essays in this book adhere to a strategy of deep immersion into individual works with which one becomes emotionally invested, sometimes called the *close reading*. As the name implies the close reading looks at the artwork closely and tries to understand all of the things it is trying to do, what it is actually doing, and how that transition works. The close reading is generally not concerned with personalities, sexual orientation, or social implications - it is concerned with content. F.R. Leavis, the British doyen of the close reading in the 1930's, gave his work a moral spin that was popular in its day while the American school of New Critics, who also championed the close reading, favored a more Puritan approach wherein a work of art was seen as a self-contained, self-sufficient formal artifact, isolated from the culture from which it sprang. This position would have wide ranging support within the arts, particularly with the American schools of abstract painting and word poetry that accepted those ideas as a matter of course. In opposition to the American school Leavis and the Europeans were open to examining the society, the biography of the artist/author, and even the emotional response of the critic while maintaining that the work of art itself must remain the primary focus. I see my own work being closer to the Europeans as I have little sympathy for the American Puritan tradition. As I see it anyone who thinks that artworks can be "self-contained" is delusional, and headed toward the dull and barren landscape of formalism and conceptual art – something I would not wish on anyone.

If I have developed much longer essays about some films while others get only a couple of paragraphs, it is because the longer essays are about films that are more important to me, and I've spent more time thinking about them and have more to say. For example *Pop Goes the Easel* shows my obsession with Pop art, particularly its British variant The Independent Group and the work of Pauline Boty; the chapter on *Women in Love, The Rainbow* and *Lady Chatterley* – grouped around the novels of D.H. Lawrence - display an enthusiasm for his writing that goes back to my youth; *Gothic* shows my interest in Romanticism, Mary Shelley and *Frankenstein*; and *Dante's Inferno* clearly displays a fascination with the Pre-Raphaelites and their muses and models, particularly Lizzie Siddal. In effect, these are the essays that I wanted to read but no one bothered to write them so I was forced to do it myself. All my essays follow that line of reasoning, that is, I would much prefer for someone else to do it as it only takes a couple of hours to read an essay but it can take a lifetime to write one.

I would like to thank my friends, as always, who provided valuable input often without being aware of it, and to my family who supported me emotionally through the process. I hope you enjoy the book and continue to enjoy Russell's work, whether you make him a part of your "family" as I did many years ago, or not – there is always something there to discover anew no matter how many times you may have seen the films. I never got a chance to thank Mr. Russell personally as did some fortunate others, meeting him in a pub or on the street, but I hope this book is a thank you of sorts – somewhat mongrel, crude and unfinished in many respects but I don't think Russell would mind – as for myself I wouldn't have it any other way.

Three Short Films

KNIGHTS ON BIKES: A ROMANCE (1956)

Knights on Bikes: a Romance was Russell's first film from 1956 when he was 29 years old – although it's only ten minutes long Russell develops his film not along narrative lines but rather from situations and episodes – a telling feature. The film's main character is something of a romantic dreamer, another aspect of this early film that would reappear as a constant in his work. From its first shot (an iris out) Russell evokes silent cinema as we see a knight dressed in the fashions of the 1400's, including a helmet and sword, making himself a sandwich using mass produced bread – in effect this is a modern "knight." A queen wearing a crown appears picking flowers and going along a dirt road, although looking more like a proto-hippie flower child than a damsel from court. She spots what looks like an invalid in a wheelchair being pushed by two men dressed as monks - as she proceeds to hand the man in the wheelchair some flowers he grabs her and forces her into his wheelchair; as the monks drive off with the lady we see that it is not an old cripple but a young, handsome rake kidnapping the helpless queen.

The "knight" realizes it is time to move into action but his sword is stuck in a tree stump – loosing precious time, to catch up to the kidnappers, he finds a handy bicycle parked near a tree and goes to the rescue. Unfortunately the bicycle is from the early century and rather stiff and clumsy so it takes some time for the "knight" to get his bearings, but just as he's finally got the hang of it he falls off the bike and hurts himself like a little boy. He can only watch sadly as the queen is taken away – who knows what fate awaits her? The "knight" gets up slowly, dusts himself off, and limps away, sword and bike in hand, as Russell holds the down the road ending and fade out. The romantic "knight" here is truly Quixote like, but sans Sancho Panza, who might have figured out a way to catch up to those horrible kidnapping monks. The theme – that Romanticism has no place in the modern world and it is a sad lot to be a "knight" on a bike – is the basic seed from which will grow the body of work to come.

PEEPSHOW (1956)

Peepshow again embraces the aesthetics of the silent film wholeheartedly and for its 22 minute duration evokes the early work of René Clair such as *Le Voyage Imaginaire* (1926) and *Entr'acte* (1924) – it also shows the influence of Chaplin and the Keystone studios, Mabel Normand, Buster Keaton and Jean Cocteau. Even the credit sequence evokes these as we see hand drawn credits on the sidewalk from a second story looking straight down: A woman with an open umbrella has the word "camera" written with white paint on black, and as she moves on we see the name of the cameraman M.C. Plomer. We then see a title card as in a silent film: "...graduation day at the beggars academy" as we see some pretend beggars appear from behind bed sheets, as in a poor mans theater, acting as hobos begging for spare change. The man they are acting for is labeled "the boss," looking like an evildoer in a Mack Sennett film. We next see these "graduates" of the begging academy on a busy street in London plying their trade but they don't get a single taker as everyone is lined up by a wall with a peepshow where people throw the performers money over a fence – the hapless trio decide to investigate.

As in home movies people approach the camera and get so close the focus goes soft - these "amateur" shots are juxtaposed to overhead views reminiscent of Russian photography and cinema from the 1930's. The boss is upset at the loss in revenue and he wants to see this peepshow himself. Russell shoots the boss going over the fence as in a silent film with slightly mismatching cuts from close-ups of shoes running to his men waiting to hoist him up, to the boss having made it over the fence – it's a beautiful evocation of silent films but deconstructed so we see how the bits of film are put together, that is, the fundamental collage element of cinema is brought forward rather than made invisible through match cutting. Once over the fence they see a makeshift stage as a performance is set to begin. A young man made up to look like an old man enters the stage and opens a life size box wrapped as a present – inside he finds a woman dressed like a child – Shirley Ann, Ken's then girlfriend - he helps her out of the box and it appears she is an automaton or a doll come to life but a robot more in keeping with Mabel Normand's films than *Metropolis*. The old man dances and plays an alto saxophone and she starts to do a mechanical dance – the man puts the girl in the box but she comes back and puts the old man in the box – then takes center stage dancing up a storm until she collapses, like a doll – wild applause follows as coins from the audience rain down on the stage.

The beggar gang kidnap the old man in the box and haul him away as the doll awakens and her movements are suddenly those of a normal woman. She looks around, in a pantomime style, and sees that the man has been kidnapped. The robbers take the coffin size box to a Victorian park where the boss demands that his men throw the box in the river but one of the men, wearing a bowler hat, balks at the idea of murder – they hit him over they head in the manner of the Keystone cops and go off to dump the box in the river. The doll steps up and revives the bowler-hatted man. "What have they done to my father?" reads a title card as they become a team to rescue the old man. On the run they find the alto saxophone and take it along as Russell shoots the high energy chase in the style of the Keystone Studios.

Once they spot the kidnappers the bowler hatted man and the girl seem to have a plan – they anticipate them from a second story and as they run by and at just the right moment the girl drops the alto saxophone down on the box as the old man reaches out his arm and catches it – no doubt this instrument is perhaps as magical as the magic flute in Mozart's opera and so it turns out to be. As the men are about to toss the box into the Thames the old man appears, like a pied-piper playing his alto saxophone – the beggar gang start to dance uncontrollably and the old man leads them away – Russell shoots this in the style of Jean Vigo, using a parallel tracking shot along the river. The bowler hatted man and the girl, now a couple, start dancing for joy, following the gang that wind up in the river, the box serving as boat. The girl and her father along with the man make up a new family that dance away joyously down the foggy strand. Russell's film evokes a bygone Victorian London with few props and locations. The creation of a family unit would preoccupy Russell for the remainder of his career and here we see the germ of that theme brought to life in the manner of a music hall skit.

AMELIA AND THE ANGEL (1958)

Amelia and the Angel is an odd film in many ways as it is both naïve and sophisticated and unlike his two previous films it is ambitious – its themes of guilt, innocence and redemption would preoccupy Russell for the remainder of his working life. It integrates various stylistic devices to show absolute innocence unprotected – innocence in the form of a little girl in the modern world – and in the process it uses the various layers of London present in 1958 from Victorian to contemporary. Nothing quite like it had been seen before in British cinema. One can see immediately why Huw Wheldon sat up and took notice.

As Russell himself describes the film, *Amelia* had been made just after his conversion to Catholicism, suggesting a profound spiritual need that had gone unfulfilled. Despite the lack of dialogue the film is emotionally powerful and coherent with various strains of thought sharing the stage comfortably - this complexity is beautifully concealed underneath a deceptively simple plot line. Russell provides voice over commentary treating the material like a fairy tale, but at times commenting facetiously on the action. Russell said in interviews that his film was influenced by Jean Cocteau's *Beauty and the Beast* and Albert Lamorisse's *The Red Balloon* but we can also see the influence of *The Bicycle Thief*, and *The Little Fugitive*.

Amelia, a nine year old girl is set to perform as one of a group of angelic ballet dancers in a show the following evening, but she cannot wait to show her angel wings off to her mother and takes the wings home against the express wishes of her dance instructor. Amelia's brother takes the wings to play with them in the park and in some rough play they are quickly destroyed. Amelia then embarks on curious odyssey, part *Zazie in the Metro* and part *Orpheus in the Underworld*, through the streets of West London, in a desperate attempt to find some replacement wings. The title role went to Mercedes Quadros, and it is a dynamic and engaging, fully realized performance full of wonderful small moments. She finds a dog wearing wings (for a circus act) but she immediately sees that, while they would be perfect if they were larger, they are far too small. The narrator sarcastically intones in voiceover: "If only the dog had been a Great Dane!" and

Amelia smiles mischievously as if it had been her thought. She meets market traders, street performers and bohemians. She wanders through The Crystal Palace, the Highline Station, and Paxton tunnel which all give a very strong postwar feel to the film, of a place in ruins and of strange Victorian buildings that no one knows quite what to do with, or perhaps even what they were for – this even gives the film a slightly chilling science fiction aspect, seen later in Russell's *Lonely Shore*. It's a child's vision of London and everyone she runs into helps in some way until she finds an artist's studio with a real angel, or perhaps a prosaic artist's model dressed as one – the artist climbs a ladder to heaven (suggested by a studio painted with clouds) and gives Amelia a new set of wings (to the music of Bach) and all is set right.

The film showed an intense and precocious talent idiosyncratically able to channel a very British Victorian/poetic sensibility that was also self-reflexive, ironic, and modern – an unusual combination. The 30 minute short seemed to permeate everyday places such as parks, streets and humdrum middle class interiors, with the character of lived experience – moreover a lived reality that resonated with the characters regardless of how theatrical they first seem. Russell seemed to already have his keen eye for obsessive framing, careful observation of details, and a strong sensitivity regarding people's interior lives, allowing his actors space to create a character or simply to show their own character – something interesting was always happening often under the most mundane circumstances such as a man playing with a dog. Another characteristic of *Amelia and the Angel* was that it referenced the avant-garde films of Jean Cocteau, Rene Clair, the work of the Free Cinema movement, the Keystone Studios, the ne0-realist cinema of De Sica, and the shot selection of Lumiere and Eisenstein – all with seeming effortlessness and a complete lack of pretension – an astonishing achievement for an amateur film.

3

The BBC: Monitor & Omnibus

JOHN BETJEMAN: A POET IN LONDON (Short/1959)
Russell's first work for the BBC was a 12 minute film on the obscure British poet John Betjeman. When Russell suggested the film Wheldon replied "a bit second tier", acknowledging that Betjeman's work might not warrant a film but Russell insisted saying, "it wouldn't cost much."[25] Even in his first film Russell tried to interject fictional aspects, having actor friends dressed in Edwardian wardrobes impersonating the poet's past relatives, but Wheldon made him take it out – unfortunately the footage is lost.

Russell's film starts seemingly in medias res showing the busy London weekday bustle concentrating on areas that had inspired Betjeman to write poems – this makes sense as Betjeman was an urban poet in the spirit of Baudelaire and the French school rather than conventional British romantics who sang the praises of Nature. Russell's early work owes a lot to the Free Cinema movement in its use of hand held cameras, natural light, and spontaneous situations captured on the fly. We see this on the first shot as Russell moves in as Betjeman walks toward us along the steamy rail station in central London, Aldersgate (now The Barbican). Betjeman explains that the station has changed over the years and he goes into detail of why it was better before and recites a poem dedicated to it: "Monody on the Death of Aldersgate Street Station." Then Russell performs an unusual move – while the poet is waxing poetic about the beauty of it all Russell openly contradicts the poem by showing destruction, decay, peeling walls, and destroyed columns – one understands that WWII had ended only 15 years before. Russell here is not so much claiming that Betjeman is wrong but rather using his poem to create a cinematic poetics of his own, using the poem in counterpoint to his images, as if construction and destruction were having a conversation.

He then cuts back to Betjeman in London as he reads a poem called "Business Girls" where the images line up with the text again. The poem is an homage to working girls who must find a way to navigate through the streets, subways, and buses to get to work on time in sleek, modern skyscrapers – seen in the bustling business district of Westminster - that the poet, and Russell, both clearly loathe. Betjeman then reads *The Olympic Girl*, another homage to sexy London girls (real or in street advertising) and his sadness at now being a bald, old man who no longer stands a chance of being with any of them except in his imagination and in his art. Russell doesn't go melancholic with Betjeman but has great fun cutting quickly to various sexy adds all over town, finally going from a billboard showing a cartoon drawing of a young woman playing tennis to a real woman putting away her racket in its wood frame, that the author mentions in his poem. The film ends with a trip to his childhood home of Hertfordshire and his traumatic memory of going hunting with his father as the poet walks off away from us into the heart of the town – an inversion of the opening shot where he was walking toward us in London. Despite its short length the film veers from nostalgia, to social criticism, to whimsical reflections on aging, to very serious reconsiderations of childhood trauma. The film seems to end in medias res with nothing resolved or concluded – really more in the spirit of Albert Camus than Graham Greene (two contemporaries) – but that aspect also reflects Betjeman's poetry that had an absurdist, existential edge, balanced by a profound humanism - but the settings and the self-deprecating irony were always British to the core.

SHELAGH DELANEY'S SALFORD (Short/1960)

Shelagh Delaney was a playwright who in 1960 was 22 years old but had already written two plays, one of which, *A Taste of Honey*, had become a hit play and then a film directed by Tony Richardson. *A Taste of Honey* was part of the Kitchen Sink British New Wave movement and the film's success meant that it was shown abroad along with *This Sporting Life*, *Saturday Night and Sunday Morning*, and *Billy Liar*– these films were the first view that people abroad had of contemporary life for working people in England and it was a revelation.

Despite her newfound star status Delaney didn't move to London to be with the beautiful people – the "best and the brightest" - but stayed on in Salford, a small port town near Manchester and so Russell went there and the two came up with a plan for shooting a documentary that would include shots where she would pretend the camera was invisible allowing Russell to shoot from unusual angles and close-ups not ordinarily available to documentary filmmakers – in a sense they would make a fake documentary and then edit those parts together with real documentary material where Delaney would answer questions while looking into the camera; in effect, they improvised a film about her life at that moment, and about the city of Salford in 1960. That mix of acting and documentary done on the spot was standard practice within the Free Cinema movement that Russell was familiar with. This practice eventually went out of fashion as many within the documentary field sought to find the high ground of "pure documentary," but it has come back again in recent years, with a vengeance, with "reality television." The use of Kitchen Sink school here is consistent with Russell's insistence on the subject of the work dictating the form of the film itself – Delaney's work was closely associated with the Kitchen Sink school and her play, *A Taste of Honey*, became one of the landmark films of that school and of the period as a whole, and so Kitchen Sink it is.

The film begins in medias res as a circle of women, including Delaney, group themselves around a pram in front of a busy shoe store – a classic urban situation of meeting people briefly on the street before rushing off. The camera tracks along as Delaney moves on with her dog through downtown Salford. We get a text over image explaining that

Delaney was born in Broughton, Salford in 1939 and *A Taste of Honey*, her first play, premiered in 1958. She enters a modest house in the suburbs and there is a seamless match cut to the interior of the house from the stairs as she comes in. She asks someone off camera "It's me - any food in the house I'm starving?" A man's voice asks off camera "who's me?" Delaney replies: "who do you think?" and goes into the kitchen without acknowledging the camera. After this section, which was scripted and blocked, the film shifts to a real documentary with Delaney addressing the camera.

She explains that despite having lived in Sweden and France she always feels a terrible homesickness and "must get back as soon as possible – to England – or Salford, I don't know. The peculiar thing about Salford is that it's like a total drug. It's got everything you could ever want." Russell shoots the rooftops of Salford with the factory chimneys in the background and then the vibrant open air market that Delaney goes into raptures about – explaining that the place is full of vitality in a way you don't see in London or other places, and the language, including the insults and slang terms, the forthright way of speaking, are all very grounded in the place and that is what makes it so special. The fact that Delaney would focus on the language – "it's alive and it breathes" - makes perfect sense. Russell did not have the means to use direct sound outside but recorded the market separately and then juxtaposed it with the film footage so we get a sense of what she's talking about. She mentions that some people had been working the market for decades and have seen different generations of customers – she also mentions the proliferation of kids, whom you see everywhere. Russell always had a very special relationship with kids from his first early work and he has great fun showing working class kids playing with discarded furniture and trash lying around.

Delaney is then seen at the docks in front of ships coming in and out of the harbor and she talks about how despite the constant movement it "seems somehow to be dying." We see old buildings crumbling and neglected – in one case a whole block in ruins and a church for sale – "and down by the river it's even romantic if you can stand the smell." Russell shows a young couple with an umbrella walking by the river and looking at the foamy polluted water without much concern. The shots of a lone kid playing with a soccer ball in an alley or a woman sweeping her small backyard area are priceless evocations of the time and place. A brilliant stationary shot of a single street full of kids and moms (the men being at work) is the best short scene in the film and reminiscent of Nigel Henderson's photography from the same period, but of course Russell is able to move in for close-ups and even over the shoulder cross-cutting as people talk and enjoy the day.

Delaney then goes into some length about the restlessness of young people, some of whom don't know what they want but they feel tethered and anxious – meanwhile many low income people in Salford are being moved to housing estates outside the city where there is nothing but large multistory housing units all looking exactly the same. As she drinks her tea Delaney explains that it takes many years to develop a close-knit civil society with a sense of pride and culture and that these new estates are "sterile places where people have to start again from scratch." Russell shows these council estates exactly as Delaney describes them. She goes on to explain that after all of the years of schooling kids are lost, as she was lost, not knowing who they are or what they should do so they get menial jobs in the city or wherever they can. "I got lucky with my writing but so many aren't lucky and this is the tragedy." Russell is able to do cutaways to small details as Delaney talks, such as her habit of taking her hand holding a cigarette and with one finger circling the teacup. Delaney wraps up: "For the young this restlessness is just starting and for the old it's behind them – but the for the middle aged, those between it's too late to change and do something and too early to give up." As a final shot Russell focuses on the Salford train station full of people and then pans over the city and its many factory chimneys, the city looking like one enormous organic machine – "restless" as Delaney says - and alive.

A HOUSE IN BAYSWATER (Short/1960)
Bayswater is in West London and was in the postwar era a working class area that was quickly gentrifying by 1960, making way for modern council flats. Russell lived there for a time in the 1950's and this 28 minute documentary – his longest up to that time – features interviews with the live-in housekeeper and the tenants most of whom he knew personally from his stay there. The most extraordinary part of the film is unquestionably the end when Russell forgoes formal documentary narrative and enters the world of poetry, shooting extensive takes done in slow motion set to music. Interestingly the Hungarian maestro István Szabó made *25 Fireman's Street* in 1974, which is also about the "memories" of a Victorian building before it is demolished – each tenant sharing a fragment of their lives – but of course Szabós feature-length film is much more

ambitious with several layers of history coming into play. Russell's film is very much of a moment in 1960 where these very different people from all walks of life suddenly find themselves sharing living quarters, but in both films the building itself is a character who remembers.

Russell's opening shot gives us the typical anonymous grid of apartments going up with an enormous crane hauling up concrete. He quickly contrasts this to the house in Bayswater that is from the Victorian era as in voiceover we are introduced to Mrs. Collings, the housekeeper who lives in the basement. She narrates the early part of the film that introduces all of the tenants/characters that live in the building. Her voice has a strange sing-song quality that seems to be from another time and when she says "of course I'm a widow" it means that her husband was most likely killed in the war. She explains her duties and we see her chugging milk up the stairs as she introduces people floor by floor. For the first time in Russell's work the film utilizes the musical structure of four parts tied together by thematic lines as in a symphony – something similar to what he would do later with *Mahler*. Here the first part is the introduction of the various tenants by Mrs. Collings as they sleep in the early hours; in the second section each tenant talks briefly about why they live in the house and we see a fragment of their lives; the third section would be the slow movement where some tenants get a more developed scene centered around an event; in the fourth and final section, shot in slow motion, we see a dreamlike ballet of motion as the tenants reprise their roles for the finale.

She first introduces "David Hearn, he's a photographer." Hearn was a good friend of Russell's and they collaborated on another of the films for the BBC *Watch the Birdie*. We see a close-up of Hearn pretending to be asleep as Russell asks all of his friends in the building to ignore his camera and even to pose in certain situations that are a typical "day in the life" as was often done in Free Cinema. He had the film he wanted already in his mind and set about as much to "document" as to construct a portrait of the place he knew. On the second floor is James Berle a painter whom we also see sleeping, improbably from directly above his bed looking down as if he were a model in a painting. On the third floor is Helen May a teacher of dancing and "today she is giving one of her rare performances. It wouldn't mean much to you – before your time- but years ago she was a rather famous person." We see her sleeping as well wearing a net to keep her hair tidy. On the fourth floor is Miss Croft, a retired lady who lived for many years in New York as a housekeeper, sleeping soundly wearing pajamas. Finally we get a couple, Tom and Lou who work in a wine cellar. We see the couple also from above snuggled together for the night.

Tom is the only person from the sleeping sequences that gets up and he takes over the voiceover explaining that he's lived there for seven years. He explains that the other tenants seem to him more bohemian but he and his wife Lou are more family oriented as we see him wash his face in the small bathroom. He complains about the lack of hot water that is unavailable unless you make it yourself using a kettle. Mrs. Collings explains that there is only one phone for the building and at 12PM she shuts it off. Russell uses beautiful overhead shots to show people meeting up in hallways and stairs, talking to each other intimately – certainly a different world to the one to come in the following century.

In the following sequences we see each of the people we have been introduced to but they explain themselves briefly or they interact without acknowledging the camera as instructed by Russell. In many cases he is able to build up a short film within a film, as when a young girl comes to visit Helen May for some dance instruction and Russell is able to use the shot/counter-shot method usually not seen in documentaries as it requires camera set-ups and knowing where your "actors" will be moving. Ms. May helps the girl prepare a "moth dance" for an upcoming theater production and we see her as a teacher, very conscientious and old school.

Mrs. Collings talks about her love of Portobello road market where most of her furniture and many of her clothes come from – she jokes that she might even find a man there eventually and Russell shoots some prospective men that might suit her. Russell accompanies this scene with some whimsical music as we see Portobello Road market as it was then, including horse drawn carts taking furniture to people's homes. We then see the various people we've met during the day, making lunch, talking with neighbors, making a painting.

There is an extended sequence of David Hearn the photographer as he shoots a naked model on the roof of the building lying in an old bathtub that covers a lot of her body. Hearn explains that he sells these pictures of women to magazines and can pay his rent but his real work is doing photography as a daily journal where images tell the story of his life without words. Russell himself of course also did commercial and erotic photography before he got his job at the BBC but Hearn continued on and had a long successful career as a photographer. There is then another extended sequence of Miss Croft, the old retired lady who spends her day feeding hungry pigeons and birds who come to her window knowing there will be food. Her sequence is broken by found footage of Manhattan seen from the air – we remember that she worked in the city for 23 years before moving back to England so the found footage is almost a memory or a dream floating over the city – we are suddenly inside Miss Croft's mind – a lyrical passage normally outside the domain of the documentary.

Mrs. Collings talks about the people who have died in the building and are no longer there but Russell shows us the people there now, preparing lunch or a cup of tea thereby joining the living and the dead in the rituals of day-to-day life. A final extended scene takes us to a theater where the dancing teacher and her pupil are both performing – Helen May recreating a "work from 1920" and her protégé, the young girl, doing her "moth dance." Russell shoots May's dance recreating von Sternberg's shots in *The Blue Angel* – as if the aura of the 1920's were something May carried around with her – her pupil's dance reminds us of *Amelia and the Angel*.

Then Russell performs his magic. Seeing Mrs. Collings on the couch relaxing we hear her in voice over as a knock is heard on the door. She explains that after 11PM she would never answer the door no matter how hard they knocked "even if they knocked the house down." Then we see footage of a door being knocked down as part of a demolition crew tears a building down. Russell then shifts the music – by John Hotchkis - to a repeating piano performing a hurdy-gurdy motif that turns melancholic. We see slow motion shots of all of the tenants doing ordinary things but now in slow motion moving in space as if they were all dancing, not just Helen May. The shot owes something to the work of Jean Cocteau's *Orpheus*, Federico Fellini's *I Vitelloni* and especially Jean Vigo's *Zero for Conduct* where the boys in a boarding school have a pillow fight and while the feathers are flying Vigo shifts to slow motion, allowing him to create an opening into the interior lives of the boys.

As in Georges Perec's *Life: a User's Manual*, it is as if the apartment building itself were remembering the people that once lived there and conjuring them in a series of instants that lead to a collective portrait. In that apartment building humanity is encompassed by the lives and memories of all its residents and all the places they have touched, the facticity of their existence and what they have left behind is what finally touches us. We see characters fall through space to their beds and do an impromptu dance on the foyer, we see Ms. May and her pupil after the performance walk in slow motion through a wall of festive balloons and confetti – perhaps a celebration of their performance - but it looks like they are still dancing through space moving away from us. It's a beautiful final shot and a wonderful portrait of a neighborhood and London itself in the transitional year of 1960 – between the austerity of the postwar era and the swinging sixties. With *A House in Bayswater* Russell came into his own, pushing the documentary towards a poetic realism and a more lyrical musical structure – a discovery from which he never looked back.

LONDON MOODS (Short/1961)
London Moods is the closest that Russell ever came to making a promotional film – in this case about the city of London in 1961, a city on the cusp of the revolutions of the 1960's. *London Moods* falls within the category of a "city symphony film" that includes films such as *Berlin Symphony of a Great City* (1927) that gave the name to the genre as well as *Apropos de Nice* (1930) and *Man With a Movie Camera* (1929). These radical films, that avoided traditional formats, were meant to be panoramic portraits of a city, centered around the editing, using the cutting of the film in a musical sense, with counterpoint between scenes offering different movements at different speeds and rhythms, precisely like a symphony.

London Moods starts promisingly with close-ups tourists pointing their cameras directly at Russell's camera and taking pictures but then goes into a traditional display of the various foot guards with their large traditional bearskin hats and shots of cannon being fired along with parades and military marches – while the end of the war was only 16 years earlier the heavy emphasis on police and cannons is incongruous for a film titled *London Moods*. Russell finally seems to have some fun with a large store that sells postcards and he moves in for the first time to close-ups of various cards, from Elvis to the Queen to a monkey to Brigitte Bardot – very much in the Pop art style of the *British Independent Group*. In one funny edit, worthy of Bruce Conner, he cuts from a young Queen Elizabeth to a cannon going off. Then we see a more traditional London: the pigeons in Trafalgar Square, the double decker buses, the tourist boats along the Thames, Big Ben, etc. Then Russell focuses on some Rockers (as opposed to Mods) going off on their bikes dressed in leather, very much in the style of American fifties rock idols such as Elvis and Eddie Cochran.

Russell tends to group his shots together to make ensembles rather than focusing on differences, as was typically done with the city symphony films, so all of the signage shots are grouped together, then all of the food shots, and so on. This creates a more traditional montage that one might see in *Life* magazine or one of the Sunday supplements using still photography. Russell has great fun showing off the new fad for exercise machines, some with rather dubious qualities, that he pairs off with comical music cues – he cuts from this to a very somber piece of music. From a new glass building in the international style he pans to an empty lot with grass and trash. From some foliage Russell slowly pans to a strange horizontal monument made of stone – a soldier in full uniform lies down at rest or death. Monuments to soldiers from WWI and wreaths falling apart from age turn the film in an elegy to a lost generation who died too young in the war.

Russell then beautifully dissolves his scene from the statue of the soldier to the river Thames looking very black, then to the Houses of Parliament and Westminster Cathedral as the music swells, and finally to the many busy bridges in London at midday. The film begins with cannon and ends as an elegy to those that gave up their lives in the war. In between is contemporary life in all of its freshness, absurdity, quotidian life, faddishness, and work ethic. Russell brings his own sense of humor and sensibility to the nine minute panorama of London in 1961 and it should not surprise us that the film is elegiac and comical, idiosyncratic and conventional, surreal and real.

ELGAR: PORTRAIT OF A COMPOSER (Short/1962)
When Russell first proposed a film on the life of the Romantic British composer Edward Elgar, who by the 1950's was considered passé, it did not go well. By 1962 Russell had made over twenty films for the series and felt ready to move into longer and more ambitious films, and so he made his pitch to *Monitor* concentrating on Elgar's forgotten prominence and the need to rehabilitate his status for a new generation of younger viewers. *Monitor's* boss Huw Wheldon replied: "The BBC is not a rehabilitation center. Your story is romantic cliché. It's flabby. It has no backbone."[26] Russell was stunned as he had wanted to make a film about Elgar for years and had what he considered a solid screenplay that was ready to go. Russell, in desperation, spoke about Elgar's life, including the unlikely, but apparently true account, that while in his fifties Elgar liked to slide down the local hills in the Midlands using a tea tray. Wheldon at first couldn't believe it, as he, like most people who were at all aware of Elgar thought of him as the stuffy, elder statesman of English music – someone who was wheeled out occasionally to perform at

graduations and funerals – his "Pomp and Circumstance March No. 1" is popularly known as simply "the graduation song" in the US although hardly anyone knows the composer's name, and his "Land of Hope and Glory" is, in England, a virtual second national anthem. Russell knew Elgar's biography by heart and after hearing his stories Wheldon reconsidered and told him: "Forget your screenplay. Film it exactly as you told it."[27]

Elgar is a biography of the British composer born in 1857 – the same generation as Claude Debussy born in 1862. Now he is now best known for his melancholic cello concerto as well as *The Enigma Variations* that was composed in 1899, as if closing out the century of Beethoven, Brahms and Wagner on a completely different note. The work was small-scale, heartfelt, unpretentious, and ironic –ever shifting from whimsy to tragedy and from irony to heart-on-sleeve emotions. In short, *The Enigma Variations* was a radical harbinger of things to come, as it not only quotes past works but also hints at the revolution in music that was just around the corner. Here Russell helpfully explains the work and what it meant to him:

"The theme on which the *Variations* were based was never stated and people have been trying to guess its identity ever since. There are fourteen variations – each represents a person, for example, his wife is the first variation and the composer himself is the last; in between we have musical impressions of an amateur pianist, an actor, a music publisher, a pretty girl with a stammer, Bulldog Dan, a cellist, and a mystery person identified by ***; and so on, the perfect subject for a mini biopic."[28]

One can easily see the attraction to Russell. Because of Elgar's provincial background he was always the perpetual outsider, socially and musically, and he was a staunch Catholic in a time when this was looked down upon by the upper classes. The British classical music world was then dominated by established academics – similar in many respects to the art world in the same period - and Elgar, like Russell, was self-taught; he was also regarded with some suspicion due to his Catholicism and his humble origins that in the highly class-conscious world of Victorian British society meant he was segregated, in a de facto sense, from the jobs, the clubs, and the gatherings of "polite society." Elgar saw all the good reviews and the glittering prizes go to others with far less talent and little to offer except what the academy regarded as "serious music," that is, pastiche versions of Brahms and Beethoven. This difficult and unprofitable situation made him cranky and melancholic.

The innovative 56 minute *Elgar* was the hundredth program for *Monitor* and the first that featured re-enactments but it begins with a traditional black and white photo of the composer as an old man with the word ELGAR in a bold modern font – the words PORTRAIT OF A COMPOSER follow in silence. The word "portrait" suggests something different from a biography as the former are often more subjective. The film then cuts to the composer as a boy riding a white horse over the Malvern Hills of the Midlands around Worcester at top speed featuring elaborate zooms and fast dolly shots that follow the horse and rider as they gallop along to Elgar's "Introduction & Allegro for Strings." This sequence, with sweeping dramatic tracking shots, done from a moving car, goes on for some time as the music fades and the voiceover introduces the composer's life story. Russell makes clear here that Elgar's inspiration is not in any sense academic but inspired by being at one with nature and the landscape around him; but the tracking and dolly shots are so dramatic that they also call attention to themselves, in effect, insisting on the presence of a film author and not trying at all for any kind of "objective" point-of-view.

Wheldon reads his own text explaining that the Elgar's were a lower middle class family and we see them playing with a dog in front of a modest house in the country. His father owned a little music shop, working as a piano tuner and Elgar was entirely self-taught. We see him practicing a baroque trumpet concerto on a cornet, a violin, and a flute as a teenager – the elaborate lace curtains behind him are all that is needed to suggest the time period. "He was one of those people to whom playing an instrument came naturally. He said later that his knowledge of orchestration was founded on these childhood experiences."

In one of the most imaginative and unusual set pieces the voiceover explains that when some lodgers were staying at the house that happened to play the violin and the oboe he wrote a duet for them. Russell places his camera in the appropriate room, but the lodgers playing the duet are almost completely hidden by a large screen showing various scenes from Queen Victoria's life at the center, surrounded by dogs, cherubs and lace – classic British kitsch from the period. Russell's camera then beautifully cranes up and over the screen to catch a glimpse of the two amateur musicians giving young Elgar's early composition a heartfelt reading. The short scene is superb as it suggest Elgar's shyness about composition at this point in his life purely with camera movement. Russell then explains that there was no question of Elgar going to University, and at age 15 he started to work in his father's shop.

In one of Russell's more idiosyncratic sequences the voiceover explains that Elgar liked to play jokes on people by hiding in trees and then jumping down on them as they walked by, but that he was also a committed church goer and went regularly to the Catholic church for whom he wrote a motet – his first mature composition. While we hear the motet Russell expands the scene to include extended documentary shots of the protocol of a traditional Catholic mass, including the incense being swung on a metal canister. Typically Russell cuts from this very serious scene to close-ups of odd looking men with strange expressions on their faces as if they might have mental health issues playing in an orchestra. The voiceover then explains that Elgar's first serious job in music was as a conductor in the local lunatic asylum. In one extraordinary extreme close-up one of the inmates is falling asleep while playing traditional British music from the turn of the century. The voiceover explains that Elgar walked the three miles to the asylum twice a week for seven years – a building that we see from behind bars looking like a Victorian prison.

On the positive side Elgar was much in demand as a teacher "with his bold, good looks." He also used his musical talents to serenade young women with some friends who formed a quintet. A beautiful shot of five top hats on a table with music playing gives the story its punctuation. The camera pulls back to a second story room as the aforementioned young ladies have some tea while gossiping, laughing, and listening to the music as the quintet is giving it their all. In voiceover we hear that "In 1886 at age 29 Elgar met the woman who would transform his life." But the images show only a game of badminton playing on a beautiful spring day with the camera very high up on a crane so we see it below us with foliage all around as if we were on a tree top. "He was bounded by the Worcester hills and somehow lacked the drive to cut himself loose. Carolyn Alice Roberts would change all of that." Alice as she was known had been a piano student of Elgar and "like many students had fallen in love with him." She had been brought up with the idea of service of some kind but up until now her life seemed purposeless – now that was to change as she was determined that Elgar would become a great composer, recognized and suitably compensated for it – that became her mission in life. The strong willed Alice also went her own way and put aside her yearly income and her dreams of becoming a novelist to marry Elgar and start a family. She contributed to his music not only as a muse but as the writer of his choral works, becoming a lifelong collaborator. Russell shows their growing intimacy with a beautiful metaphor using only hands – we see a close up of Elgar playing the piano and suddenly Alice's hands join in for a four handed version of *Salut d'Amour*, a short piece dedicated to her. Elgar is quoted from one of his letters in voiceover: "We rode up the hills on donkey's – never have I been so happy." Russell shows Elgar hiding in a tree and waiting for his new wife to come strolling by before jumping down on her and chasing her through the woods before they fall down laughing in a field.

Elgar gave up his teaching jobs and full of hopes they set off for London hoping to get noticed by music publishers and the music establishment. Russell uses a one second cut to documentary footage of London from the 1890's, the streets clogged with horse drawn carriages and pedestrians in top hats. Their enthusiasm quickly drained away as neither the music publishers nor the establishment wanted anything to do with the provincial composer. While in London Elgar had a chance to hear the new music from Germany and France and he was, as is common among self-taught people, the perpetual student absorbing everything and always learning. Elgar and his wife became sick and depressed in freezing cold London – he offered his services in the London papers as a piano teacher but not one person responded – the Elgars had no choice but to go back to Worcester. On returning Elgar bought a bike and we see an extended sequence, set to his first symphony, of him riding around the hills as a young man - mirroring the scene on a horse that opens the film.

The voiceover tells us that life in the small town was "dull, provincial and frustrating, teaching school kids the violin and piano." Nevertheless, rather than feeling left out, unappreciated and isolated to a great extent he thrived in his hometown and its musical circles – whether it was the local glee club or the *Worcestershire College for the Blind Sons of Gentlemen*. Elgar, ever the autodidact, gave his all to concerts and methodically continued to learn composition on his own well into old age. While Elgar was doubtful about his chances Alice was "adamant that he become a recognized composer and relentlessly pushed for it to happen by writing letters, correcting proofs, and creating music paper by hand with a pen as they could not afford sheets of blank music paper with the staff already printed." In arguably the most beautiful scene Russell ever filmed of marital bliss he shows them both at a work table, Elgar smoking and composing while Carolyn painstakingly makes staffs with a ruler and pen – not a word is spoken as we hear Elgar's *Serenade For Strings* – the "no dialogue" rule was something that Wheldon imposed on all of his directors and Russell here smartly uses it to his advantage in one of the most moving scenes in the film that he repeats later in a flashback as Elgar lies dying.

Using portraits of the actual people and places Russell's voice over explains that it was the German conductor Hans Richter who would play Elgar's music abroad and write about him as the "genius of British music," eventually making his name, starting in Germany. Russell then cleverly uses the actual postcards written by Elgar to his family as he visited Germany and explains his new triumph. The doyen of German music Richard Strauss chimed in and claimed Elgar to be the first genius of modern music in England. Fortunately there were dozens of postcards, all wonderful, so Russell had ample material. On his return from Germany Elgar would write *The Enigma Variations* that would seal his newfound fame in his home country — even becoming Sir Edward Elgar. Russell shows photos of all of the subjects in the *Variations*, all posing very seriously for posterity in photographer's studio as was common at the time.

Russell illustrates Elgar's triumph using one of his favorite set ups, seen first here, of children with sparklers at night running through a wall of fireworks. This is followed by an extraordinary shot of Elgar and his daughter skating down the local hills on a tea tray, laughing in the sun — this is the scene that convinced Wheldon to give Russell a shot at making his film. The following pictures show Elgar with his friends looking both dapper and very full of life and humor. This sequence in particular must have changed people's ideas about who Elgar was and what his music was all about, exactly as Russell predicted.

In the voiceover we are told that finally Elgar received the recognition that he and his wife had fought for; British royalty wanted him to write music for them and universities wanted to give him honorary degrees — in voiceover one writer explains succinctly: "Elgar's music reaches the people." On the word people Russell shifts to a series of documentary vignettes from the early teens that last eleven minutes as we hear *Pomp and Circumstance*. The BBC footage is extraordinary, particularly one long shot that follows a double decker bus as people get on and off as it travels along. The fact that his music was used to rally the troops was something he was proud of but as the carnage of the war became obscene he developed mixed feelings about both the music and the British war effort. Elgar had warm feelings about Germany — there would be no "Sir Elgar" without the Germans — and found the war as insane as the many writers who described it. As Europe set about destroying itself Elgar moved to Suffolk to get as far away as possible from it, but Russell doesn't show Suffolk but rather the carnage in long sequences of the war set to Elgar's music. He smartly juxtaposes jingoistic footage of soldiers marching robotically in unison in London to cheers from the war-hungry crowds, to soldiers dying in the trenches in France and Germany – all scored to Elgar's *Land of Hope and Glory*.

In 1918 after the war Elgar was offered the commission to write a symphony of "peace" but any government commission was now "an abomination to him" and he refused. Instead he wrote perhaps the saddest of his works – his cello concerto – arguably his last great work. After 11 minutes of documentary footage Russell cuts to that cello concerto and shots of the Midland forest in the fog – then to the death of Alice Elgar in 1920 as we see a long road full of trees that ends in darkness. This is followed by the most surrealist shot in the film – of a large stage – far larger than Elgar's house – his furniture is sporadically arranged but covered up by white sheets. A billiard table sits in the middle of the stage also covered in cloth but with three microscopes resting on it. We are told that Elgar, after his wife's death, stopped composing and developed a fascination with looking through microscopes at bacterial life and spent hours in this pursuit. As Elgar walks through this vast space it is as if he were already dead, inhabiting some Platonic realm of forms.

He was brought back to London for celebrations, parades and official dinners. He described one parade that used his *Land of Hope and Glory* as a "ridiculous charade – airplanes, loudspeakers, horrible, loud, mechanical, no soul, no romance and no imagination." We see him driving back home in a car and Russell, as he had done earlier with the bicycle and the horse, has extended shots of Elgar driving through the hills in a convertible. Elgar became the elder statesman of British music, lauded but out of touch with the wave of Modernism that came in the twenties and thirties with the music of Schoenberg, Bartok, Stravinsky and Berg.

Towards the end Elgar became ill and had to stay in bed so he arranged it so his bedroom would face the Cathedral and the hills around Worcester. There he would listen to recordings of his music and "by his own account drift through his memories in search of those moments and people and places that had brought him happiness and fulfillment." On those words Russell cuts to a two minute sequence of flashbacks from Elgar's life – some flashbacks repeat earlier scenes but some are new, including a beautiful shot of Elgar and his wife flying a kite during a blazing sunset. We realize he has died when the music comes to and end and the camera pans from the open window to the needle on the gramophone going in a circle after the music is over. The last shot in the film is a photograph of Elgar as a young man – an inversion of the opening shot of a photo of the composer in his final years. But ultimately as in all of Russell's work the physical aspect of the location takes on major importance as one can sense the hard English light, and feel the density of the wet, chilly morning air of the Midlands as the camera surveys the desolate beauty of the small town of Worcestershire and the British countryside – a landscape that permeates all of Elgar's music.

THE DEBUSSY FILM (1965)

Russell was busy making his debut feature *French Dressing* in 1963 and 1964, returning to the BBC in 1965 to make the most self-reflexive film in the series for the BBC. *The Debussy Film* (1965) is a feature length film that begins with a contemporary film crew arriving on location at a large chateau with a fire engine to produce the appropriately dramatic fake rain for a funeral procession. This film within the film is to be a biography of Claude Debussy, but Russell is now pushing the boundaries and he immediately blurs the lines between various periods in Debussy's life and 1965, the time that the film was shot. Even the overly dramatic fake rain carries over into the following scenes of a young Debussy (Oliver Reed) falling in and out of love in 19th century Paris (signaled by a one second shot of the Eiffel Tower) while reading overwrought Symbolist writers and going to art exhibits by J.M.W. Turner – an artist that much influenced Debussy's dissolution of sounds within a very narrow tonal palette.

Russell then cuts to a completely incongruous, baffling shot of a young, very sixties looking woman wearing contemporary clothes, perhaps a model, being shot full of arrows. Russell: "Near the start (of *The Debussy Film*) was a girl in a modern T-shirt being shot full of arrows by teenagers on a beach. You hesitated before you turn *that* off!" (emphasis Russell). While Russell does not explain the shot, the modern girl, being shot with arrows is clearly a reference to St. Sebastian as he is often depicted in classical paintings – it was also a favorite motif amongst Symbolist artists and writers. As usual Russell was being historically true to the material - in fact Debussy did collaborate with the neurotic Italian poet Gabriele D'Annuzio who wrote the scenario to a five-act mystery play, based on the story of St. Sebastian, with sets and costumes designed by Léon Bakst. On its premiere in Paris in 1911 there was scandal and the Archbishop of Paris requested Catholics boycott the production - the cause of the outrage was that St. Sebastian was played by a semi-naked young woman rather than a semi-naked young man, as was traditionally the case. The resulting ban limited the production's success and the piece failed to enter the classical repertoire, although it was revived by enthusiasts of Debussy's work. In the 1960's Leonard Bernstein and his young protégé Michael Tilson Thomas brought the production back and it became something of a cult hit. As usual with Russell he used this bit of trivia in Debussy's history to create his own beautiful and scandalous sequence – and a perfect opening to his biography of the radical composer.

Debussy sought to create collaged soundscapes where tonality and atonality clash and play off one another in melancholic, languorous works, sliding around the tonal scale, at the opposite end of the spectrum from Wagner's "total work of art." In this incongruous shot of a modern female St. Sebastian the same thing has been accomplished visually with the classical, liturgical image turned into farce, as if Russell was accepting Debussy's gambit and taking it to its logical, and absurd, limit. Claude Debussy was the man who, according to Pierre Boulez, the composer and music theorist, created the first modern music with *Prélude à l'aprés-midi d'un Faune* in 1894; by using simultaneous consonances and dissonances he opened the floodgates, or soundscapes, that would later make way for Bartok, Stravinsky and Schoenberg. Russell's opening here brings up many questions aside from the sixties "Pop St. Sebastian." Whose funeral is it? Why is the film's director (Vladek Sheybal), who is so knowledgeable about Debussy, also so sardonic, blasé and resigned?"

The film moves from the fake funeral in the rain to the director feeding a line to a child playing Debussy's son: "It seems he was a musician." Even the director seems unsure. Oliver Reed as Debussy asks astute questions of his director about the composer often defending him against accusations of unfeeling carelessness, or outright sexism, in regard to his female companions. Just who is right in this argument remains an open question, but as Russell's authoritative voice over makes clear Debussy drove his female companions crazy or to suicide (or both) – coldly leaving the wreckage he had wrought and then moving on. In some cases Russell uses an actor's very contemporary physiognomy, facial expressions and hair style and contrasts them to those of the Belle Époque, so different physical appearances from different time periods share the same screen space to emphasize a disjunction or a fundamental incompatibility. For example Oliver Reed's Debussy looks like a troubled, repressed, 19th century man and Annette Robertson, portraying Gaby Dupont his mistress, looks very much like a liberated, 20th century woman from the sixties – the fact that they are always at each other's throats makes a great deal of sense.

In one beautiful sequence the camera slowly pans from the film's director absorbed in discussion to an outdoor luncheon on the grass in which the women in Debussy's life set out to picnic in the summer of 1897. The transition in which the past and present cohabit works brilliantly establishes the emotional connections between actors and the people they are portraying and the scene collapses the two time periods. We see the short space between 1897 and 1965. Russell does not draw attention to his poetics, as does Ingmar Bergman who in *Wild Strawberries* (1957) has a camera perform a similar function. On the contrary the movement is quick and moves on rapidly to other business, nevertheless the poetics are no less effective.

This time shift is elaborated upon when the actors and the roles they are playing meld into one at a contemporary party for the cast and crew. Reed/Debussy and the director step into an apartment where festivities are in full swing with the latest hit music on the turntable, *You Really Got Me* by the Kinks. The actors dance to the music with abandon and Reed, in a contrary mood, takes the Kinks record out and puts on one of Debussy's most quiet and contemplative works. Annette Robertson/Gaby Dupont challenges Reed's move by using the music to do an impromptu striptease that delights her fellow players. To throw more fuel to the fire she throws her panties at the record player and the needle jumps as Reed/Debussy throws her daggers with his eyes. She clearly is challenging not only the actor, and by inference Debussy, but the very idea of serious music and what it might be used for. The juxtaposition of the Kinks with Debussy inevitably leads to the question of just what constitutes contemporary music. Are the Kinks Debussy's heirs? Russell posits the question but does not answer it. The relationship of the actors beautifully mimics the relationship of Debussy to Dupont. The two identities fuse at that moment in a way that is both emotionally and aesthetically coherent and satisfying.

The Debussy Film brings to the forefront the film crew as a temporary, close-knit family of actors and technicians who are together for the duration of the shoot, at times playing games such as having Reed/Debussy in a "duel" with another actor, Vernon Dobtcheff, who plays Maurice Maeterlinck, the Symbolist writer who specialized in decadent fairy tales that would, presumably, stimulate adult imaginations with sudden frisson's that conflated pain and pleasure, sex and death. The two actors shoot each other with rubber darts from modern plastic toys but speak their lines as if they were Debussy/Maeterlinck. Their absurd play, in a conservative 19th century mansion from Debussy's time, is telling about the childishness of actors on a set generally, but more importantly we begin to understand Debussy's subsequent failure to produce work after that initial early success. His inability to reconcile that childish selfishness and narcissism which drove him on in his hungry years, with his adult emotional life, that he seems to have found unfulfilling, leaves him in limbo.

It is in this period, starting in 1900, that Debussy meets informally with a group called *Les Apaches* (*The Hooligans*) to debate the new radical arts of the coming century, and discuss their status as "artistic outcasts." Debussy spends his time playing games like an adolescent but can never finish his opera based on *The Fall of the House of Usher*, the Poe story to which he devoted the last twelve years of his life. The one opera that he did finish, *Pelléas and Mélisande* (based on Maeterlinck's play of the same name), is so enigmatic and its themes of guilt, sexual repression, and the impossibility of reconciling with death, are so dark as to make certain the opera never received the attention it deserved in its own time. It would only find champions in the 20th century that saw the opera in Freudian terms, and as the last stages of a decadent Belle Époque strangled by social contradictions, sexual repression, and the unmitigated greed of a "gilded age" where there was room only for a fortunate few at the top. The inevitable catastrophe waiting in the wings – WWI – finally brought that "Belle Époque" to a close but as Félix Nadar, the photographer of choice for the rich and famous, so well put it (having lived it) in his autobiography: "Belle-Époque? Yes, but Belle for whom?"[29]

By the early 20th Century when Debussy was creating his final masterpieces, his Symbolist, dreamlike music, after the destruction of Europe in WWI surely seemed like small potatoes - there was no energy present. His vital vocabulary of modern sounds had already been co-opted and enlarged upon by Arnold Schoenberg, Alban Berg, Igor Stravinsky and others who revolutionized classical music. Debussy was caught between a century that he helped bring to an end and a new one that he seemed not fully able to understand. His retreat into boyhood games shows us in stark terms that are both comic and tragic, the end of the line. The funeral at the beginning of the film was, of course, Debussy's own.

ALWAYS ON SUNDAY (Short/1965)

Always on Sunday is a 45 minute biography of Henri Rousseau, written by Russell and Melvyn Bragg, and is perhaps the most moving of the BBC films – it was also the last film under the supervision of Huw Wheldon. The title refers to the then popular film

Never on Sunday (1960) and to Rousseau's status as a Sunday painter before retiring from his full time job as a clerk in a tax collector's office in late middle age to pursue his beloved hobby full time. Russell's opening shot is of Rousseau, alone, climbing the outdoor steps of a massive neoclassical building's basement for the last time as he retires quietly with no fanfare. Russell cuts immediately to Rousseau's small but tidy apartment as he puts away his tax collector's uniform in moth balls with some regret – he was born into extreme poverty so he appreciated his full time job rather than felt restricted or undermined by it. In voiceover Rousseau himself explains his situation in a matter-of-fact style. Rousseau was an iconoclast and a radical without aspiring to be either, he simply wanted people to like him and his work but was always encountering incomprehension, abuse, and ridicule. Completely out of sync with the academic Salon art of his time – an art that he loathed – he was also the odd man out with the Impressionists, who found him a naïf, uninterested in the fugitive properties of color and light and the realities of the contemporary world that formed the basic subject matter of their work. Rousseau observed present day realities but only to expand the vocabulary of his incredible imagination. Rousseau generally didn't get on with artists or art world people but rather with the local tradesmen and shop workers in his neighborhood – he wanted to be like them painting 9 to 5 Monday through Friday and resting weekends.

In an inspired bit of casting the naïve painter James Lloyd, who Russell met in a group exhibition of naïve art in London, plays Rousseau, giving him the temperament of someone who has lived a long life and been disappointed more times than he is willing to remember – the temperament of a man who knows his time is drawing to a close and he has come to accept it. James Lloyd, as Russell anticipated, understood Rousseau perfectly and provided an authenticity – even in the awkwardness and the silences – that takes the film to another level entirely. Russell shows him taking his paintings in a wheelbarrow (which is historically accurate) to the yearly Salon but always being turned away. Like Edward Manet he loathed the official Salon but he also desperately wanted to be a part of it. Later he would find greater acceptance with the Salon des Indépendants – despite their misgivings they recognized an original and Rousseau showed his work alongside that of Degas, Seurat, Redon, Cezanne and Toulouse-Lautrec – the new radical artists of the day. Like Claude Monet Rousseau was also the butt of many jokes, sarcastic put-downs, and horrible reviews but he took it in stride – but unlike Monet Rousseau realized that, for better or worse, he was part of no school or movement, he simply had to stand on his own.

Russell unsparingly shows a group of grotesque bourgeois types in close-up, some eating and drinking while viewing the exhibition of Impressionists and Post-Impressionists at the Salon des Indépendants after having paid their one franc to get in – another historically accurate detail. They go for a laugh or to see the new outrageous work – the term "Impressionism" itself comes from a sarcastic and scathing review by the art critic Louis Leroy in 1874. Russell here again uses the many voices and sounds in the film in a completely revolutionary way, applying an overall "sound design" before the term existed. Russell's soundtrack was always one of his great strengths during his BBC years and a large reason for that success is due to the person in charge, Stan Morcom, who worked on six films with Russell. Aside from *Always on Sunday* Morcom did the sound work for *Isadora*, *Dante's Inferno*, *Dance of the Seven Veils*, *Song of Summer* and *The Debussy Film*. For example, sound is used expressionistically, not to be "artistic" but to convey thought - while the bourgeois audience is heard on the soundtrack their laughter is overlaid into a disjointed cacophony, no doubt as Rousseau would have heard it. Jarry's cryptic asides punctuate certain scenes by being brought forward in the sound mix, because of their importance to Rousseau – he would have been attentive to whatever Jarry said. The film uses two voice-over narrators, Melvin Bragg and James Lloyd, that we might call the objective and subjective voices, each bringing in a different aspect of the artists life into relief as in a cubist painting – Cubism being a movement that Picasso acknowledged owed a debt to Rousseau's work.

Rousseau married twice, first in his youth to Clémence Boitard and later to Josephine Noury. When not married he always sought out female companionship to make his life whole and wrote love letters to a variety of women, many of whom never took the naïf artist seriously. Russell accentuates that isolation with the artist always alone in medium-long shots – other people are always off to the side of the frame or in the background out of focus. Like many artists his main consolation was his work, to which he remained devoted. He lived long enough to know Picasso as a young man. The Spaniard had recently moved to Paris and was then working out the pictorial problems of one of the most radical, difficult paintings ever made, *Les Demoiselles d'Avignon* (1907); a work that was, for the time, outrageously vulgar, aggressive, and obtuse - displaying an encyclopedic knowledge of art history and riffing on that history with devotion and mocking sarcasm in equal measure; this aggressive assault outraged everyone from friends to critics, to his rival Henri Matisse. Rousseau is said to have congratulated the fledgling artist on his new painting, telling him that they were the two greatest contemporary artists, Picasso in the Egyptian style and he in the modern style.[30] It is not known how, or if, Picasso replied to this astonishing remark. Picasso's admiration would prove to be important as, aside from throwing memorable parties for him, one of his good friends Guillaume Apollinaire was not only the best poet of his generation but an influential art critic who would, after some skepticism, eventually come around to Rousseau's work and write about it, giving the artist his first taste of success in the art world. After Apollinaire signed off on Rousseau's "authenticity and genius" the wealthy classes who purchased art started to buy the paintings in the last years of his life.

In Rousseau's early years when he first started showing at the Salon des Indépendants the uncomprehending audience of pompous twits during an opening is shown by Russell in a burlesque manner by depicting the laughing gallery-goers as they would have been seen by Alfred Jarry, the great proto-surrealist writer and Rousseau's one friend who understood his genius and was able to write intelligently about it. The typically serious voice over commentary by Bragg hilariously describes Jarry as a "Pataphysical midget!" This is a description that surely would have caused the highly sensitive Jarry to fire the loaded pistol that he carried with him on his bicycling tours of Paris!

Jarry here is beautifully played with extraordinary emotional force by Annette Robertson, who also played Debussy's mistress in *The Debussy Film* the same year; here she fully inhabits the role proving herself equal to the difficult part. Robertson plays Jarry as a haunted, resentful, anti-social misfit full of rage and sarcastic fury always aimed at the powers that be. Jarry was a genius who knew he was doomed to be misunderstood and to die an early death, always swinging wildly from overdoses of coffee to an alcoholic haze on a daily basis. When we first see him Russell shoots him on his beloved bicycle, in a tracking shot that mimics *Jules and Jim*, even using very similar music from the film, so we get a sense of his high adrenalin mindset, trying to accomplish as much as possible in the time he had. Jarry's acerbic wit spared no one, including himself - his work was an explosion of creative genius that borrowed heavily from commedia dell'arte of the past and the working class music hall comedy of the time. He loathed the art world almost as much as he hated the literary salons of his day. While music halls specialized in brief sketches that skewered the upper classes and famous politicians Jarry's work took different a different turn. Being well versed in classical European literature Jarry cleverly simulated conventional heroic plays and historical novels (even the Bible) but turned all of that well intentioned sophistry on its head so the moralizing narratives became absurd. In some sense he took the satire of *Don Quixote* to the next level pushing it to the breaking point. Nothing like this aggressive humor would be seen again until it started to appear during WWI with Dada and the surrealists novels of Philippe Soupault and André Breton, finally flowering in the revolutionary period of the 1960's with *Beyond the Fringe, This Was the Week That Was,* and *Monty Python's Flying Circus*. But while Jarry was there first he paid dearly for it by being ignored or openly ridiculed in his lifetime. Jarry was not only the first to recognize Rousseau's genius but someone that could talk about the work with the artist on a regular basis – something that proved vitally important for Rousseau's development.

Their moving friendship is visually developed in a few quick scenes that touch upon Jarry's brilliant play *Ubu Roi* (1896) (*King Ubu*) that used comical, episodic, non-sequiturs in the tradition of music hall comedy but mimicking "heroic" novels and plays. It was obvious to the audience that first saw *Ubu Roi* that Jarry was making fun of those in power at that moment, skewering the proverbial stuffed shirts and over decorated pompous ladies who constituted the ruling classes in 1896. Russell juxtaposes the overbearing bosses and their lackeys on stage with those in the audience to full effect. He shoots the theatrical piece using idiosyncratic and deliberately eccentric framing and off-kilter use of perspective and space – finding filmic equivalents to Rousseau's work with panache.

During the performance of *Ubu Roi*, when the women in evening gowns sitting in the front row nearly faint upon hearing the fist word in the play, "shitter," Jarry can only take delight in his small victory. As the audience scream or get up to leave Russell shoots them suddenly wearing grotesque commedia dell'arte fake noses and wigs – no doubt this is how Jarry saw them. Russell takes a page here from Jean Vigo's *Zero for Conduct* (1933) that also used commedia dell'arte masks and props for much the same reason: to satirize the ruling class. The same couple we saw earlier eating while openly laughing at Rousseau's work is seen again (still eating) horrified by the word "shitter" and looking for the exit.

Jarry's iconoclasm, collage aesthetic, along with his sarcastic working class humor, is in many ways a precursor to Russell's work, something we can see in Jarry's comic opera, *The Pope's Mustard-Maker* (1907), the last theatrical work he completed the same year he died of alcoholism. The opera is loosely based on the legend of Joan, the female medieval pope, and contains the usual Jarryesque smutty jokes, puns, and lively songs full of wordplay and innuendo. The opera ends with the pope celebrating, in song, the spiritual value of enemas. As to be expected the work was not staged in Jarry's lifetime and remains unproduced. One day the world might be ready for *The Pope's Mustard-Maker*, but perhaps the only person who could have done it justice was Russell.

Always on Sunday is very different from both avant-garde documentary work and conventional Hollywood films. Let's take Van Gogh and bring in two cinematic examples, one avant-garde and one conventional. First, Alain Resnais' and Robert Hessen's avant-garde documentary *Van Gogh* (1948), using black and white film, explores Van Gogh's work up close – literally, as we see only fragments of paintings - in some cases we are so close the image is abstract. The cutting is paced to the contemporary classical music composed by Jacques Besse and a voiceover written by Robert Hessens. This collaged fragmentary approach can make it seem as if all of Van Gogh's body of work were composed of only one painting that we never see as a whole. Resnais does not try to enter into the mind of Van Gogh but to use the film to explore his work and the ideas or concepts of the clash between nature/culture and the physical/spiritual that interests Resnais – fair enough.

Secondly the conventional Hollywood film *Lust for Life* (1956), by Vincente Minnelli, about Van Gogh takes the opposite approach by having a film star (Kirk Douglas) imitate Van Gogh's appearance and go through the motions of being "inspired" or "going mad" as the case may be. We see artifice and effects, costumes and sets, that look like the places in his paintings but everything has the look of a staged scene in an opera – once again Van Gogh's inner life and his interaction with the world (such as it was) is nowhere to be found even with a running time of two hours. Russell dares to explore Rousseau's inner life and his society; we see his relationship to his contemporaries, his friends, his enemies, and to the world of the Belle Époque to which he belonged. There are no special effects, as he does it all with writing, camera movement, framing and cutting.

When Apollinaire and some of the their mutual friends play a practical joke on Rousseau and invite some fake dignitaries from the art world to visit his studio – again with wigs and make-up from commedia dell'arte - Rousseau drops a pot of stew on their expensive shoes making sure the visit comes to nothing. As the scene unfolds Russell shows that Rousseau is clearly more concerned about that lost stew, that might have lasted a few days, than any sort of glittering prizes that the dignitaries might have bestowed. Russell was always perceptive about poverty and its effects on artists as they try to make a go of it in a world that is highly unlikely to be receptive to their work and they, sooner or later, come to realize it. Their heroism and their occasional small victories are all the more meaningful for being expressed not in grandiose set pieces or with a full orchestra guiding our emotions (as in *Lust for Life*), but in simple scenes, such as a pot of stew falling on the floor.

Towards the end of the film, and of Rousseau's life, the artist shows his work to Leonie, a shop assistant that he was having relations with but who adamantly refused to marry him; she dresses up and pretends to be a wealthy collector coming by to look at his work as a lark. Leonie can only laugh hysterically as he shows each painting, carefully mentioning the full name of each canvas. Then Russell performs his magic and the laughter and Rousseau's naming of the work become a duel of sorts as each of them seems to use the laughter and the title of the works as a weapon, baiting each other, and hitting each other over the head. Russell then cuts to close-ups of each of the works showing the paintings in full - but suddenly the laughter is not just Leonie's but a whole group of people laughing together but Rousseau soldiers on; only then do we get close-ups, as in Resnais' *Van Gogh* but here the close-ups carry more weight, being part of a larger narrative, being, in effect the response to the laughter. Russell slowly builds up his montage, speeding it up, ending on a static shot of the empty sofa where Leonie was sitting – she had left without Rousseau being aware of it – the relationship is over.

Rousseau's response is to begin a new painting and carry on. He died in 1910 of gangrene, from an infected wound, in a hospital alone. Russell shows only a close-up of Rousseau waiting to die and then a long shot of him along with a row of empty beds in a hospital giving us a horrifyingly intimate view of his isolation in his final moments. One senses that Russell felt that artists were, in effect, always alone, and their longing for love and companionship was compensation for that loneliness – certainly with Rousseau his solitude is self-evident from the first frame when we see him outdoors by himself exiting a stone neoclassical basement that looks like a mausoleum, to the final shot of him, again alone, in a room full of empty beds. But Russell doesn't end his film here - in a work that shifts so easily and so quickly from melancholy to joyous, and from loud to silence, Russell provides a wonderful coda. In a flashback we again see Rousseau as a snappily dressed, upbeat, middle aged man, while on the soundtrack we hear the jaunty music associated with his early years, taking his paintings on a wheelbarrow to see if he can get them into the Salon or the Salon des Indépendants – always pushing forward – as if he were the servant of his work, merely a laborer doing his job, which is how he saw himself.

ISADORA DUNCAN, THE BIGGEST DANCER IN THE WORLD (Short/1966)
Isadora Duncan, The Biggest Dancer in the World is a 65 minute film on the American dancer Isadora Duncan as the film chronicles the various landscapes and urban views, from San Francisco where she was born, to New York, Paris, Moscow and Nice – all places that she called home. These landscapes correspond to the voice over narration but the staged scenes are shot in a documentary style with a hand held camera and the documentary shots have highly theatrical music cues to highlight their staged reality – again the presence of counterpoint, paradox, and a distinct collage effect. Isadora Duncan is shown dealing with uncomprehending administrators in the US, Europe, and the Soviet Union - all oblivious to the creative impulse in her and in themselves, regardless of their political leanings. They manage over the years to wear out her body but not her spirit. Russell's politics were fundamentally humanist. He loved creative people because of their unwavering emotional commitment to their work and to each other. When artists spoke truth to power he was with them every step of the way, and when they made a mess of their lives he fleshed out their emotional realities, putting them in a historical context, without being condescending or superior. Duncan's overtly dramatic personality is given the stage – literally and figuratively - as her emotionally overextended life found her always playing catch-up and on the run. Unlike *Isadora* (1968) written by Melvyn Bragg, a Russell collaborator, and directed by Karel Reisz, a fellow apprentice at the BBC, which turned Duncan's life into romantic melodrama, Russell, with less time and money, explored Isadora's contradictory and complex life in depth, constructing a narrative that is as multi-faceted and complex as his subject.

Russell starts his film as a voiceover in the manner of the "News on the March" sequence from *Citizen Kane* that gives us a rapidly paced rundown of Duncan's life that is somewhat overwhelming in its compression, as Russell intended. This is similar to *Kane's* multifaceted approach in its bravura opening, where Welles mimicked various genres from newsreels to gothic horror, and from avant-garde cinema to stock footage. Russell takes the plunge but in his own peculiar way adding vaudeville, silent cinema, and absurdist sarcastic humor into the mix. Russell begins with some hand drawn letters, reminiscent of circus script, spelling out "Isadora" one letter at a time as a group of voices recite the letters as if counting down. Once into the film proper Russell wastes no time and from the rear of a theater stage we see Isadora dancing naked to an outraged audience. But Russell has speeded up the footage so it resembles a silent film giving it an element of the absurd – we will see the same scene from the opposite side of the stage later at normal speed but miss the naked dance as the cops (that seem more like Kops) bring the show to an end. The typical authorial male voiceover from newsreels explains the historical circumstances and the date: "Police break up a performance in Boston by Duncan and arrest her for indecency, October 20, 1922."

Later she parties hard, dancing on top of a grand piano, with the film once again speeded up and edited to the popular music of the period. From this hectic motion we get a feel for Duncan's frenetic pace but also get a good sense that she is running away from something. We are told in voiceover that Duncan and her husband, the Russian poet Sergei Yessenin (Alexei Jawdokimov), were both arrested and deported for throwing her piano out the window of her hotel, giving us the impression that Duncan was closer to the spirit of a rock n' roll goddess than to Adele Astaire, Fred Astaire's sister, who was also a professional dancer in the twenties but performed traditional dances in supper clubs, cabarets, and private parties for the rich.

In one of Russell's most inspired edits he cuts from Duncan rushing into the ocean to commit suicide while a one legged man on crutches falls into the water trying to save her, to a couch from the twenties with various female legs seen dancing the Charleston upside down and speeded up as in a vaudeville routine – surely this is only a cut that could have been made by Russell. "April 19, 1913" explains the voiceover as we are told that Duncan's two children and their governess were drowned in the river Seine as the car they were in stalled and the chauffer got out to restart it but the car slid into the water. Russell shows us only the chauffer holding the car's crank and staring into the river as some ducks pass by oblivious to it all.

Duncan wastes no time after her failed suicide attempt and we next see her partying inside a grand car, with a small orchestra (including a tuba) incredulously packed into the convertible, as Russell cuts to a suicide note written (in blood we are told) by Sergei Yessenin her husband who had hanged himself in his hotel room in Russia "December 27, 1925." Russell smartly cuts to Yessenin's legs dangling and spinning in fast motion as if he were dancing even in death, or as if the frenetic pace of the twenties were so powerful that even death could not bring it to heel. But typical of Russell despite the brilliance of the sequence he doesn't linger on it and quickly moves on. Finally we get the announcement of Isadora's death, strangled by her scarf in "Nice, December 15, 1927" as it got caught in the wheel hub of the convertible she was riding in to yet another party.

From this frenetic and beautifully orchestrated turbulent opening we get a second, slow movement, with a shot of an older English gentleman holding an open umbrella in a cemetery – he is sitting on a large headstone that makes for a good chair and wearing heavy British winter clothes. Russell holds his still shot as the voiceover, now assumed by Russell himself, explains that one of Duncan's few steady friends during her chaotic final years was the writer Giles Stokes who eventually wrote a biography of Duncan, with "the definitive account of her last days in Nice." Stokes was a young man in the twenties and he gives us a portrait of the woman he knew then. Russell cuts to a close-up of Stokes as he gets more into his story – his professorial manner and calm cadence suit this slow movement. One can also see why they were friends as he seems to be at the opposite end of the spectrum from the hyperkinetic Duncan – they must have balanced each other out nicely and been able to understand each other instinctively. Russell dissolves from Stokes to a young Duncan dancing, in slow motion on the beaches in California "where she taught herself how to dance." Young Duncan is played by Russell regular Judith Paris while the older Duncan is portrayed by Vivian Pickles in a fearless performance giving us Duncan's flaws and insecurities as well as her genius in equal measure. Pickles then was a full bodied woman as was Duncan herself - but the American dancer was clearly someone confortable in her own skin, someone who was, in a sense, always expressing herself through her body, always dancing, and Pickles gets that part of Duncan's personality just right.

Duncan had a life that would put most soap operas to shame – it was also consistently lived at the level of ecstasy and frenzy that only Russell could possibly do it justice. Duncan was not a dancer in the traditional sense in any form that we can imagine today. She was a revolutionary who thought of dance not as entertainment, or even as "art," but traced its roots to a form of sacred ceremony where the boundaries between folk dances, religious rituals, social play, and everyday movements were all incorporated into a holistic form of expression available to all. Duncan more than once said she had little interest in "dance" in the traditional sense – she was after some form of communion with a higher self, with the elemental life force that we all carry with us and are a part of. In effect dance was a form of spiritual healing and connection more than a performance per se. She led the way to future innovators as different as Merce Cunningham and Daria Halprin. While her philosophical underpinnings – linking dance to ancient Greek models – was somewhat far fetched since no one in Duncan's time, or today, knows what such dances were like, the spirit of the endeavor was honest and visionary.

Russell shows her brief liaison with the sewing machine magnate, and profligate playboy, Paris Singer (son of inventor Isaac Singer), in brief staccato sequences that are comical but show the complete lack of understanding between them leading to an inevitable Jazz Age break-up. As Russell paints her Duncan was suspect in her choices of mating/life partners and he treats this aspect of her life, via voiceover, with some irony. The union with the sewing machine mogul produced one child, Patrick; with Duncan's child, Beatrice, from a previous relationship with Gordon Craig, a famous modernist theater designer, she had a family to feed and Singer was very wealthy in the American Gilded Age sense of the term. He was also notoriously unfeeling and unreliable, shifting from spendthrift to miser depending on his mood, keeping mostly to himself and his life of luxury in the various cities in which he owned homes.

Russell spends some time documenting the most life-altering event in Duncan's life, the drowning of her two children, Patrick and Beatrice, along with their governess, in the Seine in 1913 when their chauffeur accidentally let the car slide into the river Seine and everyone drowned. Rather than showing the drowning as a single dramatic scene (as would happen in a conventional film) we see it in slow tracking shots and multiple dissolves, some underwater, that repeat throughout the film, as in a nightmare that keeps repeating – in effect the film seems to enter into Duncan's consciousness exploring her grief and guilt from the inside. Despite her strong will, as Russell shows her, Duncan could never escape the memory of her children, regardless of how fast paced or outrageous her life became in the roaring twenties. Duncan pushed all the buttons and burned all of her bridges without once hesitating – but she did look back and Russell's film takes advantage of those memories as they come to the fore in flash cuts and short disjunctive bursts that are like electro-shock treatments visually represented. In one section of the film dedicated to the drowning, seen earlier in the fast paced fake newsreel, Russell cross-cuts from a slow dance by Duncan in one of Singer's outrageous mansions to the children and the governess in the doomed car, scored to the music of Erik Satie; but here in the second viewing of the scene everything is slowed down in tracking shots and close-ups as we already know where the car is headed thanks to the earlier scene so the tragic aspect does not need elaboration. The final shot is of a doll surfacing briefly on the Seine before going down finally into the dark waters.

While Russell's visuals are sympathetic to Duncan's emotional roller-coaster lifestyle the voice over narrator takes a more jaundiced view, often commenting with some irony about Duncan's idealism and her allegiance to Communism – that Russell clearly thinks is something of a joke. Duncan's commitment, as with so many others of the period, seems to have been heartfelt but not clearly thought through. The reality gap between her, at times, ostentatious lifestyle and the political ideas inherent in communism – that would abolish wealth as such - never seems to have bothered her in the slightest. As such she was one of many "café Communists" of the period. Of course one could make a good case that she was hardly alone in living out a realpolitik of magical thinking – one need only remember that Pablo Picasso and André Breton were Communists but preferred to see the revolution and the "triumph of the people" from their expensive hotel rooms on the French Riviera. Russell does give Duncan the last word here as during her stay in the Soviet Union she visits some bureaucrats to ask for money for her children's school but the Council of Ministers, who are dining in a vast luxurious room typical of any czar, but without the polite manners, can't be bothered. Duncan calls them pathetic fake communists to their faces and she is duly showed the door.

To give Duncan credit, when it came to helping those who didn't have enough to eat much less enough to pay for dancing lessons, she gave as much as she got and more – at times ending up destitute herself. At one point Russell shows her on the way to China, lost in the middle of nowhere. Her car breaks down and the love letters that she always carried with her – enough to fill a suitcase – fall off the back of the car and scatter to the winds in a beautiful scene worthy of Andrei Tarkovsky. She hopelessly tries to retrieve her letters – and in a sense her past - flying off and scattering to the winds. Her intense desire for a community of like minded creative people all living together – classless, free and equal - was similar in many ways to Van Gogh's and Felix Valloton's more anarchist ideals seen in an earlier generation, in which people would live in a proto-hippie communal environment, free of money or power games, spending their time creating poetry, music and beautiful art. She was fixated on this possibility of making an Eden on earth and was wholly committed to it, whatever the personal cost.

The closest that she came to discovering this paradise was in Moscow after the Revolution where she was given an old run down, unheated palace – taken from some down on his luck aristocrat - and some children to take care of. There was no shortage of orphans and unemployed dance/music teachers in Russia after the Revolution needing a roof over their heads. Russell uses documentary footage to great effect giving us a brief but powerful glimpse into the devastation of post revolutionary Russia.

Duncan called the children her "Adorables" and taught them in her own manner – what we would now call a progressive education where they learned everything from math to literature, history and dance – all at their own pace. Her plan was to have a school of hundreds that would be so popular, and produce such wonderful results, that many other schools would be created all over the country – her dream was to eventually have her many "Adorables" in an open field dancing with her to the "Ode to Joy" sequence from Beethoven's 9th symphony.

But as Duncan discovered this ideal place of learning did not have a place in the "new society" of the Soviet Union anymore than it did in the hard-headed capitalist empire of the USA. As Russell's film makes horribly clear Duncan was never at home in either the workshops of the Soviet bureaucrats in Moscow or on the playgrounds of the ultra-rich in New York – she was, despite her fame, always the odd woman out, becoming one of the first true 20th century outsiders – like Henri Rousseau, Frederick Delius, Henri Gaudier-Brzeska, Erik Satie and Alfred Jarry – all subjects that preoccupied Russell and for whom he undoubtedly felt an affinity. Russell conflates her final two relationships with the poets Sergei Yessenin and Mercedes de Acosta turning the character of Yessenin into a hopelessly romantic fool who – as is often the case - made up for his lack of talent with superb abilities as a self-promoter with a highly dramatic, witty, and sexy presentation that left audiences agog. As to be expected Yessenin committed suicide in his hotel room in 1925.

In later life the French Riviera and Paris were her home ground as she made a reasonably good living by playing in extravagant parties and private gatherings, amusing the ultra rich in soirees that would sometimes go all night. Interestingly Fred Astaire was also in that part of the world doing the same thing but in a café/cabaret circuit that provided a more regular income – one wanders what Astaire and Duncan would have made of each other? Russell shows us Isadora putting on just such a show - a "fantasia" dance sequence performed by kids for some bored, wealthy expats. These "Greek" themed parties (as well as "Egyptian"), at times accompanied by musicians, dancers and acrobats were enormously popular in the twenties among the well to do. The dance we see is constructed along a mythic "Greek" theme that seems totally absurd, and the kids involved seem to sense it, barely containing a laugh. Russell's camera angle literally takes side with the kids and we see her from their point-of-view as a ridiculous old woman making a fool of herself. It is one of the few moments in Russell's work where he seems to be overtly cruel to his central character – his close-ups here are almost unbearable. Duncan is drunk and oblivious as the children inevitably conjure memories of her "Adorables" in Moscow, and of her own drowned children. The way she flails hopelessly in circles, oblivious to the people laughing at her, is one of Russell's most devastating sequences.

The south of France is where the American rich went to party and booze it up, escaping the prohibition of their own puritanical country until the stock market Crash of 1929 brought the party to an end and everyone had to go home. Prohibition was finally ended in 1933 but Duncan never lived to see it, dying in 1927, after yet another bruising after-party where she was strangled by her own hand painted scarf as it got caught up in the wheels of the open air luxury car where she was a passenger. F. Scott Fitzgerald was there too for the parties in the Riviera and he documented the decline and its after-effects – the famous hangover - with great sensitivity in *Tender Is the Night* and *The Crack Up*. Fitzgerald and his troubled wife Zelda met Duncan, in the last years of her life, in a Paris café where a drunken Duncan performed for tourists who would sometimes give her money or buy her a drink. By then neither Scott nor Zelda have much to say about it, except that Zelda used the attention that Isadora was getting to steal the salt and pepper dispensers as a joke – a typical strategy for the Fitzgerald's towards the end when there was not much left to say.

Russell doesn't have the heart to show this but ends his film with a fantasy sequence - a triumphant Duncan, leading her "Adorables" (seemingly numbering in the hundreds) to the ecstatic "Ode to Joy" from Beethoven's 9th symphony as she had always dreamed it would one day happen. A fitting end as Russell grants Duncan her wish - but he also leaves no doubt that, even before her tragic death and the Crash that brought the roaring twenties to a close, by 1927 the party was over, the Crash merely turned out the lights.

DON'T SHOOT THE COMPOSER (Short/1966)
Don't Shoot the Composer is a biography of Georges Delerue, the composer who did the music to many of the great French New Wave films, starting with *Hiroshima Mon Amour* (1959) along with a vast body of work comprised of over 60 films by 1966 that encompassed small documentary films and Hollywood spectacles. The film was produced by *Sunday Night*, a television series for the BBC that ran from 1965 to 1968. Their

most justly famous effort was a retelling of Plato's *Symposium* set in contemporary London, written, directed and re-titled *The Drinking Party* by Jonathan Miller.

Since this is a biography of a still vital and working composer, whose primary body of work circled around the filmmakers of the French New Wave, this film is a riff on that body of work from France that would initiate a new chapter in the history of cinema. His title references Truffaut's masterpiece, *Shoot the Piano Player*, from 1960. Russell was a fan of New-Wave films, especially *Jules and Jim* and *Breathless*, and it shows in all of his work from the 1960's. He had hired Delerue two years previously to work on *French Dressing* (1964) and they had hit if off, both being enamored of the romantic classical repertoire, particularly Debussy and Ravel - they were also close in age, hardcore film fanatics, and working class artists with young families to support.

Russell's film begins with a blatant, outrageous lie, oddly akin to Orson Welles' strategy in *F is for Fake*. By 1966 he had a bigger budget, more screen time (50 minutes), and he could do his own voiceovers if he chose to, as in this case. With beautiful black and white photography that mimics Truffaut's film we see a car from the 1940's Film Noir era arriving at La Cascade, a Parisian café near the Bois de Boulogne. Two sinister looking men exit the car and walk towards an embankment on the nearby river, have a suspicious looking conversation, and return to their car where a driver awaits them – the whole of the scene is beautifully orchestrated by Delerue and we hear Russell's voiceover explaining that the composer is highly sought after in Europe for music in films and that what we are seeing is the score for his new film as yet unseen in England. The men drive off to another café as one of them nervously looks at his watch and comments to his friend in the back seat who is always smoking and wearing dark glasses, like Godard. The men enter the café and signal to each other as the Godard lookalike starts to play pinball as in *My Life to Live* as the other man again checks his watch that we see it in close-up to a musical crescendo. A policeman routinely checks in and the men notice him with suspicion while drinking espressos. Another beautiful shot shows a Parisian street as the men make a run for it to the car and drive to Georges Delerue's house and bring him outside, forcing him into the backseat as they drive off. They take him to a secluded part of the river near the Bois de Boulogne and one of the men reaches into his coat – we assume for a gun but he offers Delerue a cigarette – not a last one before execution but as a thank you for having orchestrated this 5 minute sequence.

The nervous man with the watch was Russell himself while the Godard lookalike was John Drummond the producer and editor. They take Delerue back to his house and wire him for sound for the interview in a comic sequence that is speeded up to Delerue's fast paced, music hall style orchestration, that he used so well in Truffaut's *Jules and Jim* – we also see Ken Westbury the cinematographer set up the shots. Drummond and Russell hardly make for an inspiring Jules or Jim but instead tie up Delerue to a tree with a microphone wire, perhaps a leftover trick from the earlier sequence when they were gangsters going café to café. Micheline, Delerue's wife, and young daughter come and join in the fun. Later Russell uses a director's viewfinder so absurdly close he wouldn't be able to see anything but blurs as his sound-man uses a boom as if it were a trombone. This self-deprecating sense of fun and the absurd suggests a modesty that Russell lost as he went along but it is very much present here – perhaps made even more manifest by the presence of the master composer.

Delerue and family get fed up with these English madmen and make a run for it as Russell and his crew give chase, as in a Mack Sennett film. Russell gives some biographical information in voiceover as we see Delerue at the piano creating his orchestral soundscapes after seeing a film "only once or twice." Over a beautiful shot of a Paris street at night seen from a moving car Russell explains that the Delerue's go into the city to see a film every night of the week except Friday – the maid's night off – and that the couple met when he was working in bars, dance halls and in the theater where he met his wife who was an actress, despite the fact that his ambition as a young man had been to become a classical composer of serious music. This is very close to the character of Charlie in *Shoot the Piano Player*, something that Delerue acknowledges later in the film while talking about the composition process.

Seeing six films a week was not so unusual then and many Cinephiles of varying ages did the same. Russell creates a beautiful match cut of Delerue and his wife walking into a movie theater and then he cuts to Charlie (Charles Aznavour) in Truffaut's film walking into a bar to play the upright piano as if they were the same man. Truffaut shot his film without sound, Italian style, and then he added sound, dialogue and music after the fact so Delerue had to mimic Aznavour's playing, adjusting to the actor's sudden shoulder movements or looks into the audience when he relaxes. Russell sets up a screening where he recreates what he is is talking about so we see it in detail. Delerue explains while looking at rushes that he escaped from factory work as a young man by studying and devoting himself to music, eventually going to the Paris Conservatoire where he studied with Darius Milhaud, someone who became a role model as Milhaud worked in every sort of musical venture and was not, in any strict sense, a purist or an academic.

Delerue then goes on to explain a disagreement with Truffaut during the scoring for *Jules and Jim* where they working on the lovely vacation by bicycle sequence. The director wanted different types of music for the various locations and moods but Delerue suggested something more complex that would be, by coincidence, close to Russell's own method. The composer wanted one single theme that would unfold from one end to the other acting as a kind of counterpoint to the images, ignoring the usual parallels between picture and music, where they were always emotionally in sync. This meant that at times the music would be slow and melancholic and the images would show a happy trio, or vice versa, but what one gains is a more complex sensibility, truer to the film as a whole - Truffaut agreed. Russell then shows us the beautiful sequence with Delerue's music to see how this counterpoint worked.

Of course Russell was by 1966 already a master of using this technique in his own work, particularly with his films on composers. Did Delerue ever want to compose "serious" music? "Yes, but now my life is built around film music – I want to enjoy the benefits of a varied life – in this way I feel more useful than if I just wrote symphonies. I live with cinema people – I don't shut myself up in an ivory tower. The cinema is a living art, a work of collaboration and I like this sort of life." Russell himself might have said the very same thing.

At the halfway point *Don't Shoot the Composer* shifts toward more serious territory without a break. Russell cuts to a short documentary about a heart operation performed on a young woman that Delerue had scored. The maestro explains that for reasons of economy the producers could only afford a string quartet so, very much like Russell, he used the limitation to his advantage using the heartbeat as his launching point to the score. Russell asks the composer if he would still compose music for films if he were financially independent – Delerue says yes definitely he would continue on with the life he has now. Delerue and Russell then decide to collaborate on a mini film-within-a film where the maestro would score and then conduct music for a film Russell would make of Delerue's family life. Typically Russell uses a favorite motif: people walking in a dense forest, hand in hand, to start the proceedings. There are mini-narratives, of sorts, that are developed. First Georges and his wife flirt with him rowing a boat and her on shore keeping up – followed by a typical French get together for wine and cigarettes – these segments allow Russell to use long tracking shots with the couple as in *Jules and Jim*. We see Delerue conducting the orchestra from the piano when his daughter comes up interrupting the playing by slamming down some rebellious "wrong" notes – Delerue follows her improvisational lead and the score winds down with her impromptu suggestion as the couple on screen embrace. Russell here doubles the fiction in a tongue in cheek meta-fiction as the "fiction" on screen and the "reality" of the composer laying down the soundtrack to it are both faked.

In a radical shift in mood and music Russell shows one of Delerue's small documentary efforts on a cathedral that is dramatically lit like the moody set to an Italian opera as the mood goes appropriately dark and the music baroque. Russell shows areal shots of a castle, by day and night, with Delerue's music and we can see the effect immediately. From these benign shots Russell cuts to a "Danger/Death" sign. We are suddenly transported to what looks like a vast refinery with miles of roads – almost like a city – but completely empty except for Delerue who appears to be acting as our guide as the music becomes spectral and otherworldly, as in a horror film. The oil refinery – a "machine city" – that is near Marseilles and is run by computers without humans present except for maintenance people is the subject of another short. The music seems to anticipate *2001: a Space Odyssey* and *Ikaire XB-1* two radical and revolutionary science fiction films from the sixties. Delerue's score to the oil refinery was felt to stand on its own and was played separately in the concert hall without the film. The theme, according to Delerue, is that "natural resources such as fire and energy from oil can be used for the good of the world or the evil."

On the word evil Russell cuts to footage from the Vietnam War, then an active conflagration that would last several more years into the following decade. He uses documentary footage of a young man completely on fire running away in shock but helpless and not knowing what to do. It's absolutely harrowing film footage that is then intercut with the refinery and with American soldiers in Vietnam using a flamethrower. We see that the badly burned man collapses, his skin has turned to charcoal. The soldiers then scorch farmsand whole fields with their flames – we also see buildings on fire in an unnamed city – whole blocks as in an apocalyptic film. This is all scored to Delerue's dramatic music. Russell concludes in voiceover that these forces of energy that are harnessed are neither good or evil but can be used either way – "the choice lies with man himself."

Russell's final shot is of an incongruous concert grand piano on fire, but he runs the film backwards so the piano goes from being engulfed in flames back to its original clean state as the credits roll. Russell's radical shift from the playfulness of his opening shot parodying the New Wave to his charming encounter with the Delerue family as we find out about his work as a composer hardly prepares us for final third of the film but that is precisely what Russell wanted – to shock. A vision of catastrophe and the lures and promises of an advanced electronic society – where its industry run by quiet, efficient machines seems to go wrong - the illusion of technique becomes a nightmare.

Despite the voiceover disclaimer the film suggests that man is inherently violent and that such destruction is bound to keep recurring, until it engulfs us completely, electronic brains and all. The fact that such horrific violence can happen anywhere, anytime – "the choice lies with man himself" – is brought home. Certainly the piano – Delerue's instrument of choice – going up in flames is a reminder of the fragility of civilization, culture, and the small moments with family we treasure and that Delerue kindly shares with us – a fitting portrait of a maestro in his prime living in an age of anxiety.

DANCE OF THE SEVEN VEILS (Short/1970)

Russell's tenure at the BBC ended on a high note in 1970 with a color, one hour film on the life of Richard Strauss, *Dance of the Seven Veils: a Comic Strip in 7 Episodes on the Life of Richard Strauss (1864-1949)*. The title's "Seven Episodes" is a reference to the seven veils in *Salomé* (1905), Strauss's fever-pitched opera of sexual hysteria, misogyny, necrophilia, and revenge, loosely based on Oscar Wilde's unwieldy play from 1891 – the title also references comic strips along with a suggestion that rather than a story there would be "episodes" – such up-front allusions in the title to both high and low culture, as well as to episodic narratives, makes clear Russell's radical shift in the intervening decade from straightforward documentary films to a new hybrid cinema that would blend documentary/realism and fiction/fantasy into a new, as yet unnamed genre. Russell loved Strauss' music but hated his politics and his stuffy, Victorian narcissism – and he managed to put all of his conflicted feelings into his work with great humor and sensitivity – the film opened a new chapter for Russell that he would explore over the next decade. Unfortunately the Strauss family was horrified by the film and refused to let the music be used, going so far as to sue the producers, knowing that without the music the film could not be shown. The matter went to the courts where it was decided to shelve the work for fifty years.

While Strauss was fundamentally apolitical and more drawn to Richard Wagner's bombastic mythmaking than to fascist ideology per se, the sado-masochistic and homoerotic elements, the caricature of Weimar Berlin and Nazi Germany that Russell presented were too much for the established institutions of the time. Even in its only screening the film begins with a disclaimer from the BBC: "*Omnibus* now presents a new film by Ken Russell: *Dance of the Seven Veils*. It's been described as a harsh, unkind, violent caricature of the life of the composer Richard Strauss. This is a personal interpretation by Ken Russell as it reveals certain real and imaginary events in the composer's life – some of them are dramatized sequences of the war and the Nazi persecution of the Jews – these include scenes of considerable violence and horror."

Forewarned we open on a bare bones stage – two perfectly symmetrical small groups of audience members are placed at the left and right of a soundstage, like parentheses, while in the middle a conductor's podium has been raised ten meters off the floor – a conductor in silhouette climbs up and begins to conduct Strauss' symphonic poem *Thus Spoke Zarathustra* – based on a work by Nietzsche. Strauss in voiceover informs us: "The end of mankind is approaching! To the squalid and helpless men I will reveal the superman!" On cue we get a close up of a very romantic looking young Strauss (Christopher Gable) lit like a god in a Wagnerian opera, or perhaps an ironic comic operetta such as *Orpheus in the Underworld* as we are suddenly outdoors in the prehistoric era. In a parody of *2001: a Space Odyssey* that also used the same music Strauss stands up and we see that he is a caveman dressed like Buster Keaton in *The Three Ages* (1923). He comes out of his cave and, in all seriousness, gives the sign with his hands for the holy sacrament in the Catholic liturgy for the beginning of the Mass.

Christopher Gable was a ballet dancer before an illness forced him to switch to acting - he was Eric Fenby, the shy young composer's apprentice in *Song of Summer* - and here he performs a magnificent take-no-prisoners portrayal of the various "variations on Richard Strauss" that Russell has written for him. It is the best performance of his short career and the equal of the best performances that Russell got from so many great actors across the years. The young Strauss/Caveman, spear in hand, leaves his cave – Russell shoots from the "heroic" angles associated with classical cinema but now the heroism is turned on its head, it is put into quotes – this is heroism in shatters.

Immediately after leaving his cave Strauss improbably finds himself in the midst of an outdoor Mass with a large crucifix attached to the side of a rocky cliff, with a flock of bare chested priests flogging themselves into a frenzy – a bit further on he finds a bevy of nuns rolling on the ground in another outburst of religious hysteria, some holding up crosses and one mad nun swinging a smoking thurible that in the Catholic liturgy announces the arrival of a priest. One bold nun, Judith Paris – Elizabeth Siddal in *Dante's Inferno* - takes her rosary and lassoes Strauss with it as he takes it into his mouth sensually - this begins an orgy in which the nuns start to kiss and lick Strauss with abandon and drag him to the ground to fuck him.

In the midst of the orgy we get a change of music: we suddenly hear Strauss' *Salome* as the anti-heroine of the opera makes her entrance wearing a sixties silver mini dress. From atop a rocky crag she sees poor Strauss has been tied to the ground as one nun, dancing like her family of sisters, takes off her habit to fuck the helpless composer who then engages the nun in a wild dance of uninhibited copulation. At this point we are barely five minutes into the film but surely nothing in the history of Catholic imagery has been seen that comes even close to the outburst of sacrilegious insanity that is *Dance of the Seven Veils* - but does Russell have a method to his madness?

At a certain point it all gets to be a bit much, even for Strauss, and he makes a run for it as the screaming, dancing, nuns chase him down – the nun with the rosary fights to bring him back to the orgy but in the struggle Strauss pulls of the habit from Judith Paris and we see that she is bald – she turns to the camera in horror in a beautiful close-up as she slowly caresses her face in shame and sensuality – Strauss' aesthetic conundrum in a nutshell. The young Strauss seems to have been smitten by Salome and he goes in search of her in the woods. He finds not only Salome but a bevy of nymphs worthy of William-Adolphe Bouguereau cavorting in Russell's favorite falls in the Lake District. Strauss wisely joins in the dance with the creatures and he leads them on a ballet like dance through the forests and lakes. Since Gable could actually dance ballet Russell takes advantage having him dance with his new friends over the shallow part of the lakes so they look like they are not just walking but dancing on water.

Salome, in multi-colored pop art makeup, gives Strauss a garland of flowers and dances solo with him while the nymphs look on, as nymphs always do in 19th century European academic art. We are told in voiceover: "Strauss is the real superman as he has turned

Nietzsche's long philosophical poem into a short symphonic poem!" As Strauss' overheated music continues we suddenly see the young Strauss in a new role: wearing an officer's uniform from the Austria-Hungarian Empire – a nod to Eric von Stroheim's *Foolish Wives*. Finding himself in an opera house he tries to seduce every woman in the audience going from box to box where the elite have their seats, often with food and champagne. After a few rebuffs he finds a woman who is finally willing to dance with him and they perform a pas-de-deux – unfortunately she seems to pass out from the ecstasy in the manner of a silent film, and Strauss helpfully reaches for a nearby food tray offering the woman a chicken leg – he then proceeds to drink champagne from her boot (a cliché tradition in romantic literature/cinema) bringing the dance to an end. On cue the woman's husband challenges Strauss to a duel but the maestro quickly dispatches him, jumping to the stage where he performs another pas-de-deux with Salome herself. The audience erupts into wild applause, then a standing ovation! Clearly we are inside the mind of the fevered Strauss (or Russell?) and have been from the start of the film without any cues or clues. Russell here forgoes even fundamental narrative plot lines in favor of episodic vignettes that either flow into each other, or he uses jump cuts to move things along, more in the spirit of Monty Python than Godard – but what always unites the various parts is the nearly constant music of Strauss.

Russell shifts to a parody of silent films with Strauss as a Wagnerian Tristan and Judith Paris who is now Isolde as they sacrifice a king who "dies" as if he were in a Mack Sennett comedy. Men in tuxedos hiding behind a bush seem to see the proceedings and laugh hysterically. In voiceover Strauss speaks: "Once again a noble hero is mocked! Did I detect in some of these detractors the 'voice of the people?' I did! And in my music I mocked them." We next see Strauss as Don Quixote on a horse with a lance ready for action – most improbably (again) he sees a procession of the nuns seen earlier carrying large statue of Jesus and Mary on their shoulders. Don Quixote and his companion Sancho Panza (on a donkey) charge the nuns and Don Quixote knocks over the statues of Jesus and Mary with his lance. The statue of Jesus falls on top of Strauss knocking him off his horse. The nuns helpfully get Jesus off the flattened Don Quixote who reflects: "A hero's lot is not a happy one!" He delivers his line to the camera (as in vaudeville) while Strauss music continues into the next scene.

Strauss as an older man, dressed as a conductor in tux and tails, leads a musical group of Aryan musicians along with a military band. Strauss switches to full military uniform to play the cymbals as men in formal suits – the bourgeois audience personified - panic and run for the hills but the Aryan orchestra outflanks them and literally tortures them with Strauss' music played in their faces. They have no choice to fall to the ground and beg for mercy as Strauss continues to pound them with his *Radetzky March*. Another triumph for Strauss: "The "people" are defeated!" His victory means that he wins the heart of Isolde who now takes care of him like a housewife – helping him with his housecoat and doing the laundry in the outdoors, hanging bed sheets in the trees of the forest.

Judith Paris does a great job of going from sex starved nun to put upon housewife, at one point clobbering the maestro on the head with their new baby, in the form of a doll. We next see Strauss fucking Isolde in a bed placed in the middle of the orchestra as Russell himself conducts from the pit – as Strauss reaches climax so does the orchestra as Russell conducts, as one would expect, with abandon. Russell then has some fun parodying *The Sound of Music* – he uses one of the hills in the Lake District to stand in for the Austrian Alps as a couple with a child, all in traditional 19th century clothing, cross a stone bridge as we hear Strauss in voiceover: "Most unfortunately the allies declared war but something good did come from it: my *Alpine Symphony*!" Strauss' megalomania is made clear as we hear the bombastic music and witness the "happy German family" as in a silent film with Judith Paris doing a wonderful imitation of Julie Andrews in the "hills are alive with music" sequence from *The Sound of Music* without saying a word.

German soldiers, in rags and badly wounded, interrupt an outdoor picnic that the Strauss family is having but they are dressed in WWI clothes. Out of the blue the soldiers proceed to kill his son and rape Isolde. While Strauss watches the proceedings, hands tied, he sees that Isolde is enjoying the orgy of men on top of her. Fortunately it was all a nightmare and he wakes up in the hills of "Austria" and all is well as Isolde and his son give him a hug. Then comes the heart of the film with Strauss in voiceover: "Our beloved fatherland needed a leader - a supreme architect who can redeem our German nation. We needed a superman!"

We are back at the same staging as the beginning of the film with a large stage with the audience as a parenthesis left and right, but now alongside a conductors podium at the center is the German Reich orchestra with three Nazi banners in bright red and black. Ominously the music from *Zarathustra* returns as the camera tracks forward. Adolf Hitler comes up to the conductor's podium to give a speech as the audience that flanks him give the Nazi salute. Hitler gives a speech using his usual body language that we are familiar with from newsreels but we don't hear a word – only Strauss' music. Hitler is suddenly atop one of the stony crags in the Lake District – Russell shoots him from below as if he were a Wagnerian hero - he topples the statue of the Virgin seen earlier and it falls to the ground shattering as the nuns kneel in shock and horror. Hitler comes down from his perch as if he were the new master in the house as the music to *Zarathustra* continues – he then crushes the skull of Mary with his boot - the nuns are stunned and freeze up not knowing what to do. Suddenly one from their group – Isolde as a nun - comes and offers Hitler the statue of Jesus which he takes and throws to the ground as it suddenly becomes a Swastika. As Strauss' music concludes Russell pans up from the Swastika to the nuns, now all dressed as Hitler youth, giving the Nazi salute including Isolde up front proudly looking at her new leader – a superman has replaced Jesus.

Then comes the most controversial part of the film. The Swastika, that had been a Cross, suddenly becomes a Star of David held up by "the people" still wearing their top hats but now looking penitent. As Strauss' music goes for its grand finale the camera pulls back to reveal that the Jews are about to sacrifice a steer. With Hitler observing carefully and the Nazi youth behind him a Rabbi proceeds to cut the throat of the animal. Blood flies everywhere hitting the Nazi youth on the legs as Russell cuts to Hitler giving a speech and then to the blood soaked knife in front of the Star of David as Hitler finishes by flailing his arms wildly, as if conducting the finale to Strauss' music.

We next see Strauss as an older man with Isolde in front of his palatial house raising the Nazi flag – but in voiceover Strauss gives a disclaimer: "I have said before and I will say again that art and politics should be forever separate, yet there are moments for exceptions – the Nazis was such a moment. Of course I never came to terms with the Nazis – it is they who came to terms with me." The images show otherwise. Isolde picks some flowers from the garden as Hitler's car and entourage arrive for a visit to their house that looks like a castle in a children's book. Servants literally roll out a red carpet as Strauss, acting like an obsequious lackey, bows before the Nazis and plays his *Violin Concerto in D Minor*. Hitler, bemused, strolls with his bodyguards to the tune (literally) doing a "goosestep dance" to Strauss' concerto, as Russell shoots his sequence using a tracking medium shot, as in a Hollywood musical. Hitler is so taken by Strauss' welcome and his violin concerto that he accompanies the maestro on the piano as Herman Goering, inspired, begins to dance (badly). Strauss and Hitler then do a dance together in which they both end up playing the violin concerto as the Nazi entourage and Isolde dance around an outdoor banquet table. Clearly the scene owes much to Mel Brook's masterpiece *The Producers* (1967) that, in its sublime "Springtime for Hitler" sequence satirized both Busby Berkeley's deranged sense of mechanical order and Nazi alignments a "purity and essence," conflating them into an absurd populist musical. As they sit down to eat the beer flows and Strauss gives gifts to all the guests of one of his records with the swastika in the center instead of the title – Hitler in turn gives Strauss a medal and the composer kisses Hitler and they go off arm in arm. Strauss in voiceover: "I was the pride of Nazi culture, honored the world over, I was also the richest conductor the world had ever known. I was in demand everywhere." This is perhaps the only accurate and honest statement that Strauss delivers in his voiceover monologue.

Russell shows Strauss conducting in a sound studio as his music is being used as a soundtrack for a Hollywood film set in the royal courts of Versailles – an absurd melodrama that Russell parodies in black and white as the actors, using silent film acting and staging, go through an outdoor picnic with silly game playing and pseudo-ballet dancing, much like the one we have seen with Hitler and Strauss but now replayed on the courts of France. Russell makes the connection between the Nazis and European royalty, both bound by insipid emotional clichés, kitsch culture, and the music of Strauss that was (and still is) enormously popular in Hollywood. As we see Strauss conduct to the silent black and white film a fight breaks out in the audience between a young Nazi and an old Jew – the Nazi carves the Star of David on the old man's chest with a knife and Russell cuts to close-ups from the silent film of people kissing and laughing, then to Strauss conducting furiously as the whole audience breaks out into a fight – one woman's eye is bloodied in a nod to the Odessa Steps sequence from Eisenstein's *Battleship Potemkin* but Strauss carries on oblivious to the violence - Russell's cuts imply that the maestro is conducting not only the music but the violence as well.

In the only scene without music Joseph Goebbels comes calling as an older Strauss waits nervously with his wife Pauline (Judith Paris again) as Goebbels explains that Strauss has made the mistake of writing to a famous Jewish writer, Stefan Zweig, about a possible collaboration on a future opera. Goebbels is threatening and pleasant at the same time – exactly as he was described by the people of the time – and demands a letter of apology to Hitler himself. This scene harkens back to Russell's earlier films with a more traditional staging – the acting ceases to be cartoonish and becomes recognizably real as both Strauss and his wife are terrified, knowing that even "friends" of the Reich, if they made a mistake, could end up in serious trouble. The brilliant Zweig wrote *The World of Yesterday* – perhaps the best evocation of the Belle Époque by someone who lived it – and was friends with Thomas Mann and other exiled writers living abroad making him a known enemy of the Reich. The fact that the Nazi's knew Strauss had approached Zweig meant that they were reading his mail and probably also tapping his phone. The Strauss' had good reason to be terrified – the maestro had no option but to write the letter of apology to Hitler. "I have never been politically involved or motivated...your devoted..." As he writes his wife takes a mask of Strauss as an old man and puts it on him – at that moment he begins to act like an enfeebled old man, as if the letter and the mask had aged him half a century on the spot.

Strauss as an old man is next seen walking in the ruins of Berlin after the war reflecting on the tragedy of the war: "Our own barbarism had been perhaps exaggerated but there can be no doubt – but has it not been crushed by another barbarism, equally harsh?" With Germany in ruins Strauss moves to London in 1947 hoping to rebuild his career there and put the Nazi episode behind him. We see Strauss, now presumably in London, take to the same tall podium again with the same audience at the far left and right as he again begins to conduct *Zarathustra*. Being old he now has trouble climbing the tall stairs to reach the podium but once there he conducts with such youthful abandon and bravado that he rips his old man mask off and becomes, once again, the youthful Strauss – Zarathustra! But as the credits roll we don't hear Strauss but Ella Fitzgerald sing *By Strauss*, a song written by George and Ira Gershwin (Strauss's American contemporaries) that parodies Strauss' waltz beat:

> *Away with the music of Broadway!*
> *Be off with your Irving Berlin*
> *O I give no quarter to Kern or Cole Porter*
> *And Gershwin keeps pounding on tin!*
>
> *How can I be civil when hearing this drivel?*
> *It's only for nightclubbing souses*
> *O give me the free 'n' easy waltz that is Vienneasy and*
> *Go tell the band if they want a hand*
> *The waltz must be Strauss's*

The Gershwin's hilarious and sarcastic lyrics are both a tribute and satire of Strauss' music – it is a beautiful way to wrap up *Dance of the Seven Veils* as Russell's film does exactly the same thing cinematically. *Dance of the Seven Veils* pushes the limit on every aspect of biographical cinema. Even the traditional "rational" voiceover has been obliterated, replaced by the ravings of a completely unreliable, narcissist first person narrator, Strauss himself. To add insult to injury Russell used Strauss' actual writings to hoist him on his own petard. While the film is influenced by classical comic ballets from the 20th century, such as *Parade*, *Pulcinella*, and *The Love of Three Oranges*, as well as Surrealist films such as *L'Age d'Or* and *Entr'acte*, that all used elements of the absurd, the film goes far beyond such works to challenge the ideas we hold about storytelling, history, and entertainment – it does so by employing surrealist elements present in all of the works mentioned but pushing them to heretofore unknown territory that tested boundaries in every sense.

In *Dance of the Seven Veils* narrative cohesion is blindsided and pushed off a cliff; theatrical asides that might be from vaudeville are stuck in historical realities that make of mockery of historical realities; narrative roads merge into dead ends; conventions collapse on each other like a house of cards but no one seems to care; parody and tragedy try to outsmart and upstage each other as if they were in a circus; cartoon kitsch and biblical allegory keep crashing into each other as in a nightmare; obscene adolescent transgressions finally get their day while adults wear masks that nullify their philosophies and their pretensions. In *Dance of the Seven Veils* "narrative" itself is a nullity. The anarchist satire all came out at once with no let-up, as if Russell had been holding it back for years but could no longer contain himself. Interestingly *Monty Python's Flying Circus* shares many subversive elements with Russell's film and came out at around the same time (1969). Caution is not a word that was much used by Russell and in 1970 he dives into the deep end with his Strauss biography as if sure he will never look back. For better and for worse Russell was right, *Dance of the Seven Veils* would become the template he would return to for the rest of his career – his work for the BBC was done.

B

The BBC 3: Ken Russell, Pauline Boty and *Pop Goes the Easel* (1962)

FOUR ARTISTS IN LONDON, 1962

Perhaps the most fascinating film from Russell's magnificent BBC series of films for *Monitor*, and one of the seminal short films of the 1960's, was *Pop Goes the Easel* (1962) a 42 minute portrait of four of the young British pop artists then residing in London: Peter Blake, Derek Boshier, Peter Phillips and Pauline Boty. The latter was one of the few women pop artists in a field dominated by men. She died at the age of 28 and this is the only record we have of her speaking for herself on film. Boty was an actress, dancer and a model as well as an artist. She managed to make a living from the former professions while she worked and promoted the latter using her small but growing celebrity status as a platform. She was one of the presenters on an early BBC radio weekly arts review and so was relatively well known in London media earning a brief cameo appearance in *Alfie* (1966) as one of Michael Caine's girlfriends. Boty was also a dancer on the then popular, now legendary, British music show *Ready Steady Go!* and she also worked in TV dramas and on stage at the Royal Court.

Of course this wide exposure proved to be a double edged sword as Boty was, even after her death, accused of being a "dolly-bird" who traded on her looks to promote work not worthy of being shown. This facile and mysoginistic criticism was not laid to rest until long after her death, at the exhibition in 1994 *Pauline Boty: Artist and Woman*. Boty's work was both of its time and at once removed from it – she was different from the boys that made up the world of Pop art in London in the early/mid 60's. What were those differences and how did Russell present them in *Pop Goes the Easel*? Even more importantly for our purposes how did Russell and Boty collaborate on her segment of the film?

This is the writer Ali Smith (born 1962), who featured Boty as one of the characters in her novel *Autumn*, explaining Boty's work in the context of 1960's Pop art:

> "Pop art revels in, is excited by and transfigures the throwaway. It grew out of the newly opened sensibilities of its artists to the pop detritus of the everyday, the culture of multiple replication of images, of movie and music icons, advertising, comics, magazines, cigarette packets, beermats, trash – a manifestation of what Boty herself called "nostalgia for NOW. It's almost like painting mythology" she said, "a present-day mythology – film stars, etc… the 20th century gods and goddesses. People need them and the myths that surround them because their own lives are enriched by them. Pop art colors those myths."[31]

This statement mirrors Parker Tyler's *Magic and Myth of the Movies* (1947) in which he makes correlations (then new) between films stars and mythologies of past civilizations, principally the Greeks and their gods. By this definition Pop art was not in any way critical of these myths but was an artistic deployment or display of those myths, somewhat analogous to Greek sculpture (as Tyler phrased it). In contrast to this artistic reverie the writers of the period, who were also keenly interested in myths, were highly critical as we can see in Roland Barthes' *Mythologies* (1957), Theodor Adorno's *Minima Moralia* (1951) and Claude Levi-Strauss's *Wild Thought* (1962). In effect the writers saw myths from the outside even if they, particularly in the case of Barthes, were, in fact, inside, as he was writing about the myths in contemporary Western culture generally and Paris in particular.

Whether it was Barthes in the realm of the essay, fictions such as *Betrayed by Rita Hayworth* by Manuel Puig, or even poetry such as *The Age of Anxiety* by W.H. Auden, writers tended to see myth skeptically, as a totality that expressed the interests of power, fate, and dark historical forces that were obscure and mysterious. Meanwhile artists sought a way to enter inside of myth by creating totemic artifacts that *embodied* myths in their own culture – perhaps the ultimate manifestation of this idea is the work of Andy Warhol. The difference between the writers and the artists is crucial to understanding Pop culture, particularly its British variant that sough to align itself more with the writers. In Russell's film Boty also references Derek Boshier's explanation in which he describes how popular images of American power seduce the mind: "...they infiltrate you at the breakfast table" explains Boshier, but then he continues, "one shouldn't be frightened because it is possible to possess those images in turn, through the use of imaginative play." In effect, one could "possess" these powerful advertising images via Pop art. Was Boshier right or did Barthes have "Mythologies" in his pocket?

Certainly in 1962 when the film was made this was a very current idea, not only with artists but also philosophers. In 1955 Herbert Marcuse, the most popular and accessible of the Frankfurt School writers published *Eros and Civilization* in which he outlined a Utopian vision of contemporary society, one that had a profound influence on Boty's generation coming up in the sixties particularly with creative people. Marcuse accepted the death rattle of Communism as a fait accompli after Stalin's death camps became common knowledge but to find some sort of political ideal he, like Barthes, reached further back than Marx to the French anarchist Charles Fourier, who said explicitly that love and sex could be the motors to a free society and that it was only the coercive and restrictive mechanisms of "reason," "work," and "duty" – espoused by the ruling classes (for obvious reasons) - that repressed and distorted these fundamental desires in human beings.

Eros and Civilization imagined a future where individuals would be freed from the fetters of capitalism and where their true instincts – presumably inclined toward sharing, dreaming, play, and sexual gratification - would finally be given not only free expression but more importantly (for Marcuse) a coherent social role. In effect Marcuse rejected Freud's *Civilization and It's Discontents* (1930) arguing that sex, friendship and solidarity could overthrow the established order – an order based around the idea of competition being the major organizing factor around which society was built. This new society imagined by Marcuse would be based around equal participation, a balanced distribution of wealth, and free love – a proto-hippie communal life that has a long lineage, not only in Europe but in the 19th century in the USA, with Walt Whitman and various

Pantheistic, anarchist, proto-hippie groups that were then popular. This idealism did not last very long, either in the 19th century or in the 1960's. The "hippie" was pronounced officially dead by the San Francisco hippies themselves in 1967 – ironically the same year that the hippie phenomenon became a media sensation, via television, with the famous "Summer of Love."[32] Nevertheless this battered but unbroken idealism proved to be an all important catalyst for much of the subsequent work not only of the British Pop artists of the sixties but for creative people working in various mediums, from music to fabric design.

In *Pop Goes the Easel* each of the four artists was given their own segment and in the last ten minutes of the film they all come together in Boty's flat for a drink and to talk about their new work. For the first time in a documentary the soundtrack was composed of current pop and electronic music. As was usual for Russell by 1962 aside from actual documentary footage some of the scenes were staged and shot as a documentary and some were left to appear staged, these were then orchestrated in the editing to radically different musical cues. This is the London based critic David Allan Mellor describing the film: "In their segments they (the men) coolly mime the fascinated poses of fandom and masculine heroics drawn from cinema's past."[33] They also indulged very seriously in the male clichés of large cars, American advertising, guns, pin-ups, and accelerated urban speed. Russell nevertheless put their "heroics" in quotation marks using camera angles that mimic the traditional shot selection of action/adventure cinema, but he placed these shots in mundane English contexts, such as a suburban street or outdoor market, so they became absurd. This self-deprecating dry humor had a decidedly British sensibility. Russell also mimicked various genres of film treating them as a style whose tropes were at his service – often going so far as deploying two styles simultaneously and having one play off the other as in free form jazz – something also being done by Godard and Truffaut in their early period.

For example Russell conjures the cinema-verité style of Free Cinema in certain shots that were carefully staged such as Derek Boshier having breakfast with some Kellogg's corn flakes, and he mimicked American action films such as having Peter Phillips being driven in fancy convertible through town using a wide angle lens, but both shots were staged and lead to unexpected conclusions not available to their respective genres. By 1962 Russell was a master of this stylistic counterpoint but in other set pieces he used a highly theatrical staging that crossed over onto surrealist cinema or television variety shows, and to add to the ambiguity already in play these were incongruously staged with real people in actual apartments and studios; in some cases the non-actors seem self-conscious and going along merely for the fun of it – a characteristic familiar from amateur films, avant-garde shorts, and grindhouse B-movies of the same period. Some critics of the time argued that Russell was merely throwing everything at the viewer to see what might stick in order to keep viewer attention from flagging, but others argued that there was a more thoughtful plan involved that made sense of Russell's collage aesthetic. Was Russell using a variety of genres in the same film merely as a form of provocation? Let's look at the film itself to search for some answers.

Pop Goes the Easel begins with a pan over a large wall collage with various postcards of classical paintings and images taken from current magazines featuring mostly contemporary people that in one way or another exemplify modern life. The collage emphasizes a *democracy* of aesthetic content, where a Botticelli sits easily next to a picture of Marilyn Monroe – they not only carry the same aesthetic weight, but they have in turn become raw material for a new work of art, the collage itself – a work that was in Boty's studio and was created by her over a span of years; it was lost after her death so Russell's film and some color pictures taken by photographer Lewis Morley are the only evidence we have of this marvelous collage. We see icons of femininity from various times, from Elizabeth Taylor to the diminutive princess in Velazquez's *Las Meninas*; there are some 18th century ladies from engraved prints and even cupid makes an appearance via Bronzino. Male heroes such as Elvis and Cliff Richard, a local British heartthrob and fifties rocker, are also seen as creators of a new music that was faster, more visceral and sexual than any previous pop music. The camera then pans down to Huw Weldon, who for a moment appears to be a part of the collage as his head is framed in an empty white space, but then he begins to speak, welcoming the viewer to his *Monitor* series and introducing Russell's film. Weldon explains that Pop artists "take as serious subject matter contemporary film stars and pop musicians as well as Hollywood genre films and that they do this not tentatively but with utmost relish."

Wheldon is the authorial voice over narrator as he introduces Peter Blake, explaining that he is the "leader of the group, and the elder statesman at age 29, who had already exhibited professionally in the USA and in London." Blake in five years would go on to worldwide fame and fortune by creating the cover to The Beatles' *Sgt. Pepper* album. He is shown in a garden methodically cutting a large doorframe in half for one of his assemblage pieces while in voiceover we are told that he comes from a humble working class background in Kent where his father was an electrician. We are then introduced to Peter Phillips who was then 22 and still a student at the Royal College of Art. We see him in his studio putting lacquer on a frame to a finished painting based on a collage – behind him is a magazine cutout of a model's face, an actual gun, and a book on Chagall. Phillips is clearly caught in a world of violence, adverts and classical modernist art. Boty is then introduced as "having just turned 24 yesterday and she has just started to show her work publicly." She is shown sitting in a desk making a collage. We are then introduced to "Derker Boshier, also 24, who comes from Portsmouth and has just finished the Royal College of Art." He is shown hammering some nails into a crate that contains one of his large paintings. The shot emphasizes that the artists don't have the means to have assistants so must do all of the work to put shows together themselves. Wheldon explains that Boshier "like the others, approaches the world of the present day, the world of the teeming city, with the keenest possible enjoyment."

On the word "enjoyment" Russell cuts to a Ferris Wheel in an amusement park as the four young artists, finally together, seem to be embarking on a typical Free Cinema "day in the life" segment shot with a hand held camera. The leader of the group, at least in their social space as it is shown, is clearly not Blake but Boty. It is also clear the two are familiar with each other whereas Boshier and Phillips are relative strangers who have been forced to be together for the shoot. The footage was shot silent as we hear Bobby Darren's hit single from 1961 *Goodbye Cruel World* – the song has a hurdy-gurdy playground theme and that may be why Russell chose it. The film shows the four artists driving bumper cars and playing various games at the fair strongly suggesting that the artists were still, in some sense, kids. The first close-up in the film is of Boty as Boshier off camera lights her cigarette – this is a shot that would be bookended in the final moments of the film with another close-up of Boty.

Russell then shifts gears and subtly moves into collage cinema with the four artists shooting rifles at targets – the target being a favorite motif of Pop artists on both sides of the Atlantic. At that moment Russell cuts to found footage of a Hollywood Western from the 1950's with a cowboy shooting a rifle at the camera, then back to the artists shooting – with accelerated cross-cutting the film satirizes rhythmic montage; it is also as if the four young artists were defending themselves against American popular culture in the form of the Western. But wasn't a large section of British Pop art, not only the four principal artists of Russell's film but also Eduardo Paolozzi, Richard Hamilton and David Hockney, constantly displaying an adoration for American pop culture? Clearly Russell here is stating bluntly that his film is as much a work of Pop collage art as the work of any of the four subjects of his film and he can use this collage to not only illustrate the life and times of these artists but also critique their ideas using the medium of collage itself.

The film casually pivots to a comedy sequence with Peter Blake in bed pretending to be asleep dreaming while the novelty song *Brigitte Bardot* by Jorge Veiga from 1961 plays on the soundtrack. Russell then cuts to a scene from Bardot's *Come Dance With Me!* (1959) as we see her in a sexy nightgown seductively (and absurdly) playing with some curtains - this is followed by a slow pan of Blake's studio/live-in space. Blake pretends to wake up wearing striped pajamas looking like a little boy surrounded by toys and adolescent collage works featuring pretty girls from fan magazines – Russell is clearly satirizing Blake's mindset as fundamentally adolescent but doing it with images. Again the critical function happens in the collage within the film, not in the voiceover by Wheldon that was written by him and was always positive, informative, and conventional. Russell finishes the pan on a note of absurdity as Blake opens his closet to put some clothes on and we see that the door is completely covered in images of Bardot. Blake explains he has done "doors" (photo-collages on door panels) of many celebrities – real and fictional - including Frank Sinatra, Superman, The Everly Brothers, Shirley Temple, and Laverne Baker – all American icons. Clearly these are religious shrines made to Pop gods that rule over the hearts and minds of the young in 1962. There follows another comical sequence in which Russell cuts rapidly to close-ups of still images of handsome male Pop idols of the time such as Bobby Rydell, Elvis, Fabian, and Frankie Avalon, ending on a close-up of a very serious looking Blake, already balding and looking like a middle aged man, drinking a cup of coffee. Is Russell here taking the piss out of Blake or simply showing him alongside some of his heroes? With Russell it could be both, but it's a question that he leaves hanging.

Russell then shifts again to a more unusual format that he would, unfortunately, rarely explore in the future, avant-garde films. Russell's camera performs a slow pan of one of Blake's collage pieces while on the soundtrack we hear a very earnest and serious Elvis for one minute being interviewed before leaving for his adventure as a G.I. in the American Army. While this displacement of image and sound was commonplace in avant-garde films by 1962 it was not seen before in a documentary film, especially one shown at the BBC. Blake explains that what we have been seeing is his "love wall." Clearly Blake, like the other artists in the group is heavily indebted to fan culture, and fan illustration, which was enormously popular in the fifties and sixties – many doors and walls were decorated with collage. We then see a montage of Blake's collages, with a heavy emphasis on female iconography and the ubiquitous "pin-up" but ending with a life-size self portrait by Blake wearing a myriad of buttons of his heroes and holding an Elvis fanzine, while we hear James Darren's hit song of the time *Her Royal Majesty*.

Russell's film collage then turns toward Phillips as we see him, improbably, in the back of a large American convertible being driven by an African American in an impeccable suit while on the soundtrack we hear jazz: Cannonball Adderley's *This Here* (1959). Russell mimics the shots common to action driven American cinema but nothing much happens except that the driver drops Phillips off at his suburban studio and then waves goodbye as he drives off – again a shot sequence quotes American action films but then, on cue, fails to deliver the goods as the film veers off in another direction entirely, as if Russell were saying: "that's enough of that." We see the young artist, barely out of his teens, in his apartment framed by his new work: large Pop paintings that seem to contain a catalog of Pop iconography such as no trespass stripes, stars, targets and the ubiquitous word of the moment: GO. The paintings seem quite pre-meditated to sell but they lack the "confident imprecision"[34] (Thomas Crow) and individuality of Boty, the humor and love so ever present in the work of Blake, or the eccentric cornucopia of influences in Boshier. The soundtrack switches to the more avant-garde jazz of Charles Mingus' *Folk Forms Number 1* (1960) and Ornette Coleman's version of *Embraceable You* (1960) establishing a connection between modern modal jazz, modern art, and Russell's cinematic collage.

We see Phillips make himself some instant coffee in a kitchen completely covered with a collage from various magazines – emphasizing the collage element again - while a woman nearby casually reads a magazine. Phillips then walks to an adjacent room where a young blonde woman is playing pinball somehow suggesting that the circus atmosphere we had seen earlier has permeated the studio – this is confirmed when Russell cuts to Phillips's paintings that do, in fact, resemble the graphics found in pinball machines – accentuated by the sounds of the machine that accompany Phillips's paintings as his camera pans and tilts, playfully moving in and out of the paintings onto the room itself. This section ends on an absurdist note as Phillips takes a real looking gun, or prop, and with a rather blasé look on his face pretends to shoot the woman playing pinball who shoots back with her finger. Clearly violence is a major theme here despite the ironic - even cheeky – sense of humor deployed throughout.

Violence of a kind continues on with the Boshier segment as two wind-up toys – a gorilla with a Union Jack flag and a robot with an American flag - crash into each other and the gorilla is knocked down. Boshier then picks up the clear winner, the American robot, as he goes on to explain his interest in the American influence on England that he calls "infiltration via advertising." He then points to one of his paintings, depicting a box of Kellogg's Corn Flakes, an American cereal. Perhaps to bring home Russell's point about violence and bring the absurdity of the fake "relaxing at home moments" to a climax Boshier while making himself some breakfast expresses delight in the free gifts inside of these cereal boxes as he proceeds to pick one out of the Kellogg's box which turns out to be a plastic toy bomb that we see in close-up. Here Russell seems, again, to be expressing a critical approach to Boshier's unabashed enthusiasm for American culture, suggesting darker historical forces.

Boty's segment is completely different as she is shown in various, highly theatrical sequences with sexy costumes and poses including extended shots where she is shown playing with her hair before a mirror and putting it in various styles suggestive of the silver screen's long history of vamps from Dietrich to Marilyn. While some have attributed the label sexist to this aspect of the film, it seems highly unlikely since some of the artists featured in Russell's *Monitor* series were not only women but outspoken radical feminists, such as the playwright Shelagh Delaney with whom he also collaborated. Moreover with Boty Russell discussed her segment and she played a major role in the narrative creating a short film that is a "day in the life" – a popular format of the period that Russell had used previously – but then they turned that single minded, sometimes overly earnest style, on its head by replacing day with night, in effect opening the door to subconscious narratives. Boty wrote the piece and Russell, aside from directing, suggested locations.

Boty's sequence starts with her in a very long, modernist, circular hallway placing her artwork on the floor. The hallway was actually the headquarters of the BBC but the way Russell shoots it in high contrast black & white film the space is very dreamlike. Putting artwork on the floor or against a wall is a very typical activity in art school so the teacher can see the work just outside the classroom for a quick critique. A group of very serious adults, clearly representing authority figures, come and step on Boty's artwork - she slaps one of them on the face as a creepy, older, androgynous woman in a wheelchair comes toward her with obvious malicious intent. She is dressed in black with unusual dark glasses, like the assassin from the future in Chris Marker's *La Jetée* (1962). Boty runs away down the infinite hallway with disconcerting jump cuts to her frozen still in shock. She finally escapes into an empty elevator, but as the doors close when she turns the woman in the wheelchair is inside the elevator with her and comes toward her. As Boty reaches for the emergency phone she wakes up in bed to the sound of her doorbell.

There is a cut to Boshier ringing the bell while Blake goes to wait for her to come out by sitting down on a stone garden sculpture that looks like a sepulcher in a cemetery. They look up at her window and Boty makes an appearance fully dressed and made up in front of another stone figure – part of the building's decorative work – fading from the elements into ruin. This part of the film is accompanied by a wonderful score of distorted electronic music produced by the BBC Radiophonic Workshop that also had a hand in the soundtrack to the popular, contemporaneous, *Dr. Who* series, and influenced the sound distortions and layering process in *Sgt. Pepper* five years later.

In Boty's apartment the artists make themselves confortable as they have obviously been there before. Boshier and Phillips sit and make fun of some adverts for space travel while Blake and Boty get down to some critical analysis going through Boty's recent collages. They are obviously close friends as we listen to Boty's comic explanations for the origin of certain images in the collages while Blake's spot on critical take create a great sense of intimacy between close friends that is unique to documentaries about artists where such scenes are often forced and unnatural. As we see Boty's collages in close-up we notice that they are as likely to be influenced by English Victoriana as Hannach Hoch's harsh Dada works – pictures from American musicals mix freely with 19th century engravings in the manner of Ernst but brought up to date with pin-ups of film stars and pop heroes. As Boty relates her love of Hollywood musicals Russell cuts to the Astaire/Rogers film *Shall We Dance* (1937) and the Gershwin's song *They All Laughed* – Astaire's dancing, and Shirley Temple's tap number flash by in a matter of a few seconds. We then see Boty dressed as Fred Astaire but miming Shirley Temple singing *On the Good Ship Lollypop* while looking and gesturing straight into the camera.

While women dressed as men was a commonplace by 1962 Boty's strange amalgam of both Astaire and Temple is highly incongruous, unusual and disturbing.

After Boty's sequence, so different from the others, Russell cuts again to the four artists in a London outdoor market surveying the goods with Blake clearly in the lead as he was a known scavenger in Brixton market who constantly collected material for his collages and constructions. The scene is shot silently and we hear the recent pop hit *Duke of Earl* (1962) by Gene Chandler in which the songwriter imagines that he is so motivated, positive, and on the go that he assumes "royal" status and he asks his girlfriend to join him becoming the "Duchess of Earl." By inference the four young Pop artists are, in effect, "royalty" in the world of art and culture.

Russell then cuts to the strangest section of the film – an actual documentary of a wrestling match that is intercut with the four artists, in close-ups pretending to be engaged and entertained, but it is clear that the shots do not match up and the close-ups were in fact done at another location to be intercut later in the editing. While violence of one sort or another has been ever-present in the film, from nightmare sequences to toy bombs, this particular sort of feigned violence geared principally to theatrical spectacle, seems to come more from Russell's mind than any interest the four young Pop artists might actually have in wrestling. Certainly wrestling would continue to preoccupy Russell in arguably the greatest such scene ever shot in *Women in Love* but its place in *Pop Goes the Easel* is incongruous and tilts the balance toward Russell's eccentricities and away from his presumed subjects. As we see the absurd theatrics of the "fight" we hear a countdown as often happens in such matches but it is the song *Let's Twist Again* by Chubby Checker, a massive hit in England from 1961.

Russell then cuts to Boty's studio where the four artists, joined by other members of their generation such as David Hockney, dance like mad while others stand aside and smoke and try to talk over the music and noise as is typical of such parties. It's particularly gratifying to see Hockney jump up and down like Jerry Lewis at his most elastic while Blake does a dignified version of the twist, and Boshier cuts a handsome profile doing the dance properly and effortlessly; but of course it is Boty who steals the show with her incredible dancing (with a boa) and her sheer bliss in being alive – at one point dancers move aside and provide a circle for her joyous performance. Russell cuts from overhead long shots to hand held medium shots on the dance floor to close-ups, including a smartly dressed inter-racial couple dancing and another couple, oblivious to the camera, kissing while moving to the music.

Russell saves his most moving cut for the end, as we see documentary footage of the artists working to the music of Bach's glorious *Brandenburg Concertos*. Russell's point here is very clear – it is the Pop artists who are the new creators of what will one day be "classical" art. First up is Blake painting one of his collages, then Boshier painting while smoking a cigarette, then Boty. As we see her very deliberately painting while sitting in her studio Russell slowly, smoothly, tracks in for a rock-steady close-up thereby negating the "documentary" aspect and entering the territory of drama – the drama of the human face. After a few seconds Boty stops painting and looks down at the floor, clearly aware she is being photographed she holds the pose looking very serious and determined – it's a beautiful moment and an appropriate one on which to end Russell's sublime masterpiece.

2. RESPONSES AND POP HISTORY

What are we to make of the Boty/Russell collaboration? The film had its detractors including the writer Sue Tate who, in her book on Boty's work, quotes the film historian and theoretician Laura Mulvey: "Woman could be the bearer of meaning, not the maker of meaning."[35] Just how one can achieve one without the other is something neither Tate nor Mulvey explain, since it seems likely that everyone who is alive is both making meaning and bearing meaning at all times, even if they are not aware of it - those who are aware (at times to the point of crippling self-consciousness) are sometimes referred to as artists.

This is David Alan Mellor who seems to have a clearer vision of the Russell Boty collaboration:

> "In Ken Russell's 1962 documentary she (Boty) back-combed her hair before a mirror, a fantastic, mythical, flora, re-born from one of Leonara Fini's paintings from the close of the 1930's into the epoch of Pop. Boty appears in direct contrast to her male fellow RCA painters...as she is located within troubling narratives of eccentric femininity drawn from the cinema's past...Her masquerade in Russell's film...instances a certain idea of the production of beauty; precarious

> and excessive at the same time, rooted in representation and paradoxically forecasting the performed photo-mechanical comedies of female identity (Cindy Sherman in particular) of twenty years in the future."[36]

Mellor's astute analysis of Boty's intention is on the mark but what he does not mention is that Russell brought his own eccentric, antiquarian sensibility to bear on Boty's very contemporary Pop ethos. This made for a strange and extraordinary hybrid film where death appears in several forms, from a specter in a wheelchair, to the modern coffin/elevator, to the Victorian stone sepulcher outside Boty's apartment that is italicized when Blake gets up from it, and Russell holds the shot so we see it empty from above – a stone figure of a woman reclining and sinking into the ground and eternal repose. Boty's collaboration with Russell – her nightmare – was unfortunately prescient but also charged with insightful, uncomfortable, critical insights, very much like her artwork, where Boty used feminine and male icons to consistently question the norms of beauty, idolatry and power and to place those "norms" within the context of human frailty and mortality – elements completely missing from the lexicon of Pop art. This explains why she was the outsider in the art world of her own time and even later when American Pop became canonized and institutionalized. Clearly the questioning, reflective, dialogic work of Boty had no place in Pop's triumph in the marketplace.

When Russell's film was made Boty had just finished the Royal Collage of Art in 1961, majoring in stained glass as women were not allowed directly into the painting program. While the sort of art that we would recognize as Pop started in the in late 1940's in London – with Eduardo Paolozzi's small hand-made collages - it is a movement more associated with American artists based in New York. The London version being very much DIY while the Americans simulated the mechanical effect of magazine or billboard advertising. As Ali Smith pointed out Pop artists on both sides of the Atlantic expressed an interest in detritus, influenced by Kurt Schwitters, as well as a fascination with contemporary popular culture and advertising, seeing them as legitimate subject matter for fine art – but there were also major differences. Where Boty and her young British colleagues differed from their American cousins was that their works tended to be more personal, consciously hand made, and self-deprecating, embracing contradictions, while the Americans emphasized a cool, superior, single-minded irony that simulated machine produced imagery.

The Americans also put an emphasis on a much larger size – mimicking the heroic scale of Abstract Expressionist painting. This "heroic" scale was cleverly put into quotation marks by the Pop artists based in Manhattan, creating works that were, in a de-facto sense, ironic in its very size since once this "heroic" size was conferred upon soft drinks, film stars and cans of spaghetti the result was a celebration of American consumerism drenched in a sarcastic irony that was loud, in-your-face, and peculiarly American. The forlorn Abstract Expressionist artists, only recently the toast Of the town, felt their work was being ridiculed and marginalized – Willem de Kooning even accused Andy Warhol of "destroying art."[37] He meant of course destroying a particular kind of art that he and American artists of the postwar era excelled in creating – an art that fearlessly examined existential fears and the fragility of life – the will to live in the face of oblivion - in effect Post-War American abstract art was fundamentally serious – even heroic - and it was being replaced, they thought, by a series of visual jokes and puns that were fundamentally superficial.

But there was another difference between London and New York Pop that many critics never mentioned because it does not deal with form, which is relatively easy to talk about, but content, which is difficult. Boty and the London school of Pop artists were European and had all been through the war, even as children – they had a *tragic* sensibility that was ingrained into them. One can also hear this in the songs of Lennon/McCartney, in the plays of John Osborne, and in the music of Harrison Birtwistle – all British artists from Boty's generation where the tragic aspect of the human condition sits alongside moments of great joy and a feeling for the momentary pleasures found in the everyday – it is all one package. In effect these artists were closer to Ingmar Bergman or Alain Resnais than to Warhol or Lichtenstein. There was also a more emotional connection to the European art of the past. Boty was as likely to reference older masters, such as François Boucher or Edward Manet as she was contemporary consumer culture – Boty and her British colleagues were interested and invested in that *dialogue*.

Meanwhile for American Pop artists the art of the past was part of an image repertoire available in books and magazines – not much different from shopping catalogs. Their work referenced the vast encyclopedia of images that could be recycled and marketed. For example when Andy Warhol painted the Mona Lisa using a silkscreen image it was not in order to be in dialogue with Leonardo da Vinci, or the Renaissance per se, but to show how the image was simply yet another commodity, another luxury good, another "brand" in the marketplace, no different from Coca-Cola or Elvis – in effect it was a conceptual artwork that used the Da Vinci work to express an idea. Boty and her family of artists in London were interested in forming a dialogue not a concept. For example, Warhol's *Marilyn* portrait (done shortly after she died) from his *Death in America* series was just such an icon, but when Boty painted Marilyn Monroe in *The Only Blonde in the World* her iconic status was present but subsumed by Boty's insistence on Marilyn's freedom of movement within a constricting frame. This is Marc Kristal:

> "The Only Blonde *pays tribute to Marilyn as unsinkable and eternal – a model of beauty glamour and empowering sexual awareness, rather than a casualty of Hollywood's spectacle. Pauline's rendering shows how the star, her full-figure image taken from a publicity photo for Billy Wilder's 1959 classic* Some Like it Hot, *seeming to emerge from between two fields of brilliant green (decorated with abstractions reminiscent of the artist's Hollywood musical paintings) breathlessly on the run, face ecstatic, shapely legs in racehorse motion, her vibrant body about to burst from a shimmering chrysalis of chiffon."*[38]

Boty accentuates Monroe's joy-of-life in the midst of pain and her self-created feminine persona is living dynamically alongside a strong feminist identity – Boty embraces these contradictions rather than make any attempt to efface or resolve them with easy ironic ripostes in the manner of the New York School.

Boty nevertheless would become more disillusioned with her idealistic approach to American consumer culture toward the end of her short life becoming more political and more consciously feminist – anticipating the generation of artists that would come up in the 1980's who were much more savvy about images and their effects, coming to be known collectively as "the pictures generation." Marcuse himself became disillusioned and wrote a sequel to *Eros and Civilization* nine years later titled *One Dimensional Man* (1964). In this book Marcuse admits to having been naïve – American consumer culture he claimed, was far more insidious than he had imagined. It had learned to use people's desires and feed them spurious, simple, often infantilized, addictive short-term pleasures. Over a period of time these "myths," in the form of advertising, popular cinema, television and radio, enslaved the masses to constant, ever newer, ever more extreme gratifications necessitating constantly shorter attention spans, making a counter-attack that was thoughtful or reflective virtually impossible. Marcuse sought some answers in his book and this is how he put the problem:

"*The consumer society and the politics of corporate capitalism have created a second nature of man which ties him libidinally (sic) and aggressively to the commodity form. The need for possessing, consuming, handling and constantly renewing the gadgets, devices, instruments, engines, offered to and imposed upon the people, for using these wares even at the danger of one's own destruction, has become a biological need (emphasis Marcuse).*"[39]

To his horror Marcuse realized that Capitalism could even take presumably "critical" or "radical" artworks and bring them into the fold of consumer objects in the marketplace. For example artworks supporting radical political ideologies, such as those found in the Situationist International, the French *Narrative Figuration* movement, or the feminist and radical art of the sixties, could become easily co-opted and recycled as "avant-garde art" and placed in its proper "context" within corporate museum installations. As such they would then take their place in the market, *signifying* radicalism. Of course once "radicalism" is signified as a category in the market it ceases to be radical, because it is putting itself in quotation marks, it is, in effect, quoting "radicalism," therefore it is no longer dangerous, no longer radical. As its reality as a consumer object grows in status (and its price in the marketplace grows accordingly) its radicalness drains away until there is nothing left but a very expensive "piece." One might call this horrifying takeover the art version of the "tongue eating louse," a parasitic isopod that enters fish through the gills and slowly eats the organism from the inside out leaving only the shell and the tongue – a nightmare parasite surely but one that makes for a good metaphor. But how was this takeover possible in the complex social organism of art? Why was it so difficult to see?

The cynicism of Pop, the poker-faced refusal of complexity, the affirmation of low culture, the overwrought mechanical-style, the soft-boiled adolescent humor, the ironic twists and turns - these became the staples by which we came to recognize American Pop art and the artists fully accepted, as a matter of course, that they were producing commodities for the marketplace. Warhol even liked to joke that he made very large work in order that his paintings would fetch a higher price in the marketplace.[40] This advertising art/fine art doubling, or mirror image, that in Pop was front-and-center, would become the template for a large portion of American art well into the next century. It is a system that is still in place in art schools today in the USA and beyond - whether the conventions are those of formalist abstraction, Pop, Post-Pop, or conceptual art – they are all now as academically entrenched as the Salon art of another age.

What Marcuse explained in simple language (unusual for the Frankfurt School) was that the struggle was no longer in the streets, but inside your own mind. Writers as different as Michel Foucault, and Roland Barthes took that idea and ran with it in new interesting directions. For example Marcuse and Barthes believed that "the revolution" (without ever clearly explaining what that might be) could now come only from the marginalized classes that capitalism had ignored because they had no way to purchase goods within a capitalist system – therefore they were, in the literal sense, excluded from manipulation. This rather far-fetched his idea would in turn be overturned by Giles Deleuze, Jean Baudrillard, Giorgio Agamben and other philosophers later in the century. For the new group capitalism excluded no one – the "authenticity" of the "the streets" was one of capitalisms favorite testing grounds – the place where rookie ideas are born to be either ignored or consumed – gobbled up and spit out in the market – nothing more and nothing less.

At that point capitalism's victory was not only pronounced by every news outlet at the end of the Cold War (1989) but, around the same period it announced its triumph, more "sotto voce," inside the minds of anyone who came into contact with it. Its conquest was complete and excluded no one. Boty's work captures that transition from the first flush of idealism, to its annihilation - her collage paintings perfectly expressed that dissolution, not rhetorically like Marcuse, but visually. Boty's field of collage/painting was fragmenting and coming apart at the seams, in some cases only partially visible, going off the page, leaving the middle empty, as if the society that produced these images was coming undone, fragmenting, or disappearing, as indeed it was. The fact that she could sense this in the very early sixties, and turn that observation into beautiful works of art was an extraordinary achievement. The collaboration between Boty and Russell was bound to produce something fantastic, unusual and profound – and so it proved to be.

3. 60'S COLLAGE ART: VERTIGO AND NAUSEA

In *Pop Goes the Easel* Russell not only moves effortlessly from documentary to drama to comedy but he does so within a single take, as we saw in the final shot in the film. This is a remarkable achievement considering that such nuanced, experimental, formal techniques would not be in place until much later in the decade in the work of Bergman, Fellini, Godard and Antonioni. Russell also cuts from found footage, as was being done by avant-garde filmmakers such as Bruce Conner, to narrative documentary, and from highly theatrical set pieces to footage of Brixton Market and various parts of London that were the habitat not only of the four Pop artists but of Russell himself. In effect the film is not only a portrait of the emerging artists but of the city in a transitional moment from fifties postwar black and white austerity to sixties color, liberation, and cultural dominance. It is not a period that would last very long but Russell captures the mood as that first wave of creative energy broke out into the open.

Pop Goes the Easel is the first Pop film that did not simply illustrate collage but was itself a work of collage art - one of the seminal films not only of the 1960's but of the century as a whole – it is crucial in understanding that pivot from the early century's classical style to the radical, collage-centered, utopianism of the 1960's, and then, shortly after, to the collapse of that idealism and its subsequent fragmentation and destruction in the marketplace driven art-world of the Reagan/Thatcher years - a catastrophic annihilation from which the art-world never recovered, except in the marketplace where it was reborn as a luxury good – making its occasional pretensions to "radicalness" all the more strange, anachronistic, and pathetic.

We can see that sixties social/narrative disintegration in a clearer sense with the work of the fabled film auteurs of the period who left us clear and beautiful examples of this collapse; for example we can see it in Bergman's work as it transitions from *Smiles of a Summer Night* (1955) to *Persona* (1966), in Fellini as he travels from *Variety Lights* (1950) to *Toby Dammit* (1968), in Antonioni as he goes from the melodrama of *The Lady Without Camelias* (1953) to the negation of melodrama in *The Passenger* (1975), in Godard as he travels the difficult road from the romantic charms of *A Woman is a Woman* (1961) to the hard and bitter truths of *Tout va Bien* (1972), and in Pasolini as he navigates his sensibility from the impassioned neorealism of *Mamma Roma* (1962) to the meta-fictions of *Teorema* (1968).

It's a crack-up and a dissolution, not only of classical narrative but of storytelling itself - a burnout that was also chronicled by the novelists of the time, most brilliantly, and literally, perhaps by Joan Didion in *The White Album* (1979). This is her helpful summation:

> "We tell ourselves stories in order to live. We look for the sermon in the suicide, for the social or moral lesson in the murder of five. We interpret what we see, select the most workable of the multiple choices, we live entirely by the imposition of a narrative line upon disparate images, by the "ideas" with which we have learned

to freeze the shifting phantasmagoria which is our actual experience...By way of comment I offer only that an attack of vertigo and nausea does not now seem to me an inappropriate response to the summer of 1968."[41]

As Didion makes very clear storytelling by 1968 was problematic or impossible but vertigo and nausea were not only prevalent but an appropriate response to the time period. In effect by the end of the sixties storytelling's norms, in both the novel and cinema, were finished, except as pastiche. But there was then, as to be expected, a search for new ways to tell stories or at least to describe "The End." Writers as different as Norman Mailer, W.G. Sebald, Julio Cortazar, and Umberto Eco, among others, sought answers to these problems. Eco's wonderful book *The Mysterious Flame of Queen Loana* goes further and literalizes that search, and, like Sebald, brings the novel form itself to a beautiful conclusion. There would, or course, be many more novels written after these works but whether they acknowledged it or not they were occupying a different planet.

Russell himself backtracked and fumbled in the post-sixties era and was never able to reach the heights of his extraordinary run of 32 films at the BBC – all but two made in the sixties. *Pop Goes the Easel* condenses that transition – from classical storytelling to a more fragmented, at times abstract, episodic narrative. Russell pulls out all the stops mimicking Free Cinema and Surrealist films, English vaudeville, New-Wave films, avant-garde cinema, action films, and the more liturgical films of Dryer and Eisenstein, cutting beautifully with an ecstatic pleasure in the form of the film itself – improvising like a mad composer. Something else to keep in mind is that there was always in Russell (and Boty) a bomb throwing anarchist lurking within and in the sixties he felt free to occasionally bring that aspect of his sensibility to the surface – later, especially in his Hollywood phase, this aspect of his personality was held in check. But Russell never balked at the influences – be it a master from the distant past (Botticelli in *The Debussy Film*) or a director younger than himself (Truffaut in *Don't Shoot the Composer*) he wore his influences on his sleeve.

The collaboration between Russell and Boty stands as one of the high points for both artists. They also became friends and Russell used Boty as an actress in his subsequent film, a biography of the Hungarian composer Bela Bartok. Mellor remembers seeing *Pop Goes the Easel* as a 13-year-old when it was shown in 1962: "It was something completely else. It promised an England on the threshold of something wonderful. A new world was in formation."⁴² Indeed it was - that world didn't last very long, but in that short decade it did burn brightly, and its light even today – like that of a dead star – is still visible to us and likely to continue to shine for some time.

As for Boty herself she became pregnant in 1965 but during a prenatal exam she was diagnosed with incurable cancer. She refused to start chemotherapy that would have necessitated an abortion. Her daughter Boty Goodwin was born in February of 1966 and Pauline Boty died in July of that same year at the age of 28. Her daughter was given for adoption to her parents, then in their 50's, and she was renamed Katy Goodwin as the name Boty caused the parents too much pain. Her husband, the successful literary agent Clive Goodwin, died eleven years later at the age of 45 from a cerebral hemorrhage. In the brief four year period that Goodwin and Boty shared a flat in Cromwell Road, seen in Russell's film toward the end, their place became a central station for artists, writers, filmmakers, and musicians (including Bob Dylan) as well as fellow artists, known and unknown.

After her death her work was stored away in a barn on her brother's farm and it was forgotten for nearly 30 years. Her work was saved from the dustbin by David Allan Mellor and his friend the academic historian Sue Tate, who kept the work until it could be given a proper retrospective first in 1994 and again more extensively in 2023. In November 2019 the New York Times profiled Boty in their popular "Overlooked No More" series titled: *Pauline Boty, Rebellious Pop Artist*. Boty's daughter Katy died in California from a heroin overdose in 1995 aged 29. In 2023 a plaque was erected at Pauline's Cromwell Road home and studio - the brief ceremony was attended by surviving family, friends, and admirers, including her long time friend, now Sir Peter Blake.

P

The BBC 4:
Dante's Inferno: The Private Life of Dante Gabriel Rossetti, Poet and Painter (1967)

Dante's Inferno: The Private Life of Dante Gabriel Rossetti, Poet and Painter (henceforth *Dante*) was made for the BBC's *Omnibus* series so no longer had the restrictions of time that were an aspect of *Monitor*. Russell took full advantage, making a feature length film – the subject matter certainly warranted it as the poet/painter's life puts most melodrama to shame. Even at 90 minutes there is simply too much biographical fireworks forcing Russell to choose what to emphasize and what to ignore. *Dante* is the most satisfying screenplay in all of his early work and arguably his best overall – it was written by Russell and Austin Frazer who also wrote the dialogue and did the voiceover narration.

The screenplay sticks to historical facts altering to compress events, and he follows a sequential narrative, using jumps in time only for emotional punctuation; but the film has dream and memory sequences that flow into the narrative without markers so there is no direct break between dream, memory, and reality – an aspect of filmmaking introduced to the feature film only a few years earlier by various directors such as: Federico Fellini (*8 1/2*), Andrei Tarkovsky (*Ivan's Childhood*) John Frankenheimer (*The Manchurian Candidate*), and Ingmar Bergman (*Wild Strawberries*).

By 1967 Russell had made over twenty films and had a crew that he trusted and who knew his working style. Unlike much of his work – even later after his tenure at the BBC - that uses flat, high temperature "television lighting" the director of photography Nat Crosby for *Dante* instead opts for high contrast black and white cinematography to mimic the paintings of the Pre-Raphaelites and the results are brilliant and singular – his best effort in a long career. While Russell wanted to originally shoot in color – and went so far as to do color tests in the pre-production period – budget restrictions forced the BBC to go with black and white. Ultimately this probably worked in Crosby's favor as the cinematography has more in common with Gothic horror from the silent period (*Caligari, Nosferatu*) than with Russell's previous biographies and the interplay between paintings and "reality" flow beautifully one into the other. With costumes by Shirley Russell, design by Luciana Arrighi, and editing by Michael Bradsell and Roger Crittenden the team set to work on what is arguably Russell's masterpiece from his BBC period.

As is typical for Russell at this point he begins before the credits in medias res: we are looking straight down on a grave that has been just dug up at night illuminated only by torches while on the soundtrack dramatic music – Prokofiev's 3rd *Symphony* - builds up to a crescendo as a coffin is hoisted up by ropes. This opening scene beautifully illustrates Russell's point about compression in drama, using every second to show something meaningful even if the audience has no way to know what is going on – it doesn't matter because they will know later and make the connection themselves; of course to work like this you have to trust your audience and see them as partners rather than passive spectators. When it reaches ground level the coffin is opened and there is a decaying corpse inside dressed in feminine clothes; a male hand reaches in and removes a book as the camera moves in for a close-up of the skull, it's flesh still partially covering the bone in a horrifying rictus. Then the music quiets down dramatically as the credits roll with silent film title cards – a technique Russell has used before. The subtitle *The Private Life of Dante Gabriel Rossetti, Poet and Painter* references the elaborate wording of 19th century writing, immersing us in its aesthetic even in the font.

After the credits we see a large bonfire as Dante Gabriel Rossetti (Oliver Reed) jumps through the fire toward the camera along with a group of very angry young men – the Pre-Raphaelite Brotherhood – making a scene and screaming wildly: "Down with the old masters!" "Away with the pretty ladies!" They are setting copies of old master paintings on fire – we see a Gainsborough and a Renaissance lady go up in flames along with other paintings already consumed. As an audience we ask ourselves immediately: Who are these madmen? Frazer answers us in voice over: "Arson, raping, riot, civil insurrection are terrifying Europe. The date is 1848. In England rebels conspire to overthrow the Royal Academy of Art. The rebels are students and idealists. They are against industry, state religion, and official art. They would replace these with notions of honor, truth and beauty, quite unsuited to our times. This infatuation with the deeds of knights and damsels has led them to join together into a Pre-Raphaelite Brotherhood." 1848 saw uprisings not only in England but all throughout Europe. Political movements and ideals then were not only academic but streetwise, rife and ready for action: socialism, democratic radicalism, anarchy, liberalism, republicanism, corporatism, and plutocracy were tested and brought to trial in short lived takeovers, revolutions, and acts of terror that spread like a brush fire across the entire continent. A fire destroying the art of the past (if only in copies) is the perfect metaphor for the period. Through the flames Rossetti sees a female knight in shining armor (Judith Paris). It's a woman with long beautiful hair holding up a sword – perhaps an erotic dream image for Rossetti but he seems more troubled that aroused. Why? We don't know yet. The image suggests both Joan of Arc and a resurrection of Maria the female robot in Fritz Lang's *Metropolis*. Clearly we are in the thick of it here after only three minutes, exactly as Russell planned it.

Just what does Pre-Raphaelite mean really? The Brotherhood was a band of young men who were mortified by the art of their own time – a not unusual circumstance. What made them different was that they perceived that industrialization and "progress" were the primary enemies that must be destroyed. They saw mechanization and industry – then relatively new - as leading inevitably to the atomization, dehumanization, and eventual destruction of culture and perhaps of civilization itself. In a sense our own time is something they foresaw and fought to keep from happening. Needless to say they lost that war but what they left behind in their struggle – their art - is worth a look. As a counter to mechanization they posited an agrarian economy and Quattrocento Italian painting – an art with abundant, minute detail, intense primary colors, and complex compositions. For them the break with this tradition happened with the adoption of a simplified classicism that gave primacy to concepts, using sober and subdued colors seen first in the work of Michelangelo and Raphael, and later with the Mannerists, who succeeded them – hence the assignation Pre-Raphaelite. The most revered, successful, and powerful artist of their own time was someone that they hated: Sir Joshua Reynolds (whom they dubbed Sloshua Reynolds). He followed along the lines of High Renaissance art, using simple, classically balanced compositions and somber colors but with looser brush strokes (hence Sloshua) and quaint British themes. The Brotherhood sought a clean break from this tradition, not by going forward (as did the Impressionists a few years later in France) but by going backward.

Dante was christened Gabriel Charles Dante Rossetti and came from a family of erudite Italian immigrants, the second of four children. He grew to not only develop a love of Dante's Alighieri's work (changing his name accordingly) but came to identify with him, particularly his very romantic unrequited love for Beatrice. By an early age Gabriel, as his friends called him, had translated Dante's *Divine Comedy* into English and was deep into his search for his own "Beatrice"- the fact that the story of Dante and Beatrice ends tragically did not seem to deter him. For artists to also be poets at the time was not considered unusual – the British had William Blake behind them - and many people were amateur or Sunday poets/painters simply for the pleasure of it, sharing their work privately, similar in some respects to the way people now share photos and video clips without considering themselves photographers or filmmakers.

Aside from Rossetti the Brotherhood was composed of William Holman Hunt, John Everett Millais, and five other members who do not figure in Russell's film – but he does include Edgar Burne-Jones the artist; William Morris, the textile designer, artist and poet; Algernon Swinburne the writer and playwright; and John Ruskin the critic who was an older, patron of the Brotherhood. Russell keys on this particular group – particularly Morris - because they would be closer to the wives: Jane Morris and Elizabeth Siddal – and his main focus is the emotional/sexual relationship between the couples. He even leaves out key players in the story such as Walter Deverell, a ranking member of the Brotherhood and Rossetti's roommate who "discovered" Elizabeth Siddal by first asking her to pose; and Rossetti's brother William, the critic and literary editor, who helped get Gabriel published.

A few words about the group that he does focus on: William Morris found the whole fine art business bunk and decided, about 70 years before the Bauhaus, that there should be a return to basic crafts such as furniture making, panel design and weaving. Christina Rossetti was a poet concentrating on religious themes and children's poems – her most famous work, still read in school in England, is *Goblin Market*, a first edition of which was illustrated by her brother. Algernon Swinburne was an aesthete and alcoholic who wrote about many taboo topics of the time such as lesbianism, sadomasochism and atheism – his radicalness made him an ideal companion (and subject) for the Brotherhood. John Ruskin theorized the destructive influence of industrial capitalism early on becoming a forerunner of the movements toward environmentalism and sustainability. Ruskin also championed the work of Turner and the Pre-Raphaelites, along with a neo-Gothic style that he favored over "modern" architecture which he found pompous, boring, and eclectic, without any clear identity of its own – the radical modernists of the early 20th century such as Adolf Loos and Le Corbusier agreed with him (eschewing his love of hand-made craft, preferring industrial made, machine like, products) duly obliterating Victorian architecture within a generation. By 1848 the battle lines were clearly drawn and Russell dives into the deep end from the get-go.

One crucial element to the success of *Dante* is the sound design – a term that did not exist in 1967. The person responsible was Stan Morcom who also did the sound for *Always on Sunday*, *The Debussy Film*, *Isadora*, *Song of Summer* and *Dance of the Seven Veils*. Sound film was, from *The Jazz Singer* onward, something that served the images and the narrative – as the word served implies (from the Latin serviō: "to be a slave") narrative would be the master, the images a trusty servant, and the sound a slave. But the sixties and seventies saw a major shift, even a break, with that cinematic tradition. The change occurred first with Godard, who from *Breathless* onward had used music differently. He didn't only use it simply to cue emotional responses, as in traditional or classical films, but as a counterpoint to diegetic urban sounds such as car horns or café noises. He used music as punctuation, as an ironic aside, as a heartfelt reminder. He also used diegetic sound musically rather than simply as background noise, while the sudden start/stop motifs in the musical sections called attention to their existence by italicizing it. His soundtrack completely revolutionized how sound is put to together in a film – after Godard all of the sounds, dialogue and music need to be seen as one larger "orchestral soundscape." Russell adopts this technique and then goes further – by imposing not one but several distinct voices in the voiceover narration of the film - this is a major innovation in the history of narrative film – but what do we mean by "voices?"

The "authorial voice of reason" that was Huw Wheldon's trademark is now gone – Frazer's voiceover falls into the category of unreliable narrator – leaving us in a pinch since we must now navigate the uncertain waters of mid 19th century London on our own. While Austin Frazer – who not only wrote the narration but spoke it - at times uses the "objective" narrator who gives us basic information, at other times the voice is judgmental, or ironic, and, most fascinating of all, at times it takes on the characteristics of the main characters mimicking their speech and slang. The aural part of *Dante* – thanks in large part to Morcom - is a chamber piece for voices, something like Dylan Thomas' *Under Milk Wood* but taken to another level entirely because the voices interplay with images, narrative and music to create a highly complex work. There are two primary voices: Frazer's voice filling in the historical information that is pertinent and Rossetti's voice as he recites his poetry. There are also secondary voices – the wives and mistresses, the patrons and the poets.

Russell's film stands at the forefront of this revolution in sound coming to achieve equal footing with the image. When Orson Welles was asked in the 1970's what he would change, if anything, in his early work, he said: the sound. He made up for that oversight with his masterpiece *F for Fake* that takes full advantage of the "orchestral soundscape." Godard also kept pushing the envelope of sound to the point that in 1990 ECM Records released the complete soundtrack to his film *Nouvelle Vague*, including music, dialogue and diegetic sounds – the record company simply took it for granted by that point that this constituted modern music.

This layering of voices is crucial if we are to be as immersed in the world of the Pre-Raphaelites as Russell himself, entering into the mind of Dante Rossetti. Russell cuts from the bonfire ablaze with paintings to the model Elizabeth "Lizzie" Siddal (Judith Paris), Rossetti's "Beatrice" made flesh. Siddal is the woman that Lucinda Hawksley, Siddal's biographer, believes to be the first super-model, which is probably true as she was not only Dante's model, but the muse of the Brotherhood as a whole, and when the work was written about in the press she was mentioned – everyone in the art-world knew Lizzie, someone who was herself a poet and painter. Later in the film we see her working on a watercolor *Clerk Saunders* (1857) with Dante posing for it, as he did in real life. As was often the case the picture relates to a story wherein a woman named May Margaret meets the ghost of her murdered lover, Clerk Saunders, who materializes in order to renew his marriage vows. This narrative is clearly Gothic and anticipates in many ways her own life and that of Rossetti. Siddal had been drawing since childhood and had developed a raw, more direct style without the idealizations common at the time – in many ways it looks forward to the more intimate work of Berthe Morisot, Edvard Munch and Pierre Bonnard. Because of her financial situation she did not start to paint until she met Rossetti who taught her the basics. In any case, whatever her innate talents, her chances in the art-world of the period would have been minimal (to put it kindly) because of her sex and she understood those odds – to her credit she persisted and eventually got some recognition for her work as well as her modeling – but clearly the effort took its toll.

We first see her in a small metal bathtub, the size of a coffin, posing for *Ophelia*, by John Everett Millais (Derek Boshier), one of the most incandescent and justly famous paintings of the 19th century. As we see her in close-up Frazer's voiceover states: "The Pre-Raphaelite Brotherhood have fished a stunner from the milliner's near the Haymarket. She is working class but respectable. Unusual for the Haymarket..." Frazer's tone here is not objective at all – on the contrary it is familial, intimate, somewhat sarcastic. When he says that the Brotherhood "have fished a stunner" it is their slang he is using; we are expected to know what a milliner is (a hat maker); and we presumably understand what it means for a woman to be "near the Haymarket," that is, she might be looking for companionship, a client, a husband, or merely a hat, as the Haymarket was the area for women's hats and pretty shopkeeper's assistants who modeled them; when Frazer notes with approval that "she is working class but respectable" the narrator displays a racist mindset with regard to the working classes that was then commonplace and acceptable.

The voiceover continues as we see Millais working on *Ophelia* observing: "He (Rossetti) drifts between being a poet and a painter, whatever impresses most, requires the least effort and pays best. Millais has money – or rather his parents have. Rossetti hangs about, hoping to acquire the method of painting without working at it, or if not the method, as least the model." Here the voice is ironic, even scornful, but the images are romantic and show the two friends – both in love with Siddal – sharing a glass of wine and seriously working. Again Russell has the push/pull he wants between text/image so we are emotionally inside the drama rather than merely watching it from the outside – the end result being that the film is more viscerally powerful, or as Russell said "it goes inside you." Millais was played by another non-actor, Derek Boshier, a painter in the then emerging Pop Art movement in England – Russell had met him a few years earlier when he had made *Pop Goes the Easel*. This follows Russell's tradition of using artists to play artists.

John Everett Millais was perhaps the most talented of the Brotherhood and produced the masterpiece that almost everyone is familiar with: *Ophelia* (1852), with Elizabeth Siddal taking the role of the princess who drowns herself because she cannot have her prince Hamlet who has gone mad, and even goes mad herself. Millais might have had some intuition about engaging the young Lizzie as it would come to have haunting parallels to her own life. Interestingly, long after the events, when Rossetti and Siddal were dead, the remaining Brotherhood admitted that *Ophelia* captured Lizzie as she was in real life better than any other work they had made. In the long, cold sittings in the tub, with Siddal wearing a wedding dress, Rossetti is more direct than Millais even "suggesting a proposal of marriage - eventually" and so they go off on a date to Russell's beloved Lake District and its dramatic waterfalls and rocky hills where we are told that "Miss Siddal acts with the instincts of her class" which means that she puts her prospects for marriage and financial security first. On screen we hear Lizzie say, in her working class accent beautifully delivered by Judith Paris: "That's enough'a posing recite me a poem." Rossetti does recite and her enthusiasm for the sentiments it expresses infuriates the poet as he considers it only a rough unfinished work – the fight that ensues is filmed in long shot as they circle one of the lakes – in exasperation Rossetti pushes Siddal and throws her hat off a cliff as she chases him down laughing. These are cliffs that Rossetti would return to years later as an old man, perhaps looking for some consolation that he had once been loved – and it is where Russell eventually ends his film.

When next we see her Siddal is posing in a formal classical style depicting the Virgin Mary framed by a window, with Rossetti drawing furiously, framed by an enormous elaborate baroque frame – this frame-within-frames was something that Russell consistently used in his work and also a favorite motif of Romantic artists who sought to create a self-referential secondary theme ('this is a flat work of art') that would act as a counterpoint to the main theme, usually religious or spiritual. From Rossetti working and looking straight at the camera Russell cuts to a daring extreme close-up of Siddal's lips and tongue as she speaks, but on the soundtrack we hear Rossetti's poetry dedicated to Siddal – at this point we are completely inside the head of Rossetti and no one else seems to exist except the couple – exactly as it is for young people in love. Lizzie and Gabriel would have been in their mid twenties at this point. For Russell the power of film is that it can get you not just pretty surfaces but inside someone else's head – this had been the domain of the novel but the post-war auteur filmmakers, including Russell, saw that they could loot that technique and make it their own.

After a comical sequence that shows us Siddal refusing to have sex with the poet/painter until they are married the Rossetti family comes to pay a visit to the artists studio and the strain between Christina Rossetti – also a poet – and Lizzie becomes evident. Still their relationship moves ahead despite the fact that, as the voiceover explains: "It is unbecoming for the personification of a spiritual ideal to display an appetite" meaning that Rossetti is put off by Siddal's needs. Lizzie is a woman and that is bound to create problems for anyone in the throes of an idealization. This was one of the major issues not only for Rossetti but for the Brotherhood as a whole – they could not see that their ideals created insurmountable problems that made life impossible, not only for the people around them but for themselves.

On a personal level their Kantian idealization of women as personifications of "the sublime" could not withstand the day-to-day *management* of a relationship. In short, like the romantic poets of an earlier generation they could rhapsodize about "Love" but could not be bothered to talk about their problems, cook a meal, or change diapers. On the social and artistic front their romantic idealization of the era before Raphael, that is, before the 1400's, was fundamentally absurd and bound to run into trouble once this ideal was let loose in the world at large. That era was well described in detail by the historian Barbara Tuchman (*A Distant Mirror: The Calamitous 14th Century*) as one of "furious follies," constant battles, dangerous alliances, stupid games, bad food, dangerous drink, bitter animosities, and constant struggle – she also described the knight as "a terrible worm in an iron cocoon." This single sentence helps us to understand the reality of knights far better than all the Pre-Raphaelite paintings put together. The romantic chivalry of the knights for some reason persists even into our time but has no historical basis in fact – ironically the closest film that we have to the actual facts is a comedy: *Monty Python and the Holy Grail*.

The Pre-Raphaelites were essentially fantasy artists but they didn't know it - this is arguably why the work of their contemporary Turner stands up better over time: He seems to have been actually involved in the era in which he lived — he was obviously fascinated by how the new trains interacted with the landscape. Even today his painting *Rain, Steam and Speed* (1844) gives us a good sense of the fear and awe that the machines inspired. When one sees Turner's primitive steam locomotive in the midst of a sudden downpour one can already see the bullet trains, driverless cars, and stealth bombers to come — it's all there.

Frustrated by Lizzie's reluctance to have sex until she is wed Rossetti turns to other models for inspiration and sexual relief - although Siddal's biographer Lucinda Hawksley claims that there might have been more complicated circumstances at work — an abortion or miscarriage putting her off the subject for a period of time. In any case Siddal suffers since Rossetti will not marry her, and a friend suggests laudanum, a sedative and a cure-all of the time that was also used as a recreational drug. Russell brutally uses comical fairground music to cross cut between Rossetti's new model girlfriend and Lizzie's newfound addiction to laudanum.

In another beautiful display of conveying two meanings at once in contrapuntal opposition Russell stages a deep and harrowing fight between Lizzie and Christina Rossetti — the two clearly dislike each other but cannot, under the rules of that period, say anything directly — every word is tinged with double meanings. Russell at a certain point cuts out the direct sound, and has Christina in voiceover reciting "In an Artist's Studio," one of the most tender and heartfelt poems she ever wrote (years after the fact) about her first visit to her brother's studio to meet Lizzie: "One face looks out from all his canvases, one selfsame figure sits or walks or leans, we found her hidden just beyond those screens, that mirror gave back all her loveliness, a nameless girl in freshest summer greens, a saint, an angel every canvas means. He feeds upon her face by day and night, and she with true kind eyes looks back on him, not as she is but as she was when hope shone bright."

The two women seem to make a truce and part company — Russell in his compressed style has said all he needed to say about the scene. This aspect of his work, where two contradictory ideas are expressed at the same time, is a constant throughout the BBC films but comes into its own with *Dante* as a force to be reckoned with. To better understand it we might apply a scientific principle to the idea from particle physics: If all matter is both particle and wave we have to think two different contradictory ideas at the same time to even get a basic understanding of matter. So it is with drama – everything else after Russell's work, and that of his fellow auteurs, is merely melodrama, or worse, a naïve simulacrum of drama, a pastiche that does not know it's a pastiche.

William Holman Hunt becomes the first art star in the Brotherhood - for a silly painting of a goat painted in minute photographic detail – of course it being the Brotherhood the painting is also a Biblical allegory titled *Book of Leviticus on the Day of Atonement*. Hunt is generous to friends but Rossetti typically treats him with condescension – in an outdoor setting where Hunt is painting a female model posing incongruously with a grandfather beard and a crown, Rossetti steps up and removes it placing it on Hunts' head and then starts to sing gibberish as a joke.

Hunt goes out of his way to introduce him to John Ruskin, the most respected and powerful man in the art world of that time. Ruskin approves but in a comical twist (which is historically true) he consistently calls Lizzie "Ida" – but he was so powerful that they let him have his way. Of all the Pre-Raphaelites Ruskin prefers Millais until he runs off with his wife and so he turns his attention to "Dante and Ida" preferring Siddal's more raw and direct drawings to Dante's. Rossetti seems nonplussed but smartly goes along with whatever Ruskin says – the eccentric writer then invites Rossetti to his estate where he promises 150 pounds a year each to Lizzie and to Rossetti (a very good sum at the time) – demanding that Siddal spend some time in the south of France, known then as an area of health spas to people recovering from tuberculosis or other disorders. When Rossetti offers him some snuff as a thank you, Ruskin, with his fussy art-world humorlessness states blankly: "Art is my stimulant Mr. Rossetti!" While Dante tries to stifle a laugh he indulges himself and relaxes into his newfound wealth. Ruskin also gives Lizzie one pound of "ivory dust" – considered then either a sexual stimulant and/or a cure-all. The Victorian age had a medicine chest full of quack cures and the dust was one of the most expensive and obscene, coming from elephant tusks. Back at the studio with Siddal Rossetti sneezes as a joke and the whole boxful of "ivory dust" goes flying – Lizzie, covered in expensive dust, can only scream out: "I wish he didn't call me Ida!"

The Rossetti household enters into some cash but the poet/painter squanders his days chasing models through farm fields and going with them to the circus while Lizzie recovers in France reading his love poetry that gets sentimental about her "friendly eyes."

Again the vast gulf between sentiment and reality is made abundantly, and absurdly, clear. Russell inventively cuts quickly between Siddal dunking herself over and over in an outdoor thermal bath to Rossetti and one of his models laughing on a Ferris Wheel – the editing speeds up until they become flash cuts – at which point the model and Rossetti collapse on the ground in an embrace and Lizzie collapses in exhaustion on the beach, fully clothed. This kind of montage, pioneered by the Soviet school and Sergei Eisenstein, is used for non-dialectical purposes here, to show the emotional strain, the hunger to experience life, and the pain that each caused the other without directly meaning to – but it also serves to suggest the deep connection between Rossetti and Siddal, as even when living in different countries they seem to reach orgasmic relief at the same time.

Lizzie returns to London and decides to surprise Rossetti in his apartment, finding him with one of his models. As the model leaves in a huff she finds another model coming up the stairs and starts to laugh uncontrollably. Of course this is the moment that the Rossetti family and Ruskin have chosen to come pay a visit from opposite directions. Russell directs the dramatic explosion sure to follow with his typical humor – made clear by the music cues – turning the drama into a burlesque. Ruskin arrives first and encounters a huge row – Lizzie takes a new case of "ivory dust" that Ruskin has brought and throws it out the window hitting the Rossetti family on their fancy hat covered heads, covering everyone in white dust. Then comes the most unusual and beautiful transition in the film as Russell cuts from the white dust flying to a knight in shining armor with a sword flailing around in a deep white fog- the white dust and the white fog beautifully dissolve into each other but we are at a loss as to what is going on until a short poem read in voiceover (by William Morris) explains that that what we are seeing is the struggle between good knights and evil technology/progress, in the form of a train – the fog is from a nearby steam locomotive that the good knight is engaging in battle – a pointless battle of course but heroic failure is a strong part of the romantic mythos.

As Russell depicts it the knight (Morris) is on the verge of defeat until Rossetti shows up, in a bicycle, using an umbrella as a sword. Saved by Rossetti Morris and the Brotherhood retire to Oxford to regroup. Clearly Russell is taking the piss out of the Pre-Raphaelite effort against technology but he does not fail to take into account their heroics, such as they are – and in the long run who is to say that they weren't right? From Russell's vantage point in 1967 to be against progress and technology seemed somewhat fanciful and absurd – after all Russell's film was first shown on television, the most advanced tech of the moment; but from our vantage point, more than half a century later we can say, with some sense of anxiety and regret, that the Brotherhood, although clearly eccentric Luddites, may have been right in the long run, that is morally right, but they didn't stand a chance of being heard in their own time (or ours) – their romanticism, as Russell shows, was delusional and doomed.

At Oxford the Brotherhood convene in a church, which makes sense as they all professed to be deeply religious, expressing fundamentalist moral beliefs and spiritual longing; presumably they were also in thrall to the Medieval period, detesting their own time. Oxford, full of old churches and public buildings, as well as the University itself established in 1096, was ideal for them. But Russell shows that the young men have underground currents of emotion that run deeper than *any* established institution or text – and he does so without a word. Amid incongruous organ music that is modern Rossetti cautiously walks about the altar as if he were in doubt, while Burne-Jones and Morris position themselves in medieval nooks looking like dead saints; meanwhile Swinburne leans over a stone sepulcher of a life sized man in repose and kisses the stone head on the lips taking his aestheticism to its logical conclusion. The kiss is shown in the traditional close-up used in romantic films with the appropriate lighting, which of course, is not to be found inside churches, that are typically dark - we are clearly inside the mind of Swinburne himself.

Still in the church Rossetti spots Jane Burden (Gala Mitchell) and is captivated – he approaches her sitting in a pew and chats her up but we only hear the organ playing as Morris (who will later marry Jane) looks on, a stained-glass angel appropriately behind him looking over his shoulder. Rossetti steals some flowers from a nearby grave as a gift and introduces her to his Brotherhood, starting with the poet and model Swinburne who sticks his tongue out sexually, and to the others, who are all clearly sexually captivated by her – at one point they all lunge forward towards her like hungry animals – as the organ music dies down Rossetti calms the Brotherhood down and explains that Miss Burden has agreed to pose as Queen Guinevere, in one of their murals representing knightly love and chivalry. Again the Brotherhood's ideals and the reality we see completely contradict each other in ways that they are oblivious to. Stealing flowers from a grave to give to his newfound infatuation conflates death and sex in a way that the Brotherhood always sought to create in their work but rarely achieved – and it also anticipates Rossetti as a defiler of graves.

Following the events in the church the Brotherhood find a setting more amenable to romance as Rossetti, William Morris, Burne-Jones, Swinburne, and Jane Burden share a punt – a flat-bottomed boat with a square-cut bow used in the small rivers around Oxford. Morris rows and steers as the men serenade Jane by reciting poetry, looking longingly at her beautiful face. In Gala Mitchell Russell found someone whose large dark eyes, pale skin, and luxuriant hair really does resemble a Pre-Raphaelite muse. As the poem is recited Burne-Jones and Swinburne repeat the refrain Beata Mea Domina (My Beautiful Lady) in a chorus that is both charming and absurdly comical because it is clear they would all simply like to jump on Miss Burden but the social rules and the crowded punt make that impossible.

Jane Burden (later Jane Morris) is to be the subject of many of the Pre-Raphaelites' best work. We next see her in a static interior shot standing on a long narrow board stretched between two ladders posing as Lady Guinevere as Rossetti and his fellow Pre-Raphaelite Brotherhood are making a large wall painting in the Oxford Union. Her idealized image, especially her incredibly luxuriant hair, would preoccupy much of the Pre-Raphaelites' efforts for years to come. In this scene, that establishes her as the new muse of the group (replacing Lizzie Siddal), she is frozen in a conventionally heroic neoclassical pose – a style much in favor by the Brotherhood – at which point she suddenly starts to chew gum and play with a Yo-Yo. This is one of the most brilliantly timed visual gags in a work that is not primarily a comedy. To a modern audience a Yo-Yo might seem to be a modern invention but it was extremely popular at the time of Morris and Rossetti, and had been known in England since the 17th century. The visual pun shows the model's boredom while posing for long hours but also her complete indifference to the pompous rhetoric of the male artists below her. In Russell's work it is often women who throw a monkey wrench – or a spanner as the English call it – into the pretentious endeavors of egotistical men. Such a scene puts into doubt the Pre-Raphaelite ideology of classical order and ideal beauty that they so earnestly believed in and sought to create in their work. It suggests strongly that such endeavors are Platonic fantasies that have little, or nothing, to do with the everyday world as it is. Russell gives voice to two contradictory sentiments or voices within the same work to ecstatic effect for we can never be sure of where the film will go next, or where our sympathies should lie – rather we must think about it and come to our own conclusions. Lizzie shows up to see what is happening with Rossetti and his friends and realizes immediately that Jane Burden is now the new muse of the group.

As in *The Debussy Film* Russell also uses the women in the film to express facial gestures to match the present moment – mid 20th century – while the men's faces are securely tied to their own present, that is, mid 19th century Victorian society. Yet these gestures by women are never aggressive but discreet, indirect, implied – often they are asides that they cast at each other as they get their bearings, almost like a secret language, but for the men they reserve the straightforward gestures that are expected of them. This repressive and destructive state of affairs sets up a situation where their struggles are not merely those of male/female but of fundamentally different ways of being in the world – the men entrenched (in the trenches as it were) in their own time and society, fighting for survival, and the women harkening toward some future independence for themselves that they sense but cannot yet reach. The wars that men and women fight are never named and the battles are never marked but Russell shows them ongoing and brutal. When Lizzie comes to see Rossetti and the Brotherhood working with their new muse she is devastated and takes it like a punch in the stomach - and Rossetti knows it - twisting the knife by sarcastically greeting her: "Ah Miss Siddal – and what brings YOU here?"

Swinburne helpfully explains the mural to Siddal: "Mr. Rossetti up there is painting Lady Guinevere, a libidinous whore, who left her husband King Arthur for Sir Lancelot." Russell here for the first time employs a technique he will use later in *The Music Lovers* during the *Swan Lake* sequence: as someone describes a work of art (or a ballet) the film cuts away from the art toward the artists at work and we make the connection: Lady Guinevere (Jane Morris) leaves her husband King Arthur (William Morris) for Sir Lancelot (Rossetti) – we see each in close up looking straight at the camera, but presumably at each other, in a brilliant series of matching cross-cuts. Swinburne continues as the visual motif repeats: "While over there William Morris is painting a white-hot adulteress called Isolde (Jane) who left her husband, King Mark (William Morris) for Tristan (Rossetti) and inspired by these promiscuous legendary stories, over there, Ned-Jones introduces an appropriate Cupid." The Cupid is hardly necessary as we get the triangle that is to come with Russell's usual intelligent mise-en-scéne and compression.

There are many times throughout the film that Russell cuts away to the work of the Pre-Raphaelites particularly when Rossetti, his sister, or Swinburne are reading poetry in voiceover. We might take these cuts as simply illustrating the efforts of the Brotherhood but we would be missing something important. Russell is both performing a critique and using their work to create a collage poetics of his own. The Brotherhood assumed that they were creating works that illustrated heroic stories and myths so their models were always "Guinevere," "Ophelia" or "The Virgin Mary" but what Russell shows is that these works were made not by one person but two – artist and model – in effect when Russell shows us the work what we see is not Guinevere, Ophelia or Mary, but Lizzie – it is Siddal who is *present* – it is she who helps to make that work what it is, it is she who transports the viewer from the chaos of contemporary England into the world of myth. What Russell gets (that the Pre-Raphaelites missed) is the "transience value" (Freud) of the modeling job – one might say the 9 to 5 of posing and making art. For the Pre-Raphaelites everyday life disappears and makes room for a deeper, truer reality, a mysterious ordering which transmits, in some cases, the almost mystical certainty that the universe makes sense. Russell goes with them down that road but he also does the opposite – he is aware of the passing of all that is beautiful and meaningful, (Siddal laughing while putting on a wedding dress) like the Impressionists before him, and he gets it down in black and white. This happens not only when Russell focuses his camera on drawings and paintings but also in Russell's montage that juxtaposes their work with their lives.

In the scene following the Oxford Union mural all the Brotherhood marry at once – a compression of real events - and we see them exiting the cathedral in Oxford to the usual celebrations and Mendelssohn's *Wedding March* – Morris to Burden, Rossetti to Siddal, and Edgar Burne-Jones to "Georgie" McDonald (a close friend of George Eliot) – but the voiceover uses the 19th century slang term "spliced" that signified to be married. We see Siddal and Rossetti walk along the Lake District as she reminds him that they have known each other ten years – his only reply is "so it is my dear." On that cold note Russell switches to slow motion as they continue walking with Siddal looking at her new husband apprehensively – their short marriage already problematic - and Rossetti seemingly oblivious – but is he?

In slow-motion we hear his poetry in voiceover while Mendelssohn's *Wedding March* continues playing softly: "The sea stands spread as one wall with flat skies, where the lean black craft like flies seem well-night stagnated, soon to drop off dead. Seemed it so to us, when I was thine and thou wast mine, and all these things were thus? Could we be so now?" Clearly Rossetti is feeling much more than he lets on. During the voiceover we see the couple playing on the beach, as Rossetti pushes Siddal around in a wicker wheel chair for old people – both laughing hysterically like kids - then Russell recreates the favorite motif of Romantic painters as the couple, their back to us, look out in long shot to the vast waters in front of them, perfectly still as in a painting. The vastness of nature for the Romantics was always tied to eternity, to the fearsome, the sublime, and the unknowable – the old fashioned wheel chair is emotionally moving as, of course, Siddal will never get to be old. As the *Wedding March* continues we see, via cross-cutting, that Rossetti has become obsessed by Jane Morris, while Siddal sits melancholically at her garden, during a picnic, consoled by Christina, for having lost her baby. At that moment Morris decides to start acting like a chimp - the men seem to get behind the game by playing along, but the women just look on bemused or horrified. Again two contradictory emotions, the tragic and the absurd, play out at the same time.

As the Brotherhood are having a lunch Siddal, now married to Rossetti, feels sick – it is Swinburne who notices that she is pregnant and Siddal chides her husband for not having bothered to notice. As he walks her home they go by the Haymarket area as the voiceover reminds us: "A place for those in search of pleasure and hats, for this is where Lizzie worked twelve years ago before the hysteria and her addiction to laudanum." Lizzie stops halfway and remarks: "Such a short step from shop to street aint' it Mr. Rossetti?" Then she starts treating him like a customer on the lookout for whores: "Give you a good time gov, you knows you likes it." The night does not end well – Lizzie asks for some laudanum and Rossetti reluctantly gives it to her. As Siddal begs for Rossetti to stay with her he runs out as if being chased by demons.

While Rossetti ignores his wife to run off with Jane Morris he assumes that Lizzie will wait for him – instead she commits suicide by drinking an overdose of laudanum leaving behind a suicide note. As she drinks we hear her poetry in voiceover: "I am gazing up toward the sun, Lord, remembering my lost one, Lord remember me. How is it in the unknown land? Do the dead wander hand in hand?" She puts on her wedding dress before lying down to die and Russell beautifully cuts to Siddal posing years earlier for Millais' *Ophelia* also in a wedding dress, and then to her wearing the same dress but inside a coffin waiting to be buried. The cuts are fast but emotionally powerful – nothing like them had been seen before as they generate multiple meanings, like a collage, but within the framework of a narrative film.

In a gesture of his love (and guilt) Rossetti puts the only copy of his poems in the coffin with her as a parting gift despite his sister begging him not to do it realizing they will be worth a fortune in the future. Even Siddal's biographer expresses uncertainty about the causes for her suicide, particularly as she was pregnant at the time – something she had long wanted, having survived a difficult stillbirth. Hawksley: "Perhaps Lizzie had again felt her baby stop moving inside her and knew it was dead, or maybe she felt she could not risk the possibility of another stillbirth and its miserable repercussions; perhaps her postnatal depression had tragically led her to believe she would be a bad mother and brought about a decision not to bring her child into the world, or maybe she thought of motherhood inside such a tormented marriage was overwhelming. We will never know."[43] Siddal was 32 years old.

Russell dissolves from a close-up of Siddal dead, eyes closed, to a golden oriental mask also with eyes closed – a favorite artifact of the period - the mask is worn by a woman dressed as a doll or automaton playing the mandolin. The automaton was Freud's vision of the Uncanny in human form that we would see later in Fritz Lang's *Metropolis* – a favorite motif of the Enlightenment that makes a final appearance (taking a bow of sorts) in Fellini's *Casanova*. Swinburne in a drunken thrall begs at the automaton's feet calling her a "poisonous queen." As the camera pulls back we realize we are in a whorehouse. Clearly we have entered a stage of decadence, alcoholism, drug addiction, and frivolity – the very opposite of what the Pre-Raphaelites stood for and sought to achieve in their life and in their work. The voiceover identifies it as the "Grand Turkish Room - the establishment most favored by the Brotherhood."

Seven years later, in desperate need of money Rossetti pays to have the poems dug up by a grave robber so he might sell them to a publisher and finally make his fortune, which he proceeds to do. The voiceover informs us that Rossetti is suffering from insomnia, addiction to whisky, and a new drug that has come on the market, choral hydrate, known simply as "choral," a strong sedative that was used to counter the effects of insomnia, but also used as a recreational drug as it induced a hypnotic effect. The desecration of his wife's grave is appropriately rendered like a horror film but out of sequence as if the very memory caused a short circuit in Rossetti's mind: Black clad men in a fog carry a coffin while Jane Morris looks on horrified but in another pastoral setting far removed from the burial – then we see the coffin again but resting one of the crags in the Lake District with Rossetti sitting nearby tentatively taking his book of poems from his coat to place in the coffin, but not before Siddal's hand reaches from inside the coffin to take them. There is a short cut to Swinburne as he kisses the face of the automaton, which then cuts to Rossetti taking the poems resting by the head of Siddal's corpse – an imaginary nightmare event that never occurred as grave robbers dug up the coffin and took the book.

Another extraordinary cut takes us from a close-up of Siddal's decaying skull to a painting of her in her youth, looking ethereal as she always did in the work of the Brotherhood. This match-cut is one of the most beautiful in the history of cinema but unlike the famous match-cut in *2001: a Space Odyssey* (bone to space ship) Russell doesn't linger on it – his need to compress forces the film to rush past the match-cut to Rossetti unconscious on a couch – clearly suffering the effects of chloral – he then pans down to a drawing on the floor of Siddal as Mary Magdalene – at which point an incongruous primeval pet armadillo walks over it, like a harbinger of a pre-human primeval world - this is another sequence that tells us much about the poet/artist's state of mind without a single word.

The moment the grave robber comes and hands Rossetti the book of poems Russell, in one of his most brilliant edits, cuts to Lizzie looking alive and well, laughing herself silly in a bathtub full of water, dressed as Ophelia, the princess who drowned herself because she could not have her Hamlet. Millais paints her in the small tub but later in the finished painting puts her in a lake full of beautiful flowers painted in minute detail and bright colors, as we would expect from the Brotherhood. Haunted at night Rossetti takes a lamp and goes up to one of his own framed drawings of Lizzie, and he sees himself reflected on her face, as in voiceover we hear Rossetti recite one of his poems: "This is her picture as she was. It seems a thing to wonder on. As though mine image in the glass should tarry when myself am gone. I gaze until she seems to stir until my eyes almost avert that now, even now, the sweet lips part to breathe the words and yet the earth is over her. The drips of water night and day giving tongue to solitude. Yet this, of all love's perfect prize remains save what is secret and unknown." In a daze he goes back to the Haymarket area where he first met Lizzie, as if hoping to find her, and sees himself reflected in a milliner's shop, an old man with glasses. A prostitute approaches him and asks if he needs some company. In an homage to *Citizen Kane* Russell pans up to the sign and we see that it is the milliner's where Siddal worked selling hats, and as he pans down in a single take Rossetti sees Lizzie next to him in the glass and he pushes her away terrified.

He returns home to take an overdose of laudanum hoping to die the same way as his wife and passes out on the floor as a snake crawls over his face. Immediately we get into Rossetti's mind as he – now young again - is walking about the Lake District looking for something - he finds Lizzie's coffin lying by a waterfall - he approaches cautiously. Rossetti removes the lid and takes out the book of poems but as he gets up to leave Siddal rises from her coffin and tries to take the poems back. He is so scared that he looks to commit suicide by jumping off the falls to his death but wakes up at his home – his young ex-mistress, now housekeeper and companion, Fanny (Pat Aschton), has saved him by forcing him to throw up the laudanum.

Jane Morris comes to take him back to her husband's house is Oxford to recover and Fanny lets him have it before they leave: "Don't mind me, you carry on girl, I'm just part of the furniture – he tried to kill his self he did and it was me that saved his life. Me nursed him I did. She can have you! Look at you. You can hardly walk, you can hardly see. A blind cripple. Well she's bleedin' welcome to you! I'm fed up with waiting you hand and foot." At their rustic estate William Morris dedicates himself to weaving – something he became an expert at - while Jane and Rossetti play at romance. "You don't mind sharing?" asks Jane as William tries to embrace his wife in bed but she laughs him off.

William decides three's a crowd and packs off to Iceland to learn more about the Icelandic sagas that intrigue him, a historical fact, leaving the field clear for Rossetti and Jane. In the one nude scene in the film Rossetti pulls the cover from the bed revealing Jane naked as we hear him in voiceover reciting another love poem, now dedicated to her - the close-ups use extreme high contrast lighting exactly the way the Pre-Raphaelites saw the world. Russell contrasts this warm scene by lamplight to William Morris in the frozen fields of Iceland by himself, dressed in a fur blanket like a primitive – a state he always sought but now he seems to have some second thoughts, alone in a vast field of fog and trees – he screams to himself: "And yet indeed if I must live alone, if fellowship is but an empty dream, is there not left a world that is mine own? Am I not real if all else doth but seem?" There is no answer but the chilly winds of the mountains – a scene that Russell shot in the Lake District at mid-winter.

William Morris' two little girls, Jenny and Janey inspire Rossetti to write some new sonnets. The voiceover explains that: "Morris can sweat it out in Iceland and Fanny can peddle Rossetti's paintings in the art market – a critic (anonymous) can attack his published poems, for these are clouds beyond this earthly paradise and Gabriel gives not a damn. He savors only the joys and the bliss of a happy family life." One of the girls asks Rossetti to be her daddy. Jane Morris sees a doll with no eyes and freaks out running inside the house in a panic attack. The doll, like the oriental mask and the life size sepulcher that Swinburne kisses, are signs of theater, deceit, and mystery. At night she asks him if he wants a child of his own and he says no, "can you see me as a father?" She replies "no" and we next see her standing on a boat, her arms outstretched, as in a painting by Arnold Bocklin the Romantic painter – the boat moves away from the camera and the lake reflects the sky so it appears for a second that she is floating through the clouds - Jane Morris leaves Rossetti.

Finally finished as a lover, as an artist and a writer, Rossetti is shown staggering on the lakeside hills that he always loved walking and playing adult games with Lizzie, now alone, walking always as if searching for something. The voiceover explains: "His mind had become clouded with chloral. He hears and sees the dead. They wait on him accusing, condemning, as he accuses and condemns himself, endlessly." Rossetti in voiceover answers: "The lost days of my life, until today, what were they, could I see them on the street lie as they fell?" Rossetti again sees the knight in shining armor before the bonfire as in the beginning of the film, but now we see in close-up that the knight is clearly Elizabeth Siddal. The close-up of the fire dissolves to a stream of white water from the falls of the Lake District as Rossetti continues on his perambulations as we again hear him in voiceover, when suddenly another voice, Lizzie, joins in for a call-and-response:

Rossetti: *Ah dear one we were young so long, it seemed that youth would never go, for skies and trees were ever in song and water in singing flow, in the days we never again shall know. Alas, so long!*

Siddall: *Then was it all spring weather?*

Rossetti: *Nay, but we were young and together. Ah dear one I've been old so long it seems that age is loathe to part, and though have they still the art that warmed the pulses of heart to heart?*

Siddall: *Then was it all spring weather?*

Rossetti: *Nay, but we were young and together. Ah dear one you've been dead so long...*

Rossetti sits to rest and reaches out to the camera but the official voiceover brutally answers him this time: "Too late old man, you had your chance. So, till choral kills you console yourself with the bottle and your muse." Fanny comes to fetch him but he throws his empty whisky bottle at her and she leaves cursing him. We last see Rossetti in silhouette standing up with difficulty and walking away - a bent over old man. One is reminded or Eliot's line: "Do not let me hear of the wisdom of old men, but rather of their folly." We most definitely get that here.

Rossetti's heartfelt poetry comments on his dissolution as an old man - as if a part of him, his younger self, were taunting the washed up artist and poet but it is also a heart-rending elegiac sequence where we feel the full gravitas of Rossetti's loss, his tragic mistakes, and his final dissolution. Russell at the very end cuts to the credits using fake stereoscope cards with the image on one side and text on the other, sometimes changing sides, with soft, distant carnival music as in a traveling circus that is leaving town. The text/image stereoscope cards draw an equivalence of sorts between words and images, or poetry and painting, which were also the twin pillars of Dante Gabriel Rossetti's art – a collective art of sorts (like cinema) because portrait art is never made by one person, it is made by at least two people: artist and model – and in the case of recluses who forego the model, using themselves, it is their immediate world, regardless of how small, that is their partner in art, for poets and artists are never isolated in a "space" – on the contrary they are always in a *particular* place and time - those feelings and coordinates are definitive and inescapable. In the case of the Pre-Raphaelites that dangerous, ever-changing world that they inhabited is now lost – Russell recreates it in a studio in London in 1967 and gives it to us as a work of art – a film that reflects on the nature of fine art, memory, and transience. This is to some extent ironic as Rossetti's sought to escape from his own contemporary London into a medieval paradise that he never found. But when Dante created his art he was (unbeknownst to him) not alone. There was the regular input from the Brotherhood, from those artists he hated and those he loved, from those that he laughed at, and those that he stole from – and most important of all were the physical and emotional bonds between him and his muses and models – co-authors as it were of their art, known as Pre-Raphaelite: Jane Morris and Elizabeth Siddal.

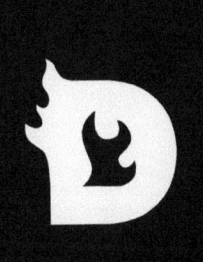

The BBC 5: *Song of Summer* (1968)

There were, over the years, a handful of films that Russell considered to be his best, when he was invariably asked – this was one of them. *Song of Summer* is a 74 minute film made for *Monitor* concerning the difficult relationship of the early 20th century British composer Frederick Delius (Max Adrian), who had become crippled and blind in his old age due to syphilis, to the master's apprentice, the recently graduated 22 year old Eric Fenby (Christopher Gable), who was an aspiring composer in his own right and comes for a time to work as Delius' assistant in France – a short stay that ended up lasting for six years. The official name for Fenby's job was amanuensis – but for the young man it was something of a shock to go from living with his parents in Scarborough, North Yorkshire to living in France with one of the most ornery, irascible and cosmopolitan composers in the world.

It is Fenby who provides the voice over narration based on his memoirs, written in 1936, so we see many of the scenes from his point of view, although, significantly, Russell sometimes steps back from Fenby and we see things from a more traditional "objective" point of view, and at times even from another character's point of view. Russell had wanted to make a film about Delius for some time but there was too much information – Delius went through many periods, friends, lovers, and living situations, from the US to France to Denmark. These included long stays in Paris where he probably contracted the syphilis, in the city's brothels, that eventually killed him – there were so many stories they could never be pared down to 74 minutes. But once he read Fenby's memoirs he realized this was the way into the life, not by showing bits and pieces of his overall life trajectory but by focusing on one specific incident towards the end of his life when a young provincial Englishman came to help him arrange his final works while he was in the countryside in France in Grez-sur-Loing, near Paris.

Fenby took the delicate job of helping Delius to finish orchestrating his works in his final years from 1928 to 1934. Without his help Delius's final years would have been non-productive as well as physically difficult and emotionally traumatic. A difficulty they would have as working partners is that Fenby was a confirmed and very earnest Catholic and Delius was an acerbic, hard-core atheist, often expressing his atheism in sarcastic asides. It was an uneasy partnership where Fenby even became Delius's nurse in the final stages of his illness – a job he was not suited for and that probably traumatized him.

The paintings and drawings of Edvard Munch, a contemporary and friend of Delius whose work the composer used to decorate his house, populate the film and act as a sounding board to the delicate and difficult relationship. Delius owned Munch's *Death of Marat I* (1907) and *The Kiss* (1897) along with paintings by Gauguin and other Post-Impressionist masters. Munch's hardened winter aesthetic seems to permeate the summer landscape in a way that Fenby himself would not have been conscious of until much later. Russell smartly uses the paintings, particularly a Gauguin nude and Munch's *The Kiss*, as a counterpoint to narrative action or to comment on it, treating the paintings like an on-stage chorus.

Russell's focus on the corporeal tends toward the direct, even brutal approach sometimes seen in Bergman's work of the 1950's. In these works humans are very much seen as animals in the wild, or in the captivity of "civilization" (always in quotes) learning the rules of the game, often the hard way, with problematic results that are depicted with great sensitivity. Humans in these works are essentially a part of nature without being conscious of it. Russell's approach is similar and shares with Bergman that sensitivity about people's fragile interior lives. Early on when Fenby takes his tuning fork to the beach – the North Sea - to test his ear for musical notation Russell shoots him in an exquisite shot, in front of a teeming and restless rocky coastline with waves of water just beyond Fenby's reach – everything in sharp focus. As Russell frames his shot Fenby is a part of the wild ocean and the rocks - they are all one – even if Fenby himself is blissfully unaware, wearing city clothes to the beach like a man who could not be bothered with such a messy, nasty interaction. In terms of audio the sound of the ocean, the wind, and the musical tuning fork are all, in a fundamental sense, sounds produced by nature and the soundtrack mixes them all with a pantheistic delight that is lyrical and ravishingly beautiful. Fenby makes a notation about the sound of seagulls that seem to have inspired him, and Russell dutifully shows us seagulls, but it will be Delius who will set their flight to music in his *A Song of Summer*.

The opening shot of the film was to have been Fenby playing the organ at the movie theater in his hometown to a Laurel and Hardy film (*Way Out West*) but it was cut due to the fact that they could not get permission to use the film so we only see Fenby, innocent face in sheer delight, as he watches the film while playing music. This was an unfortunate loss – Roger Crittenden explains:

> "Cinema enjoys ignoring the three dramatic unities of time, place and action, insisted on by Aristotle in his Poetics; however, in this sequence (of Fenby at the organ with the film playing) we, ironically, built a filmic reality that ostensibly observes those unities whilst simultaneously ignoring them: the film on the screen was made in America in 1937, the audience was filmed somewhere in England, probably in the 1950's, and Christopher Gable as Fenby playing the organ was shot in 1968 in London. Edited together they represent an event in the 1920's in a cinema in Scarborough, North Yorkshire."

Crittenden, who helped to edit *Song of Summer*, makes an astute point – like the "Frankenstein monster" of *Prokofiev: Portrait of a Soviet Composer*, singled out earlier for having been made of bits and pieces shot far apart in time and place *Song of Summer* is also put together in a similar fashion creating a new (post-Aristotelian) poetics.

Since for Russell it would be the biographical subject that would determine the form, in *A Song of Summer* he avoids the collage element, the quick cutting, and the omniscient voice-over narration that we hear in most of the biographies. Here the voiceover is handled by the central character as he looks back and Russell follows Fenby's lead, cautiously exploring Deilius' world, exposing layers like peeling an onion. He also took a page from Ingmar Bergman's *Summer Interlude* (1951) – another film about looking back in anger, frustration, regret, and ultimately reconciliation, with the emotions forming an interlocking puzzle that, ultimately, come to make up a life.

After Fenby's arrival the beautiful French maid (Elizabeth Ercy) wakes Fenby up and we see a print of Munch's *The Scream* directly behind the bed – the combination is incongruous and shocking. We see that Fenby is already nonplussed by so much input and he immediately gets more confortable as he is introduced to the rules of the house by Delius' wife Jelka (Maureen Pryor) explaining how things will be done – like clockwork – so Delius has a well grounded, organized life and he can devote himself completely to composing. Fenby is so reticent and quiet that Jelka wonders if he can even play the piano. Clearly Fenby is repressed, frustrated and wound up to the point he might break at any moment – perhaps this is related to his strong Catholic faith that he seems to hang on to for dear life – French maids or not.

He is called by the sound of three bells - Delius asks for the radio to hear some music. Beethoven's 5th is playing and Delius goes on a rant about the "note spinners: Beethoven, Bruckner and Mahler! A complete waste of time!" Fenby quite can't believe it as for him Beethoven is one of the immortals of music. "Forget the immortals!" screams Delius "and listen to nature." Mid sentence Delius suffers a painful stroke and Fenby feels helpless as the maestro asks Fenby to get "the Bruder" who is the athletic German male nurse that can carry Delius around like a sack of potatoes when needed – he can also read classical German literature in the original which is a favorite pastime.

In one of Russell's most beautiful shots Fenby at a desk studies one of Delius' scores in front of another Munch painting of a haunted looking young girl sitting naked, somewhat awkwardly on a bed, her arms folded dramatically over her sex. The painting is Munch's *Puberty* (1894) and is the perfect accompaniment to his meditations as behind the girl is her own shadow that Munch has painted as if it were a living specter, a dark amorphous ghost that might swallow up the girl at any moment. It is clear that Fenby feels the same way but he is unable to articulate it – Russell with a single static shot is able to convey all of this succinctly and then moves on to the next scene quickly as Fenby is asked to read Mark Twain, one of Delius' favorite authors. Russell beautifully intercuts Jelka and Fenby reading in a Wellesian touch – back and forth - so we get a sense of time passing. His wife reads Nietzsche in close up: "My suffering and my fellow suffering what matter about them? Do I then strive after happiness? I strive after my work! Well, the lion hath come, my children and I Zarathustra has grown ripe - my hour has come! This is my morning, my day begins!"

Fenby's first few weeks are taken up purely with reading as Delius is too tired to think about composition. In voiceover as he walks the grounds he regrets the time spent with no change in routine but Russell's panning camera contradicts him - we have noticed a young, interesting looking female neighbor who Fenby has missed, too engrossed in his reading and daily walks. Fenby wasn't gay but only married in 1944 after temporarily leaving the Catholic Church – the couple had two children. Clearly it took some time for Fenby to unwind and the film beautifully articulates the contrasts between the multiple barriers he has erected, as a young man, to Delius' up-front, take-it-or-leave-it informality.

Finally Delius has the inspiration and energy to start composing and calls Fenby in, humming a tune (out of tune) that the young scribe is supposed to get down on paper. Fenby doesn't know what key it's in and has no way of knowing the notes – they finally figure out that Delius must sing out the notes rather than hum but it's no good – Fenby gets very frustrated and has to leave the room in tears – he runs to the train station perhaps to run away but comes back to the house, defeated. Jelka tells Fenby he must stand up to the maestro and tell him directly what he thinks of his last score and Fenby refuses as he thinks it's very poor and doesn't have the courage to say it. Delius is brought in by the Bruder who places him on a sofa, under a painting of a nude woman, Gauguin's *Nevermore (O Tahiti)* (1897). Delius asks Fenby directly what he thinks of his music and the young apprentice, behind another painting by Munch smartly goes to the piano and plays his music, explaining in detail what he doesn't like – but when he uses the word "weak" Delius throws him out. The contrast here between Munch and Gauguin, winter and summer, Fenby and Delius, is very strong as both men struggle to understand one another but they are very different people inhabiting different worlds.

Jelka, ever the conciliator, interjects, bringing the two antagonists together to listen to a recording of a Delius masterwork. Russell crosscuts close-ups as everyone is very moved by the music. Delius suggests starting again the following day in the music room fresh. This is taken as a victory for Jelka and she and Fenby go off to the woods for another celebratory walk – as usual Russell shoots in medium long shot so we see the amazing countryside full of trees. She explains that Delius' opera *Hassan* has just come back from the publishers and needs to be proofed and she asks Fenby to do it – she's determined to keep him there for the duration. She is reminded that this was the last piece he wrote before he lost his sight – they were in Norway where they befriended Edvard Munch, and Percy Grainger, the eccentric English composer was there as well helping out. She recalls having traveled all over Europe looking for a cure that was never found and complains bitterly that they never play Delius anymore on the radio. Clearly she is totally devoted to Delius despite his wandering ways that, in the long run, cost him so dearly. The next morning the men are hard at work - finally with success - on *A Song of Summer*, despite a few setbacks here and there – "you forgot the pizzicato!" - and Jelka is happy in the garden planting new flowers. Later they celebrate their first success with champagne.

Delius at one point wants to hear a recording of *Ol' Man River* the American song by Jerome Kern and Oscar Hammerstein, sung by The Revelers and made popular in the 1920's. At the time in Europe this would have been like playing primitive world or folk music and Delius, like Bartok, Stravinsky, and others was fascinated with American roots music and borrowed liberally whatever he could use. Delius recollects how much he loved Florida and the "singing of the negroes." After Bradford, an industrial northern city, also home to David Hockney, he was demoralized and looking for a new start – America gave it to him in 1884. Interestingly it did so for David Hockney as well but in Los Angeles in the 1960's. Delius' father was in the wool business and refused to have his son be a musician and so he was packed off to Jacksonville, Florida. There he met an organist who showed him "everything he wanted to know about harmony and counterpoint. I didn't realize his worth as a teacher until I went to study at the Leipzig Conservatory."

Delius was always radically anti-academic and he shows it here, explaining that it was in those surroundings in Florida with African Americans singing and partying that he first felt the need to express himself in music – Russell moves in for an extraordinary powerful extreme close-up as we see Delius talking with his eyes closed. Russell had wanted to include elements of Delius' life that were well known but not official, until many years later when a biography came out that exposed that Delius had fathered a child with one of the African American women but simply left mother and child behind once he left the US for Europe. Russell made up for this later with his short novel *Delius: A Moment With Venus* that explores that ground. Once ready for bed Jelka and Fenby carry Delius to his bedroom as the three of them together form a triangle exactly as in *Jules and Jim* when the two men carry Catherine forming a trio. In Truffaut's film of course they form a ménage-a-trois but in *Song of Summer* it's a beautiful visual representation of a new family, of sorts, created by music.

In one of his most exceptional shots Russell shows Fenby and Delius outside waiting for the sun to come out with Fenby sitting facing the camera and Delius in profile in his wheelchair, face to the sun – this is the shot used in the poster for the film. Rather than the standard over the shoulder cross cutting, typical for dialogue scenes, Russell opts for the Wellesian two shot that is dynamic and clearly places the dominant Delius in the foreground with the uncertain Fenby further back, but both in pinpoint focus. Delius says that he understands why the ancient Persians worshipped the sun – the maestro always had more sympathy for ancient religions that worshipped nature that he saw as more enlightened than modern religions that had abstract "gods" that would reward and punish people according to certain dictates.

As the men wait for the sun Delius goes into raptures about nature and his friend and fellow composer Percy Grainger (David Collings) makes a dramatic entrance sliding down the roof of the house landing by Delius' side. Grainger starts to play games with a tennis ball like a child, throwing the ball up to the roof of the house and then running like a madman to the back of the house to catch it – something possible only with the magic of film but Grainger makes it seem like a lot of fun and worth trying. He then carries Delius' off into the woods as if he were on a bicycle rather than a wheelchair. For this part of the film Russell uses Grainger's music *Handel in the Strand* that has a sarcastic "jolly jaunt" underside to its neoclassical foundation – perfect for a fast stroll in the forest as Jelka and Fenby run to keep up.

Later Grainger and Fenby play some sensitive piano duets indoors - contemporary music with harmonically unresolved intervals being pushed back and forth by the two players as the others quietly listen as if they were at church. As the music dissolves to a symphony the two men carry Delius up a local hill so he may experience nature, despite his reduced faculties, while Jelka brings up the rear in a stately procession that looks almost religious – and of course it is in a sense religious, since Delius, despite his atheism was an unashamed Pantheist. Russell zooms out so we see his beloved Lake District (again) that he used as a setting. Russell wanted to shoot the film in Grez where Delius' house still stood but finances made shooting in France impossible, so he used Surrey, Scarborough, and The Lake District. To italicize the religious aspect of the pilgrimage Jenka stops by a small waterfall and picks up some water with her hands to splash on her face, then looks renewed or blessed as the men soldier on. As they climb higher they encounter snow and keep climbing with Delius looking like a mad tyrannical King in exile, his eyes always closed, his mouth always humming a tune that we can't hear as Russell uses *A Song of Summer* throughout. As they reach the summit Russell uses Wellesian deep focus so the little group is seen within the sublime vastness of nature, of what looks like an unexplored planet full of wonders.

Back indoors in one of the most heartbreaking of Russell's set pieces Delius and Grainger recall another time, just before Delius went blind, when they carried him up another mountain in Norway so he could see the sunset for the last time. Everyone remembers this a joyous occasion but then we see that Jelka has a different idea without saying a word – Russell cuts to a flashback from her point of view trudging up the Norwegian mountain looking depressed and miserable in the snow – Grainger is sweating and uncomfortable but not saying a word as they carry the egomaniacal Delius up to the top, on his throne, where it is full of clouds and rain making it impossible to see. Shooting clouds and rain in the Lake District was easy and Russell takes full advantage as the trio struggles on. When they reach the summit the clouds part and Delius can look at the sunset, eyes wide open like a madman, trying to take it all in before it goes dark. This is a beautiful use of counterpoint as the dialogue suggests one thing but we see another, harsher reality.

Russell cuts from this dark pilgrimage to see the light to a more lighthearted romp by the two young men – Fenby and Percy- as they race in the woods and throw a ball back and forth, with Russell's camera performing a parallel tracking shot, again as in *Jules and Jim*. As usual with Russell the scene is quick and ends just as it was beginning with Fenby falling from the exertion and Grainger running off backwards down the country road: "So long Fenby! By the time you get back I'll be gone! And true to his word Percy is gone.

We miss him immediately as he was such an eccentric, energetic and childlike character, and no doubt that's how it was for Fenby.

On his return to the house Fenby runs into the mysterious young female neighbor who is incongruously wearing a large beautiful hat in the woods. They stop to chat and she explains that she's from Kent and he introduces himself as being from Yorkshire. She asks if the woman who used to live in the house, who was an artist, and a friend of Jelka's, has painted him and explains that the two women shared Delius. When Fenby is shocked she asks him if he goes to church, then explains that the local priest who used to live in her house was a peeping-tom, and that the Delius house was full of models when Jelka was still painting nudes – "all of those women with Jelka and her girlfriend crazy about Delius, and then it was too late." Fenby doesn't seem to understand much of what the woman is saying but is saved by the three bells – Delius calling.

Delius wants to dictate some music but Fenby took so long he's forgotten it – the imperious Delius doesn't even ask what the young man was doing. As he apologizes Fenby is framed by another Munch painting of a sleeping nude looking like a mortified corpse – it's as if Fenby is inside the painting, caught in the web of Munch's dark, brooding artwork, almost anticipating Francis Bacon's more nihilistic despair. As Fenby explains the young neighbor Delius, sitting his wheelchair with his wife behind him, asks Fenby sarcastically if he intends to marry the girl – explaining that "an artist must never marry although one can amuse oneself with as many women as one likes - but for the sake of your heart never marry because it is fatal! Love is madness! You're a fool if you ever marry!" Jelka is behind him in tears while he talks, unable to stand his withering sarcasm. The sensitive Fenby is embarrassed for her and asks to be excused as Jelka runs out of the room to the garden where she and Fenby regroup. "There are times when I wonder if I can go on." Says Jelka with Fenby behind her listening intently but not knowing what to say.

She explains that she's never stood in his way, whatever he wanted to do, providing the perfect conditions for work. Fenby attributes his cruelty and selfishness to his illness but Jelka refutes him crying as Russell moves in for a close-up as Maureen Pryor does a great job conveying both her unbounded love and admiration for Delius and her horror and disgust at having to witness his many betrayals first hand over a span of years. She explains that he used to leave for Paris and not return for days, and then the affairs with women that led to abortions she would have to arrange. "But I knew he'd always come back to me!" Jelka is distraught and in tears but Fenby, although he wants to, can't bring himself to give her a hug, and she runs off.

Distraught himself he goes to his one refuge from the storm – the local church – empty but for the local priest (Russell in disguise) fucking a young girl in one of the pews. True to form at first Fenby only hears something but then sees the priest and his lover. His only comment is: "will you hear my confession Father?" There is no reply. This scene was not in Fenby's memoirs – he told the story to Russell as they talked about that time period and he was surprised when he saw the final film and not only was the scene included but Russell himself was the parish priest! Clearly Russell's own uneasy relationship to Catholicism is embodied in the small role that he must have enjoyed playing.

We then see Fenby and Delius on a small boat sailing the local waterways – actually the Lake District - as Delius chastises Fenby for his religion. "This humbug has paralyzed music all along – what Catholic has ever written a piece of music worth hearing?" Fenby counters with church plain songs and Haydn's *Creation* oratorio but Delius rejects the very idea. We then hear Delius' own *Requiem* on the soundtrack as we see the two men in long shot, Fenby rowing against the wind. Delius' *Requiem* (1916) was not overtly religious but was written as a memoriam to all the artists who died in WWI, some of whom Delius knew – some critics at the time accused the composer of sacrilege but he took that to be a complement. Delius: "Human beings are incredible – they'll believe anything to escape reality." Finally ashore Fenby has learned to carry Delius on his back like the Bruner and he places him gently in his wicker wheelchair. Delius is inspired and has some new ideas. We hear Delius' music as Russell pans to the expansive water moving swiftly in long extended takes set to music. Russell gets literal here as Delius explains that the flute "suggests a seagull flying" and Russell shows it – of course we remember that Fenby had the idea first when he was still at home in England but it's Delius who gets to turn it into real music in *A Song of Summer*.

While we see them working together Fenby in voiceover explains that after six years he felt his job was done, and as Fenby prepares to depart Delius has a final gift for him, a pocket watch on a chain "so you may remember our years here." Fenby is unlikely to forget but Jelka puts the watch in Delius' atrophied hands and then ceremoniously passes it to Fenby who is clearly moved. Fenby explains that the years with Delius were difficult but they resulted in the completion of several pieces of music and at least one masterpiece: *Song of Summer*. Russell plays some music but on a loop from a 35mm recording on magnetic tape thereby accommodating the needs of the visual sequence requiring repeats. Nothing was sacrosanct and everything was basically raw material for the poetics of sound and image - in a sense Russell here re-created Delius' music via a modernist collage (sound loops) but one that is transparent and flows perfectly with the rest of the film.

Fenby returns to England to supervise the publication of Delius' music and his sisters welcome him home with a party where everyone is dancing to American jazz music, but clearly Fenby is as alienated in this environment as any character in a Munch painting. After the party he suffers a nervous breakdown and looses the use of his legs and it takes him some time to recover – he then receives a telegram from Jelka still in France telling Fenby that she is soon to be operated on for cancer and he must come immediately to help at the house. Upon his return Delius becomes emotional at hearing Fenby's voice again. Yet we see some differences in Fenby – he kisses Delius on the forehead and jerks his head for the smoking Bruder to leave the room, with some authority. Fenby is growing up on Delius' watch. From then on it is a matter of attending to the maestro in his final days as a nurse – the doctor tells Fenby to stop asking him if it will be alright as it is obvious that Delius is dying of syphilis and he has only a few days left. Jelka returns from a successful operation and she and Delius reconcile knowing their time together is almost at an end. After the death he is stretched out on the living room sofa as Jelka and Fenby listen to the BBC news speak about Delius' death after a long "undefined illness." They then play *Song of Summer* as Jelka pours flowers from the local garden over Delius' body – an event that actually happened that closes Fenby's memoirs.

Fenby and Russell worked together on the beautifully detailed script, and the 62 year old Fenby also coached Max Adrian and Christopher Gable on their line readings, recalling that the final effect was "disturbingly lifelike." Russell recalls asking Fenby to come onto the set but he was, as one would expect, shy about seeing the young actor portray him in the film, to say nothing of Adrian as the imposing Delius. Fenby said he would prefer not to come to the shoot but as Russell recalls in his autobiography one day Fenby did come:

"Then came the day when we were shooting Fenby's arrival at the Delius household in France, a meeting which prophesized disaster. The gauche young Fenby had been shy and tongue tied, Delius rude and boorish. It ended with Fenby almost in tears and a deathly silence. Before I could say "cut" there was a sob from a darkened corner. It was Fenby himself, the real Fenby. He told us over lunch that he had slipped in unnoticed and found himself transported back in time to the day of his arrival, the memory forcing from him that cry of anguish which had remained stifled all those years."

Unfortunately after seeing the completed film Fenby suffered another breakdown and it would be a year before he fully recovered and returned to work.

In a more glamorous Hollywood film certainly Fenby's altruism, kindness, and generosity would have been rewarded with a kind, solid mate and some success on his own as a composer. Not surprisingly the facts are different and Russell sticks to them as they are far more interesting than the romantic clichés of most composer biographies. Fenby was, by his own admission, "completely burnt out" by the experience with Delius that he recounted in *Delius as I Knew Him*. In later life Fenby gave up trying to be a serious composer and instead became artistic director for the Bradford Delius Festival in 1962, eventually becoming the Professor of Harmony at the Royal Academy of Music. He composed occasionally for films – his most famous collaboration was with Alfred Hitchcock in *Jamaica Inn* (1939).

Despite remaining busy he never produced a body of work that he might call his own - he realized toward the end of his life that he had devoted the major thrust of his artistic energies to Delius and to the seven full scores that they finished together. Of these works it is still *A Song of Summer* that is most remembered. Fenby, as an old man (Delius's age when he met him), recorded the music with the Royal Philharmonic Orchestra producing a record released in 1981; this is considered by many to be the definitive recording of the work and it remains a final testament to their difficult friendship. Toward the end of his life he rediscovered his Catholicism and died while he was approaching his 91st birthday in February of 1997. Since he was born in 1906 he was a true child of the century – he's buried next to his wife in Scalby, a small village in Scarborough, England very close to where he was born and raised and from where he started that long journey to France and to Delius – a journey that came to define the remainder of his life.

s

Independence 1: From *Diary of Nobody* to *Savage Messiah*

THE DIARY OF A NOBODY: THE DOMESTIC JOTTINGS OF A CITY-CLERK (1964)

In 1964 Russell took a detour from *Monitor* to make *The Diary of a Nobody: The Domestic Jottings of a City Clerk* so his first independent film, without Huw Wheldon, was still under the wing of the BBC. *Diary of a Nobody* was a thirty-eight minute black and white film adaptation of a novel from 1892 that Russell made in the style of a silent film with touches of Kitchen Sink, shifting from one to the other depending on the content. As in his *Monitor* work there is a constant voiceover that in this instance reads from the novel by George and Weedon Grossmith. The book as well as the film is a drama/comedy about a clerk, Charles Pooter (Bryan Pringle), who is tired of having only adventurous heroics and extraordinary tales get all of the attention in the book world and he seeks to – in a sense like Cervantes with *Don Quixote* – provide an antithesis.

Pooter publishes a diary about what he believes is his very boring life as a city clerk, going to work and then coming home to his wife and having dinner. The book had its supporters in the early 20th century - Evelyn Waugh called it "the funniest book ever written"[46] and George Orwell was influenced by it in his wonderful novel *Keep the Aspidistra Flying*. As Russell shows Pooter's middle class family, especially his wife Caroline Pooter (Avril Elgar), are crazy in the best way possible. Gilles Deleuze once made the wonderful remark that it is impossible to fall in love with someone unless they reveal their own madness or insanity for that is where their charm lies.[47] The novel revels in madness or eccentricity but in a minor key – all very much behind closed suburban doors. Russell was always a master of making the interior lives of his characters visible on screen and he does it here in his first independent film, making it clear that Charles' life is not as boring as he thinks it is – Avril Elgar's performance as Mrs. Pooter is a hoot. Russell updated the time to the present, 1964, but wisely kept the text from 1892 as it was. The use of silent film makes a great deal of sense as the book was written just as Edison, Lumiere and Melies were getting ready to change the world – the film seems to exist in a suspended state of magical realism – an alternate universe between the turn of the century and 1964 where silent cinema and Kitchen Sink happily meet. Unfortunately the Grossmith estate did not like the fact that the film had been updated to the present time and they withdrew their permission to use the text, giving the film extremely limited distribution.

FRENCH DRESSING (1964)

Russell would move tentatively into feature films with *French Dressing*, an absurdist comedy of manners, shot in the style of his *Monitor* work in black & white by cinematographer Ken Higgins who had worked on John Schlesinger's *Terminus* (1961), one of the landmark films of the Free Cinema movement. Like *Terminus* the film has an incongruous winter feel despite the summer setting. Russell mimics the style of the French New Wave with snappy romantic dialogue concocted by Peter Myers, Peter Brett and Ronald Cass. Despite some good set pieces, the film falls flat and did not do well financially. *French Dressing* presumably takes place in Gormleigh-on-Sea, a rundown seaside resort, but the film was primarily shot at Elstree Studios near London and on location at Herne Bay, another more up-to-date seaside town. The plot centers around the poor, local deckchair attendant who decides to turn the towns fortunes around, as well as his own, by hosting a film festival, modeled on Cannes, and hiring an actress from France to come and inaugurate the launch, and hopefully initiate a sex scandal of some sort, putting the festival on the map.

Of course nothing goes as planned, and in a style made popular by Jacques Tati, there is a lot of physical humor that the actors are able to deliver on cue as Russell surrounded himself with some old pros, such as Roy Kinnear, who knew their comedy. The main problem with the film was that the characters remained cliché types without ever becoming involved in their characters or their situation. The film seemed to be a series of skits that were amusing and often beautifully framed but emotionally uninvolving. To add insult to injury Vittorio de Sica, Neil Simon, Cesare Zavattini, Britt Ekland, and Peter Sellers would team up two years later to make *After the Fox* (1966) – a classic satire with more or less the same plot but with the location shifting to a sleepy Italian beach resort that, unfortunately, is not to be found on any map.

Italy and France throughout the sixties produced a number of amoral sex comedies that were part screwball comedy, part melodrama, part "knee trembler," and part vacation film. These films were short on plot and long on charming and/or sexy episodes that were, at times so disconnected they came close to resembling avant-garde works. These adult escapist films did not travel well to the USA, for obvious reasons, and received limited distribution or were never officially released there. Films such as Richard Lester's *The Knack and How to Get It* (1965), Roger Vadim's *The Nutty, Naughty Chateau* (1963), Sergio Corbucci's *Totó, Peppino...e la Dolce Vita* (1961), and Michel Boisrond's *Catherine & Co.* (1975) exhibited a profound moral relativism and an ironic and anarchist sensibility with regards to all rules, questions of class, and conventions (including those of cinematic continuity). In many cases, such as *Catherine & Co.*, insult was added to injury as the film openly made fun of the excesses and absurdities of a capitalist society. *French Dressing's* attempt at this format seems half hearted at best - as Russell described it himself:

> "The film industry was not ready to accept TV directors. Everything was done by the book, improvisation was frowned upon and there was little team spirit...a film director has to be a psychiatrist but it was too late as far as *French Dressing* was concerned – the film was a flop...a very unhappy film as far as I was concerned."[48]

There are some comments by Russell here are that are worth pursuing. While improvisation in the theater and on television was a commonplace, in studio films it was very rare and looked down upon as a sign of unprofessionalism. Improvisation was, presumably, reserved for lowbrow television and highbrow avant-garde films, such as those made by the American independent filmmaker John Cassavetes. Russell in his television work extensively used improvisation and allowed his actors to develop their characters on the run, assuming he could then cut out all of the things that did not work. But the conventional studio films didn't work like that - the cast of *French Dressing* in particular wanted their director to tell them (like a psychiatrist as Russell said) exactly what the situations and motivations were. Russell returned to the BBC, bruised but hungry to give it another shot.

BILLION DOLLAR BRAIN (1967)

Russell got his second chance at features three years later in 1967 with *Billion Dollar Brain,* the third installment in the "Harry Palmer" series – an early franchise film based on novels by Len Deighton. Palmer (Michael Cain) was a working class version of Ian Fleming's James Bond – wearing glasses and out of fashion suits, living in a cold-water flat, drinking beer rather than martinis, and never getting the girl. John McGrath was chosen to write the script by producer Harry Saltzman who had made the first two in the series, *The Ipcress File* (1965) directed by Sidney Furie, and *Funeral in Berlin* (1966) directed by Guy Hamilton. The first two Harry Palmer films were finely tuned, Cold War narratives that were lean, down-to-earth, with brilliant craftsmanship all around, by cast and crew. The two works perfectly balanced dry working class humor, traditional action sequences, and Le Carre style spy drama - the subtle cold war anxieties, and the brutalities of the time were allowed space to come forward giving the films some depth, that the Bond films lacked. While the Harry Palmer franchise would seem ready-made for Russell – being about a cantankerous, working class outsider - Russell's film seems to spin its wheels without going anywhere in particular, and while the ride is often enjoyable, the film is slight and lacks the substance of his television work.

On the other hand the film is, in many respects, ahead of its time anticipating the anxieties about computers and AI that were present in 1967 but would become much more prevalent and urgent in the following century. The film also has many pleasures unrelated to its overly-plotted script by McGrath, that follows the genre rules in a paint-by-numbers, tongue in cheek style popular at the time – in that respect *Billion Dollar Brain* is closer to *Casino Royale's* (1967) self-conscious, episodic absurdities than to *Torn*

Curtain's (1966) earnest, cold war paranoia. One pleasure is seeing Françoise Dorléac play Anya, a triple-crossing secret agent – this would be Dorléac's final role before her tragic car accident and she chews up the Pop scenery and costumes with an irresistible charm and presence. The other pleasure is seeing cinematographer Billy Williams and Russell play with the spy genre and its outrageous settings, seemingly becoming adolescents for the duration of the shoot – they play an infectious game.

Harry Palmer has left MI5, the British Secret Service, to work as a private investigator and finally make some money. An extraordinarily beautiful opening shot of London at dusk, reminds us of his early *Monitor* film *London Moods* but now in color and wide screen. An unseen man enters a building and searches Palmer's apartment – we see a series of still life's giving us clues as to Harry's single lifestyle – meager, small and depressing. Palmer enters and we see that the intruder is his former superior at MI5 Coronel Ross (Guy Doleman), who wants him back at MI5. Palmer insists he's doing fine and throws Ross out. The beautiful shot of Palmer talking tough but holding a box of *Kellogg's Corn Flakes* that he has just purchased (and subsequently spills on the floor) visually puts his tough guy persona, and to some extent his masculinity, in quotation marks – something that Russell does repeatedly throughout the film until the end when he brings the theme to resolution. These shots do not undermine Palmer's masculinity but they put it on the dock so we think about it as a running motif throughout the film.

When Ross leaves Palmer receives a phone call and is given a job to take a package to Helsinki containing six virus-laden eggs that have been stolen from a secret British facility. In Finland Palmer meets Anya (Françoise Dorléac) a beautiful agent who takes him to meet her boss Leo Newbigen (Karl Malden), an old friend of Palmer's from their spy days. Leo is clearly in love with Anya and she is playing him but Leo takes the team to a secret room where a computer issues the orders - Harry notices that the computer has the same voice that ordered him to Helsinki in the first place. Palmer surmises that he cannot trust anyone but plays along so he can get paid, but before he can make a move he is abducted by his former superior at MI5, Colonel Ross again, who coerces him into one "final mission" for the British government getting the eggs back. In Helsinki Anya tries to kill Harry while seducing him, but then confesses that the computer told her to do it - Harry is saved by Colonel Stok (Oskar Homolka), an old acquaintance from the KGB who is onto the scheme and playing his own game.

Leo offers to pay Harry off but Palmer now says he wants to go in as a partner and take half the money in order to meet the boss. The pair then go off to Texas to meet the top man who is running the computer - an oil tycoon named General Midwinter (Ed Begley) – a name straight out of Terry Southern – who proudly displays his "billion dollar brain" – a massive room full of computer hardware dispensing orders to agents worldwide, including an insurrection in Latvia that he thinks will trigger the fall of Communism worldwide, that he will lead, eventually becoming ruler of the "free world." Russell had the finances to shoot an actual computer – the most advanced at that moment – the *Honeywell 200* at their headquarters in Charlotte, North Carolina. When Harry first sees the computer he intones glibly: "No more need to think." He seems to get the gist of AI right away – one of the true wonders of genre films is that insight, for the hero, is invariably instant, and so it proves to be here. The imposing, futuristic location for the billion dollar computer rivals *Dr. Strangelove's* bunker and has the added benefit of being real. In a train bound for Moscow all of the principals gather for a showdown and as predicted Anya betrays Leo pushing him off the train and taking the eggs.

Leo finally sees the light of day and offers to help Harry stop Midwinter's scheme that could trigger a world war. Midwinter is leading his private army across the frozen fields of Finland into Latvia for the Armageddon. Leo is killed in the process but Harry finds a way to get information to MI5 about the invading private army and the British find a way to break the ice with bombs. Midwinter's convoy plunges into the ice and the freezing water and all of the vehicles and men, including Midwinter himself, sink into an icy Baltic grave. This scene is probably the best set-piece in the film directly quoting Sergei Eisenstein's famous *Alexander Nevsky* battle sequence where all of the horses and men fall through broken ice made of wood painted white. Russell had the finances to use a giant tank at Pinewood studios with slabs of polystyrene to represent the ice, and he used actual vehicles instead of miniatures. Russell may be quoting Eisenstein but rather than the Russian master's tragic heroism what we have with *Billion Dollar Brain* is closer to Welles' existential, tragic absurdity from his own incomparable battle sequence in *Chimes at Midnight* where we survey all of that extensive effort and only death to show for it. Heroism of a military sort is always a fool's errand for Russell (and Welles).

Russell here takes *Billion Dollar Brain* beyond its genre boundaries as we sense the horrifying pain and horror of those deaths by drowning in icy, dark waters – we see it as they stare oblivion in the face and are helpless to do anything about it but remain in their vehicles that will soon become their tombs. The scene offers no affectations of emotions, as we see in James Cameron's *Titanic* (1997) where we can actually see underwater in the middle of the night in the north Atlantic while reveling in the doomed romance – in Russell's film when the men sink into the dark mass of icy water they are simply gone forever.

Harry regains consciousness and aid arrives in the form of Colonel Stok, the old KGB man who introduces Anya to Harry as his new agent – Stok is also besotted with Anya and the story here will no doubt repeat as Anya, the all around survivor, is now a Russian agent. To thank him Palmer offers the eggs to Stok but is brushed off. "We don't need them – we have our own ideas." Apparently the Soviets are also working on germ warfare and are ahead of the game. Back in London Harry delivers the eggs to MI5 and Ross promises Harry a promotion if he stays on board. When he opens the box full of eggs he finds it is full of chicks – the eggs have hatched. The chicken/egg joke seems a bit shallow and meaningless after all that sound and fury. Nevertheless *Billion Dollar Brain*, like the previous Palmer films, was a financial success, with mixed reviews, but it was the last official release in the Palmer series as Caine moved to Hollywood (literally and figuratively) to focus on action films and historical epics – in any case Russell finally had his foot in the door and *Billion Dollar Brain* remains a cult favorite among aficionados of the genre.

THE MUSIC LOVERS (1971)

The Music Lovers is a biography of Peter Ilyich Tchaikovsky (1840-1893) concentrating on the period in which he was briefly married – as usual Russell focuses on the marital relationship in the life/history using it as an entry point for understanding the man and the music. Melvyn Bragg, who wrote *The Debussy Film* and *Always on Sunday*, wrote the beautifully articulate, complex script based on *Beloved Friend* the posthumously published letters of Barbara von Meck, Tchaikovsky's wealthy, reclusive, aristocratic patron. But Bragg, the polymath and cultural historian, shifted the point of view from von Meck to a series of fragments consisting of flashbacks, dreams, and fantasy sequences from specific points of view that were then assembled in the editing using the music as counterpoint. Bragg clearly took a page from *Citizen Kane's* (1941) multiple viewpoints, but *The Music Lovers* is more fragmented, for despite the multiple time frames in *Kane* there is an underlying classical structure at work, tied to the "mystery" of *Rosebud*. *The Music Lovers* avoids this classical foundation in favor of an episodic structure, so, unlike *Kane* Bragg incorporates fantasy sequences that at times blend in with memory or "reality." What Bragg focuses on with *Kane* is what Jorge Luis Borges called the "labyrinth structure" of Orson Welles's masterpiece. Bragg would use this "labyrinth structure" repeatedly in his work, including his own version of *Isadora* (1968) directed by Karel Reisz, with Vanessa Redgrave as Isadora Duncan.

The moment *The Music Lovers* begins, even before the credits, we are fully immersed in the labyrinth of Tchaikovsky's life and the people that loved him and his music and wanted to be a part of it. As he was wont to do in this phase of his career Russell starts at full speed, in media res, so the viewer is immediately forced to figure things out for herself without a narrative introduction. Russell had learned from his BBC work to condense his material and simply avoided traditional exposition, not because he wanted to rebel against the rules, but because there was no time to bother with it.

Not everyone enjoyed being suddenly in the middle of something from the get-go and then having to play catch up. Pauline Kael, the reigning doyenne of American film criticism at the time – via *The New Yorker*, a magazine that espoused the viewpoint of the cultural ruling elite in New York and championed the cause of belles-lettres (such as it is) wrote of the film: "...a sprawling, incoherent mess that fails to do justice to the brilliant composer..." She also ranted against Russell in her thankfully short essay that all of the director's work and *The Music Lovers* in particular were like two minute coming attraction trailers stretched out to 90 minutes. But as we have seen Russell used the "kaleidoscopic condensation" of the trailer as a *method* early on while working at the BBC. Kael's mediocrity aside, *The Music Lovers* is lovingly put together by Bragg, Russell, and the editor Michael Bradsell so we may view it many times and see something new every time – the wonderful attribute of a well constructed cinematic labyrinth.

Typical of Russell he would get into trouble not only with critics but with the authorities again, this time in the Soviet Union, for making Tchaikovsky's tortured homosexuality a major thematic thread that runs through the film. Tchaikovsky's (Richard Chamberlain) interior life is given as much screen time as his public persona and the two are played off in beautiful movements set to the Russian composer's music. Before the credits roll we see Tchaikovsky and his boyfriend, Anton Chiluvsky (Christopher Gable), rollicking in a Russian popular winter festival with dancers, acrobats and frenzied partygoers. Some of the characters that we will meet later are seen at the festival wearing masks so already there is a dreamlike quality to the opening. The festive scene unabashedly ends with Tchaikovsky going down a slide – Russell shoots it from the composer's point of view - as he reaches the bottom laughing in delight the diegetic sound is pushed to the background and the music takes over as the titles come up.

Russell shot this scene, as he did a lot of his work, in the "Italian style," that is he filmed to playback. This involves playing music during the shoot (for the actors) but filming without sound and adding dialogue, sound and music in post-production. This procedure is more costly, as it means time spent in studios with actors doing sync sound but it allows the director great freedom during a shoot with more complex choreography that could be coordinated and adjusted on set. It also enables the director to talk to his actors during the performance as was done during silent films. This format enabled Russell to use more compact, lighter camera equipment that did not require sound muffling such as the Arriflex IIC that could easily be hand-held, even being confrontational, and going directly up to actors - something Russell wanted for *The Music Lovers* as it gave him the opportunity to use his camera as a "character" within the piece rather than standing outside the action as a spectator.

Post-credits we see arguably Russell's strongest set piece – an extraordinary scene establishing several points of view at the same time using Tchaikovsky's Piano Concerto No. 1 to establish the rhythm and pacing. But Russell goes further – he uses his camera and the editing to mimic the mind of the character as we see their thoughts, memories and fantasies – to do this for one character and make it work is a feat but to do it for four separate characters at the same time, in counterpoint, is a remarkable achievement. Russell's advantage here is that memory as such is not a stable entity but a malleable organic one – it dies and is sometimes resurrected, changes or slips sideways into something else. The film makes little distinction in scenes between memory, dream, public events, and personal dramas. The film in that aspect borrows from Fellini's *8 ½*, Has' *The Saragossa Manuscript*, and Tarkovsky's *Ivan's Childhood*, among others made in the sixties that first charted the use of dreams not as separate "dream sequences" (as in *Spellbound*) but as an integral, concurrent, part of the film narrative itself.

As the scene opens Tchaikovsky's staunchest supporter and benefactor, the musically radical but socially conservative Madame von Meck (Izabella Telezynska) makes a dramatic late appearance, in a horse drawn cab, at the premier of his concerto at the

Moscow Conservatory, with Tchaikovsky himself conducting from the piano. Her hasty entrance is intercut with Tchaikovsky's troubled thoughts as he starts his concerto – now considered one of the great works of the century and part of the standard repertoire. Chamberlain could actually read music and play the piano and he gives a strong performance as the guilt riven and overly sensitive Russian genius. This scene is also where we see the inner lives of Tchaikovsky's sister, Sasha (Sabina Maydelle); his brother Modest (Kenneth Colley); and Nina Milyukova, (Glenda Jackson) Tchaikovsky's wife to be, as we see them come together for the fancy dress premier.

All of these characters are "music lovers" to a fault and they all get their interior lives displayed. This scene uses each of the three movements as a springboard for a variety of stylistic and formal cinematic devices – it is arguably the finest instance of contrapuntal editing set to music in the history of film. It's only remote competition is Sergei Eisenstein's famous "Potemkin Steps" sequence from *Battleship Potemkin* (1926) but in that film the unfolding of events – an attack by Russian troops on their own people – is fundamentally sequential, even as the portions of time are broken down into ever smaller segments, slowing down the action into powerful individual "scenes within the scene" that interact in extraordinary counterpoint. Russell's film is not in any sense sequential, using character's memories, dreams and segments from their everyday life at various points – all brought together by the music – so one is able to make sense of their lives without traditional exposition. With *The Music Lovers* we are dealing with the interior lives of four very different people alongside a structuring "main event" – the premiere of the piano concerto. This leaves Russell the possibility of radically different sorts of temporal segments within the scene, each using different tempos, different lenses and filters, even different film speeds, as one scene is shot in slow motion using the slow second movement. Russell takes full advantage of all of the options available to him, shifting from dream to memory to the actual "live" event in a dizzying display of the possibilities of cinema.

Nina's daydream, triggered by the appearance of young military man in the audience, is a typical romantic vignette, shot with soft filters, using fast cuts and making full use of the up-tempo segment of the concerto. We see Nina and her dream officer in a Hansel and Gretel carriage in a romantic park scenario worthy of Fritz Lang's silent, romantic period. As they cross a fairy tale bridge they throw an empty bottle of Champagne overboard while laughing and toasting themselves silly. When Nina wakes up from her fantasy she looks around but her dream man has departed, being uninterested in the new music. Russell then shifts to a flash-forward where Nina has written a letter to the officer and invited him to her room, but she discovers, to her horror, that the officer was not a gentleman, as he beats her in a drunken haze before leaving her on the floor, in despair at once again having made the wrong choice. From her small, impoverished and cluttered room, we see her world without Nina having to say a word.

Sasha, Tchaikovsky's sister has a more dense and complex memory/dream, set to the slow movement of the concerto, in which she is clearly in love with her brother in an unrequited, incestuous bond that may be linked to Tchaikovsky's homosexuality. In her sequence she is carrying flowers in a forest in slow motion. She clearly loves her husband and their children and cherishes their family time together vacationing in an idyllic lakeside dacha. She remembers boating on a lake as Russell shoots the children, also in slow motion, in a scene that recalls the Impressionist paintings of the period. From her selective memory it is clear that while she adores her brother she finds his homosexuality repugnant. Their sequence is shot in an actual forest using natural light without filters. Its extreme use of slow motion turns the forest into dream space, as well into one of the romantic tableaus popular in Tchaikovsky's time.

In a series of repeated flashbacks Tchaikovsky remembers seeing his mother die horribly, dragged from her deathbed and forcibly immersed in scalding water – a cure at the time for cholera. As a boy he doesn't understand his mother's pain or the men's wish to help, by placing her in a bath of scalding water – a presumed "final cure" that only ended towards the beginning of the next century. The guilt over his inability to save his mother haunts his life and his music in a way that he himself seems not to understand but it leaves him groping for answers even as it is clear that in all of his music those tensions and contradictory feelings have found expression.

After the concerto Nicolai Rubinstein (Max Adrian), the elder head of the conservatory where Tchaikovsky works as a teacher, tells the young composer his work is immature, verging on wild atonalities that are whimsical and unmusical. Russell shows Rubinstein's rejection is due in equal parts to his conservative nature and his jealousy of Tchaikovsky's genius. Something else that he does – when Rubenstein sits at the piano and mimics Tchaikovsky's concerto to display its "unmusicality" – is that he makes clear that this music, despite its heavy doses of Romanticism, was the first step to the harsh, jagged dissonances of Stravinsky, Bartok and Schoenberg. Russell very smartly both ostracizes Rubenstein for his short-sightedness but also seems to show that he – like Tchaikovsky – had some insight regarding this new music to come, but, unlike the young composer, he was horrified by it. Despite Rubinstein's disparaging comments Tchaikovsky gains some success as a young composer of promise and even Rubenstein praises him to Madame von Meck to secure funding for his conservatory playing one of his pieces on her grand piano.

Nina wins Tchaikovsky with another letter promising her unconditional love. The Romantic composer is immediately taken with the idea of this letter as it triggers his imagination and he, despite protests from friends and family, feels that he must answer the letter or, like the hero of his opera *Eugene Onegin*, suffer eternal damnation. He does answer and in a quick montage he is officially married in an Orthodox ceremony. Then comes the honeymoon as the composer finds himself in a private train compartment with his new wife. As Bragg's script suggests Tchaikovsky seems to harbor some hopes that he can learn to live with a woman, at least as brother and sister, in effect carrying over into adulthood the relationship with his own sister, now married with children. What Tchaikovsky did not seem to understand was that Nina was a highly sexual woman – some in her circle even suggested she was a nymphomaniac. But we need to remember that in that time period the term nymphomaniac was bandied around and applied to any woman who openly sought out male sexual companionship, since healthy women were presumed to not have sexual agency – any woman that did was considered to be sick (nymphomania), depraved, or insane. This longstanding idea, that clearly had no basis in fact, was internalized by many women themselves and was the cause of enormous psychological problems. Sexual autonomy in women was finally, and "officially," declared to be a part of human physiology by Sigmund Freud a few years after Tchaikovsky death, but the idea – as a populist trope - refused to be put to rest and persisted well into the 20th century.

In a perceptive, and comical series of two scenes taking place at the same time – as written by Bragg – Tchaikovsky and Nina, as husband and wife, attend an outdoor performance of *Swan Lake* in St. Petersburg Park where they are having their honeymoon. But Chiluvsky, Tchaikovsky's ex-lover is there and he coyly introduces himself to Nina as an old friend - as the performance gets under way Nina responds by telling him "my husband wrote this music." Clearly it's going to be a long day and Russell primes the moment by juxtaposing the events of the ballet – a Romantic hero destroyed by his illusions – with Tchaikovsky's marriage. Chiluvsky mischievously explains the ballet to Nina pointing out the characters on stage but Russell cuts to Tchaikovsky, his sister and Nina in the starring roles of *Swan Lake* as Chiluvsky's makes points that Nina doesn't have the experience to follow but that Tchaikovsky understands completely as his ex-boyfriend gives him some sly looks, seeing through Tchaikovsky's "marriage."

The composer can't take the pressure of Chiluvsky's snide innuendos and pulls his wife back into the park and a nearby Camera Obscura – there, in a dark rotunda we see a rounded white tabletop with a projection of the scene outside that shows people promenading – suddenly the camera stops at a couple getting frisky as the man tries to get a woman down on the grass behind some trees but she rebuffs him as the crowd watching the silent proto-film all laugh and nervously giggle, except for Tchaikovsky and Nina who can only look at the aborted heterosexual union with horror as a mirror of their own sexual frustrations. The scene was actually shot in one of the follies in West Wycombe Park in London – an outrageous palace for the amusement of 18th century dilettante aristocrats and it serves Russell well as the structure's sense of erotic play and ruinous decay perfectly mirrors Tchaikovsky's situation.

Their alcohol-drenched train ride back to Moscow from the St. Petersburg honeymoon uses expressionist lighting and quick cutting as we witness the physical revulsion that the composer experiences by being in an intimate situation with a woman. This is accomplished without a single word being spoken in a tour-de-force sequence of incredible emotional power. The scene was shot partially with a hand held camera in tight quarters, so close to the actors that we see only fragments of faces. Russell also placed a camera directly above the compartment looking straight down as if the actors were specimens in a jar, intercutting these and slowly building up speed, to the rhythm of the music as the train car sways, causing havoc with the inebriated and disoriented husband and wife using staccato crosscutting from one to the other in time to the music. Russell used Tchaikovsky's *Manfred* and *Pathétique Symphonies* blending them in the mix, as he had done before in his BBC work. For Russell the importance of finding the right sound to the image was the number one goal – the sanctity of the musical work was secondary.

Clearly Tchaikovsky and Nina are drinking heavily to alleviate the tension and fear and at one point Glenda Jackson as Nina, in a fearless and brilliant performance, takes off her uncomfortable red corset – as wives are wont to do – that to Tchaikovsky looks like the rib cage of an animal about to devour him. His repressed homosexuality here is at breaking point. Nina collapses unconscious, her head rhythmically bobbing from side to side with the train compartment and Russell brutally uses this movement as a metronome to keep the beat of the music – he simply shows no mercy here as we are completely inside the mind of Tchaikovsky as he realizes what a nightmare this "honeymoon" has become. Nina's breasts and pale feminine skin, covered in alcohol, seem to horrify the composer as his disgust reaches the point where it looks like he might vomit at any moment.

During initial screenings of this scene from *The Music Lovers* some people in the theater were gasping, or shrieking while others were laughing, as it was a scene of such visceral intensity that nothing like it had been seen before. Russell shot this sequence in the studio recreating a 19th century private railcar placed on rubber wheels that crewmembers then shoved back and forth to a recording that was playing live so the crew and the actors would be synchronized with the music.

Tchaikovsky at one point looses the patronage of Madame von Meck when she discovers his homosexuality from Chiluvsky, who is jealous and angry that his lover would be so extreme in his denial that he would marry a woman to shield his homosexuality. Bragg's script smartly chooses a moment of triumph for the composer to deliver the blow - an evening party celebration at von Meck's spectacular mansion sets the stage. In one of the most beautiful shots in the film some children with fire sparklers run in a line along a wall covered in a lush fireworks display creating a dreamlike, nighttime space of wonder and innocence. Russell smartly intercuts this shot with a close-up of his lover Chiluvsky whispering in von Meck's ear – we don't hear a word he says but von Meck's reaction makes very clear what has happened. Once she understands the situation the wealthy matron stages a hearty laugh, as if she were amused by the news that clearly horrifies her. Russell then cuts to Tchaikovsky literally locked out of his luxurious home – a gift provided by von Meck along with a monthly stipend. Fortunately for the Russian master his need for a patron was just at that moment coming to an end as his conducting career was making him a wealthy man.

Conducting was a viable profession for composers from Bach to Bernstein and Tchaikovsky took full advantage of his fame to secure lucrative contracts written up by his brother. Russell uses the triumphant *1812 Overture* to score Tchaikovsky's ascent to stardom and immortality. This is shown in brief, staccato tableaus, as he goes from impoverished conductor to established, world famous maestro, ending in Tchaikovsky conducting to an adoring crowd. Russell's imaginative play here is fully operational as in one shot, suggesting the absurdity of the sudden arrival of fame and wealth, Modest swings wildly from an enormous golden bell and is later showered with Rubles from adoring music fans - as the Rubles fall on the ground Modest gleefully scoops them up in a parody of American musicals.

After this bravura montage scored to the triumphalist section of *1812 Overture* comes one of Russell's most imaginative uses of cutting – the equal in every respect to Kubrick's match-cut in *2001: a Space Odyssey* (1968) from an animal bone flying mid-air to a space ship. Russell stages his beautiful match cut as he goes from the screaming and adoring crowd filling the soundtrack and the busy frame while Tchaikovsky "conducts" them, to a silent, deserted park in winter with a bronze statue of Tchaikovsky in the same position as conductor, hands in the air in triumph. The scene was carefully staged from the same point of view and the same focal length lens so the match would be perfect. We see Tchaikovsky suddenly turned into a statue, but the park is empty in the midst of a heavy snowstorm. While the camera tracks backwards through the falling snow the music fades to the local sound of snow and wind. The scene beautifully comments on the complex nature of fame, fortune, and legacy.

Nina by now is aware of her husband's homosexuality but rather than confront him directly she begs him that "people can change," repeating the saying like a mantra but to little avail. Bragg very smartly here has the line repetition perform a double function: on the first reading she is telling Tchaikovsky that he can, if not become a heterosexual, at least warm up to the idea of it slowly and she will help him; but as a second reading she is speaking about herself, saying that a woman from the Russian lower classes who has slept with many men and had a difficult life can become the admired wife of a famous and wealthy composer – she doesn't need all of those men, *she* can change. Tchaikovsky disagrees and runs out of the room mortified as Nina scrapes the rug with her nails, and curls up in a fetal position, defeated. Strangely she moves her head side to side as in the railway carriage when she lost consciousness, as if she remembered that trauma and it caused an involuntary movement of her body.

While having dinner with Modest in later life and reminiscing on old times, his brother casually mentions that Nina, now Tchaikovsky's ex-wife, has been institutionalized in an asylum. We then see Nina, at first being pimped out by her mother to men, while she tells her unsteady and delusional daughter that famous composers want to share an intimate moment with her. In one of the most haunting scenes in the film Nina, already at the asylum, head shaved, lowers herself onto a grating where men's filthy hands try to reach through the metal from their underground cells. Tchaikovsky seems unable to withstand the guilt any longer and he drinks tap water, knowing it is probably contaminated. At first his brother makes fun of him telling him that he only drinks wine and hasn't drunk water in years, but then realizes he has consciously poisoned himself.

Shortly after Tchaikovsky develops cholera, the same disease that killed his mother, and he is given the same treatment, as his body is immersed in a bathtub of scalding water. In the penultimate shot we see his corpse on the bathroom floor, his skin boiled, and his face looking out at the world in terror and pain. Russell then cuts to the bars of the insane asylum we saw earlier, but now from the outside, where Nina stares out at us in a tight close-up greeting us from behind the iron bars of her cell with a nod, and just the hint of a smile, as if she recognized us. In a no-holds barred performance, Jackson actually shaved her head for the scene, but her face is nothing like Dryer's Joan of Arc – ethereal and saintly – Nina is simply tired, beaten, and traumatized. She then turns away from us and shudders after which she lowers her head to her folded arms to finally rest in a classic pose of acceptance and closure as Russell's masterpiece fades to black.

SAVAGE MESSIAH (1972)

Russell would wisely use the same talented technicians, writers, and actors that he had with him over the years as a team. His first wife Shirley Russell, who outfitted the BBC films also worked on the biography of Henri Gaudier-Brzeska, *Savage Messiah* (1972), and Derek Jarman returned from *The Devils* to do the set design for one of Russell's most heartfelt efforts. The cinematography was by Dick Bush, who had worked with Russell on *Isadora Duncan, The Biggest Dancer in the World*. Since Russell could not afford music he found copyright free recordings of Scriabin, Prokofiev and Debussy in Russian records that he used extensively throughout the film.

Financing proved to be impossible as producers and money people didn't think a film about a little known French sculptor stood a chance with a public that wanted action, adventure and biopics about famous people. Realizing that the screenplay and his hand picked crew were ready he decided to finance the film himself by mortgaging his house. As predicted upon release the film was panned or ignored by the press and the critics, but fortunately for Russell it was something of a hit with audiences and he kept his house, eventually even making money from the work. With this basic team that he had collected over the years the director had a solid group that he trusted, and if there was a chance that he would be forced to "live in the streets," as he put it, he was ready to give it his best shot, and *Savage Messiah* would become arguably Russell's finest work.

While it might seem that self-financing would put added pressure on the shooting the opposite was the case. Brian Hoyle:

> *"No longer beholden to a big studio or other outside financiers, Russell became liberated. He was working on a scale far closer to his final BBC films and enjoying a level of creative freedom he had arguably not experienced since his days filming* Amelia and the Angel*...at the same time the crew, many of whom had been employed on* The Devils*, were also noticeably happier working together on this smaller project. Indeed, Jarman would later remark that it was the closest Russell would ever come to making a home movie, and it shaped his own desire to make films primarily for the camaraderie."*[49]

Savage Messiah would be their second and final collaboration as Jarman would go on to write and direct some of the most stunning films ever made by a British director becoming "British cinema's leading religious filmmaker"[50] despite his lifelong atheism. *Wittgenstein* (1993), a biography of the radical German philosopher and *Caravaggio* (1986), a biography of the iconoclastic Italian artist, are unthinkable without the work of Russell.

Gaudier-Brzeska was a French sculptor in the early 20th century and the subject of a short study by the eccentric but gifted American expatriate poet Ezra Pound but Russell primarily used a book by Jim Ede whose biography included Henri's partner, the writer Sophie Brzeska. Ede had acquired Sophie Brzeska's estate in 1927 shortly after her death, and he based his dual biography on the couple's correspondence, including letters written from the front lines during WWI. Ede also came up with the great title *Savage Messiah* that is appropriate as Russell himself was something of a savage messiah. The book was admired by the director who wrote:

> "The story will ever be an inspiration to anyone down on their luck with a belief in their own talent, despite the hostility of those who should know better. Here was a tale worth telling on film...I wanted to show artists as workers not people who live in ivory towers, it was about passion and sweat, it was about revolution and fuck the art dealers...It was austere and simple...my least glamorous film...There was a chance I'd end up on the street but I felt I owed Gaudier something...he taught me there was a life outside commerce and it was well worth fighting for."[51]

Russell gave the leads to Dorothy Tutin, a stage actress in London of great emotional range, known primarily for her gritty roles in early kitchen-sink British theater, and to Scott Anthony who was a newcomer. Anthony became inspired by working on the film transforming himself from an actor to an artist, choosing photography as his medium.

Henri Gaudier-Brzeska was a vital and brilliant sculptor, the same age as "the lost generation." He made sculptures that were playful and complex, indebted to the multiple perspectives of Cubism and using very traditional materials from sculpture's long history, stone, wood and marble. As with the work of the Cubists in Gaudier-Brzeska the classical and the contemporary collided, sometimes literally as we see in his sculpture of a bird colliding with a bomb. This was inspired by his time in the trenches of WWI, where he eventually lost his life at the age of 24. That his work would not be well regarded in his own lifetime goes without saying, but fortunately he subsequently developed a following, particularly after the popular study by the influential Pound.

Russell picks up Gaudier-Brzeska's life as he studies human anatomy in a library in London by making careful pen and ink drawings. In real life the French artist was born Henri Gaudier in Saint-Jean-de-Braye but changed his name, honoring his Polish partner Sophie-Brzeska who was considerably older. The sculptor had met the governess and aspiring novelist in the Bibliotheque Sainte-Genevieve in Paris, and started an intense, lifelong relationship. In the spirit of the suffragettes the freethinking Frenchman changed his name to Gaudier-Brzeska but they never married. Both Brzeska's were intense, creative people who did not care at all for social norms, rules of conduct, or proprieties – they were true bohemians even down to being poor and having to choose between art supplies and food.

Gaudier-Brzeska's stay in London was both charmed and tragic. While scouting local London galleries he fell in with the Vorticism movement championed by Ezra Pound and the irascible British artist and writer, Wyndham Lewis. Vorticism was a homegrown ham fisted cubism – a British beer version of the fine French wine made by Picasso and Braque. As the two bohemian lovers settle into a dingy basement, with large barred up windows near the ceiling facing the street, Ms. Brzeska gets to work on her writing, furious at herself for not being able to finish her novel, while Henri carves stone madly into the evening. In one of Russell's most spectacular uses of location – always one of his strengths – the Brzeska's visit a quarry next to a beach and Henri jumps from stone to stone screaming the masterpieces that he will create from the stones under his feet while Sophie does an impromptu dance. They eventually fall into each other but Sophie refuses to have sex with Henri – she seems to have an aversion to physical contact perhaps precipitated by an earlier trauma.

Strapped for cash Henri gets a job making a work of traditional sculpture for a wealthy, aristocratic general in the English army. The general's rebellious suffragette daughter, with the unlikely name of Gosh Boyle (Helen Mirren) soon befriends the sculptor and she takes him to meet her Vorticist friends at an avant-garde club where slumming tourists mix with louche gallery owners, and Vorticist décor mixes with odd, and dangerous, alcoholic drinks that were then popular, not only in England but also France. Jarman here gets to shine as Russell's very low budget did not allow him to do much set designing, as he had in *The Devils*, but, rather, had to rely on location scouting. Jarman found places in London and Paris that looked like early 20th century places and then slightly altered the facades, or rented an old car that was parked nearby to provide period flavor.

But with the Vorticist club Jarman was able to construct it from the ground up in a studio and he created a masterpiece of set design smartly using the hard diagonals and faux cubist forms that the Vorticists loved giving them bright primary colors, bringing a dose of modernity to the club, as he had to the town of Loudun. Gosh does a highly spirited number called "Votes for Women" that she doesn't seem able to finish so Henri jumps to the stage and suggests she strip turning the suffragette performance into an absurd and bawdy burlesque that delights the audience. Mirren brings a dynamic energy to the part of Gosh as she seems to take delight in bringing this multi-faceted suffragette to life. Before the cops burst in to close their show they decamp laughing. He becomes one of her lovers, as Sophie seems to be uninterested in having a sexual relationship and he feels the need for intimate female companionship.

Henri spends time in the general's expansive mansion decorated in the pompous high Victorian style of the time, complete with the requisite stuffed animals, historical prints and paintings of landscapes and horses. In an extraordinary shot Gosh, completely naked, descends some stairs while she pontificates about being a suffragette and wanting to give some meaning to her life via politics or art to alleviate the boredom and limitations of her aristocratic background. While Gosh seems hemmed in by her wealth, Mirren uses her voice to express her character's narcissistic mindset, shifting easily from emotionally earnest rebel to ironic manqué bohemian, and from playfully seductive vamp, to self-disgusted oligarch. From this exchange it is clear that Gosh is taking quite a lot for granted, and that she has a lot of growing up to do. She tells Henri she is considering being an artist, perhaps even a sculptor. Upon hearing this Henri suggests that she become familiar with quarrymen rather than poor bohemians like himself – a caustic remark that seems to bring the relationship to a close.

A friend and supporter Angus Corky (Lindsay Kemp) hosts a soiree for the Brzeska's but Lionel Shaw (John Justin), a prestigious gallery owner, seems to not take either Brzeska very seriously and makes a point of it. Sophie counters his upper-class sarcasm with a song – improvised by Dorothy Tutin – in a magnificent performance where she finally seems able to express her fears, her arrogant bluster, and her contempt; all of the things she seemed unable to get into her novel finally find their release as she ends her song with a fake laugh, scatting "ha-ha-ha" with a controlled fury. The song is met with incredulous applause even from the jaded Shaw.

Corky even gets some prominent people to come for a studio visit but Henri blows the meeting, infuriating Sophie who cuts vegetables for a pot of Polish stew with Freudian determination, chopping carrots and cucumbers down to size, while doing some pontificating herself – and still angry about that unfinished novel. Lionel Shaw confronts Gaudier-Brzeska at one of the dinner parties taunting and challenging him to come up with the goods and put his money where is mouth is. The French sculptor accepts the challenge, suggesting the haughty Shaw come by in the morning to his studio to see a new piece of work – a naked female torso in stone – a sculpture that does not exist so Henri spends the evening drinking strong coffee and making it from the ground up with a hammer and chisel, with bits of stone flying in all directions.

In the early morning the beautiful life size female torso is finished but Shaw, as one would expect, is absent, never having taken the artist seriously. Henri takes his heavy work, in the pouring rain, to Shaw's gallery and throws the piece through the glass front shattering it, while screaming. The way Russell shoots the scene it is clear that because of that missed appointment by Shaw Henri realizes that he will never make it in the art world of his time, and this infuriates him in a way he can only express by throwing his work inside the gallery, knowing it is to no avail.

In desperation Henri joins the war effort and is sent to the front. At one point he makes a carving using a rifle butt. He also writes long letters to his beloved Sophie that are the backbone of Ede's biography and Russell's film. At the Vorticist club some friends of the sculptor casually mention that he has died at the front. Having enlisted in the French army, he had received a decoration for bravery before being killed in the intense trench warfare at Neuville-St. Vaast in the north of France near the German border in the summer of 1915. The cemetery there is called Maison Blanche and is the largest in France from WWI with over forty-four thousand men buried there.

Russell cuts with great sensitivity and economy from the Vorticist club to the Brzeska's empty studio. To see it suddenly bare and silent is startling – its barrenness suggesting Sophie's despair as she stands in the middle of the large space in tears, destroyed, looking as if she had been kicked in the stomach. Above her through the barred up window near the ceiling we see, at street level, young men marching off to war, and women singing patriotic songs and urging them on. We know of course the horrible, pointless, outcome of that war in terms of human loss and sacrifice, the mistakes made after the armistice, and the next world war to come only a few years later.

But Sophie-Brzeska would never see any of this – she also never finished her novel. Unable to work after Henri's death, she suffered from what we would now call Post Traumatic Stress Disorder, eventually becoming homeless. She died alone, in an asylum for women in 1925. But Russell doesn't need to show us this last part of her tragic life, rather, he cuts to what remains: Russell slowly and lovingly pans Gaudier-Brzeska's surviving works at eye level, in museums through France and England, set to a melancholic prelude by Claude Debussy. It is a fitting tribute to the artist and his few surviving works, while the film as a whole can be seen as a testament to two people who risked everything for their art and the emotional connection they found with each other – as if intuiting that their time would be brief they packed as much into their short lives as possible. That Russell was able to examine the complexity and contradictions of their lives, as well as their social conditions, the divisions within the art world of the time, the strong emotional connections and societal disconnections – the all-important facticity – in which those lives were lived, all in 90 minutes, is a testament to his genius.

Independence 2: Ken Russell & D.H. Lawrence

WOMEN IN LOVE (1969)

Russell would develop a lasting and satisfying relationship with the work of D.H. Lawrence (1885-1930), the radical British writer that would last from 1969 to 1993. While the first of these ventures was actually suggested to him by the producer Larry Kramer Russell quickly realized there was an affinity there and he wisely pursued it further. *Women in Love* is arguably the best film adaptation of a classic novel ever made. Lawrence's book was published in 1920 when Lawrence was 35, and came after the cataclysmic changes brought by WWI and just before the onset of the Roaring Twenties – a historical tipping point. What made the book controversial for the time is that it opened the 20th century novel to the contemporary reality of everyday sexual and social mores, especially for younger people, that was radical for its time and seen as a breath of fresh air – in the US F. Scott Fitzgerald's *The Beautiful and Dammed* (1922) performed a similar function, that is, it discarded the proprieties of Victorianism and described reality as it was rather than as it should be – not everyone was pleased and both novels had their detractors - but one hundred years later both books are now considered part of the cannon of Western literature.

Russell shifts the time frame slightly to the mid 1920's so the war is further in the past and the coming catastrophe of the economic Crash is just around the corner – he wanted to get the Belle-Époque (obliterated by WW1) that in Lawrence is still present, out of the way, concentrating on the way young people sought to find new ways of living, of mating, and relating to one another on a day to day basis. There was no nostalgia for the past in the 1920's as it was all death and destruction if you looked back – the only way was forward into the future, full speed ahead, the sooner the better, and Russell gets that sense of urgency better than anyone had before or since. The film and the book chart the trajectory of two sisters, the Brangwen's, Gudrun (Glenda Jackson) and Ursula (Jennie Linden), who grow up in the bleak Midlands of the early century, an area that is, like Russell's own home town of Southampton, both close and far from London.

To pair off the sisters Lawrence created Rupert Birkin (Alan Bates), a free spirited, sarcastic iconoclast, light on his feet and with a quick wit to pair with Ursula; and Gerald Crich (Oliver Reed), a wealthy, troubled and anxious industrialist who is all heaviness and tormented self-doubt for Gudrun. Rupert is more or less a stand-in for Lawrence and he espouses the same ideas often word for word. Lawrence believed that the great disaster of the civilization that he inhabited was its poisonous hatred of sex and a fear of death that was so staggering humans were willing to believe anything rather than accept mortality. Moreover this fear causes our intuitive faculty to atrophy - for Lawrence this "superpower" was of supreme importance if we were ever to become fully realized human beings. In effect one had to fight the forces of civilization and the powers that be to realize oneself – there was no escape from this struggle.

Women in Love would feature one of his strongest scripts written by Larry Kramer but his original screenplay featured changes in the novel's plot to make it more oriented toward cinematic action and less dialogue and interior monologues that in Lawrence were extensive. Such radical changes were considered normal, particularly by Hollywood producers, as it was thought that novels generally were un-cinematic and so needed to be changed in order to accommodate cinematic storytelling. This is why in adaptations of classic books before Russell it was commonplace for screenwriters to leave out most of a novel and simply write new material deemed "cinematic." Russell rewrote the script from the ground up with Kramer so that it was true to the novel, even having characters coming in after the half-way point (a no-no in Hollywood), and leaving in many of the long monologues and discussions without changing a word.[52] The result was a success on all fronts. Russell was not only ready to move on from the BBC but he realized he decided to follow up that hunch about Lawrence, adapting *The Rainbow* and *Lady Chatterley's Lover*, (with a title change to *Lady Chatterley*) resulting in some of his best and most deeply felt independent work.

As in his television films Russell also used extended, highly charged dramatic scenes, as in a play, drawing out the various characters so they are, as in Lawrence's novel, fully rounded individuals, and symbolic representatives of their particular class and sex. The Brangwen sisters are poised between the end of the British Empire and the beginning of the post-colonial, post-industrial age – they belong to that transitional generation who in their childhood might have gone in a horse drawn carriage to hear Tchaikovsky conduct his 6th symphony, and then in older age might have seen the story of The Beatles breaking up on the BBC – something that in fact did happen to Igor Stravinsky, who was the same generation as Lawrence but lived far longer, until 1971.[53]

Russell brought in the cinematographer Billy Williams (*Billion Dollar Brain*), composer Georges Delerue (*Don't Shoot the Composer*) and costume designer Shirley Russell, who had worked on many of her husband's BBC films. Together they created one of the masterpieces of sixties cinema. Ironically *Women in Love* is a film that was copied by Russell's old bosses at the BBC, basically re-inventing the format for classic novel adaptations, bringing the whole genre into the modern world – this would prove to be the most popular and profitable format for the BBC for years to come, with adaptations of Jane Austen, Charles Dickens, Henry Fielding, George Eliot, and even D.H. Lawrence, coming to the small screen long after Russell had moved on.

During the 1920's when Lawrence was at the peak of his powers as a novelist the ground was ever shifting and despite the era's generic epitaph as "The Roaring Twenties" it was a difficult period with extreme uncertainties, misunderstandings, estrangements, polarization, and confusion. One can most clearly see this in Hemingway's short story collection *Men Without Women* (1927), Dos Passos' *Manhattan Transfer* (1925), and Jean Rhys' *Quartet* (1928) that all masterfully captured the feeling of the time by people who were living through it. Russell and his team carefully present a color scheme, a dress code, and a manner of speech that typifies the era. But film historian Caroline Langhorst makes the astute comment in her essay on Russell's films that the decade of the 1960's played a crucial role in the film, not in its setting or its costumes but in its tone of rebellion, already present in the novel:

> "Lawrence invites the reader to abandon the priorities of human visual perception, and embrace other ways of knowing and touching the world. This rejection of ordinary perception corresponds to the 1960's countercultural fervor for "breaking on through to the other side"...Jackson's sassy portrayal of the free-spirited Gudrun, in turn, is of an explorative, curious nature, accentuated by her flapper haircut and the style that merges 1920's and 1960's bohemia and permissiveness."[54]

Russell and Kramer follow Lawrence's lead concentrating on the sister's dissimilar response to the men that they are attracted to, their stiff and stilted Victorian upbringing that they long to overthrow, and the uncertain future that looms large with the 20th century opening before them in all of its glory and terror - people looked askance with both delight and horror at the possibilities with some justification. Russell puts Lawrence's ambitious, multi-faceted worldview with all of the various stratified classes in British society on display, allowing the epic scope room to breathe, mimicking the high strung novelists condensed, high octane prose style in which several pages might be devoted to a character's thoughts but when they finally speak it might be only a short prosaic line – but we know the thought behind it so the line has a certain power. The actors – that at this point were his company - all beautifully deliver for Russell and give the simple line readings their full subtext.

The film takes place in the Midlands mining town of Beldover that Lawrence was familiar with. The proceedings begin in a midst of a wedding ceremony for Laura Crich, daughter of the town's wealthy mine owner, Thomas Critch, to Tibby Lupton, a naval officer - all of the main characters meet here, as in a play, and it is clear that the Brangwen sisters are on the lookout for prospective mates, in the style of Jane Austen, but things do not play out as in Austen – Lawrence was writing after Freud, and despite the fact that he did not agree with him, was very much in his shadow. When Laura and Tibby, in an act of spontaneity run to the church they have to pass a graveyard that they are oblivious to, but Russell sees it and italicizes it. At the church each sister becomes fascinated by a man that Russell shows in traditional match cuts: Gudrun by Laura's brother Gerald Crich and Ursula by Gerald's best friend Rupert Birkin. Ursula is a schoolteacher and

Rupert is a school inspector so they have previously met. We see how she remembers his visit to her classroom in a flashback, loudly interrupting her standard botany lesson with a suggestive discourse on the sexual nature of the catkin plant. Clearly she is upset, discombobulated and intrigued by his talk and by him - the lecture is interrupted by Hermione Roddice (Eleanor Bron) a wealthy landowner who has a troubled relationship with Rupert that is rapidly disintegrating into cruelty and indifference. She also takes up the catkin plant but Ursula loudly rings a bell bringing the proceedings, and the classroom lecture, to an end.

In one of Russell's funniest set pieces in the film, using one of the simplest set-ups (showing you need very little to work with if you have a lot of ingenuity) Rupert and Hermoine are in a tight close-up as she speaks – to no one in particular – about the necessity of all mankind becoming at some point one large brotherhood, stateless and classless, equal under the sun. As the camera pulls back we see that they are in bathing suits sharing a hooded lounge chair. As the camera continues pulling back we notice that Rupert is reading a newspaper with the headlines "Miner's Strike" that completely contradicts Hermoine's laudable philosophy. Suddenly Rupert interrupts and says he disagrees: "Mankind is not all equal at all, quite the contrary, differences in quality are obvious, but everyone seems trapped by social bonds and rules that are antithetical to spontaneous acts of love or violence that are natural to human beings." Hermoine calls him an egomaniac – an epitaph hurled at Lawrence more than once. As the camera continues pulling back we see the beautiful pool and the servants making a mockery of Hermoine's altruistic humanism. Russell achieves this in one simple camera movement. Then he shifts to close-up again as Rupert spills some champagne on himself that Hermoine starts to lick off his body. He seems nonplussed and kisses her on the forehead to make her stop. Clearly their sexual relationship is already at an end.

During a picnic at Hermoine's country estate Rupert gives a verbose, comical and sarcastic explanation of the fig and its similarity to the female sex – as with the theatrical plant discourse earlier in the classroom clearly Rupert is fixated on sexuality as the prime mover not only in plants but animals and humans. Hermione devises a typical entertainment of the period, in which some of the guests, including the sisters, are to dance in the "style of the Russian ballet." As in his film on Isadora Duncan Russell mocks the pretensions to "high art" of these dinner parties as the music is a dirge like parody of "serious" classical songs while the women prance around the room simulating ballet like movements – even they are giggling. But the film is also very accurate in its depiction of such entertainments that referenced ancient Greek or Egyptian themes that were enormously popular in the 1920's. Rupert becomes disgusted with the boredom and the pretensions of his own class and tells the pianist to play some Ragtime so everyone can at least dance and have some fun, which they begins to do. Hermione, mortified by having had her party hijacked takes Rupert aside and strikes him with a stone paperweight on the head – as if saying alright, you want "spontaneity" here it is! Rupert begins to bleed and stumbles out the door to the countryside.

There Russell creates perhaps his most Lawrencian moment as Rupert takes off his bloodstained suit and proceeds to walk naked through the forest, cleaning himself with some wet leaves, bonding with nature, like an animal rolling on the ground. The scene is both erotic and completely in keeping with Rupert's (and Lawrence's) philosophy that humans had to learn to become civilized animals and the way to do so was to seize upon any opportunity to commune with nature by improvising with it, like a piece of jazz music, but the instrument in this case was one's own body – an idea that was then not only new but also the very antithesis of Victorian era proprieties.

At the Criche's annual picnic, to which the whole town is invited Ursula and Gudrun ask Gerald for a boat so they might go and picnic together and he provides it – the actors here do a fine job of hinting at the massive amount of subtext in very simple lines ("a picnic basket – that's the idea?"). Russell's beautiful mise en scéne is up to Lawrence's complex intertwining narrative. The women find a secluded spot and both sisters find the solitude in nature amenable to expressing themselves - Gudrun dances before some Highland cattle while Ursula is singing a popular song. The dance is confrontational and somewhat disingenuous and dangerous as she is clearly taunting the bulls to come and get her – again Lawrence's symbolism is clear, and perhaps too obvious, but he was under the spell of Freudian metaphors and he pushed them to extremes in order to make a point about his own genteel, Victorian generation. He could never resist sexual symbols and saw them everywhere, which is odd considering he disdained Freud's work considering it too programmatic and polarizing – for Lawrence there were as many different forms of sexuality as there were humans on earth so to try and scientifically classify human sexuality and organize it into a system was at best problematic.

Gerald comes when he sees that the cattle are running scared from Gudrun's modern dance. Demanding to know what she's doing with "his cattle" Gudrun calls him out on it asking: "how are they *your* cattle? Have you eaten them?" He calls Gudrun's taunting behavior, driving the bulls mad, "impossible and ridiculous," and then out of the blue proclaims that he is in love with her. Gudrun's only reply is a curt: "that's one way of putting it" - but they shortly make love in the woods and discuss sex and death. She lightly mock slaps him and he cautions her: "you struck the first blow." Gudrun takes flight and continues her dance of provocation extolling: "and I shall have the last!"

At the party Laura and Tibby are swimming naked in the lake and Laura goes underwater as a joke but doesn't come up. Tibby goes after her but he also disappears under the dark waters. Gerald dives in to save them but he can't see anything in the fading light. Everyone thinks the worst and the lake is drained using the nearby dam and that is where they find the two naked bodies, dead and entwined in each other's arms trying to save each other. In *Women in Love* Russell, not for the first time, adopted a modified version of Soviet montage using the edits to create metaphors. This is spectacularly evident in a cut from the two dead young lovers in each other's arms to Ursula and her lover Rupert entwined in the exact same positions after coitus. As this second couple slowly separate, their heavy breathing, glowing, sweaty skin, and sexual vitality stand in brutal counterpoint to the dead couple. For the radical Russian director and for Russell this "collision-montage" created a conflict or opposition that then produces a new idea – in this case the symbiosis of sex and death, which was the foundation of Lawrence's work. This is one of the most brilliant uses of editing since Eisenstein and Russell must have had it planned out before the shooting stage for the match cut to work exactly.

Russell had previously used this very sort of match-cut in Dante's Inferno, where towards the end of the film, after Lizzie Siddal has committed suicide, Russell cuts from Lizzie dead on her bed wearing a wedding dress to her many years earlier, also wearing a wedding dress, as she poses for the painting *Ophelia*, but now full of life, laughing in the small metal tub the size of a coffin. The match-cuts that Russell offers in these two films are peculiar to his own sensibility about death that mirrors Lawrence, but has its own strain of Gothic mysticism closer in spirit to Dante Rossetti.

For Lawrence death was not merely a matter of accepting the inevitable, it was a belief that humans are made for death, as is everyone and everything else that we know. Lawrence reasoned that once an individual accepts one's common status as an "animal in nature living amongst other animals" some form of healthy communion with nature would inevitably follow – including presumably the desire to not simply exploit nature for its resources at all cost thereby turning the natural world into a commodity. Lawrence intuited, long before the 20th century got rolling, that once nature was turned into a commodity humans would not be far behind in including everything else such as culture, war, art, history, politics, and finally, in a last act of desperation, basic human resources and humanity itself. In effect Lawrence saw the 21st century as a vague outline and it terrified him – his novels in a sense are sermons from the pulpit of literature akin to *1984* and *A Clockwork Orange* – a warning to avoid catastrophe.

Lawrence was also one of the first artists to see all of man's creations, from manicured gardens, to cars, to cities, as a part of nature since an animal made it – and while a city may be more sophisticated, structurally, than a bird nest, it is only a question of degree, not of kind. This idea was one of Lawrence's main contributions to the arts and it is one that, unfortunately, has not yet found a home. This is why Lawrence hated religion - it was not so much the ideas or the commandments, and certainly not the spiritual aspects. What he despised was its pretensions to a fundamental superiority over animals, and eventual immortality for all the good people in a heaven beyond the reach of mere wants, needs, or physical laws. Lawrence was highly spiritual but when he went on a spiritual pilgrimage it was not to Jerusalem or the Vatican but to Taos, New Mexico to commune with Native Americans and their Vision Quest. For Lawrence, as for William Blake, the way to spiritual knowledge was not through passive acceptance of orthodoxy, or a book of rules, but on the contrary, it was a personal creative act, made through searching, discovery, and action. In short, his was an existential relation to spirituality and the eternal. Established religions taught people that they were created in the image of a God, and that they (or their souls) were immortal so, in effect, they were not animals at all. Under this anthropomorphic system concocted by Christians not only animals but all of nature was placed here for man to use and enjoy as he saw fit – and it was invariably always a "he" since many men considered women to be a part of nature, closer to the animal world than to the civilized human male.

It was only centuries of struggle, the relative liberalization of 19th century education, and the Suffragette movement in Europe that finally brought such absurd fantasies to an end, at least for large sections of the educated population. The idea that humans, particularly male humans, were somehow above nature by the decree of a God rankled Lawrence to no end, and he was, in his novels, essays, and poems, always fighting against it which is why his novels can seem, at times polemical and strident. Nevertheless, the oft-repeated attack on Lawrence by critics as a "male chauvinist," due to his constant focus on masculinity and sex, does not really stand scrutiny – he was closer to Emile Zola than to Ernest Hemingway. It would be more to the point to say Lawrence was fascinated by the human animal (male and female), trapped in a civilized cage with all sorts of codes of behavior, hierarchies, and mating habits – the resulting struggle fascinated him right up to the end with his final book *Lady Chatterly's Lover* (1928).

The evidence for Lawrence's clarity of insight – and even his proto-feminism - is made obvious in the characters of Gudrun and Gerald, for it is the free-spirited and sarcastic flapper Gudrun who is the active agency in the book (and the film) whereas Gerald is, despite his strong masculinity, wealth, and power, a passive character who reacts to others and seems always somehow stilted and unsure of himself – Oliver Reed does a magnificent job of showing us Gerald's self-hatred, his spiritual vacuum, even in scenes where he has no dialogue. Gerald's feeble attempts at an autonomous will are possibly due to his overbearing mother who constantly belittles him. Clearly he loves and despises her but can do nothing about it so an impotence of action set in probably quite early. We see Gerald naked at the picnic when he jumps head first into the lake that would later drown the young couple, his strong masculinity clearly in evidence. Ursula makes the comment, while admiring his body, that he "has a lot of go." Yes, replies the skeptical Gudrun, "but where is his go going?" Both women laugh but the question is more to the point than they realize.

We are treated to Gerald's macho faux heroics as he abuses a horse by forcing it to chase a train - this was considered a normal pastime of the early century for landed gentry. He then pushes the horse towards the train taunting it – much like Ursula's taunting of the bulls – drawing blood from the animal's haunches. The women see this and are duly horrified, screaming for him to stop, but Gerald merely rides off laughing. In one of the most brilliant set-pieces in the film Gerald then visits the mines with his father where he performs another macho act by treating the men who work for him with contempt making sure he instills fear and respect amongst the workers. In his inspection he sees that one man is having trouble lifting the heavy coal pieces to the conveyor belts and he dismisses him out of hand. Even his father expresses some trepidation at his son's callousness but Gerald won't have it any other way – he treats the men like he treats his horse, a thing to be used until it is no longer useful. His father mentions that Gerald has gotten rid of the program of free coal given out to miner's widows and the son merely reminds the old man that the mine is not a charitable institution. In the best shot in the film father and son ride off in an immaculate white convertible surrounded by grubby men and women covered in black coal soot. No Marxist filmmaker has ever delivered such a potent image of irreconcilable class differences, impotence, and rage. The reason Russell (who was not a Marxist) is so successful is that he concentrates on the emotional aspect of the men and women who depended on the mine but also hate it – as well as the owners who depend on the men but despise them (because they are the cause of guilt) but they need each other and so Gerald and his father are safe even in an open car as it slowly makes its way through the proletarian crowd. That tension is palpable and creates an explosive set of possibilities – an explosion that finally did happen in Moscow in 1917 only a few years earlier with the Communist October Revolution in Moscow and so it is indelibly in the minds of all concerned as a possibility – like a land mine lying just under the calm surface of things – everyone is on tiptoes and always on the lookout for signs of trouble.

In the most famous set piece in the film Gerald and Rupert wrestle in the nude. Originally the film diverged from the novel having the struggle take place outdoors so they could shoot from behind branches and foliage obscuring the men's sexes, but Oliver Reed was adamant that Russell shoot it as it was in the book, let the censors be dammed. Fortunately Russell finally agreed and the scene remains one of the most stunning sequences ever put to film as Russell's mise en scéne here is amongst his best. In one of Gerald and Rupert's discussions, in a fancy drawing where the men would meet after dinner for brandy and cigars, they sit in front of a roaring fire and talk – behind them Russell fills the frame with armor, weapons, mirrors and a large fireplace. Rupert suggest a "friendly" boxing match and Gerald passes, preferring naked Japanese style wrestling as a way of getting closer physically and emotionally. While Gerald cannot understand Rupert's idea of wanting to have an emotional union with a man as well as with a woman he decides to give it a try. Russell takes full advantage of the intersecting mirrors that meet at right angles with the walls, using them in an extraordinary dance between the wrestlers and the camera, suggesting both a latent narcissism and fundamental irreconcilable differences. Regardless of how close and sweaty they get intimacy seems ultimately impossible, but once they get going they soldier on in desperation of finding some connection. Russell holds his shots to get the maximum impact from the cutting, building up his scene to a climax as if the men were having sex rather than fighting wringing every possible series of angles from the mirrors – a tour de force equal in many ways to Orson Welles' famous mirror sequence in *Lady From Shanghai*. Afterwards the men seem somewhat self-conscious but as to be expected Rupert is sure they have achieved some form of spiritual or emotional bond and Gerald is unsure, depressed at having failed again, but he remains cryptically noncommittal.

Gerald's father dies in one of the most realistic and haunting death scenes on film – coughing up blood in agony – he spits out his final moments already lost to the world. Gerald inherits the mine and he seeks consolation with Gudrun. She seems to take pity on him and lets him inside – when he enters her room Russell cuts to a flash cut of Gerald's mother mocking him. Clearly Gerald, like many men, has conjoined the two women – his girlfriend and his mother - in his mind and is seeking solace and comfort, as when he was a child, but Gudrun, like his mother turns him away. His only response is to say: "you seem to be reaching towards a void, and then you realize that you are the void yourself." Gerald and Gudrun are in the same room but occupying vastly different spaces with the man speaking in close-up or in a mirror and the woman listening behind him in the background out of focus. Clearly Gerald is at a crossroads and his sadomasochistic relationship, which is a constant struggle for power, that is a repeat of his relationship with his mother, finally seems to be wearing him down.

After Rupert and Ursula's wedding Gerald suggests that the four of them go the Alps for Christmas – a traditional December playground for the rich. At their rustic Inn Gudrun irritates Gerald with her interest in a new character, Loerke, (Vladek Sheybal) a gay German sculptor, who pontificates on the meaning of "art" driving Gerald crazy with his esoteric quips and ironic asides. Introducing a new character so late in the narrative was a risky move but it's Lawrence who took the gamble in his book and it worked so Russell follows suit. Loerke is a minor character in both novel and film but a brilliant creation by Lawrence – in 1920 he seems to have anticipated the effete, pretentious, manqué bohemian that would dominate the art world for the remainder of the century and beyond – an "artist" for whom ideas (such as they are) come to be far more important than the thing-itself which is perceived to be not much more than an after-effect. We see a similar character in Wyndham Lewis's *Tarr* (1918) but while Lewis was out to skewer his fellow artists of the London scene Lawrence wants to understand Loerke and what makes him tick. Certainly Lawrence would have seen Dada and Vorticist exhibitions and would be familiar with the artists of his time but this is really the first fully rounded portrait we have in a work of fiction from someone who was there.

Gerald confronts Gudrun about her relationship with Loerke and she derides and ridicules him, really letting him have it. Finally, he can endure it no longer and he attempts to strangle her. After coming to his senses he trudges off into the cold, a broken man, to commit suicide by hypothermia, alone. "I'm tired" he says finally. This is a common sentiment of many Russell characters towards the end of their lives – one thinks of Dante Rossetti, Delius, Tchaikovsky, or Bartok. In Gerald's last moments Russell holds on a beautiful long shot as Gerald cuddles up like a fetus before going into eternal sleep in the vast folds of the Swiss landscape that we see as Russell pulls the camera away and zooms out to a postcard view with Gerald only a small dot in the landscape that finally disappears from view.

Rupert and Ursula return to their small cottage in England, and while he grieves for his friend he is also upset that Gerald could never return the love that Rupert had offered. Ursula patiently explains that there is only one true love – between a man and a woman – and Rupert disagrees. On that abyss that has opened between them Russell freezes his frame on a shocked Ursula as the suddenly dramatic music leads to the end-credits. While Rupert is certainly Lawrence's alter ego *Women in Love* smartly gives all of the characters good motivations for their actions – everyone explains themselves well, even minor characters, like the older mine owner Thomas Cricht, and the annoying artist Loerke, who could easily have become caricatures, have something to say and are fully rounded human beings with their faults, their sense of reality, and their reasons. Lawrence died in 1930 at the age of 45 so Ursula and Gudrun never got a follow-up novel that would have made a wonderful trilogy - taking them into the uncharted waters of the 1930's and the war. If he had lived one can only speculate on what the two sisters, in middle age, would have made of the political polarization and militarization of the war years and the complete obliteration of the Victorian era that they had grown up with and that came to define their lives.

THE RAINBOW (1989)

Russell's love affair with Lawrence would continue twenty years after *Women In Love* with *The Rainbow* (1989), a prequel with the same sisters as central characters, but now Ursula takes center stage as we see her in secondary school, counting the days to graduation, liberty and moving to London. Lawrence wrote the book of the same name in 1915 and it was a success, paving the way for *Women in Love* five years later. Writers were at the forefront of the new radical changes in society and got it all down in black and white. Virginia Woolf put it succinctly in 1924 when she noted that not simply "society" but that the "human character" had fundamentally changed "on or about December 1910."[55] That "on or about" is clearly satirical but she meant what she said – being a modernist she could be ironic and literal at the same time without missing a beat. She went on to formulate that "relations between masters and servants, husbands and wives, parents and children shifted and when human relations change there is at the same time a change in religion, conduct, politics, and literature."[56] The shift she is suggesting is so radical that we might call it not simply revolutionary but evolutionary. Lawrence was, along with Eliot, Joyce, Kafka, Hemingway and Woolf herself, one of the modernists trying to understand those fundamental changes and Russell was receptive to that endeavor.

Fortunately Russell had the same extraordinary team from *Women in Love*, including the DP, Billy Williams. While the novel was epic in scope encompassing three generations Russell again concentrates his focus, this time on Ursula who in *Women in Love* moves to London to become a teacher and experience the culture and bohemian lifestyle of artists and writers, that was a major attraction for independent women of that time. Glenda Jackson, who was her sister Gudrun in the earlier film, now plays the mother, always knitting and giving advice from her pulpit, the kitchen, and Sammi Davis plays Ursula in an inspired performance.

To the dismay of her parents Ursula rejects the marriage offer of a local soldier, eager to go off and fight in the Boer war (1899-1902). This was one of the final colonial struggles that the British were determined to win despite the enormous loss of life. The location was South Africa and the reason for their eagerness was the discovery of precious minerals including diamonds, but the British typically put the struggle against the Boers (independent itinerant farmers) as one of Christian civilization and solid British values versus heathen savages and their primitive way of life - the British only relinquished the prize in 1961 to a white minority government sympathetic to British financial interests.

The African majority only won their independence in 1994 after decades of struggle led by Nelson Mandela who formed the first democratic government that same year.

More to the point Lawrence here is drawing out another lesson from Freud's writings – that sexual repression leads to some form of neurosis and violence in a reciprocal manner – the greater the repression the more deranged the neurotic impulses (or fetishes) and the more extreme the violence. Accepting this idea the puritanism of the Victorian era makes perfect sense – like Sparta in ancient Greece England was a warring society, an Empire always on the prowl for new colonies and always playing defense against other empires on the move such as the French, Portuguese, and the Spanish. In the classical world it was Athenian culture that was soft, liberal, fascinated by music (which they considered their highest art), plays, art and philosophy – the Spartans were too busy in wars to produce any culture as such; in fact the way we remember the Spartans at all is primarily via Homer's work – and he was from Ionia in what is now Turkey.

While mass industrialization was ever present in all areas of society at the turn of the 20th century, it was also on the verge of being remade once again by post- industrial financial speculation and electronic communication, seen first in the innocent form of the telephone. In this transitional world Ursula defies her parents and the social mores and manners of the late Victorian era, not as an act of rebellion for its own sake, but to save herself, going off in search of independence, earning her own living, and making her own way as a teacher and a freethinker. For Lawrence, like Virginia Woolf, independence for women was irrevocably tied to financial autonomy. Ursula uses the metaphor of the rainbow to signify freedom, more specifically freedom of the body and soul to express itself openly as a small, ever changing, and all too brief part of the natural world. This is not explained but is shown, when we see Ursula, in ecstatic communion with the countryside – where she and the rainbow are, for a second, *one*. It is there that she realizes that she belongs to a fragile but continuous chain of being linked to something much larger than herself that is beautiful, sublime, dangerous and perhaps ultimately unknowable.

Russell dedicated the film to the memory of his cousin and childhood companion Marion Russell who was tragically killed on the cusp of becoming a teenager. The British military had mined the cliffs and glen around Southampton in case of invasion by the Germans, and while playing on the beach, in the immediate post-war era, one of the hidden mines exploded and Marion was killed. Clearly Russell makes the connection, not only to a cousin that he loved and was devoted to, but links Ursula's story to the following generation, to which he and Marion belonged, coming of age during WWII, and in effect closes that chapter started by Lawrence and the generation that lived through WWI – that fragile chain of being again.

LADY CHATTERLEY (1993)

The association with Lawrence would end on a high note four years after *The Rainbow* with an adaptation for cable television of *Lady Chatterley's Lover* (1993) done in four one hour parts from the book by Lawrence published in 1928 two years before he died. The book was finished in Italy while Lawrence was still attempting to recuperate from tuberculosis but he knew it would probably be his last book. Russell changed the title to *Lady Chatterley*, not out of prurience certainly, but to make it clear that his version would not concentrate on the relationship of the lady and her lover, but would be primarily about Lawrence's final magnificent creation, Constance Chatterley, one of the great – one daresay feminist – women characters in the history of the novel. While a privately printed edition was published in 1928 the book was illegal and only available in censored versions - the ban was not lifted until 1959 and was finally published in the UK in an uncensored edition in 1960. One would think that after the experience of WWI (ending in 1918), where the number of people who died range in estimates from 15 to 22 million, seeing the word "cunt" in print would not drive people into a fit of moral rage, but it did. Things have not changed as much as one would think since Lawrence's time as the word fucking, when it is currently seen in print or video text, is often translated as fu&!*g, but wars hot and cold rage on, often in third world countries that first world people have difficulty in finding on a map – such is our realpolitik. The strange duplicity and unsoundness of moral outrage in human beings can never be overestimated.

American film versions of the book predictably obscured the class issues, emphasizing the sexual intrigue, while some affected lavish productions, produced primarily in England, fetishized the aristocratic wealth of the Chatterley country estate treating the wealth as part of the natural order of things – this is a longstanding tradition that goes back to the early studio system that Russell hated, and continues down to our day with parochial, shallow, reactionary works such as *Downton Abbey* (2010). Russell wisely avoided these pitfalls by following Lawrence's lead and diving into the class issues from the get-go.

While the book is called *Lady Chatterley's Lover* it explores the relationship between three people: Lady Constance Chatterley (Joely Richardson), her husband, the wealthy Sir Clifford (James Wilby), who is wheelchair bound, and her lover, the young, poor gamekeeper Oliver Mellors (Sean Bean), who is simply referred to as "Mellors." Being a servant in that society he has only one name (like a pet), and he and Lady Chatterley speak wildly different versions of English so at first they can barely understand one another. This aspect was unfortunately not translated to the film – perhaps the thinking was that it would take up too much time to develop dramatically and too much effort on the part of the audience. Of course, in the physical sense, while flirting and fucking, another form of communication happens where the corporeal expresses itself with its own language. As in the book the characters at a certain point come to articulate, and argue over, the exact nature of their relationship – language is always playing catch-up in Lawrence and when the verbal and the physical finally line up as equals one gets real communication. This observation was one of Lawrence's substantial contributions to literature, and to culture as a whole – one that we for the most part can take for granted now as obvious.

As Lawrence and Russell show once communication is firing on all fronts, physical, intellectual, emotional and spiritual, humans are able to achieve a state of grace denied (as far as we know), to any other animal; a human being can become more civilized and more of an animal at the same time – a contradiction that for humans is within reach. Some film adaptations of the book have treated Lady Chatterley as repressed – someone who manages to finally come out of the closet (so to speak) as a free spirited sexual female thanks to her lover. In the book none of the characters are repressed sexually, certainly not Constance, who freely discusses sexual matters with her sister Hilda, in a typically familial, frank manner, over drinks, laughter, as most educated people did (and still do). More importantly in both the book and the film it is Lady Chatterley who changes as the book/film progresses while neither of the men do.

Sir Clifford is in a wheelchair having suffered an injury to his spine as a soldier in WWI rendering him impotent. Being Lawrence of course this is also a symbolic castration – a metaphoric impotence also used by Ernest Hemingway in *The Sun Also Rises* (1926) when speaking of the same generation of men that came back from the Great War haunted and never the same. Pablo Picasso once wisely commented on that generation (to which he belonged), explaining that when his close friend Georges Braque went to fight in the war Picasso saw him off at the station for his military training and both men were laughing about the adventure and the danger awaiting him, as young men do. Braque fortunately returned two years later with only a slight injury when the war was over, but as Picasso put it, "the man who I left on that train station never came back."[57] It was that way for many people and Lawrence and his generation of writers, including Ernest Hemingway (*Soldier's Home*), Virginia Woolf (*Jacob's Room*), Louis Ferdinand Celine (*Journey to the End of the Night*), Robert Graves (*Goodbye to All That*) and E.E. Cummings (*The Enormous Room*) put that horror in writing so it would not be forgotten.

When we first see Clifford he is firing his shotgun from his wheelchair shooting birds, or game, as the British call it, for sport and Russell then cuts to the vast Chatterley estate, looking imperious and aristocratic. Like "Brideshead" in Evelyn Waugh's masterpiece *Brideshead Revisited*, the estate is a metaphor for a class, for a capitalist/colonialist system that made its wealth using slave and child labor, and for a genteel aristocratic social system – replete with feudal dependencies and the politics of patronage - dissected by various writers from Marcel Proust to EM Forster. It was a world that Lawrence knew well, where people in England were divided between the nobility and "the Herd."

With those opening shots (literally and figuratively) of Clifford killing birds the film immediately sets up a resonance between violence, sport, and wealth so we understand where we are before a word is spoken or the credits have even finished rolling. We go from the estate to a priest saying words typical for the period: "Ours is a tragic age..." Everyone looks up at him, tired, helpless, and bored from having heard it too many times. The generation who fought in WWI were always being told they were either "tragic" or "lost" and must have wondered what it would be like to live in world that was "comic" and "found" – they never got to know as WWII was just around the corner and would, again, shatter the world into pieces to be remade yet again - something that would not have surprised Lawrence at all but he never lived to see it.

When the young couple is being chauffeured to the coal mines Russell does a reprise of the set-piece in *Women in Love*: the immaculately white luxury convertible going to the coal mines surrounded by men covered in black soot. In this case the men are striking and blocking the entrance to the mine so no one can work and some younger men throw mud at the car hitting Clifford in the face. Unlike the earlier film where the car carefully negotiated the space at walking speed here the chauffeur, under instructions from Clifford, goes at dangerously high speed, showing the working men who's the boss. In the process they almost run over a little boy – child labor at this time was still practiced, and not made illegal In England until 1933. The boy hurts himself as he rolls out of the way but they don't stop to help him. Clifford reminds Constance that their vast wealth comes from this horrible situation that must be endured; more so, one must constantly be on vigil, showing them that you are the master and they are lucky to have a job otherwise the whole edifice might collapse – the recent Marxist revolution in Russia where the wealthy had to run for their lives with whatever fit in a suitcase, made that clear. Lady Chatterley looks around at the horrifying poverty and says: "The war between classes is ghastly, it's as if we belong to a different species." "You'll get used to it in time" Clifford shoots back, adding: "how would you like to live in a miner's hovel?" The threat is clear enough – class warfare it is.

Sir Clifford then performs a stunt worthy of any populist oligarch – brilliantly orchestrating his display of power despite his handicap. He orders that he be placed, wheelchair and all, inside one of the coal wagons and then pushed into the mine. He is reminded that the mine is blocked by the miners themselves but Clifford insists. He is pushed in and the men part to let him through – once inside Clifford, in raptures, shouts: "That's how we'll win!" Lady Chatterley just got her first lesson in class warfare. For Clifford class wars were as common as a yearly cold – and about as dangerous – one had simply to manage it carefully so it doesn't become something else, something more dangerous that can kill you. Russell's brilliant set-piece here, surpassing his earlier version in *Women in Love*, achieves many things at the same time including showing – one would say almost in a Marxist sense – the origins of the wealth of the Chatterley estate right at the beginning, in a very dramatic manner, so we are constantly reminded later – during festive balls and dinners, where this wealth comes from. Sir Clifford might forget that little boy jumping out of the way of his car almost immediately after the event but we don't.

Late in the day by the fireplace Clifford is reading aloud from G.K. Chesterton's *The Ballad of the White Horse* - a poem popular during the war with Christians - that contrasts the battle between Christianity symbolized by a white horse, and nihilistic heathenism symbolized by a black horse. Chesterton's idea was that everyone had these "horses" within them but that the black horse must be restrained and civilized – an idea later made into a more coherent book, without the mythological Christian trappings, by Sigmund Freud in *Civilization and It's Discontents*. Constance doesn't understand why the black horse needs to be trained and restrained and finds the poem overbearing - Clifford explains it's merely a symbol of all our desires: "Surely, you don't think that desire and passion should *not* be curbed at all? You think we have a right to all our desires?" Constance replies: "Why not? The black horse should have the right to his desires otherwise he shouldn't exist at all." Here he get to the heart of Lawrence in a beautiful mis-en-scéne orchestrated by Russell: As the poem is read the camera performs a slow tracking shot from Clifford across the vast room and fireplace to Constance on the opposite side of the room showing the distance between them. Clifford understands her meaning in a literal way and suggests Constance get a lover if she wants to but she tells him immediately that she doesn't want anyone else - but Russell, on her line reading, cuts to her dream that night that contradicts what she has said. In the dream Constance is riding a black horse that leads her on a footpath on her estate, but it is now decorated with the corpses of men who fought in the war looking like neoclassical statues, but decorated with roses, all dead and seemingly attached to the trees, perhaps returning to the earth. The horse leads her to a shallow lake where Sir Clifford is about to hand her a bouquet but as she reaches out to take it he grabs her hard and starts to pull her in as he goes down into the dark waters. Clifford drowns but she pulls away at the last moment. The camera pans up from the still lake to Mellors on the other side looking very much alive and ready for something to happen.

Lady Chatterley wakes up clearly distressed going to Clifford's room for some comfort but finds him in the midst of what we would now call post traumatic stress disorder – he hears men screaming with the cannons, machine guns, and sounds of men dying in battle – it is Clifford who needs comforting. Russell ends the scene by doing a tracking shot from a close-up of the two comforting each other to a long shot from across the room that's extremely effective in rending the mixed emotions in a visual sense. In another exchange in their sitting room Constance wonders why people don't walk around with their faces covered and their bodies naked. This is another clue that Constance, without being aware of it, is already calling into question the mores and conventions of her day. Since husband and wife have separate bedrooms Constance has a painting showing a neo-classical nude as decoration and poses for herself in the same manner. As she approaches the painting she seems inspired and gets completely naked, except for shoes and a chiffon scarf around her head with a look of mischief. She goes to Clifford's room and approaches his bed saying in mock seriousness: "I am your faithful servant – your wish is my command." She puts her breasts right up to Clifford's face, but instead of playing with her game, in a fit of rage he exclaims: "Stop doing this! Why are you doing this to me?" Constance apologizes and runs off crying. Clifford's physical disability affects his legs and his sexual organs only, but he seems unable to caress or explore his wife's body, as if he were afraid of a sexuality that was not strictly about penetration and ejaculation; unfortunately for the time this was not so unusual as little was known about sex except for basic facts and even these were often couched in Victorian euphemisms that were derogatory and uninformed. The net result was that there was a lot of fear, misunderstanding, and disgust – feelings that people didn't know what to do with so they carefully hid them – "polite society" was built around this collective repression and Lawrence saw through it and sought, in his writing, to not simply criticize but to demolish it – for Lawrence it was war.

Later at a festive Christmas ball at the Chatterley estate people play musical chairs – a standard game for adults of the time – and we meet the looser of said game, Ken Russell himself in an inspired bit of casting playing Sir Michael Reid, Constance's father and the proverbial cynical and sybaritic aristocrat, whose only care in the world seems to be enjoying himself, having a laugh, and making sure everyone else does too. To Constance's argument that she is doing what she should be doing Reid replies: "if that's the case you're not being kind to yourself or anyone else." This scene gives Russell the opportunity of always providing advice for Constance – a comical turn as Russell wrote the lines himself so we hear the author giving advise to his creation – not too surprisingly she takes him up on it. Later in a private conversation with free-spirited Hilda (Hetty Baynes), her sister, she makes a comment that men in some sense can't ever really enter in women's lives and concludes: "of all of the men I have known none is as real to me as my butler" – an incredulous line (by Lawrence) that tells us more about the class system in England than many long-winded essays. Constance seems to disagree but holds her tongue.

Sir Clifford at one point suggests, in a more serious tone, that Constance get a lover, and if this liaison should result in a child he promises to give the newborn the Chatterley name and fortune as the aristocratic Clifford is looking for an heir to pass on his name and his vast wealth. But it is Mellors who balks at being used; Constance comes to him when she wants tenderness or sex just as Clifford calls when he needs something – all masters and he nothing but a servant. Mellors, using his soft, even-toned, polite voice that he always uses when speaking to the bosses, explains he's going to Canada where he has a brother and start his life over.

Later with a hammer and two nails Constance and Mellors make an X marks the spot cross on a nearby tree, with two big nails, marking their time together. The lovemaking in the film is depicted naturalistically rather than with any sort of affectations of bodice ripping, or romanticism – Russell shows two human animals mating, nothing more and nothing less – which makes it, in its own way, extraordinary. The British seem to have a sensibility for the depiction of sex that belies the old joke "No sex please, we're British." Arguably the best sex scene ever filmed is to be found in *Don't Look Now*, Nicolas Roeg's film. Russell's *Women In Love* and *Lady Chatterley* are not far behind. One thing that might account for this success by the British – that stretches from Henry Fielding's novel *Tom Jones* (1749) to *9 Songs* (2004) by Michael Winterbottom – is the pragmatic aspect of British philosophy and outlook, an interest in the "brutality of fact." Certainly Lawrence's output as a writer continues this line of reasoning, waging war against the mythologies of his day in favor of plainspoken facts.

In Russell's depiction Constance's marriage is always under scrutiny – we see the looks of her maid, the emphasis on an enormous table for twenty that is only for them, the sudden pans to the chauffeur biding his time, to servants waiting for orders but frankly sizing up the situation – the regulations and separations of class are italicized with images not words. In her regular trysts and communions with the countryside of her estate, and with her lover who takes care of it, Lady Chatterley comes to realize that the class structure she lives in, and the nature of property itself is unnatural and unhealthy; this is not so much a political realization – Lady Chatterley does not become a Communist – as much as an ethical realization grounded in her lived experience. Some of the old fire of her early youth as an independent intellectual and social progressive resurfaces, where she studied in Germany with her sister, and she comes to create a space for herself, apart from her husband and Mellors, as she forges her own kind of independent freedom.

When she hears noises in the forests she asks Mellors what they are and he responds that it's the trees moving with the wind and touching each other and pleasing themselves – this is Lawrence distilled into a country walk that Russell shoots at the golden hour giving it an aspect of the fairy tale also in the book. During one of her trysts with Mellors it starts to pour rain and the couple take their clothes off and commune with the rain running through it as Russell's camera, fixed to a car, keeps up with them – this is similar to the scene with Rupert (Alan Bates) in *Women In Love* after being hit on the head by his lover he goes outside bleeding, takes his clothes off, and starts to commune with nature by cleaning himself with the wet foliage like an animal. Later Constance and Mellors, wet and naked, place garlands of flowers around their heads like crowns, as if they were the king and queen of Nature, or proto-hippies who have found their own commune, but one that sits precariously on Lord Chatterley's estate, someone who does not seem predisposed to proto-hippies any more than to working class miners. There is the crux of the problem: Lady Chatterley has jumped classes and is now straddling the fence so at some point she must make a choice. There is no escape from social structure and danger and uncertainty lurks everywhere, whatever you choose to do – or as Lawrence himself put it "There's always the hyena of morality at the garden gate, and the real wolf at the end of the street."

Michael invites his two daughters for two summer months at his estate and Constance and his sister Gilda go off in her fancy red sports car – they stop to see Mellors who Gilda is interested in meeting. Russell again beautifully contrasts the flashy car with Mellor's small house in the woods with a thatch roof that could easily be a house in the 17th century – as if the classes were separated by centuries as well as finances – Mellors and Gilda hate each other almost immediately as Mellors speaks his mind with her, something she isn't used to hearing, especially from a game keeper. As she leaves in a huff Constance tells Mellors that the world they have created is the real world and the outside world doesn't matter at all. He disagrees saying that the real world *is* the real world for him and always has been and he must adapt to it as best he can – there is no escape. She then tell him she's pregnant and they hug by the lake – the same lake where Clifford was drowning and tried to drag her in with him. It's one of Russell's best set-pieces as the couple realize that they are now a couple in a much more physically connected sense, and must navigate the world as it is and face the consequences.

At the father's estate we meet Donald Forbes (Breffni McKenna), a romantic interest for Constance before she married, who is still in love with her - he is also an artist who does slightly surreal, cartoonish paintings that Russell is clearly mocking as they look like the paintings of a not too talented adolescent. Donald talks about being an "anarchist, emotionally and artistically" while walking around a topiary maze, while wearing a tuxedo. Typical of Russell the surroundings and context give the game away as he completely contradicts what he's saying simply by being in this space – a topiary maze is surely the least anarchist space imaginable. What is it she asks that makes him pull the petals off a rose, wrap the vine with thorns around a chicken bone and then call it "the true rose?" - surely a question that might be put to many artists, then and now. Lawrence here, as in *Women In Love*, with the character of Loerke, gives us a great portrait of an artist gone off the rails, where the radical or "anarchist" rhetoric is simply absurd, somewhat akin to Dada in its anti-rationalism but without the context (WWI), or the humor – the only thing left is the philosophy that is now in the hands of a wealthy dilettante.

Unlike Donald the Dadaists were actually attempting to overthrow the society that had made WWI possible with their antics by making fun of their rules, reasons, and conventions; but knowing full well that their enterprise was foredoomed they did not wait for the revolution, rather, they made their own but with tongue firmly planted in cheek, and then they retired to the country, to a monastery, or to play chess when the next war came. In these efforts they were often putting themselves in some danger as real anarchists were, in the early 20th century, feared and persecuted by both police and vigilantes. The reason the state took them seriously (as anarchists if not as artists) is that politicians reasoned that if aesthetic categories could be proven false or meaningless, social barriers could be revealed as constructed illusions, and the world could be changed in a manner not amenable to their interests. This is why Duchamp's urinal, or the nonsense poetry of the Dada group was so incendiary while it was created (in the midst of WWI) but soon lost its power, co-opted by the surrealists as harmless amusements and pranks that were soon regarded as passé, or worse, they entered the world of Art History as relics from the past, alongside Etruscan tombs and Faberge eggs. But in the fever of the period when they were made Dada basically said to the art world, and to the establishment as a whole: "go fuck yourself" – and that was not only extraordinary but very Lawrence-like in its sentiment.

Constance, by asking that question about the rose, clearly sees through Donald as a café anarchist, a manqué artist, making him perhaps an amusing friend but certainly not a serious mate, while Mellors, whatever his faults, knows who his is and what he wants, is true to his word, and has his feet on the ground. In fact sometimes his feet are so solidly on the ground that he trips over himself, as when he admits to Constance that sometimes he is afraid of her because of her class. By comparing the men, as she does we come to understand her choice.

In one of Russell's favorite shots, that he has repeated in many films, he shoots the sisters walking in a field of flowers, in a tracking shot, talking about what to do now that Constance is pregnant – she refuses to simply hand over the child in order that Clifford's family name and inheritance should carry on after he's gone but is unsure what to do. When Constance returns to the Chatterley estate all she knows is that she must see Mellors who has quit his job. Constance comes to look for him and Russell stages a beautiful exterior of one of the hovels in the town – Russell was always a master of showing how poor people actually lived and here he is up to it, showing Lady Chatterley in an immaculate white dress, trying to find her lover in s soot covered alley full of children and mothers as the men are off working.

Later on the same lake as in the dream Constance and Clifford discuss Proust – Clifford admires the work but Constance says it revolts her as there is no feeling in the book but only words about feelings: "it's all so self-important." This is exactly Lawrence's criticism mouthed by his own creation. Constance tells Clifford she's pregnant by Mellors and he is flabbergasted and exclaims: "Dear God you ought to be wiped from the face of this earth!" When Constance asks why Clifford tells her that Mellors is nothing but miserable scum and it's impossible for her to have any real feelings for him or want to marry him. Such a thing is not conceivable. He tells she's not in her right mind. Clifford refuses to divorce her and Russell as always shoots the final fight between them at the usual table but his mis-en-scéne this time is the traditional shot-counter-shot so they are never together in the same frame.

The pregnancy forces Constance to choose between the two men, and the political and emotional aspects of the story conflate, leading to a final moral choice that will define the rest of her life. Symbolically for both Lawrence and Russell, it is with Mellors that she discovers the sublime beauty and the immense power – the density of the thing itself – of the English countryside and where she becomes pregnant. In effect she accepts herself, like Ursula, as one small part of nature, and its long, shadowy, mysterious interplays and history. Constance, with the help of her sister's speedy roadster just manages to catch the ship in Southampton – Russell's hometown – to Canada and Mellors is called to the top deck. To meet Constance he has to cross a chain link rope that says "First Class Passengers Only" but Mellors easily skips over the rope – now his turn to jump classes - and meet up with Constance as they embrace looking back at England as they leave it behind.

Lady Chatterley is a high note for Russell in many ways as it is arguably his last great film, made in 1993, when his struggles with Hollywood and conventional producers in Europe and the US were beginning to take their toll. With *Lady Chatterley* Russell returned to what he did best – Lawrence, the English countryside, and superb actors and technical people who were willing to go with him into the heart of D.H. Lawrence and that long literary trajectory that he brought to a close along with his fellow novelists Virginia Woolf, John Dos Passos, and E.M. Forster. Of course once that Modernist chapter was closed another one very quickly began in the postwar era, but that would be another story. Russell, like Lawrence, always felt more at home in a Victorian parlor, no matter how much he hated it and railed against it, making him the ideal interpreter of Lawrence's radical vision.

Independence 3: *The Devils* (1971)

In order to understand, I destroyed myself.

—**Fernando Pessoa**

There is no power relation without the correlative constitution of a field of knowledge, nor any knowledge that does not presuppose and constitute at the same time power relations.

—**Michel Foucault**

The Devils is arguably Russell's most visually spectacular work, an opinion that he shared himself.[58] The film is a fictionalized account of the brief rise and spectacular fall or Urbain Grandier (Oliver Reed), a 17th century French Catholic priest, prosecuted for witchcraft in 1634 following the supposed possession of the townspeople of Loudun, a small, rich, autonomous city-state in France that King Louis XIII wanted to make part of his kingdom. Independent city-states were normal in other parts of Europe but in France Loudun was something of an anomaly – relatively "liberal" for the time, even allowing Huguenots and Catholics to co-exist. Like many "liberal" city-states, such as Venice or Amsterdam, their primary interest was trade not religious orthodoxy. Despite their relative autonomy Loudun was still directed by the Church and by the King but the mayor of the city controlled trading contracts, taxes, defenses and fortifications. As the film opens the mayor has died passing all power temporarily to Grandier who was canon of the Church of Sainte-Croix, a powerful position with authority over the clergy and nuns in the city. Since Grandier was naïve with regard to the complex power relations at play between the mayor and the government in Paris he fails to see the machinations of the plot against him until it is too late.

Once Sister Jeanne des Anges (Vanessa Redgrave), a troubled and sexually repressed Ursuline nun based in Loudun – who suffers from kyphosis, or curvature of the spine - starts a series of baseless accusations of sexual impropriety against Grandier, with whom she is infatuated, the King (Graham Armitage) and his henchmen, Cardinal Richelieu (Christopher Logue) and Baron De Laubardemont (Dudley Sutton), assess that such an accusation might prove useful now that Loudun is between mayors. This state of transition and uncertainty is seen as the ideal moment to take the independent priest down and bring Loudun into the fold of the French state. It was reasoned that once the city was reduced to anarchy, vandalism, and violence, the people themselves would beg the King to take control, restore law and order, and make the city part of the French state.

There were good reasons for the King to want Loudun. The hapless royals were in desperate need of money as France's interminable wars with England, as well as their local wars with the Huguenots, were all taking their toll; there was also the ravenous needs of the growing nobility in competition with each other for more wealth and strategic alliances; and finally there was the absurdly lavish lifestyle of the King himself, his family and friends. The antagonisms and fractures among the various power brokers were making life difficult, and dangerous, for the royals and the wealthy elite - the predatory acquisition of new city states was at least a short term remedy. This state of affairs would reach a boiling point 155 years after the tragedy at Loudun in Paris as the French Revolution reset a new world order.

The events in Loudun proceeded as planned but at a certain point the situation starts to take on a life of its own that no one had foreseen. Once the nuns agree under oath – and the threat of death by crossbow - that they have been seduced by the "devil worshiping priest" the convent and the town become gripped by a collective hysterical madness, as the confessions allow everyone to release libidinal energies long suppressed – suddenly unexpected sexual liaisons, casual violence, and orgies become the norm. This is a situation (long before Sigmund Freud) that takes everyone, including the participants themselves, by surprise. The historical tragedy of Loudun actually occurred and has a long pedigree in the arts. There were several official academic histories but it was first made into a novel by Aldous Huxley in 1952 and then turned into a play by John Whiting ten years later. Russell adapted the screenplay from these sources but the film kept only some of the dialogue from Whiting's strong but verbose play.

The actual Father Urbain Grandier was burned at the stake in Loudun, France on August 18, 1634. He was accused of seducing an entire convent of Ursuline nuns and of being in league with the devil. Grandier was a handsome man and a popular speaker, and his canonships within the church brought him significant income and likely contributed to some envy and animosity – even his friends admitted that Grandier was promiscuous, and made many enemies as a result, but the charge of being in league with the devil was wholly rejected by all concerned. Even Sister Jeanne made an offer to Grandier to become the spiritual adviser of the convent but he rejected her.[59] To add insult to injury he publicly spoke out against Cardinal Richelieu as an unwanted predator, looking for wealthy cities to annex for the hungry King. Once he turned against Richelieu his fate was sealed, but even under torture he never confessed to his presumed crimes.

Russell brought his usual stock company of actors including Max Adrian as Ibert, a mad quack doctor, Murray Melvin as a the troubled and repressed father Mignon, Kenneth Colley as Legrand, a businessman and friend of Grandier's, Judith Paris as Sister Judith, a nun trapped in the convent only out of family necessity, and of course Oliver Reed as Grandier – he augmented this solid team with Vanessa Redgrave, one of the great aristocrats of British acting in the all important role of Sister Jeanne and she gives a brilliant, highly nuanced performance with sudden shifts in tone, using her voice like a musical instrument, to capture unresolved inner conflicts. With a fantastic surrealist set made primarily of white tiles by Derek Jarman, costumes by Shirley Russell, music that both mimicked brass-heavy medieval chants and atonal works by Schoenberg created by Peter Maxwell Davies, and cinematography by David Watkin using high contrast saturated color that mimicked the paintings of the late Renaissance, Russell had a top crew of people that understood the story and were willing to travel with him into uncharted waters. Russell's script, partially derived from Whiting and Huxley, was arguably his best. It was almost inevitable that sparks would fly and they did, igniting a firestorm of a film that, in a sense, is still banned today since Russell's final cut remains locked up – it is as if society, collectively, had decided it must remain under lock and key and in a sense the power brokers are right, *The Devils* is a dangerous film.

DEREK JARMAN

The exterior shots for the town were shot in Bamburgh Castle on the northeast English coast in Northumberland – a location also used by Roman Polanski in his extraordinary adaptation of *Macbeth*. The work of Jarman here deserves special mention as it was an inspired choice by Russell who had met the eccentric genius and liked him enormously, saying "he was the last true bohemian"[60] – coming from Russell that was indeed very high praise and one can see why he trusted the young artist (he was 29 when Russell hired him) despite the fact that he had no experience as a set designer. Jarman was clearly influenced by the aesthetic component of Carl Theodore Dryer's *The Passion of Joan of Arc* (1928) in its use of white tile and by Fritz Lang's *Metropolis* (1927) in his use of large mechanical sets that towered over the actors as a single malevolent force - he saw the overall look of the film as straddling these worlds but existing on its own plane of reality, outside of cinema history and of 17th century France - even outside of time and space itself - in its own modern and medieval nightmare world. The set, comprised of immaculate white brick walls, contribute enormously to the meaning of the film and their use was determined by practical as well as aesthetic considerations. In his original pre-production sketches Jarman used stone, and the decision to use white brick was made at Pinewood Studios where they had a machine to make brick and stone molds of every size, shape and color. Russell:

> "We experimented at Pinewood with all their molds, including those for old stone, but obviously when you use the same molds time after time you end up with an absolutely uniform pattern, so we thought; let's accept the limitations imposed on us by a machine-made product and use the most machine made thing, the ordinary household brick. The whole town is made out of Pinewood standard brick mold. But having decided on this basic material, we had to make it distinctive and put over the ideas we ourselves had about the town."[61]

For Russell and Jarman the decision to use pure white rather than the usual reds that they initially tested was inspired by one famous line in Huxley's book that is often quoted: "The exorcism of Sister Jeanne was equivalent to a rape in a public lavatory."[62] This is a line that also, not surprisingly, inspired many of Francis Bacon's paintings.[63] In effect the whole town becomes a lavatory as well as a hospital and a lunatic asylum. For Brian Hoyle the walls also serve as a reminder:

> "In an earlier scene in which Madeleine (Gemma Jones) visits Sister Jeanne (Vanessa Redgrage) at the convent to enquire about joining the order Sister Jeanne's cell seems especially claustrophobic due to the low ceilings. In addition the arch-shaped bed and the quadrant-shaped door evoke the nun's hunchback.

The white bricks here...serves to remind the audience of all the young women, like Sister Jeanne, with physical or mental impairments, who were sent to convents by their families."[64]

The townspeople of Loudon would also have seen their own city as "modern" and so its modernity is both factual – like the green lipstick worn by fashionable young women in 17th century France – and suggests our own time where we might encounter similar aesthetic, political and religious situations.

A POLITICAL FILM

The theme of the film was the working method by which sexual repression turns into the mainspring of aggression and violence within a restricted and isolated social group; and then how that social group in turn absorbs that derangement and acts on it. The film remains one of the most astute and fascinating accounts of social hysteria and sexual pathology, as well as showing the complex symbiotic – one is tempted to say biological - interaction between the individual and the state. Russell maintained that *The Devils* was his only political film, and while that is an exaggeration – political sympathy for the down-and-out is a constant in his work – it is in this film that the political becomes a primary player taking center stage.[65]

The pathology at work in Loudun is unusual and extreme but in another sense it is merely a more hysterical version of what happens in other places/times, that is, we see how a clever populist leader can use this wellspring of repression to his/her advantage, treating it as raw material, in effect magically turning suppressed rage into gold. This is why *The Devils* is Russell's most political film, in effect he is not speaking only of 17th century France but of 20th century world politics. He shows in very clear cinematic language how that "magic" works, that is, the process by which strong but inchoate emotions in populations can be manipulated toward practical political ends. The film was also brutally frank showing, in detail, various tortures used at the time by the church, as well as the protocol by which the most barbarous acts were normalized and made socially acceptable. As Michel Foucault so nicely summed up: "The judges of normality are present everywhere."[66]

The film veers from emotional traumas to self-reflexive irony and from tragedy to farce with a virtuosity not seen in Russell's work before. His scabrous humor and his deep sense of moral outrage find space to co-exist in the same film as do his sense of realism and theater. At times he throws caution to the wind and these contrasting elements fill his busy frame to bursting. For example, nuns – some with shaved heads that tells us they have been tortured by the state – frolic nude, laughing hysterically in an orgy, while others in the same shot look ashamed, confused and horrified. In effect, no clear directive is given by Russell as to how we should react to the scene, and we are free to judge and decide for ourselves. Russell uses grotesque imagery, atonal music, oblique framing, disorienting camera and editing techniques, fast zooms and flash pans to constantly keep the viewer off kilter, unbalanced, so we are inside the drama that plays out rather than merely passive observers. His camera is often hand held going directly up to actors confronting them or following them as they enter or exit a scene – it is *present*.

AN ERSATZ BIRTH OF VENUS

Russell's theatrical opening sequence might be a film within a film onto itself. Russell cues a small stage and the play being performed is an otherworldly, ersatz version of Botticelli's *The Birth of Venus* as we see a limited audience, composed of wealthy drunken elites that clearly constitutes a private performance. They are all standing except for the all-important Cardinal Richelieu who is the honored guest from Paris – he not only sits but appears to have an entourage of beautiful nuns with him some of whom appear to be horrified by the upper crust audience – all decadent, fey, flamboyant, and appearing to be more interested in partying than in the finer details of *The Birth of Venus*. Again Russell and his team hit the mark historically as such mini plays or short entertainments (often based on classical texts) were commonplace within the ruling classes – even Leonardo da Vinci staged them for his wealthy patrons in Italy, but unfortunately the sets and costumes he created no longer exist.

We first see Venus, performed by King Louis XIII as a cross-dressing sprite, portraying the god of beauty, sex, and fertility as he appears from behind some paper storm clouds to shower gold coins to those on stage with him. Russell here oscillates between aestheticized camp and psychological horror without missing a beat. The level of wealth is staggering and has clearly driven the King mad – his stage persona in drag displays a personality disintegrating into a form of decadent game playing where all norms – sexual, spiritual and moral – are merely social conventions that are either useful, useless, amusing, or boring. We understand without one word being said that the King is so powerful that he feels free to embody male and female, human and god - no doubt Nero and many other Kings passed their hours in similar productions with similar alcoholic audiences.

At first sight Louis in drag is laughingly absurd but then Russell performs his magic and as his camera, from the audience point of view, looks up at him Louis changes from a joke to a malevolent, powerful, devil – insidious, clever, and supremely dangerous. The atonal score digs in as the elements of performance, lighting, camera movement and editing create a sudden and unforeseen drama. Russell makes this magic purely with lighting, shooting from below stage level, and moving from medium shot to close-up. The shift is so sudden it takes us by surprise. Before we realize it the performance is over and Cardinal Richelieu moves toward to stage to congratulate the King. Russell again pushes the envelope as the Cardinal himself does not move but is taken while sitting in his chair pushed by nuns! Clearly the Cardinal has reached such a level of power that he need not even walk. As he reaches the stage he casually mentions *The Birth of Venus* displaying his education, but tells the King, in so many words, that its central significance is "the unification of church and state." Such a theme was nowhere to be found in the King's entertainment, or in Botticelli's masterpiece that inspired it, but the cardinal holds out his gloved hand, full of expensive rings, for the King to kiss - clearly the Cardinal has never heard the words "you're wrong" and he acts accordingly. The power shifts between the two men is brutal, forthright and without pretenses of any kind as they are locked into an alliance and they understand that to fail is to die. The King is not a fool, he understands that he needs the Vatican and can do nothing without an alliance, therefore, with good common sense, Louis gets on his knees and kisses the ring saying "amen" as if it were a veiled threat - on that word the opening credits roll.

This prelude serves to introduce the themes of the main film with little dialogue and no traditional exposition – it is one of the greatest opening set pieces in the history of film. One of the things that make it so powerful is that, like Bergman's or Fellini's work, Russell's is a tactile cinema, full of seductive, or repulsive matter. The material and corporeal qualities of the world at large come repeatedly to the surface, despite the theatrical make-up. The fleshiness of flesh is ever present as is the costuming that conceals it. Nothing is hidden in Russell's cinema as the camera, that he considered one of the central characters in all of his work, captures all of the particulars. If God, or the Devil, is in the details Russell's camera is there to show it. Not too surprisingly the film was made just subsequently to Russell having lost his Catholic faith – he had converted a decade earlier after a conventional secular English childhood. Here is the director himself explaining how he lost one faith but found another, in his inimitable prose style, where we get a good sense of his British sensibility:

"The Devils *was the last nail in the coffin of my Catholic faith, a faith that had sustained me for more than ten years and given my life purpose and direction. But my picture of God was hazing over: too much incense, too much stained glass, too much sci-fi in the sky. It was time to come down to earth. I needed a new prayer book. I found it in* The Prelude *by Wordsworth and started devotions anew in his church, where the nave was Borrowdale, the transept was Cat Bells and Grange Fell, the altar (where a memorial stands to the local men killed in the Great War) was Castle Crag, and the roof was Clouds of Glory."*[67]

Russell seems to have found a new faith in the work of Wordsworth and the Lake Poets and their more earth bound spirituality based around Nature and the seasonal cycles of birth, constant change, and death.

DON GIOVANNI

Russell early on shows the normalization of the plague that was devastating Europe as people in the streets are casually surrounded by people dying horrible and painful deaths, and with piles of corpses being carted off for mass graves as there were too many to be buried in the conventional Catholic tradition. In one sequence we witness one such death close-up where a young woman is being administered to with one of the many quack cures of the period by two "doctors," Adam (Brian Murphy) and Ibert (Max Adrian), who look like something out of Goya via Max Ernst. Grandier dismisses them by throwing the stuffed alligator they use in their rituals out a window – this is also where he meets Madeleine, his future wife, who is related to the victim and asks Grandier to perform the last rites. In these opening sequences Grandier's lifestyle is given full scope as we see his luxurious apartment, with a spiral staircase, and one of his mistresses, Philippe (Georgina Hale), casually naked, informing him that she is pregnant. Grandier takes the news in stride suggesting (as he has undoubtedly done before) that she buckle up and submit to God's will. He barely seems to take her into account, grooming himself like a narcissistic playboy. As a counterpoint to this scene Madeleine, inside the local church, confesses to Grandier (as a priest) that she loves him and they begin a more serious relationship – eventually even marrying at night in the same local church.

Nevertheless Grandier's ego gets the better of him as he tells Philippe that he seeks his own destruction in order that he might finally meet God - she can't possibly take him seriously but no doubt there is an element of truth there. For example when Grandier spots Philippe's father on the street cursing him and demanding immediate satisfaction in a duel for having seduced his daughter Grandier humiliates him and laughs in his face, clearly seeing him as an inferior, not even fit to duel with - an act of self-destruction surely as the father is a powerful man in Loudun. There are shades here of Mozart/da Ponte's opera *Don Giovanni* in Grandier's unthinking viciousness as he savages fathers and husbands, leaving a multitude of Donna Elvira's to their fate and an ever-growing group of men who want to see his downfall – for Grandier it was only a matter of time.

Sister Jeanne's highly imaginative and sexual interior life is shown by Russell in a black and white dream sequence, which is one of the highlights of the film. Jeanne imagines worshipping at the feet of Grandier in the pose of Christ on the Cross. She wipes the blood and the stigmata, or perhaps semen, from his feet reverentially looking up at him full of adoration and desire. In this de-saturated sequence Christ looks down on her with painful convictions aflame, scrutinizing her idolatry with interest, sympathy and finally desire. Jeanne sensually caresses his body and licks his open wound as if it were an erogenous zone while the crowd applauds its approval. At the end of the sequence they roll on the ground and kiss passionately as Christ seems finally unable to control himself and takes Jeanne sexually as she seems to reach orgasm while onlookers approvingly look on. Suddenly Jeanne's robes fly off due to the wind and, to her horror, her deformed back is revealed. The crowd starts to laugh at her and Grandier/Christ looks on with pity. It's a magnificent scene showing Jeanne's desires, fears, and guilt without a single word. Russell uses Wellesian deep-focus and extreme angles throughout the film but emphasizes it – even italicizes it - during the scenes with Sister Jeanne to punctuate the power dynamics in play.

Russell flash cuts from the de-saturated dream sequence to a full color close-up of Sister Jeanne gouging a bloody would into her own palm with a crucifix; this is something she hides immediately, terrified of being found out. It is clear from this short sequence that her fantasy life is cause for pleasure but also for traumatic psychic pain that she converts to physical pain as a way of dealing with it – a way of exercising some control. In the period in question self-torture was a common practice among Catholics, often made public, such as walking on one's knees to church. In a later sequence Sister Jeanne flogs her naked torso while Sister Judith looks on bewitched and sexually excited. It is clear from these extraordinary scenes that Sister Jeanne's imagination is outrageously creative and the only way she, as a nun and an outcast from the society that she came from can deal with it is to try and suppress and destroy it. This, of course, is impossible, but once she takes that destructive impulse onto the world at large she sets in motion a machinery of discipline and punishment already in place that no one can stop.

Catholic theologian Gene D. Phillips described this dream sequence with Sister Jeanne and Grandier/Jesus – referred to in the literature regarding the film as "the rape of Christ" – as "depicting blasphemy without being blasphemous."[68] Phillips, a proponent of Catholic doctrine, is seeking to walk a fine line here to make the film palatable to believers. While the Catholic Church officially criticized and banned the film there was a dissenting group within the Church (Phillips included) that saw things in a different light, that is, as an affirmation of Catholicism in the character of Grandier, who, in a sense, becomes a martyr for the cause. In this view it is the Cardinal and his henchmen who are "devils" and cynically use the institutions of the Church for their own ends. The film caused debate within the Church that continues to our day, not only in Italy but wherever Catholics felt the film confirmed their Christian beliefs rather than denied them. Meanwhile others, such as the critic J. Hoberman, based in New York and affiliated with *The Village Voice*, relegated the religious and political aspects to the background and sought to align Russell with a group of cult, iconoclastic, avant-garde auteurs with strong surrealist ties, such as Alejandro Jodorowsky, Shuji Terayama, Fernando Arrabal, and Nicolas Roeg.[69]

COUNTING CROWS
In one of the most brilliant and absurd set pieces in the film Luis, the Catholic King of France, while lounging in his massive, manicured garden with his entourage, amuses himself by shooting, and counting, Protestants dressed as crows with droll nonchalance. The sequence is shot first as a farce, worthy of Monty Python, that turns macabre as the King shoots a man in the back and kills him, then muses with ironic concern on the number of Protestants killed thus far in their endless religious wars – even the King can't keep track. Russell's violent shifts in tone are consistent throughout the film and form a part of a complex formal strategy. What holds *The Devils* together, despite these radical shifts and stylistic deviations is that Russell emphasizes the ontological dimension of the tragedy that underlies all of the sequences regardless of their content, so he is free to mix highly realistic scenes with burlesque elements within the same sequence. Russell also created one of his most memorable effects in the conflict between the grounded tragic drama and the beautiful painterly artifice of the images,

forcing them into push-pull that is orchestrated as a musical piece in a play or an opera, which *The Devils* resembles. Russell pulls the film in many directions at once – it is a kaleidoscopic vision.

A MARRIAGE WITH NATURE AS WITNESS

Despite the pathological and physical horrors on show – in some cases in graphic detail - there is one moment of respite for the viewer and for Grandier himself and that is his marriage to Madeleine a simple local woman that he loved, and that he was having intimate relations with. We see an exchange of letters between them where Russell shows Grandier on a road trip to gain the backing of the King, shot in Russell's beloved Lake District that served him well in many films. It is on that trip that he realizes that real power resides with Richelieu, not the ministers or even the King – the reason is that Richelieu controls the vast wealth and army of the Vatican. We see Madeleine read the letter in a field of flowers at mid-day glowing with natural color, health and beauty. Grandier, in some sense, like Russell himself, here rejects his Catholic faith and moves closer to "a new prayer book" as he called it, and even performs a mass, using a loaf of bread, by a lake surrounded by a majestic series of mountain peaks. It is nature that is his witness – he (Russell or Grandier) needs no other. Both men seem to take Wordsworth's line "the human heart by which we live" at face value, using it as a shield against the blows of culture (Catholicism) and empire (French imperialism) – for Russell and Grandier all "isms" are dammed in the cathedral of Nature. Just by this simple expedient in the narrative Russell shows that Grandier and Madeline are a decent couple in a world that is corrupt, decadent and fundamentally unnatural.

More importantly Russell shifts our sympathies here from Grandier as randy, narcissistic, womanizing priest, to Grandier the married man and a good mayor who wants to see his town free to prosper and who is not bound by the orthodox conventions of his day. We might say with hindsight that Grandier is an existential rebel, that is, he says no to injustice and oppression not out of a sense of nihilism or desire for political power but out of a desire for affirmation and a sense of shared humanity. Grandier the rebel rejects both the absurd condition of existence (he becomes a priest), and the one-dimensional pieties of Catholic orthodoxy (he marries), recognizing the needs and the limitations – the *fragility* - of the human condition. Camus famously asked: "What is a rebel?" His answer was: "A man who says no."[70]

An important scene that takes place outside of Loudun, aside from the shooting of the Protestant crows at Versailles and the reading of Grandier's letter/hymn to nature, is in the claustrophobic inner sanctum of the Vatican's file keeping sector where the Cardinal has gone to look for some way to indict Grandier with the correct legal language. Jarman's work shines here as a priest/clerk casually rolls the Cardinal around the vast rows of files – a scene clearly influenced by Orson Welles's *The Trial*. As imagined by Jarman this area of the church (that most people would never see) is a medieval version of Kafka's bureaucratic nightmare world but post-modern and pre-industrial, comical and horrifying in equal measure. The vast swinging doors, reminiscent of a Hollywood musical from the Thirties, have a Cross on them like a logo – again the absurd and the sinister occupy the same space. The methodology of discipline and punishment is shown not as a monolithic superstructure in the manner of Jeremy Bentham's Panopticon but rather as a haphazard series of laws and rules that are often obscure and contradictory but they are, as we would say now, all "virtue-signaling." Such statutes and laws (and the structures that support them) can become, in the right hands, useful tools – this is the crafty politicians approach to the law/prison not that of philosophers, academics or saints.

While Dryer's *Joan of Arc*, in its profound acceptance of Catholicism and belief in the sainthood of Joan was an enormous influence on *The Devils* Russell sought to bypass the transcendental ideology of that film and replace it with a very different set of principles that would not only question that faith but supplant it with a new one – *The Devils* is an ambitious film. With his more subversive work of the 1970's Russell reached full maturity as an artist and created a radical *corporeal cinema* that did not necessarily reject metaphysical truths – as we saw in his very positive reaction to Wordsworth and the spiritual poetry of the Lake Poets that exalted Nature - but consciously set out to establish a new epistemology of physical frankness, contingency, and mortality that would stand alongside that earlier religious metaphysics, and people could decide for themselves what they thought. As we shall see it is in the "Cat Bells" (the name of a modest mountain in Cumbria in the English Lake District) that he mentions in his testament where we will find the spring of that new faith.

Before his imprisonment Grandier makes an impassioned speech in the central square of Loudun – where he will later be burned alive - about the importance of freedom and independence from French imperial power embodied not by the King, whom Grandier praises (the politically correct thing to do at the time), but by Cardinal Richelieu who is mad for power and wealth. While the townspeople seem to be in full agreement Baron De Laubardemont (Dudley Sutton) and his uncertain henchman Father Mignon side with the King. They plot Grandier's demise torturing the priest's allies, including his wife Madeline to make written confessions – by then a long-standing tradition of Inquisitions throughout Europe. Russell shoots their plotting using sinister lighting from underneath creating highly theatrical, sinister shadows. Once these "confessions" are signed the priest's fate is sealed. Grandier's friends were "latitudinarian" Christians – later called Newtonian Christians - who placed a high value on reason and saw no distinctions to be made between science and faith since they were, in a sense, both seeking the truth. But Barre and his henchmen were fundamentalist Catholics for whom the words in the Bible were, literally, the only truth.

The presumptive trial – where the final verdict is already a foregone conclusion – is presided over by Father Barre, in a performance of genius by Michael Gothard, an actor who encapsulated sixties rage in every performance – particularly in *Herostratus* (1967) where he is allowed to shine as the lead. Despite the relatively conventional writing by John Whiting that Russell used Gothard turns the straightforward text of the trial into the ravings of a hysterical madman who does not understand his own sadistic needs – just as Sister Jeanne does not understand her sexual imagination. Gothard brilliantly turns his performance into a mirror image of Redgrave's but just as in a mirror everything is reversed. Sister Jeanne is repressed, that is, she holds everything in, tightly around herself, always putting up barriers, trying to stay still, exhibiting no emotions lest her real emotions be revealed. But of course in Redgrave's brilliant performance Jeanne does reveal herself, when her voice breaks, when she gives the prosecutor a sly, ironic look, we see her frustration and desire at boiling point. Gothard's Father Barre, on the contrary, is explosive, outrageously exhibitionistic, constantly moving and shouting, completely out of control – one might say possessed. At times Gothard appears to stop mid-sentence, unable to speak because he is too emotionally wound up, literally foaming at the mouth. In the drama that Russell created once these opposites meet the end result is explosive.

As Barre interrogates, exorcizes, and tortures Sister Jeanne the quack doctors, Adam and Ibert, seen earlier return to inspect her and see if she has had sexual intercourse. Here Russell takes up Huxley's line that "Sister Jeanne's exorcism was like a rape in a public lavatory." With vomit, blood, concoctions and liquids flying everywhere as Jeanne screams in horror we understand Huxley's line less as metaphor and more as a literal reality. As Ibert, with his hands covered in blood, explains to the magistrate that Sister Jeanne is not a virgin the crowd watching the proceedings seem duly horrified – they realize what has happened – Ibert has broken her hymen with one of his medieval tools. With plungers, pliers and vials they torture Jeanne until she gives the Baron the name he's looking for: "Grandier." But still the crowd seems to see the Sister as a poor deluded woman, not someone possessed by devils. The prosecutors will have their work cut out for them but they soldier on, producing love letters from various women that amuse the crowd – but Grandier in defense gives a beautiful speech about having kept the letters in case he might need to be reminded later, when he was old, that he had once been loved. As the proceedings draw to a close Grandier gives the sign of the Cross as in a mass and the crown follows his lead. Without a confession from Grandier and the town behind him the prosecution will have to proceed with caution. Fortunately for us the prosecutors – and the Church and the Inquisition generally – left meticulous records of court proceedings, detailing speeches, tortures that were administered, with exact names and dates, so we know in detail exactly what happened during the trial.

Grandier's torture is shown methodically as the process rarely varied – including the shaving of the head, the puncturing of the tongue to see if it bleeds, and the breaking of the legs to make the trip to the scaffold as painful as possible. In one of the few conventional eye-line match cuts in the film Grandier asks for a mirror before his head is shaved and Baron De Laubardemont offers him a metal basin. "Will this do?" he asks in close-up. Grandier briefly looks up at him and they exchange a series of powerful looks as Laubardemont shakes his head as if saying "you poor fool you're done for, just confess and get it over with – make it easy on yourself." Grandier understands his meaning and seems to accept it on some level but he refuses to confess and the tortures continue.

Once the flames surround him Grandier, in a final burst of energy, condemns the town for having turned against him – Russell shows us from his point-of-view the townspeople in the midst of a raucous party, as public burnings often turned into parties when the person at the stake was famous and/or beautiful. It became a circus of sorts and Russell spares no one. Phillipe is there with her new baby as her father extols: "it's not everyday you get to see daddy burn!" A last minute attempt to save Grandier from the flames by garroting him at the stake – paid for by his friends - is prevented at the last minute by a zealous Father Mignon, eager to prove his subservience to the church. Once Grandier is dead the order is given to blow up the walls of Loudun and Russell had the budget to actually blow up his set – the explosions seem to finally cause some of the townspeople to wake up as if from a dream but it is too late – the French army is ready and waiting to move in.

When the King finally makes an appearance in Loudun and sees the catastrophic violence that has been unleashed, the ruinous breakdown of social order, and the collapse of the town's fortified defenses, he seems to barely register the macabre scenes of violence and the sexual orgies taking place before him, and simply urges the townspeople to "have fun" – he understands that Loudun is now his. To bring the point home he offers Father Barre a gold box holding the dried blood of Jesus Christ – a holy relic claimed by various churches and collectors. Barre proceeds to use the box to drive out devils and the nuns all begin to roll on the ground in agony, like vampires suddenly exposed to sunlight. The King, with obvious glee, shows them, with well timed theatricality, that the box is empty and everyone but the incensed Barre starts to laugh hysterically and continue on with the orgies – the fake box was all just part of the fun. The film is a veritable encyclopedia of cinematic transgressions that went the limit, going far beyond other works that were later influenced by Russell's film, without acknowledgement. It is not surprising that the Vatican condemned the film and that it was banned in many countries – unfortunately it was also cut by censors in various places (including England and the USA) to make it palatable for distributors, creating a plethora of versions of the film that create confusion to the present day; Warner Brothers who own the film will not release it in its original uncensored form (as of 2025). A restoration of the excised sequences, taken from various countries, was undertaken in 2004 and released finally with the correct Panavision aspect ratio.

TOURISTS
What remains of Father Grandier after he is burned alive? Baron De Laubardemont collects one of his charred bones – surely the corporeal at its most basic - and then gives the phallic bone to Sister Jeanne as a souvenir. At first horrified, she then appears to be amused by it but there is also a sense of melancholy as her "victory" over Grandier is surely a pyrrhic one. She is also secretly basking in her newfound fame as tourists from Paris flock to Loudun to see for themselves the site of the orgies – another historically

accurate point. But the prosecutor, bemused as always, reminds Jeanne that this fame too shall pass. What are we to make of it? Irony? Disgust? In Redgrave's magnificent tour-de-force performance we see Sister Jeanne accepting her new status with some joy but also with the dawning realization – the horror - of what she has done. Her "lesson in life" comes a bit late in the day for all concerned, including Sister Jeanne herself, but it comes nonetheless – that is tragedy.

Caroline Langhorst's study of *The Devils* explains that Grandier's destruction might be seen as the "figurative and literal deconstruction of manhood."[71] Aside from illustrating how the term "deconstruction," at least in its academic sense, is now meaningless, one is apt to wonder what was "deconstructed" at the end of *The Devils*? Grandier was tortured, his body broken, and then he was set on fire so there would be nothing left but ashes and a few "souvenirs." Surely the point is not that his manhood (or masculinity in general) was destroyed or "deconstructed" but that his horrible death is part of a *consistent and formalized* social system that is understood to be not only "normal" but to provide "justice" at the hands of God's emissaries on earth (a Cardinal and a King). That system of punishment is shown by Russell to be merely a survival tool of the ruling elites, nothing more and nothing less. The Church and the King impose the rule of law, of normalcy, they decide what is real and what is fake, holding the miscreant Grandier in a mechanism of objectification, of domination, made manifest in ceremonies and rituals of power. For the people of Loudun this procedural narrative *is* simply modern life.

What we see in *The Devils* is that the mythical version of things is usually more persuasive, more all encompassing than mere fact – but not more true. Myth is a tale we tell ourselves in order to live, it's a fantasy, and sometimes, as in Loudun, a delusion that helps us to go on, to reaffirm ourselves – especially in times of adversity or great change - to that extent it is indispensible. Unfortunately there is only a small gap between this social identity and brainwashing - it very much depends on the point-of-view. But even powerful myths sometimes give rise to their own de-mythologization, their own destruction as it were, and here in Loudun we can see the fissures, the stress points of Catholic mythology par-excellence. Grandier steps into this fissure assuring not only his death but his necessary annihilation – his *erasure*. Ironically it would be because of Grandier's tragedy that we would remember Loudun at all as the drama/farce that would unfold there seemed like such a highly toxic and concentrated version of what happens everywhere, but under the surface – in Loudun it all came out into the open, like a transparent watch where the mechanism and the source of power are in full view.

THE SEVENTH SEAL

One precursor to Russell's film, that we can briefly examine for further illumination, is Ingmar Bergman's *The Seventh Seal*, particularly the scene where a young "witch" is about to be set of fire so she can be freed of the devil that possesses her. Block (Max von Sydow), the wandering (and wondering) knight interrogates her to find some hard "truths" and comes up empty. The girl is simply luckless and her interrogation has driven her mad – the only insight that she can provide is that there is no insight – the character of Death similarly himself explains to Block: "I have no secrets." At that point Block reaches endgame not only in his game of chess with Death but with his gamble spending years on the Crusades rather than with his family in order to find God. The bet comes up a cropper – the chimera of religious myth evaporates in the realm of the corporeal and the mundane. As Bergman himself poetically put it in an interview, "heaven is empty."[72] Bergman turns the tables on Dryer's *Joan of Arc* for now the saint about to be destroyed by fire in *The Seventh Seal* is merely someone modern, that is, someone who was in the wrong place at the wrong time. In a similar sense the devils in *The Devils* are not spirits possessing hapless nuns and hot priests on the prowl – they are Kings and Cardinals, prosecuting attorneys, clerks, and priests in good standing like Father Mignon. Their destruction of Grandier is something that is purely tactical and politically expedient – a matter of technics. By the Machiavellian code that they live by under other circumstances Grandier might have been an ally and Sister Jeanne the sacrificial victim – such are the rules of the game.

MADELEINE RETURNS

The marriage of Grandier to Madeleine is one of the counts against him in the proceedings that sends him to the stake, and while Madeleine plays a relatively minor role throughout the central part of the film, when she is being interrogated and tortured, off screen, until she confesses she returns at the end, broken in body and perhaps in spirit, as she climbs the rubble of what was once the walls and fortifications of Loudun and leaves the town probably never to return. In such times and places her future looks rather bleak – in Whiting's play at the end she becomes a hard-bitten prostitute, who entertains the tourists who flock to Loudun. This seems like a likely scenario under the conditions of France at that time but Russell leaves that part of the play out making for a more ambiguous down-the-road ending. But of course her return at the very end of the film inevitably reminds us of the earlier scenes in the idyllic natural settings in which she briefly lived as Grandier's wife and her life was beginning a new chapter. The fact that such a moment did not last long does not in any sense render it meaningless; quite the contrary, it is endowed with a great deal of spiritual and emotional weight, and so its meaning is all the more powerful and precious precisely because of its brevity.

At the coda Russell de-saturates the color as Madeleine staggers down a road lined with corpses on wheels suspended atop poles, stretching into the horizon – a warning to non-believers, Protestants, rebels and renegades that Loudun belongs to Catholic France. When Grandier's wife, dressed in rags, walks away from the ruins of Loudun at the end there is no redemptive coda, no compensatory religious platitude waiting in the wings, no metaphor as such - it is simply the end of the road. In Russell's work there is no abdication possible from the tragic and all escape routes, from sentimentality, to irony, to religious epiphany, to academic metaphor, are all fantasy of the lowest order – one simply cannot take them seriously. For Russell, the point of cinema was to produce art that helps us to understand and to face our brief time and place in the world honestly and creatively – this all important latter function is why Russell so often concentrated on artists, poets and dancers – and in this case a priest – creative people are always doing a visionary re-invention of themselves, improvising a life, as beings-present-in-the-world – they are creative with their lives as well as their art.

NUNSPLOITATION

The Devils would inaugurate a series of films that would be so extensive they would eventually create a genre of their own with the wonderful name of "Nunsploitation." These works came from all corners of the globe from Japan (*School of the Holy Beast* (1974) to Germany (*Witches are Violated and Tortured to Death*, 1973). But the countries that took most heartily to "Nunsploitation" were, not surprisingly, Catholic, such as Mexico (*Satanico Pandemonium*, 1975), Italy (*The Sinful Nuns of Saint Valentine*, 1974) and Poland (*Behind Convent Walls*, 1978). There *The Devils* seems to have triggered some latent narrative strand that exploded to the surface and gave free reign to stories and themes long latent but suppressed for years, perhaps centuries, as in some sort of strange re-enactment of *The Devils* itself. But the results in this case were, at worst, bad

B-movies, and at best, with films like *Satanico Pandemonium* and *Behind Convent Walls* the filmmakers were able to explore sexual suppression and madness within their own cultural and historical framework.

HEALTH MILITANT

What we take away from *The Devils* is not so much the excesses, the orgies, or the tortures but the sadness and despair of seeing humans destroy each other needlessly with pathological urgency. Russell got that sentiment better than any other filmmaker and set it down in a film where we witness human urges to destruction that are linked to repression – all that is needed is the right trigger mechanism – from this point-of-view we are all, as a species, kindling just waiting for the right match to strike. In the tragedy as shown by Russell it is the "reasonable" men – Grandier and his friends – who are destroyed and it is the "devils" – Louis, Barre, and his henchmen, who are victorious – it is they who seize the initiative at the right moment and seem to know instinctively when to strike the match. Even more importantly these devils see the chaos and the destruction not as a detriment or a setback but as an opportunity that must be seized before things go back to normal – their "shock doctrine" has a religious component that makes it all the more powerful. But the fact remains that their enterprise is built on the foundations of a profound death wish and sadistic impulses they hardly understand themselves – motivations that Whiting's play and Russell's film make explicit.

As Russell makes clear the only counter to this dark chaos, this exercise in the will-to-power, this collective death wish, is some form of love – not as an abstraction, as we see clearly in the "love" of the King for his people, or the "love" of the Cardinal for "God," but love in the corporeal sense. While humans certainly have the will-to-power they also have a will to health, a will-to-altruism, and a will-to-empathy. As the British neurologist and essayist Oliver Sacks so nicely (and positively) put it: "Health, health militant, is usually the victor."[73] Usually. For Grandier this sense of existing as an animal in nature – a "thinking reed" (Pascal) - eventually came to supersede his religious orthodox training. This took the form of marriage vows that he performed himself and religious services lakeside in the base of mountains that seem to go on forever – Russell's "prayer book." Grandier, his wife, and his town are ultimately destroyed but that one moment – his marriage – is something no one or nothing can take away from them, it is Grandier's and Madeline's small victory in the face of oblivion, and it is also where we may find the core of Russell's faith.

Independence 4: *Mahler* (1974)

Russell, in one of his later interviews looking back on his body of work, said that *Mahler* was the best film he had ever made about an artist[74] – the work centers around the life of Gustav Mahler, the composer and conductor who lived from 1860 to 1911 so managed to witness first hand the greatest changes in human society the world had ever seen, at least according to Virginia Woolf[75] who put the tipping point "sometime in 1910." Mahler's music charts that transition beautifully over ten symphonies (the last unfinished), as well as his complicated personal life that Russell explores thoroughly in this "compressed", two hour tour-de-force. Russell from his book *The Lion Roars*: "My intention was never to produce a factual, day-by-day account of the composer's life...what I've always been after is the spirit of the composer as manifest in his music."[76] What Russell wanted was an examination of the artist through their work and an examination of the work through the life, and he fully achieves that with *Mahler*.

The film is structured as a series of flash-backs with realism, symbolist fantasy, theatrical set-pieces, musical pastiche, poetic asides, and ironic comic interludes, all strung together on a basic narrative line: a single train ride, (which actually occurred) in which the sickly composer, beautifully played by Robert Powell, and his wife, Alma, played by Georgina Hale in a tour de force performance, are returning to Vienna from his time conducting in the United States (1907-1911). Mahler in his absence has become something of a star and because of the press people knew about his delicate health and his train route so fans greet him at each station as they cross Europe toward Austria, in a sense also saying goodbye. Each of these stops serves to trigger a memory, reflection, or dream triggered by a sudden realization that the couple makes along the way, so the puzzle of Mahler's life, despite its complexity, interlocks and comes together beautifully, like one of the maestro's own symphonies. Russell:

> *"I based the film on the rondo form in music where you present the theme and follow it with variations, then return to the theme and so on. My theme was the composer's last train journey before he died. During the journey we flash back to incidents in his life, the variations on the theme as it were. They vary from passion to comedy. Like the scherzos from his symphonies some of the scenes are pretty grotesque, too."[77]*

Russell would borrow this rondo form for his own autobiography written a decade later so it was something that was close to him emotionally and stuck with him.

With cinematography by Dick Bush, who had worked with Russell on *Isadora* and *Savage Messiah*, costumes by his wife Shirley who had worked on many of his best films, and art direction by *Ian Whittaker* who had worked on *Valentino* Russell had a team that he trusted and who understood his working method. Together they made one of Russell's final masterpieces which in some ways is fitting as Mahler himself was arguably the last of the great German/Austrian composers who dominated European music from the age of Bach (1685-1750) onwards – once one gets to the 20th century it is Russian, East European and American composers who primarily dominate while the "Second Viennese School" of Schoenberg, Berg and Webern are something of a niche discipline for academics and enthusiasts of atonality.

Mahler's ingenious credits owe something to the Secessionist work of Klimt and Schiele – Mahler's contemporaries - and constitute a short film of its own making it clear that this story will not be strictly about Mahler but about the relationship of the maestro to his wife Alma - Russell was always fascinated by difficult relationships and marriages and there is plenty of material here to work with. The film begins with a beautiful small cabin/workshop on a lake suddenly catching on fire and immediately being engulfed in flames – scored to Mahler's 3rd symphony. Russell loved dramatic opening shots and he delivers here, setting the pace for the film and acknowledging the symbolist themes that will play out later. In the following shot we see Mahler in a casket with a window screaming as the flames devour him – the title comes up using Fin-de-Siécle typography as Russell dissolves to Anna von Mildenburg (Dana Gillespie) a beautiful opera singer raising her arms as if performing an unknown ritual or sacrifice – then ominously we see Mahler's two small children posing by the lake in their Sunday best. We are suddenly transported to a rocky landscape that looks like the moon, full of holes and crags as Russell's camera pans to a slightly larger than life statue in stone of Mahler's imposing head, resting among the rocks as if it were a natural formation. The head seems to be based on Mahler's death mask. He pans again to a chrysalis of a life size woman desperate to be born – hence we have a man encased in stone who is dead and a woman who is not yet born; it would seem in this case that opposites attract: She sheds her first layer of wooly fabric and we see it is Alma as she crawls, like an animal, naked except for a flimsy elastic jumper, to Mahler's statue and kisses it on the lips.

There were certainly women in the 19th century who had melodramatic lives, there were women who had many marriages and affairs, there were femme fatales, and then there was Alma Mahler. From her first affair as a teenager with the painter Gustav Klimt Alma had affairs with a dizzying array of geniuses of the early 20th century, including Walter Gropius the founder of the Bauhaus. She became the muse of so many geniuses that one forgets that Alma was also a composer herself of some promise, specializing in songs like her compatriot Hugo Wolf, but she was forced to suppress her muse and her creativity on the urgings of Mahler who made it clear he wanted a conventional housewife not a composer – and a competitor - for wife.

It was in his work where Mahler, the socially conservative gentleman with his fastidious suits, and pince-nez glasses, gave way to Mahler the revolutionary. While he is often depicted as being the "transitional figure" between European romanticism and 20th century music that is a very limited programmatic viewpoint as it puts the 20th and 21st centuries as the "natural" endpoint of Mahler's music treating it as "proto-modern." Creating narratives (or bromides posing as narratives) to satisfy the needs of curators, such as the transparently obvious case of MoMA's enthusiasm for formalist abstraction and conceptual art presumably coming from Postimpressionism and Cubism, is invariably a fool's errand. But just as one powerful agent, such as a museum or concert hall can create sophisticated "professional" narratives one can also create lo-fi counter-narratives. For example we might see that 20th century classical music saw a falling off in quality, complexity, and imaginative prowess after Mahler, descending into trite formalist platitudes and stereotypical clichés. Further, we might say that the "baton" of classical music would be taken up, not by Karlheinz Stockhausen or Phillip Glass but by Charlie Parker and John Coltrane – they stole that fire and ran with it into new directions that they themselves could not have foreseen because they (like Mozart) were improvisers not academics. A little later in our lo-fi narrative The Beatles and George Martin started to make electronic music at EMI studios using multi-track analog tape - by then the writing was on the wall for all to see.

Mahler was a radical insurgent (musically speaking) who took a different route to the creation of music. He knew the symphonic work that had come before him inside out and he saw its formidable abundance and intensity, but he also detected a weakness, an opening. For example there had been many pieces of music devoted to the wonders of nature, and so it is with Mahler, but he saw not only the beauties and the expressive dramas of the seasons, etc. – he saw into the dark side, the chaos, the randomness, the grotesqueness, the absurdity, the interconnection of everything, and death as the ultimate goal not only for mortal humans but for physical reality itself. Mahler also put man and his social world back into nature in his capacious symphonic work – and for his contemporaries the results sounded very odd. While Offenbach and Strauss made work that put the social world at the center of their music, their waltzes and operettas were no match for Beethoven's complexity or Mozart's melodic genius. But what would happen if you mixed Offenbach's popular pulse to Beethoven's orchestral complexity, and Mozart's playful counterpoint, and then pushed these to the breaking point? This was Mahler's entry point into the cannon of Western music and the question that occupied him – we may find the answer in his music.

In Mahler symphonies a jaunty folk dance worthy of Rossini interrupts a reverie into the natural world that quotes Beethoven's 2nd symphony; a slightly out of tune military marching band (instructed in the score to play out of tune) plays over a slow classical fugue; a funeral march is juxtaposed, and at times overlaid simultaneously, over a joyous wedding song. Clearly Mahler was a fox who knew many things and wanted to get them all into his work - for him nature and human life was one very complex package than included the social world he had constructed, and the only way for him to get it all into one symphony, aside from making the symphonic form larger and longer, was to use pastiche, digressions, quotes, parody and a complex layering process that his contemporaries found confusing and/or incomprehensible. Mahler was, significantly, one of the first people to call himself a collage artist.[78] Satire, sarcasm, subversion, and parody had not been heard before in symphonies, or at least not overtly. Haydn and Mozart wrote works with humor as part of the package but these were subtly integrated into the whole, becoming part of the classical order. Mahler not only put these elements into his work, he made them insistent, with quicksilver changes of mood, violent virtuosic switch-backs, insistent off-key intrusions, and then, to add insult to injury, he put these things front and center so you could not possibly ignore them; the old guard bristled and, at least initially, rejected his music out of hand.

Mahler found few champions for his work in his own lifetime and he was only able to finance his luxurious lifestyle from his great success as the conductor of the Vienna State Opera House – one of the summits of conducting jobs in Europe, then and now. It was not until the brilliant American composer/conductor (and promoter) Leonard Bernstein championed Mahler's work in the Post-War era, that Mahler's music entered the cannon. Bernstein not only regularly scheduled his symphonies with the New York Philharmonic in the 1960's but he spoke about him in public television lectures that were meant for the general public, educating the masses about the new modern music. It was in that television work that Mahler found a new audience, un-academic, untied to traditional classical music, and therefore more receptive to Mahler's multifaceted work. In this endeavor Bernstein was wholly successful – by the end of the century not only Mahler, but Stravinsky, Bartok, Gershwin and Berg (all Bernstein favorites) were part of the regular concert repertoire, alongside the earlier masters.

Let's follow Russell's rondo structure in that final train ride to Vienna to see what the director has to tell us about Mahler. Gustav wakes up in the train compartment with his wife Alma opposite him and tells her his dream – how she was a chrysalis "struggling to be born." "Finally you've noticed" intones Alma – her barely repressed frustration and bitterness is evident in Georgina Hale's luminous performance as Alma that shifts from her adoring and carefree younger years to an older sarcastic shrew who can barely restrain her contempt and her tears. Clearly Gustav is used to Alma's attitude and he pays it no mind, as long married couples sometimes do. As she leaves to get a magazine Mahler spots a young blonde boy and a middle aged man in a white suit sharing some space in the platform – clearly the man is besotted with the boy; this is a pastiche of Luchino Visconti's *Death in Venice* that transposed Thomas Mann's story to be about Mahler as a repressed homosexual, played by Dirk Bogarde, who finally finds release (of sorts) with a young boy in Venice, but too late, he dies in the Lido while watching the boy swim out to sea. Clearly Russell will have none of it and as Mahler's 5th symphony (used by Visconti) play out Gustav is only bemused. Russell: "His (Bogarde's) characterization had nothing to do with Mahler, who was never decaying, never sorry for himself, never given to dreaming of the past. The whole thing was a bit cheeky on Visconti's part and very lazy – he played the very same theme (adagio from the 5th symphony) in every scene."[79] Russell won't abide laziness and he is true to his word here working hard to get it right - and when he veers from realism, as in introducing Nazi SS guards in a dream sequence, it is clear that Mahler might well have sensed that storm brewing long before it struck, in the same way that he foresaw the atonalities and disharmonies (in every sense) to come, as early as the 7th symphony with its grotesquely abrupt, almost comedic transitions – a provocative challenge to symphonic continuity that sounds more modern today than much contemporary music, in any genre, and puts it to shame.

Mahler feels exhausted and makes Alma draw the blinds so he doesn't have to listen to people's speeches, suffer autograph hounds, or receive bouquets from loving fans along the way. To complicate matters Alma's young, handsome lover Max, an officer in the army, is also on the train, urging her to leave Gustav and get off the train before it reaches Vienna. Max makes it clear that while she may enjoy Mahler's wealth, status, and fame it is him that she is attracted to and wants to be with - we sense that there is some truth in Max's statements. The train ride also pits Alma and Gustav as man and wife in the same compartment as they confront the reasons for their faltering marriage, their dying love, and their need to escape from the shared memories of the death of a child – memories that both bond them and tear them apart. The film also delves into Mahler's dysfunctional family as a child, his conversion to Catholicism, and the solace and rebirth that he found in the natural world – a feeling so powerful that it would lead him to become a lifelong pantheist and hiker – feelings that he expressed fully in his first and third symphonies.

As the train rolls on Mahler is upset by the noise and gets a migraine headache asking Alma if she can find a less noisy compartment. This reminds Alma of when they were young and she was in charge of creating a quiet space so the maestro could call forth his muse. The idyllic hut on the pier of a lake, seen during the credits catching on fire, is seen again with freshly painted wood, as Mahler as a young man is trying to compose but finds the noises from animals and people are making it impossible. Alma, young and clearly in love, wearing a traditional German dress, hushes the cows by removing their bells, she quiets the pan player in typical Alma fashion by kissing him, taking his flute, leaving him nonplussed, and she quiets the people at the nearby inn by giving them large steins of beer – all scored to the exuberant 1st symphony.

Throughout the film Alma wears traditional Austrian folk costumes and Mahler is dressed in non-descript city clothes making his nationality impossible to read – even their clothes (created by Shirley Russell) hint at irreconcilable differences. Exhausted Alma returns to the hut but Mahler is too busy composing to thank her. Mahler as a young man was athletic and Michael Powell gives a strong performance as the egotistical but humanist composer trying to reconcile all of his urges and commitments into a working life – he jumps into the lake without a thought and when he returns Alma has made a scarecrow wearing Mahler's glasses to chide him for his thoughtlessness. Instead of chasing her around the little studio, Mahler, more in keeping with his style, looks despondent and Alma reassures him. In arguably Russell's best romantic set-piece he suddenly picks up his wife in one fell swoop and threatens to drop her in the lake to girlish screams, as they reconcile and kiss – Russell uses reflectors and mirrors to throw the ever shifting light of the lake on to the close-ups of Hale and Powell as they regard each other and kiss, young, grateful to have found each other, and deliriously in the moment.

As the train nears its first stop a large group of fans is waiting, including a brass band. Mahler is distraught and decides to go hide in the bathroom telling Alma that if any speeches are called for she should do it. "What do I tell them?" asks Alma. "Tell them their music gives me the shits!" replies Mahler. "You shouldn't have written so many brass bands into your music" chides Alma. Hiding in the bathroom takes us on an extended flashback to Mahler's boyhood as we see a sign that says *Mahler Wines and Spirits*. Mahler as a ten year old boy (Gary Rich) is coming home to what looks like a Jewish ghetto. He spots his father forcing himself sexually on the local servant girl through a window and Russell – ever the Freudian – shoots the scene through the phallic spokes of a dangerous looking rake. Both Gustav and his brother Otto are musical child prodigies and the family, horrified by Gustav's desire to be a composer, imagine him a wealthy man about town as a keyboard maestro in the manner of Franz Liszt. His father reminds him that the greatest composer of all time, Mozart, is buried in a pauper's grave so he shouldn't even think about composition. He is made to take piano lessons that are expensive but the family makes sacrifices for Gustav's promising future as a famous concert pianist.

The piano teacher Professor Sladky (Otto Diamant) is brutally old fashioned and comically places the coins given to him inside an empty bust of Richard Wagner. Sladky also chides Gustav for wanting to be a composer telling him to keep all that nonsense in his head. After a few lessons Gustav can't take it anymore when he sees a young girl leaving Sladky's studio in tears, and goes off to the woods to swim in the nearby lake. There he finds a group of boys his own age being organized by a young man, Nick (Ronald Pickup) who is constantly playing a country accordion. Russell shoots these scenes as idealized and not happening in "nature" at all but in an arcadia, reminiscent of classical paintings. Nick himself is a stock character from country idylls – he is Papageno in *The Magic Flute* - a happy, benevolent wanderer, usually the friend of the hero. While the boys tease Mahler Nick shows him how to swim and appreciate nature in a more direct way, learning how to identify things and listen to the sounds of nature, which are constant, and overlaid together – never once the same.

Typically Russell is consistently anti-academic and here Mahler gets his first real lesson in being a composer not from the fastidious professor Sladky but from a woodsman who actually lives in nature. As a shorthand for letting us know that these lessons have hit home young Gustav runs into a beautiful white horse on his wonderings in the woods – at first terrified he then befriends the horse and then rides him, quickly mastering the animal and going full gallop. The scene is scored to the finale of the first movement to the 1st symphony as Russell uses flash-cuts, with each image lasting 1/16 of a second – a traditional technique of avant-garde films but hardly ever used in narrative films as it highlights the editing process – here it's a superb use of symbolist poetics to suggest

Mahler's instinctual understanding of nature. When his family finds out that he has been skipping his classes to talk with a woodsman they are furious and his father threatens to beat him. Gustav hides out in the bathroom where the toilet is a hole on a wood bench. His father, in a fit of rage, hits his mother and draws blood. After a few hours pass and the fury subsides Gustav leaves the bathroom, depressed and guilty – full of shame and angry at the world – all feelings that would find their way into his work.

Back on the train which is finally moving again Mahler leaves the toilet but runs into Max waiting for him in his compartment who sarcastically tells him that if he really is the great man that everyone says he is he should leave Alma to him and get a nurse for himself, since his relationship has not worked in years – suggesting that Mahler is impotent. He also reminds Mahler that no great composer has written more than nine symphonies, then asks him: "how's your tenth coming along?" Mahler throws him out as Alma comes in to tell Gustav that she has found someone to change compartments. A beautiful African woman, who is a fan of "Dr. Mahler," dressed in the haute couture of the day, has agreed to change compartments with the couple and Mahler's response to seeing her is "good heavens!" She tells Mahler that she loves his 9th Symphony because it is all about the basic harmony of nature. "You mean the music of the spheres?" asks Mahler. "No, *death*," replies the woman, "death the joker, even death the lover." There is a beautiful close-up of Alma as she closes her eyes in horror. The woman comically explains that she read about it in The New York Times. Mahler contests her appraisal saying she shouldn't believe everything she reads - the symphony is about a lot of things, including the "death of love" he explains. On this Russell cuts to Alma, furious but not saying a word.

In the next flashback we are back at the lakeside hut, Mahler is older now and married with two young daughters, in the garden with some Durer engravings of heaven and hell. Mahler teaches his two children about death and heaven/hell, explaining that spirits or souls become part of God's soul when the body dies but you can't see it. When the girls seem skeptical Mahler illustrates with a microscope and some slides. The slide appears to have nothing on it but once seen through a microscope it is teeming with life – Russell shows a short color documentary segment of a water molecule. On the word "hell" his 6th symphony gets very loud in a sudden major key as we see Durer's highly imaginative engravings of hell as Mahler explains to his girls, while rowing a boat on the lake, that hell is made up and no one is rewarded or punished. "There is nothing then" states one of the girls. Mahler replies that there is one thing: "love." The boat again puts Mahler on water, that he is associated with through the film, most spectacularly as we see him from the back composing his 1st Symphony at the lakeside hut, with the water moving rapidly behind him as if he were on a ship.

In his new compartment Mahler is sarcastically checking for Alma's lovers under the seats —and he is upset that people are always talking to him about death. While trying to lift some luggage he suffers a hear attack — saying the word Beethoven before loosing consciousness. We suddenly enter Mahler's nightmare as we see a white bust of Beethoven with painted eyes as if he were wearing mascara but the setting is a graveyard. Mahler finds himself in a coffin but upright, in the midst of an old musty European cemetery as we might see in a horror film. There is a glass window by his head so we can see his face inside the coffin looking out in terror as Alma, in a black dress is there with Max, dressed in the uniform of a Nazi SS Guard playing the trumpet to Mahler's 6th symphony. Nick is also there, the same age as when Mahler was a boy, sitting casually on a tombstone playing his country accordion. Max and Alma square off as some other SS guards in uniform come in and take the coffin to the crematorium in a processional march that includes some goose stepping that keeps time to Mahler's 6th symphony – an outrageous coup de grâce to Mahler's own funeral as staged by Russell. To top it off Alma gets on top of the coffin and dances a can-can that we can see from Mahler's point of view, looking directly up her dress to her panties as she struts to Maher's symphony as if it were Offenbach's *Orpheus in the Underworld*.

Inside the crematorium the beautiful close-ups of Georgina Hale, looking both despondent and ready-for-action, beautifully display Mahler's own fears and insecurities, as well as Alma's own complex feelings about her husband. Alma performs a "dance of the seven veils" stripping down to her knickers as Max looks on smirking and Mahler looks out in horror from his coffin screaming but we don't hear a word, only his own symphony. The coffin is placed on the rollers that will take it to the flames as Max and Alma push the button to take Mahler to the next world – Alma then continues her seductive dance as the SS men and Max watch, fascinated by Alma, the beautiful femme fatale.

Russell places black and white photomurals of Mahler throughout the interior of the crematorium and Alma dances to those as well, at one point pulling the curtain (literally and figuratively) on Gustav as she cuddles up to Max. There are some beautiful cross-cutting close-ups of Alma and Max winking at each other as this dance of death to Mahler's music continues with Alma doing a seductive stripper dance with purple feathers to an oil painting of Mahler's done in the style of Oskar Kokoshka, a contemporary. She kisses Mahler's death mask reminding us of the kiss earlier during the credits. As Mahler's ashes are brought out we see a pair of eyes still intact looking out from the urn as Mahler wakes up in a sweat.

He explains his dream and the "death of love" to Alma: "I was alive and you didn't take any notice, it was horrible" and Alma agrees – but Russell shoots her in extreme close-up, clearly emotionally distraught, so this "not taking any notice" is something important to her as well, taking us to the next segment: a flashback from Alma's point of view as we see Mahler with a beautiful soprano Anna von Mildenburg, singing one of Alma's songs, with Mahler and the opera singer exchanging lingering, romantic looks, shot by Russell in the traditional Hollywood style using eye-line match cuts. When the song concludes both of them are condescending toward Alma in a way peculiar to art and music academies with Anna calling her song "pretty, but derivative of Zemlinsky." Then they have fun playing the "derivative game" where they trade names of who influenced who, laughing at Alma's expense. Gustav tells Alma to leave composing to the professionals and to be content as a housewife as it is rough to be a composer in the world – "I don't want to see you get hurt, I've seen it too often."

On this line we switch to Mahler's memory of going to visit his good friend and colleague Hugo Wolf in the beautiful grounds of an insane asylum – in effect we are switching gears here going from one memory to another – a rabbit hole of remembrance and point-of-view. Wolf has come to believe that he is Franz Josef, the emperor of Austria and is interviewing Mahler for the job of conductor of the Vienna State Opera – a job that Wolf himself was on the verge of securing before he went mad. Mahler is there with his sister Justine (Angela Down) whom Wolf believes is his wife and he asks them to dance to a waltz which they proceed to do in the wealthy grounds of the asylum, full of topiary mazes and fountains. Wolf as Franz Josef then asks Mahler to pull his pants down, observing that he is circumcised, telling him, with a straight face, that it might be possible to graft another foreskin on but it would probably not fool Cosima Wagner, the head of the classical music world in Germany and Austria – she would simply never allow a Jew to get such a job. Wolf then goes to ponder the problem by sitting on the edge of a fountain, excusing himself as he plunges into the water as attendants come and fetch him by force.

Mahler is then joined by his brother Otto, who along with Justine, and Wolf's brother, discuss the problem of madness - Mahler is reminded that Schumann also went mad so there is a precedent for Hugo's insanity. Mahler visits Wolf in his cell – his friend is naked and filthy but still composing music that has been described by the asylum doctor as rubbish. When he sees his friend he suddenly wipes his ass with his own sheet music sheet, telling Gustav while crying uncontrollably: "this is what the critics think my music is good for!" Mahler holds his mad friend realizing that being an artist, writer, or a composer is, indeed, a dangerous occupation. Mahler consoles him by telling him: "Our time will come." Everyone agrees that what Gustav needs is a regular job that pays well to save his family and himself. Mahler is fortunate that he is not only a genius as a composer but also as a conductor, which is unusual - even more astonishing, everyone knows it. The only thing between him and the top job in Austria is that he is a Jew. This is because the keys to the music world are, as Wolf said, in the hands of Cosima Wagner, the imperious, reactionary, anti-Semitic widow of Richard Wagner, who would never allow a Jew to hold such a position. After Richard's death Cosima actively managed the music world in much of Europe, marginalizing composers such as Mendelssohn, who was Jewish, and promoting others more to her liking. Mahler realizes that Wolf has given him the answer - he must covert to Catholicism lest he end up in the madhouse himself.

Back in Alma's flashback after the song recital Mahler tells her, while clearly thinking of Wolf: "Leave composing to those too stupid to do anything else." He dismisses Alma's work – precious to her - with no thought of what it might mean to her or to his marriage. Alma is destroyed by Mahler's dismissal but shows no sign of it – she merely takes her composition with her as she exits the music room. This is a brilliant observation on Russell's part – showing how people can be utterly devastated and destroyed by something but they somehow manage to internalize it and never show it – but as Freud made clear that festering destruction ultimately wreaks havoc on a person – Alma's insecurity with her future children and relationships with men is in large part probably due to Gustav's rejection of her work.

In the following set-piece by moonlight, shot with a blue filter, Alma takes her composition and places it carefully in a wood pencil case that becomes a coffin of sorts and takes it out to the forest to bury it by a tree. Russell uses an extraordinary long parallel tracking shot through the forest of Alma crying as she finds a suitable place to dig the grave to her own music, and in a sense, also to her muse. Russell then shoots from directly above her looking down as she lies by the grave as if we were seeing her from the point of view of the departing soul of her work, and perhaps even Alma (which means soul) herself.

Since Alma Mahler's death, as one would expect, she has received a thorough re-appraisal due to feminist scholarship that puts her life into a completely different context – no longer a muse, like Picasso's many wives, but creator in her own right whose fire, like Mozart's sister Nannerl, was snuffed out by a patriarchal society that could not see how a woman might be a wife, a sister, a mother, and a composer all at once. As Norman Lebrecht, Mahler's biographer points out, there is no way to know how good Alma might have been as a composer and she tended to push the victim button herself when it suited her in later life, but that is hardly the point, as there is no question of her talent, so we are back to the moment of truth when she buried her own work, and her possible future as a composer, which is what Russell delivers in one of his greatest set-pieces, orchestrated to Mahler's 5th symphony.

Back in the train compartment Mahler is still going on about Wolf exclaiming it is horrible to see something or someone destroyed. Alma agrees: "it's terrible to destroy something that's alive. It changes you." Clearly she is not speaking about Wolf but herself. Mahler tells her that before they reach Vienna she must choose between Max and him and that her only consideration must be love and nothing else as "duty always destroys." This idea takes us to the next flashback. Mahler is back with his poor Jewish family who ask him how he's going to get the job – one family member even puts on a clown mask and wig to work in a Music Hall to make money – as a joke his sister asks Gustav if he plans to marry Cosima Wagner. "Nothing so drastic! I'll become a Catholic!" says Mahler. On the word Catholic the family expresses shock in a cartoonish, burlesque manner with a family member dressed as a clown honking a horn as in a music hall when someone says a crude joke. While the family all find the idea of becoming a Catholic risible they agree that he can, it seems, single handedly pull the whole family out of poverty by this absurd expedient. This leads us to the most controversial part of *Mahler*.

Russell here takes a page from *Dance of the Seven Veils* managing to ridicule both Cosima Wagner's doctrines and Mahler's abject, but necessary rejection of his Judaism, kissing the ring and sealing the deal. Mahler himself was an agnostic/atheist/deist who always shifted his allegiances, wary of being pinned down, micromanaging his "beliefs" depending on circumstances and who was doing the asking, but he was not a strict believer in any sense of the term - Russell has him telling Justine a line straight out of Nietzsche: "God is dead – man is the only god now." Justine doesn't say anything in return but it is clear she has other ideas, but she keeps them to herself – later we see her looking at the various objects of Catholic worship, including reproductions of classical paintings depicting the Bible, with a look of resignation and despair at a world that makes no sense and probably never will. The success of this beautiful wordless scene is due as much to Angela Down's wonderful acting as Mahler's pragmatic sister as to Russell's cutting.

The conversion scene is a brutal set-piece done in the style of a cartoon burlesque musical that begins with silent film cards explaining the action – the title card reads: *The Conversion Starring Cosima Wagner with Gustav Mahler* – of course it is Cosima that gets top billing. Russell seems to relish doing a pastiche of Fritz Lang's *Die Nibelungen* (1924) that turns the fantastical search for love and power into a joke. While this incredible, over the top, set piece starts as a silent film (scored to the 6th symphony) it ends as a musical in the manner of the rough and tumble acrobatics of Gene Kelley and Stanley Donen (scored to Richard Wagner). The scene is also parody of Wagner's *Ring Cycle* as we see Mahler (again in Russell's beloved Lake District) scaling the heights of a great mountain to reach the summit– but first he must pass through various tests "by fire and blood." As in the *Ring* there is a beautiful blonde Aryan woman with a sword – in this case Cosima Wagner (Antonia Ellis) herself in the guise of Brunhilda. She is depicted goose-stepping around in black lipstick, wearing a Prussian military helmet, and a bathing suit with the Catholic cross on her chest and the Nazi Swastika on her back. Clearly Cosima/Brunhilda has an agenda and from the looks of her she is used to getting her way.

Mahler is the aspiring Siegfried to Cosima's Amazonian Queen. Mahler/Siegfried must now kill the dragon, but for the moment he is merely carrying a large Star of David up the mountainside to sacrifice the symbol with an anvil, helpfully provided by Cosima. Once the Star of David has been put to the fire and transformed into a cross Mahler is made to jump through some flaming hoops with a Catholic Cross, which he happily does, and is then given a large sword to kill the dragon in the cave. Despite the fact that in Russell's silent movie parody Mahler looks more like Stan Laurel than Douglas Fairbanks, Gustav pulls off a miracle and slays the dragon winning the admiration of Cosima/Brunhilda, but not before the fire breathing dragon leaves Mahler in blackface like Al Jolson in *The Jazz Singer* – the humiliation of Mahler is nearly complete here as he performs kneeling in the manner of Jolson but clearly the fastidious Mahler is out of his element here.

He is then made to perform the last of his ritual trials: eating a non-kosher pig that he proceeds to do in the style of a television commercial. Once this is accomplished Cosima/Brunhilda is suddenly dressed as a Nazi officer as the music appropriately changes from Mahler's symphony to Wagner's *Ride of the Valkyries*. Mahler's conversion is now complete as he and Cosima sing a song to Wagner's well known music, and jump to the top of an enormous sword with incredible athletic prowess possible only in the world of movies – Mahler's conversion has seemingly turned him from a clumsy intellectual to a Nietzschean superman – earlier Cosima had removed Mahler's glasses with a single lash of her whip certain that once he converted he would no longer need them, and so it proves to be. Mahler/Siegfried is now worthy to lead the Vienna State Opera to triumph, and to show the victory of German art to the masses.

The fire/earth mythological world of Wagner is brought down to size (and to earth) in Russell's absurdist recreation wherein the mythological search for the Ring/Holy Grail is turned into a farce by having Mahler's "test of endurance" include the eating of pork, thereby proving his Catholic faith. The basic core of Wagner's *Ring* mythology – a unification of Greek and Germanic myths – was first put forward in a serious work of art by Goethe in *Faust* (Part 2) that inspired Wagner. In this tedious and overlong work Goethe conjoins the Romantic Medievalism of the Germanic west to Classical Greek myth. Once Faust embodies these two mythologies in a corporeal sense he is ready to marry the most beautiful woman in the history of the world: Helen of Troy. Wagner in *The Ring* employs similar elements and restructures them around a complex web of Aryan myths. Russell, in typical English burlesque style shows the bathetic elements in the "great myths" – from *Faust* to the *Ring* - to be nothing more than silly cliché's with narratives so far removed from people's real lives that they are ridiculous kitsch, phony, and irrelevant. The *Ring* is about getting the ultimate prize, a magic ring that enables the owner to control the world (whatever that means). Mahler might not have the whole world but he at least controls the Austrian musical world after his conversion to Catholicism, a job that would eventually take him to the New World and the directorship of the New York Philharmonic as once the attacks and the anti-Semitism in Austria became too much for him and his family they decided to take the difficult train/boat trip to America. Back in his train carriage, and his final ride home, Mahler tells Alma, "don't do anything out of duty, do it out of love."

Another flashback takes us to the successful Mahler having scored the biggest job in the European music world. He and his sister leave a church where he has officially performed the conversion rite (sans Cosima) with a priest and he shows his sister some Rosary beads that he has received as a gift, holding them up as if they were a key: "The keys to the Vienna State Opera!" He then makes fun of the Catholic liturgy by going to get some champagne to celebrate, intoning "Oh Magnum Mysterium!" In the Catholic liturgy this saying is related to the Christmas Nativity narrative but Mahler uses it to emphasize the "Magnum" of champagne for his upcoming celebration. As he and his sister carry the champagne bottle up to their apartment Mahler opens the door singing but is startled to find his brother Otto lying on the floor – he's committed suicide by shooting himself in the head, and left a note on some music sheets stained with blood: "One less mouth to feed – your second-rate brother." "Never do something out of duty" extols Mahler back in the train compartment.

As they near Vienna there is one more flashback that serves as a bookend to the first that occurred at the lakeside hut but now the Mahler's are older and their marriage is already in turmoil. The children are seen outside in a heavy, windy storm – a Symbolist storm as well as a natural one - as Anna, the opera singer, is there seductively pulling Mahler to her as they finally kiss and clearly enter into a physical relationship. Alma is upset because Gustav has written a song cycle *Songs on the Death of Children* (*Kindertotenlieder*). This fight between the couple is intercut to the illness of both daughters, Anna and Maria, as they succumb to scarlet fever and diphtheria. Anna recovers but after a horrible week-long struggle Maria dies. Alma is there to console her remaining daughter but Mahler is nowhere present. We then see a child's coffin on top of the grand piano in the music room, creating a macabre, gothic, still-life.

Russell suggests here that Mahler's own lack of attention to his family helped to bring about a tragedy – or perhaps this is how Alma sees it. But after this scene and the destruction of her own music and muse we can understand Alma's imperious, ice-cold façade as a mask that she has slowly chiseled over the years to conceal her disappointment and frustration – but at the same time she never stops loving Mahler – we see it all in the beautiful collaboration between Georgina Hale, Robert Powell, and Russell. She asks Gustav if he has ever put her before his music; he replies that all of his music is about her and for her, that she *is* his music. They kiss and reconcile and Max is the one who gets off the train without her.

As they arrive in Vienna Mahler's regular doctor reveals by phone to the train doctor that Mahler is very ill and has only a few weeks to live. The train doctor meets the newly happy couple as they walk through the Vienna station and he wants to tell Mahler the bad news but Gustav, in a fit of ecstatic reverie with his wife, says: "go home doctor, we are going to live forever!" At that instant Russell freezes his frame. Clearly Russell here is pointing not only to Mahler's music (which will live "forever") but to time itself having stopped. We remember that Henri Bergson was a contemporary of Mahler's and his ideas on duration and simultaneity would conclude that eternity might very well be contained in a single segment of time but such segments, while irretrievable as we follow the arrow of time ourselves, are also bound by instinctual forces – a vital impulse within us that can only be understood through experiential first person intuition, not through reason alone. Alma and Gustav, frozen in time/space, (the frozen frame) live forever in their union. As in *The Devils,* for Russell it is love – physical/spiritual/sexual love between people - that creates these precious experiential first person moments that are both inside and outside of time. Despite the bad news delivered by the doctor *Mahler* contains the most unabashedly joyous ending in all of Russell's films, and this is perhaps why it was one of the director's own favorites amongst his works.

Independence 5: *Tommy* (1975)

For a film director who's starting point was an epiphany that happened when he combined the music playing on the radio with the images in his head, being given the project to make a feature film from The Who's *Tommy* was something of a miracle. In interviews Russell called *Tommy* the best opera of the 20th century and while that is hardly much of a complement, since the competition is so meager, it is probably true – all other comers fall short by a good measure. After the genius displays of Handel, Mozart, Puccini and Verdi – all fireworks, drama, hijinks, and even social criticism, the 20th century sputtered out some weak tea (*A Rake's Progress*), some Freudian cold stews that were difficult to ingest (*Pelleas & Mellisande, Lulu*) or operas so boring that only cognoscenti with a religious discipline, or fine art training, could possibly sit through them (*Moses Und Aron, Einstein on the Beach, Nixon in China*). Tommy had something they all lacked: tunes.

Pete Townshend, who wrote the music and lyrics, provided songs that were powerful, melodic, and just like Bizet's *Carmen Tommy* is full of tunes that you *had* to hum or whistle as you went home after the opera. The main problem was that *Tommy* had been, from the start, an opera that you listened to, not one you saw acted out on stage. When the Who performed the whole opera live on stage – as they did in the famous Isle of Wight concert in 1970 - it was primarily Roger Daltrey the lead singer who sang the songs and Townsend who led the way with his *Fender Stratocaster*. Russell had to turn the piece into a drama – what he chose to do was to make a film about a boy who becomes a man and learns to accept his mother. Hardly the stuff of high drama – no *Don Giovanni* or *La Traviata* here - just a British boy who grows up in the postwar era and becomes a man. It's Pete Townshend's story, Daltrey's, as well as Russell's, and for the most part, it works.

Tommy was a two LP set, from 1969 written by Pete Townshend – a work that had, from its release been acknowledged as a masterpiece and a breakthrough for rock n' roll, as much as *Sgt. Pepper* had been two years earlier. It was producer Robert Stigwood - an impresario well known for highly successful translations of contemporary, high energy musicals into rhapsodic films such as *Hair* and *Jesus Christ Superstar* – who chose Russell, got the financing, and approved the casting, giving Russell a good budget and the green light to take the helm on all matters of production.

The Who was a London based rock group that was part of the British Invasion in the 1960's – their music was primarily a fusion of American rhythm and blues and English theatrical music made popular, and contemporary, by groups such as The Kinks and The Beatles. The Who cut their teeth in small clubs but unlike other groups they were, from the start, associated with Pop Art and the Mod movement in England – this Pop aspect led to the group utilizing "auto-destructive art" as a part of their live shows that mimicked performance art or happenings, wherein they violently destroyed their instruments at the end of their shows – a feature of their performance used by Michelangelo Antonioni in *Blow-Up* (1966) where The Yardbirds, a similar but short-lived blues-based British group, pretend to do the same. Unlike the Yardbirds who primarily did blues covers and love songs The Who were the embodiment of adolescent rebellion - raw, unsparing, and loud, anarchic rock 'n' roll – their songs often had an edge of sarcasm (*Substitute*), of complete incomprehension in the face of society (*I Can't Explain*), of disgust in the face of sexual relationships (*Bargain*), of self-hatred (*Behind Blue Eyes*), of being proudly heterosexual without apology (*Squeeze Box*), of mortification at the absurdity of masturbation (*Pictures of Lily*), of coming to understand that everything Townshend wrote was a letter to his generation (*My Generation*). The music took risks and didn't apologize for it. Also unlike other groups Townshend sought from very early on to combine rhythm and lead guitar in his style of playing creating a more theatrical style – so between Townshend's guitar format and the "performance" of auto-destruction there was already at the outset an operatic outline at work – *Tommy* merely brought it to the surface.

Three years earlier The Who had already done a ten minute song titled *A Quick One, While He's Away* (1966) – a sarcastic suite of song fragments, including the call and response known in operas, about a girl who has a short affair while her lover is away but is ultimately forgiven – the album *A Quick One* was a hit and they performed the ten minute suite for the justly famous film *Rock n' Roll Circus* (1968) so one can see a full performance in their heyday shot on film. *A Quick One* opened the door to opera and *Tommy* was the result but the idea was floating around – it being the 1960's. The Pretty Things released *S.F. Sorrow* in 1968, a psychedelic rock opera about a young man and his journey toward learning to trust people but suffering ultimate disillusionment with society. While The Pretty Things take to psychedelia, in the manner of Pink Floyd, and a meandering song structure, to mimic London's Swinging 60's, The Who use a much tighter vocabulary of solid, almost old fashioned, pop songs with strong hooks all strung together to form a simple, coherent story.

Initially *Tommy* was declared to be about Townshend's initiation into the work and teachings of Meher Baba – an Indian "spiritual master" who claimed to be God in human form. He taught that the everyday phenomenal world was an illusion and that one must awaken consciousness to imagination and divinity, becoming one with God, thereby reaching ones full potential as a human being. Subsequently in his memoirs, written many years after the fact, Townshend explained that *Tommy* was also about child abuse, and his own guilt, fame and fortune as a member of The Who in the 1960's.

The plot: Mr. Walker, a British Army captain, goes missing during WWII and is believed dead. His wife gives birth to their son Tommy. Years later Captain Walker returns home to discover that his wife has found a new lover. The lover kills Captain Walker, the father, in front of Tommy causing a lasting trauma. Tommy's new parents coerce Tommy into believing he did not see or hear anything causing the boy to disassociate becoming deaf, dumb and blind to the outside world, coming to rely on his sense of touch and his imagination. A quack claims a quick cure and he is left by his frustrated parents, in short order, to be tortured by his sadistic "cousin Kevin," to be sexually abused by his "uncle Ernie," and to be given hallucinogenic drugs by the "acid queen" as a possible cure. As Tommy grows older he discovers that he can feel vibrations far better than most people and he becomes an expert pinball player, or "pinball wizard." A doctor tells Tommy to look in the mirror and to everyone's surprise Tommy can see his own reflection. After he becomes intoxicated by looking endlessly in the mirror his mother smashes it out of frustration and Tommy is finally set free from his traumatic loss of sight, hearing and speech. He realizes that he has power and starts a religious movement that generates great excitement and fame, eventually becoming a holiday camp or retreat. In the end Tommy's followers reject him and he retreats inward but now with his senses intact and with a newfound knowledge and wonder he seems finally ready to grow up.

Russell follows Townshend's plotline but interjects a prelude and a coda to the film placing the opera in brackets that unify the work and give it a solid structure. By 1975 *Tommy* was already iconic and Russell uses famous guest soloists (Elton John, Tina Turner, Eric Clapton, Jack Nicholson, etc.) to play the various parts while the lead role of Tommy went to Roger Daltrey, the Who's singer. Townshend wrote six new songs and an overture (used also at the end) not on the original album in order to flesh out the story as required by Russell.

It is clear that the director – already an enfant terrible by this point - is channeling the American musicals of the postwar era, as he had with *The Boy Friend* that also existed in an alternate reality of polished sets and exquisite classical order. But here Russell makes some changes – the time frames are WWII, the postwar era and the present – all eras that he knows intimately so he can interject his own memories of the period; secondly he finds the fuel that can propel *Tommy's* over-the-top narrative line: the tension between this "classical order" of the traditional musical and the angry, disenchanted, anarchic energy of rock n' roll. The flat graphic style with saturated colors that Russell and cinematographer Dick Bush developed here, coming from *American Graffiti* and *Grease*, as well as Hollywood Technicolor musicals (*The Bandwagon*) would also influence films in the coming decade and beyond both in high art film (*Drowning by Numbers*) and low (*Xanadu*).

Russell always loved strong, attention grabbing openings that left room for ambiguity, for questions that need to be answered, setting up his films with a prologue of sorts as an entry to the film proper – this is of course a commonplace in music and opera but in films it was something of an oddity and at first the openings of *The Debussy Film*, *Dante's Inferno* and *Bartok* tended to take people by surprise and people would write to the BBC and ask them what it all meant - in *Tommy* Russell delivers one of his best and most emotionally involving openers, no doubt due to the personal nature of his own memories of the blitz during the war. Daltrey himself was born during the air bombing of London in 1944 so it had a resonance as they all grew-up in war-torn post-war Britain.

We begin at the Lake District on a hill overlooking the whole area as Tommy's parents to be, Nora (Ann- Margret) and Captain Walker (Robert Powell), are picnicking atop a mountain and clearly very much in love. In the following scene, also shot in the Lake District, they are making love in a lake by a waterfall – Russell shoots from a medium-long shot with close-ups but keeps it short, avoiding the cliché's associated with waterfall trysts. Townsend in his autobiography, may years after the fact, speaks about the importance of water to him as an element that has an almost religious significance and Russell takes up that idea repeating the water theme throughout the film as a constant motif. As we see Nora and Walker slow-dance in their apartment Russell cuts to a car on fire and we see that the whole side of their flat has been blown away and a child lies dead in the rubble – firemen are desperate to put out the fire as Nora and Walker run outside. Russell shows a whole street that has taken the hit from the rockets and his camera tracks along surveying the damage. Beside a fire truck some women dressed in their underwear come out wearing gas masks, single file, as in a surrealist burlesque show. Despite the theatricality the sequence has the feel of lived reality.

Nora and Walker go to a train station and say goodbye – time seems to have become compressed as it does in memory or trauma. Here Russell mimics the romantic films of the 1940's in the goodbyes and then cuts to a Royal Air force plane with Walker piloting, then to Nora in bed inside a box with a cage to enter and exit – again a historically accurate element from the blitz in which people slept in their beds but inside mini-bunkers made of a wood, like a coffin, but with one side made of wire mesh so they could see, to protect themselves in case the house should collapse on top of them. Walker's picture falls off the nightstand shattering the glass and his plane goes down in flames. As Nora is working along with other women in a munitions factory – like the one in Southampton where Russell lived - she gets the dreaded cable that her husband is missing in action and probably dead. She passes out and the bearings from the munitions fall on top of her, looking like pinballs. A few months later, as the Victory over Germany parades are underway Nora has a son in a hospital to the first song on the album, *Mrs. Walker It's a Boy,* and the opera proper begins.

Townsend and Russell waste no time at Tommy as a four year old goes off to summer camp with his mom to the song *Bernie's Holiday Camp* as Nora meets Frank (Oliver Reed) a Rocker, a greaser, and something of a grifter, who escorts the two to their bungalow but is clearly besotted by the stunning Nora as he teaches her how to swim. At first she's reluctant to start a new relationship but Frank's high spirits and sense of humor win her over and Tommy suddenly has a new father to contend with. Russell shoots Bernie's Holiday Camp using the clean and bright, saturated Technicolor images associated with Disneyland and holiday camps of the period. This sequence also strangely anticipates the work of Wes Anderson, but Mr. Anderson's limited world-view, akin to a child's, is here used ironically so we see the high spirits, and programmatic positivity associated with holiday camps; but thanks to Russell we see beyond the camp, literally and figuratively, to the reality of death and sex – the former in the form of Tommy's father and the latter in the form of Frank and his mom as they start a relationship. Russell is also making the point that these affected, happy color schemes are compensating for the post-war depression and ennui that was then prevalent and did not lift until well into the 1960's. After tucking in Tommy for the night the new couple go off singing "1951 is going to be a very good year…" in a melancholic tone – for those of us who remember the 1950's that hope, along with a gray oppression and gloominess, were ever present and Russell gets it just right.

As they undress for bed Captain Walker makes an unexpected visit to Tommy's room – his face is partially burned from the flaming airplane but otherwise looks exactly the same as in a dream, still wearing his uniform – he just barely touches his son's face then goes to the master bedroom to confront Nora and her new man, Frank. Tommy wakes up and goes to his mother's bedroom. A fight ensues and Captain Walker is killed as Tommy sees the murder and then the ensuing horror as Nora and Frank implore Tommy to forget everything he has seen and heard and never speak a word about it, causing a trauma as Tommy goes deaf, dumb and blind.

In the original version Tommy sees the murder in the mirror and he develops a fascination with mirrors but in Russell's version it gets more complicated – Tommy sees everything before him as a tableau *and* in the mirror he sees himself looking at the murder. It's a critical difference as it takes the film somewhat beyond the limited Freudian/Lacanian reading of the enactment of a mirror stage and a trauma. This is Bruce Fink providing a Lacanian reading of the scene:

> "As a true Oedipal son who loves his mother and hates those who compete with him for affection, Tommy must identify with the stranger (Frank) who carries out the deed he himself has always dreamed of accomplishing. Yet the stranger simultaneously becomes Tommy's new rival. At the very moment at which Tommy's wish for his rival's (Captain Walker) death comes true, punishment is inflected: a new rival is instated in the family triangle...What happens to Tommy's sense of self during the traumatic scene? His self-image which had originally been positive and coherent breaks down. His former sense of self shatters when he is confronted with is parents' powerful new view of him as highly dangerous: he is someone who could, with one false move, one inadvertently uttered word, destroy his whole family forever...Yet the self known as Tommy did see and hear it, and instead of blocking out the incident, he blocks himself out."[80]

While there are obvious truths to Tommy's "blocking himself out" it is also clear that Captain Walker is not in any sense a "rival" – i.e. a father figure who must be "killed" for the affections of the mother - in fact quite the contrary, Walker becomes a god like figure of purity, honor and bravery while Frank, who is by no means a "stranger," is nevertheless rather a poor substitute father because he didn't fight in the war.

Tommy blocks himself out but finds an alternative identity – or to put it in contemporary terms he finds that being deaf, dumb, and blind can be a kind of superpower – he becomes a pinball wizard (a rock star) and makes a fortune for himself and his family. But this superpower is not the ending but the beginning of his "amazing journey" back to selfhood. His treatment of Frank shows that he does not see him as a "rival" – on the contrary Tommy likes Frank and comes to love him and when he dies at the end of the film he carefully takes his hand and places it inside that of his dead mother – he accepts them as a couple, Oedipal sentiments notwithstanding.

To confirm the new family – to the song *Amazing Journey* – all three members are, literally cut from the same cloth, wearing identical 1950's fabric as they go through a set of rides in a fair including bumper cars and a Ferris Wheel which Russell shoots with the same energy and enthusiasm he showed in *Pop Goes the Easel*, where the artists who are the subjects of that film go to a fair and enjoy crashing into each other in bumper cars. Frank shows Tommy how to play a game where he uses a toy machine gun to shoot down airplanes – upsetting Nora who remembers her first husband, a pilot in the war.

Tommy becomes fascinated by the fun house mirror despite the fact that he can't see, and from an extreme close-up of Tommy's eyeball Russell cuts to Captain Walker wearing his uniform with no burns, at the top of the mountain, as we first saw him, holding a glowing ball in front of him that he holds out to Tommy as an offering. From the glowing ball we go to an arcade game of planes being shot down to one plane in the center with Captain Walker nailed to it like a cross. This image, of Walker as Christ, in turn becomes a glowing cross, symbol of Russell's Christian faith that then becomes a ball that opens to reveal two young Tommy's that fuse into one – the dream of a unified personality that Tommy must try to reach. Finally we arrive at a house of mirrors sequence – a house of mirrors that shatters Lacanian theory to bits – as the scene recalls one of Russell's favorite films Orson Welles' *The Lady From Shanghai* (1947). That film is, of course, about the final reckoning for the "Lady" of the title and the destruction of the unstable family unit she has created. Here Tommy dances like a boy possessed – until his mother arrives with Frank. As in Welles the confrontation here is male/female but the roles are very different. Nora is crying and trying to understand, and even Frank is trying to be the decent father as the trio are next seen at a Christmas party presided over (as Russell depicts it) by an angel atop a tree. The family unit is very complicated for Russell and to try to categorize or force it into a Lacanian template is pointless as it is precisely this complexity, this uniqueness that makes it work (or not).

Russell uses snap zooms on Tommy while the kids are trumpeting him, beautifully showing how alone and alienated Tommy is from the party. Ann-Margret shines here as the frustrated mother who sings: "I believe in love but how can men who've never seen light be enlightened?" – a line leveled at Frank – "Tommy doesn't know what day it is, or what Jesus is or what praying is." – sung to Tommy – then as a chorus of all party members: "How can he be saved?" As Tommy takes a little statuette of the Virgin Mary he knocks over a nativity scene, and Russell cuts immediately to a close-up of Tommy as an adult in the form of Roger Daltrey who was then 31.

As the camera pulls back we see that Tommy is at the "Church of Marilyn" with his mother, they are holding hands in a pew where the iconic actress is worshipped as a god. Worshippers bring their sick relatives, as they do to Lourdes, so they might be healed by touching the garment of Marilyn – an enormous statue made from the skirt-raising scene in *The Seven Year Itch* (1955). Presiding over the church functions is Eric Clapton singing *Eyesight to the Blind*, one of the most famous songs from the opera. Clapton's backup band is The Who, wearing monk like robes with a picture of Marilyn behind them as a backdrop. Clapton is also wearing robes with the words "Celluloid Love" printed on it while singing: "You talk about your woman I wish you could see mine – when she starts a lovin' she brings eyesight to the blind." In a hilarious re-imagining of the Catholic liturgy women wearing Marilyn masks carry metal canisters with incense in a mock procession that is visually spectacular – Russell's sense of theatrical spectacle is without parallel here as he both mocks Christianity while simultaneously invoking the Catholic idea of "having no other false gods" thereby affirming Christianity. As the crippled, blind and wheelchair bound acolytes line up to touch the garment of Marilyn it becomes Tommy's turn and he knocks over the six meter statue and it shatters – just as he did with the nativity scene.

In the following set-piece scored to *The Acid Queen*, Frank appears to be running a sleazy bordello on the borders of a run down street presided over by the acid queen (Tina Turner) singing the eponymous song as she introduces Tommy to sex, drugs and rock n' roll. Turner brings her typical energy on overdrive, all fire and fury, to the proceedings as she initiates Tommy in a tableau that Russell shoots in bright saturated reds as if Tommy were suddenly in the opera *Orpheus in the Underworld* – he also shoots extreme close-ups of Frank and Tina Turner using a wide angle lens distorting their faces as in a fun-house mirror seen earlier.

Turner has a syringe with her that looks like it might be meant for a horse as two twin girls prepare a modern looking iron maiden with syringes all around it rather than knives as the twins escort the still blind, deaf and dumb Tommy towards this ritual sacrifice. After Tommy is inside the syringes pull out with blood and then back in. Turner, doubled by superimposition, does a spirited ritualized dance around the Iron Maiden with Tommy locked inside. The Iron Maiden opens and closes in sequence – the first time it is Tommy's father inside; in the second he is covered in fake flowers with Nora at his feet looking to be in the throes of nervous breakdown as she is surrounded by munitions pellets seen earlier; in the final sequence with the Iron Maiden we see a skeleton completely covered in snakes. Frank enters the red room and drags Tommy, unconscious, out as Tina Turner finishes *The Acid Queen*: "If your child ain't all he could be now this girl will put him right. I'll show him what he could be now if you give me one more night."

The following two sequences we see Tommy abused by Cousin Kevin and Uncle Ernie – both are framed by Frank and Nora going out for the evening as a heavily made up Ann-Margaret sings: "Do you think it's alright to leave the boy with…" To which Frank always replies: "Yes, I think it's alllll-right" as he reads the paper indifferent to the situation, but as Russell shows it, when the couple come home early, Frank is aware that Uncle Ernie is a pervert who is abusing Tommy and as a warning he sets his newspaper on fire and throws it at him. Uncle Ernie is played with relish by Keith Moon, the Who's drummer - all boozy, sinister perversity. Just as Uncle Ernie is getting down to business Russell wisely turns out the lights to complete blackness for a full minute so we must imagine the nature of Ernie's abuse.

In arguably the best moment of the original record and the film, scored to *Pinball Wizard*, Tommy discovers that despite his handicap – or more likely because of it – there is something he can do better than just about anybody else – playing pinball. As Frank and Nora zone out to their television while eating and drinking, clearly anesthetizing themselves to the injuries of life, Tommy wanders outside. Suddenly instead of the usual self-conscious sets with saturated lighting and color coordinated wallpaper we are in the midst of an actual junkyard, a graveyard for cars and consumer products, shot in natural daylight – it's a startling cut as Russell seems to be suddenly taking a page from the Kitchen Sink school for one more go-round.

Russell needed to expand this scene – which is the heart of the film – to over 12 minutes so Townsend wrote out an orchestral version of *Pinball Wizard* as a prelude to the actual song, played by Elton John and The Who. Russell then cut up the song and used repeats, again changing Townsend's music to suit his needs. Tommy suddenly gets into serious trouble running into car fenders and tripping on old washing machines and televisions. Since this journey started with television it ends that way with Tommy seen through the broken glass of a discarded television set.

Tommy finds a pinball machine amongst the debris and starts to play, finding his genius. As in *Pop Goes the Easel*, where Russell also enjoyed deploying close-ups of pinball machine graphics, that were similar to Pop Art, set to music, he does so here again but in bright saturated color. Two guards come onto the scene as we see bright red and green lights all over the junkyard, as if the pinball machine had extended itself to the whole of the surrounding area – they see Tommy in the thrall of an ecstatic communion with the machine. In the early morning an ambulance arrives along with Tommy's parents. Nora is worried about his health but Frank sees the score on the machine and the potential for enormous wealth from Tommy's talent as a pinball wizard.

Wealth comes quickly as we see Frank on board a yacht with several young women in bikinis as shipmates – one is serving him champagne while another gives a manicure; Nora also drinks champagne – it seems to be the one thing they have in common now – in an overly large mansion the size of a hotel with a Cadillac convertible parked in front. From these scenes of traditional bourgeois wealth at its finest Russell cuts to Elton John as he looks straight into the camera beginning the finale of *Pinball Wizard*. John's pinball machine has a piano keyboard in front while Tommy plays a traditional machine as they square off. John is also dressed in outrageous glasses – a tradition for him by this point in his live shows – and enormous boots that lift him several meters off the ground and turn him into a cartoon character. Elton sings: "That deaf, dumb and blind kid sure plays a mean pinball! He's a pinball wizard there has to be a twist, a pinball wizard with such a supple wrist. How do you think he does it?" As the song unwinds the crowd cheers a new pinball wizard, Tommy, as Elton takes a fall, literally into the audience as he, or his boots, are carted away, and Tommy is paraded around on the shoulders of his screaming fans.

In the original version this was the song's conclusion but Russell adds a magnificent coda to it and arguably the highlight of the film. Nora, in an immaculate white bedroom, wearing a white jumper, is watching what we have seen, that is, Tommy becoming pinball champ, on television. But it's clear she's been drinking too much champagne and she starts to hear the "see me, feel me, touch me" song overlaid over Tommy on the TV screen. As she changes the channel, mortified, Russell cuts to the TV ad: an incongruous and massive royal dinner party in fancy dress that is also visually all white. The Queen at the head of the table is suddenly served a can of baked beans the she begins to eat as if they were the utmost delicacy. This TV commercial satire takes its cues from an earlier Who album *The Who Sell Out*. That album, their third, from 1967 has on its cover Roger Daltrey bathing in a tub full of Heinz baked beans, with Townsend advertising an oversized deodorant – the album satirized not only consumer culture but local British radio and a host of British norms and traditions.

While there were many extraordinary scenes done in earlier films lampooning consumer culture, from Antonioni's *Zabriskie Point* to Don Levy's *Herostratus,* Russell here joins their exclusive group with a set-piece of pure genius. As Nora dances around the white room, drink in hand, she still sees Tommy imploring: "see me, feel me, touch me." She changes the channel again but now to some contemporary royal types at Ascot dressed to impress watching the horse races and eating chocolates – another advert. Russell here beautifully jump cuts between Nora on the floor trying desperately to change channels, Tommy triumphant as the pinball wizard, and the absurd advert for chocolates that, again features royals.

Ann-Margret does a sexy, almost burlesque style, song of despair – a contradiction in terms that she makes work - running around the room as if wanting to tear her hair out while Russell's camera caresses Ann-Margaret's sumptuous curves as if they were an Arcadian landscape, shooting her from various angles so we get multiple perspectives on her legendary beauty. Further flash cuts takes us to a detergent commercial – with a wealthy couple, the woman wearing a fur coat and the man a tuxedo, improbably doing the wash, as Russell flash cuts from close-ups of Tommy to a washing machine in action.

As the set-piece climaxes Nora throws the bottle of champagne at the television which shatters as soap suds come rushing out filling up the white room. Nora starts to cover herself in suds but just as she is beginning to enjoy the suds, caressing her body in a sexualized dance, the television vomits gallons of chocolate covering the room in brown sludge as Nora gets completely covered in chocolate. Interestingly, a similar scene was staged by the Yugoslav director Dušan Makavejev in his outrageous film *Sweet Movie*, from 1974, where the lead actress Carole Laure, was also immersed in a vat of disgusting looking chocolate. Makavejev's film was a radical but post-Marxist film that was also a satire of capitalist "sweets."

In Russell's version the chocolate is soon followed by the baked beans so the soap, chocolate and beans mix together to form a repulsive consumer product akin to vomit. At one point during her wild ecstatic dance Ann-Margaret grabs a long pillow the length of a sofa and straddles it like an enormous phallus, riding the muck covered pillow through the vomit of consumerism to some sort of ecstasy. Nothing like this had been seen since the explosions at the end of Antonioni's *Zabriskie Point* but in Antonioni's film the television, with the proverbial talking head, is blown up in slow motion, but here the TV is shattered and it vomits up everything that it has promised – the flow of information, sales pitches and propaganda all come out at once in a disgusting liquid form that looks like shit. This vomiting forth is repeated, like a musical motif. It is as if the sheer moral repugnance felt by the culture at large could stand it no longer and had to let go of everything it had been forced fed for years. Like the great abstract expressionist canvases of an earlier generation, the scene offers up its own numbness and disgust as a direct challenge to established order – an order that is overfull of meanings, abstractions, rationales, theories and concepts ad nauseam. This rage embodied in ecstasy (and vice-versa) that Ann-Margaret embodies so beautifully in her dance, is the most ardently anti-capitalist, anti-classical scene in Russell's body of work. At the end the room looks appropriately like a Jackson Pollock painting but made of consumer shit with Nora on the floor semi-conscious – whether she has passed out from orgasmic ecstasy or nausea and disgust is left an open question.

Frank hears some noises and comes into the bedroom drinking whisky directly from a bottle. The bedroom is perfectly clean and white as before with only a broken television with the empty Champagne bottle inside the box, and Nora writhing on the floor. Frank, tipsy himself, can barely make his way to the bed as he barely register his wife, and passes out as we fade to black on one of Russell's greatest achievements.

In a series of highly staged tableaus the family tries for a semblance of what passes for normalcy with the deaf, dumb and blind Tommy at the center of a troubled family. In one scene Nora eats chocolates in bed – perhaps a sign of the victory of consumer culture. In another set-piece the family doctor (Jack Nicholson) in an office that looks strangely like a Victorian parlor, gives Tommy tests that prove that he can hear and see so his problems are purely psychological. In a beautiful and funny series of cross-cuts between the doctor and Nora, they flirt while looking at the camera as Frank watches from the sidelines wearing the clothes of a country squire. Nicholson does an ironic, tongue in cheek performance – as usual for him in this period - but clearly loves singing to Ann-Margaret as Nora in a pas-de-deux that shows off his fine voice.

In *Tommy Can You Hear Me*? we get a duet between Tommy and Nora but only Ann-Margaret sings, first in the Cadillac convertible then in the bedroom – shades of Hamlet and his mother here as Nora becomes hysterical and finally in a fit of exasperated rage she grabs Tommy and shoves him into the mirror and he destroys it falling through to the other side. Russell cuts to Daltrey, surrounded by shards from the mirror, falling through space to a swimming pool and sinking to the bottom. When he reaches the surface he can see, hear and speak – Tommy is healed. Unfortunately the shots of Daltrey in the pool are more "rock-star-in-a-pool" than "Tommy is healed" – Russell cuts to Tommy running through a vast field of flowers in the Lade District, one of Russell's favorite shots that he has repeated in *The Music Lovers* and *Women in Love*, and then running through a war zone in a non-descript, unnamed war, and finally at the beach as Nora climbs up the side of a mountain to reach Tommy.

He wakes up and they look at each other for the first time since he was a child, before the trauma. Russell, in an inspired shot, shoots Nora upside down – the first image Tommy sees of his mother again as he is lying down and she's behind him. It works beautifully as we get a sense of a topsy-turvy world that Tommy must now navigate without a word being spoken. On her upside-down image Russell cuts to various flashbacks from Tommy's memories, including the trauma that he now finally remembers. He tells Nora that he has a "higher path" to follow – a religion of sorts that mixes pinball, rock n' roll, and Eastern spiritualism. He takes all of Nora's extensive jewelry and throws it in the ocean and then baptizes her on the cold waters to his new faith oddly mimicking the Christian baptism, suggesting that Tommy is now undergoing some sort of Messiah complex – not that unusual in the world of rock music surely but odd nonetheless in the world of pinball and traumatized suburban boys.

The headlines from the next day's newspapers make it clear: "Tommy Speaks!" Frank seems to be in charge of the publicity department for Tommy's new enterprise – a moneymaker as Russell always loves depicting newfound wealth, as he did in *The Music Lovers* with Modest, Tchaikovsky's brother, scooping up Rubbles on the streets of Moscow. Nora proudly art directs a photo shoot for the newly famous Tommy posing as The Pinball Wizard standing on top of a large pinball as if it were the globe that he has conquered.

The film's following set piece is a change of gears and where *Tommy* falls apart in some ways as a narrative although this is due more to Townsend's original idea than to Russell's film. The song on the LP is *Sally Simpson*. Sally is an acolyte and believer in the new religion espoused by Tommy. When we first see her as a suburban teenager, she is throwing away a book by the Reverend A.B. Simpson *A Soldier for Jesus* – Simpson was an actual author of countless books on his Christian faith – into a coal fire, having converted. As she approaches a concert stage full of screaming teenagers they are held back by police, as with Beatlemania, while Frank, looking like an SS Trooper for Tommiemania pumps his fist in approval. Finally we see Roger Daltrey on stage in his persona as the front-man for The Who, handling the microphone exactly as he did during Who concerts. It is here that pinball/rock n' roll finally cross not just paths but wires, but the electrical charge is missing. Something goes wrong here and the problem lies as much with the Who themselves as the unsustainable, and finally rather weak, pinball metaphor.

The Who in 1965 was a radical rock group playing in small halls, such as the one depicted in this scene with Sally Simpson, with their Mod, rebels-with-a-cause, auto-destruct, Pop Art credentials intact. Daltrey was the leader and creator of The Who (not Pete Townshend who wrote almost all of their original material) and his working class credentials, as a metal worker, were impeccable. The Who in 1965 was one of many bands making an advanced form of music, in effect, an avant-garde that rejected academic classical music but liberally stole from it whatever they felt they could use; they also took from American Rhythm and Blues, using it as a springboard to something new that had no name – what was it? This is Greil Marcus:

> "*It was a music best suited to anger and frustration, focusing chaos, dramatizing the last days as everyday life, ramming all emotions into the narrow gap between a blank stare and a sardonic grin. The guitarist laid down a line of fire to cover the singer, the rhythm section put both in a pressure drop, and as the response to what was suddenly perceived as the totalitarian freeze of the modern world the music could seem like a version of it. It was also something new under the sun: a new sound.*"[81]

Ten years later by 1975 that sound, at least in terms of The Who, had calcified into an effete, smug and elitist parody of itself, playing to sold out stadiums - by 1975 The Who was a cover band of itself. The musical reaction against this commercialization was called Punk Rock, created in part by Malcolm McLaren and a group called The Sex Pistols who "reinvented the music whole cloth." (Marcus).

With this scene of Daltrey/Tommy playing in a small auditorium for high school kids it's as if The Who want to put Humpty Dumpty back together again and return to their roots playing in little clubs in London, but The Who are too big to fit into the tiny box. The result looks and sounds professional – and there is the problem – a solid business enterprise certainly but it's not rock n' roll – it's not that new sound. Sally Simpson is in the wrong film, she should have been at London's Ricky-Tick club, recreated at Elstree Studios in Borehamwood, listening to The Yardbirds acting as if they were The Who in *Blow-Up*.

While the pinball metaphor seems to work on first glance on further inspection it falls apart. Pinball is a solitary game while music making is fundamentally a communal art that is shared by like-minded fans. With the reciprocal give and take that comes from live performances there is a certain flow, an alchemy created in the interaction of musical performance and audience – by definition it cannot be repeated. Rock n' roll works within those communal alchemical realms that pinball does not know.

As Sally approaches the stage in a state of ecstasy Frank pummels her with his boots and she starts to bleed from a deep gash in her face. As the crowd goes wild Tommy does a bit of crowd surfing while Sally Simpson is carried away by police, unconscious, to a hospital. In an absurd sequence so outrageous that it almost works a priest, in front of an actual stained glass church, marries Sally to Frankenstein. In a matter of seconds Sally is rocking a baby carriage while looking at all of her expensive jewelry – the same jewels that Nora had on earlier and that Tommy threw into the ocean; but Sally looks to have grown bored with the whole thing and yawns uncontrollably while in the middle of a scream-fest, a Tommy concert in full throttle.

Some vignettes of working people, including machine workers (a nod to Daltrey's past) ends with trash-men throwing out yesterday's news (Tommy Speaks!). Clearly Tommy's days as a "Pinball Wizard" are numbered but some street people and bikers in leather start a gang war that is interrupted by Tommy, who arrives by hand glider ("I'm a new vibration – I'm a sensation – I am the new life") and improbably brings the motley crews together in peace and harmony. Never has the dream of "peace and love" from the sixties seemed so absurd, so kitsch-like, no narcissistic, and so pathetic as it does here – Russell turns it into a commercial but clearly no one's buying. Tommy's next stop is a gambling joint with people playing slot machines – once they see Tommy in mid-flight they get converted and start to break dance on the strand.

Tommy's grand suburban house then becomes a Mecca of sorts for people from all walks of life, as Frank and Nora hand out literature to the new flock. Finally so many people come that there is no room for them and Tommy must build a "holiday camp" – a parody of Bernie's Holiday Camp seen earlier. Soon such "holiday camps" are covering the globe with Frank an unlikely CEO and Nora the spokesperson who handles publicity. At one point people who actually are deaf, dumb or blind are coming to the camps to get a cure by touching the garments of Tommy, while Keith Moon plays an enormous organ that instead of pipes has numbers as in a cash machine – another Russell concoction that works very well to show Tommy's decline into yet another programmatic business model.

We're Not Gonna Take It is the culmination of the Tommy Holiday Camp sequence as the new flock rebel against their master, breaking every pinball machine in sight. Russell shoots the revolution as both absurd and violent but Townsend's lyrics hit the mark: "We're not gonna take it anymore, Oh you're so condescending, your call is never ending, we don't want nothin' not a thing from you; your life is trite and jaded, boring and confiscated, if that's your best, your best won't do." Townsend really writes the epitaph for The Who here. Tommy barely escapes with his life hiding underneath some sculptural pinballs but Frank and Nora aren't so lucky. Tommy first finds Nora, dead with her head resting on a destroyed pinball machine, covered in blood, and Tommy reprises the "see me, feel me, touch me" song. Frank is lying dead alongside her and Tommy intertwines their hands so at least they are together at the end.

As he escapes his holiday camp, now in flames, he goes toward the sea. Here Russell takes over the film and adds his own significant coda. As Tommy reaches the ocean the waters change and suddenly he is in a lake with a waterfall, the same place where Nora and Captain Walker made love and conceived Tommy, who now revives himself in the waters, cleansing himself of "Tommy the Messiah." He then climbs the mountain we saw earlier that his father had descended and as he reaches the summit the music, written especially for the film by Townsend, builds to a crescendo as Tommy is now ready to take his father's place and to create his own family, and make his own way in the world.

This coda turns *Tommy* the opera on its head. For Pete Townshend the family is not only the place of trauma it is the cause of it – the family is something one needs to escape from, a place of mediocrity and kitsch as well as trauma. For Russell the family is the place of redemption and healing, it is a fragile and precious link in the chain of being that stretches back to pre-history and stretches forward to the unknown. It would appear that there is a conflict here but Russell's is a Whitmanesque vision of the world, that is, it contains multitudes including its own opposite – Russell brackets his film within the warm and sacred hearth of sex and procreation – leading to the formation of a family – that is then shattered by WWII and remade by Tommy at the end as he finds that link to his father enabling him to forge his own way forward.

The opera as a piece of music, released by The Who in 1969, could certainly easily play out for its duration because one is left to ones own imagination. But in the film the episodic tableaus insistently push forward a highly structured narrative that at times turns tedious – even the vitality of the "angry rock 'n roll energy" quickly becomes programmatic and shrill. Nevertheless the great music by The Who, already well known to fans, and the sheer bluster, imaginative set-pieces, and high energy of the film propelled *Tommy* to be a financial and critical success. It also paved the way to MTV nearly a decade later, the video format that would completely revolutionize the music industry and turn the short, poetic film into a populist form.

Later musicals such as *Chicago, Rent, Moulin Rouge* and *Mamma Mia!* are unthinkable without *Tommy*. Despite its false steps, and its slides into kitsch, Russell consistently takes chances no one else would dare to take and he makes most of it work, even if some parts are greater than the whole. In Russell's version of *Tommy* the history of trauma, of the family, as well as History (WWII) itself, is remade and unmade every day. Russell's film posits that unless we recognize our sense of self and seize upon it as ours, name it and claim it, our future is bound be confused and impoverished – we will always be playing someone else's tune never our own. *Tommy* successfully claims that turf of self-discovery as an opera and as a film.

Independence 6: *Gothic* (1986)

Gothic marks another return to form for Russell as the material was ready made for his interests and temperament. The film is a fictionalized retelling of the poet Percy Shelley's and his wife Mary's visit to Lord Byron at his *Villa Diodati* in the summer of 1816 – a beautiful mansion in the style of a French chateau located by Lake Geneva. It concerns one night in particular – June 16 - in which Byron invites not only the Shelley's but also Claire Claremont (Mary Shelley's stepsister and Byron's lover) and Dr. John Polidori (Byron's friend/doctor) to his estate and then challenges them (and himself) to write a horror story. The weather was obliging as volcanic ash clouds unexpectedly blocked out the sun that summer and created heavy electrical storms and cool weather. The event eventually produced Mary Shelley's *Frankenstein* as well as Polidori's *The Vampyre*, to be remade later by Bram Stoker into *Dracula*. The most famous literary party in history deserves not a plaque or a monument in a museum but a living work of art and Russell is up to the task.

The Victorian era tended to at first despise the Romantic poets vilifying them in print but once their status as great British poets was established and they were no longer a threat, that is, once they were dead, the same Victorians whitewashed the poets and their liaisons – dangerous and otherwise - as merely eccentric geniuses with a flair for self-promotion. What made them so dangerous in their time to the status quo was their politics, which tended toward anti-authoritarian, anti clerical, and proto feminist. Another sticking point was their poetry, that ignored the traditional subject of poets (Greek myths, historical epics, biblical stories, etc.) but concentrated instead on everyday matters and concerns, contemporary reality and news events, and even the ephemeral and the quotidian, using everyday speech and colloquialisms that, at the time, never found their way into print and so were considered shocking. Poets then were supposed to stick to academic, esoteric subjects but the work of Wordsworth, Shelley, Byron and Keats opened the doors and windows of Victorian society to the real world as they found it – not everyone was pleased.

The legends that surround that meeting are so famous, magnetic and theatrical that several books have been written and films have been made about it. With a literate script by Stephen Volk that predated Russell's entry into the production, beautiful high contrast color cinematography by Mike Southon, that mimicked the romantic paintings of Fuseli and Bocklin, great young actors ready to seize the moment, and music by Thomas Dolby, bringing in his first film score, Russell had a solid team together.

At the *Villa Diodati* the Shelley's and Claire meet Byron's physician friend Dr. John Polidori, who feels himself to be a bit of a third wheel in the midst of Lord Byron, considered then one of the most brilliant and controversial poets of his time and one of the most famous people on earth, and Percy Shelley, who at age 24 was already a published poet and a media star, in the manner of Franz Liszt. The general public at that time had a passionate interest in poetry in a similar way to today's emotional investment in pop music – unlike today poets they felt the push and pull not only of their peers and the academic milieu but of the general public.

When we first see Percy he is being chased by groupies who are tearing off his clothes – this is based on actual events as souvenirs of hair or bits of clothing, not only from Shelley but other poets, were collected by fans - Mary saves him and brings him into the mansion rented out by Byron. Russell smartly used a real location – *Gaddesden Place* a grand Palladian mansion in Hertfordshire, England, rather than construct a set. While the real *Villa Diodati* was a relatively modest French style country chateau Russell opted for architectural overstatement, no doubt illustrating Byron's ego and his need for drama.

Russell cleverly covered over the modern parts of the building with sheets and added romantic paintings of the period, including Henry Fuseli's *The Nightmare* (1781) that depicts a goblin figure atop a sleeping or dead woman on a bed, arms and luxuriant hair falling off the mattress to the floor. This is one of the classic images from the era that also served as the poster for the film. This makes a great deal of historical sense as Fuseli as a young man was the lover of Mary Wollstonecraft, Mary Shelley's mother.[82] The woman's awkward position in the bed was used by Mary to describe Victor Frankenstein's bride after she was brutally killed by the monster on her wedding night in her novel *Frankenstein* so Mary was intimately familiar with the painting.[83]

While getting acquainted the guests and Byron play a game of hide-and-seek – a common pastime for the well-to-do of the period. Later in an enormous room with beautiful windows the two couples are indulging in an orgy but Russell shows them only semi-naked and grouped together in a tableau as seen in the neoclassical paintings from the period. Later in the parlor Polidori joins them and Byron gives everyone laudanum to drink but Mary declines. He then shows his guests *Phantasmagoria*, a book of horror stories, and asks his guests to read small excerpts out loud to get a taste of the material. Reading out loud during a get together was another commonplace of the time in which many people excelled as it was the one social area where mimicry, sarcasm, and theatrical posturing were not only allowed but encouraged. This reading inspires them to hold a séance gathered around a human skull during which Claire has what appears to be an epileptic seizure but Mary calls them "horrors" that would occur during their childhood with beds inexplicably shaking and doors slamming shut by themselves.

Percy goes to investigate noises in the night and discovers a grotesque creature in the barn just outside the house that seems to be excreting a material that looks like semen - meanwhile Mary speaks to Byron in the billiard room, confronting him about his intentions with Claire, revealing that she is pregnant with his child. Byron shows little interest and he casually suggests she have an abortion provided for by Polidori – they argue resulting in a physical confrontation in which Byron violently kisses Mary – clearly trying his best to emotionally rape her and scare her out of her wits but Mary holds firm showing that even at an early age – she was 18 when she met Byron – she was strong willed and had a mind of her own. It would be at the villa where she would discover her own muse and prove herself to be the equal of Byron and Shelley.

Later Byron performs oral sex on Claire but his face immediately after appears covered in blood like a vampire. Percy begins to suffer paranoid fantasies, claiming to smell an over powering scent of decay and death that terrifies him – he begins to suffer a panic attack. Mary hears a noise in the staircase and feels blood dripping on her – she looks up and sees Polidori leaning over the banister clutching a bleeding wound on his neck, claiming to have been bitten by a vampire in his room but Byron accuses him of self-inflicting the wounds – something he has done already to his hand by pounding it against a nail. Percy starts raving that the group collectively gave birth to something during the séance, manifesting fears that they can no longer control. Polidori attempts suicide by drinking cyanide but is stopped by Byron.

Mary is horrified by the hallucinations everyone seems to be having – perhaps due to the laudanum that everyone but her has been drinking - and attempts to flee the house inadvertently crashing through a glass door, passing out. Russell shoots the scene quoting Cocteau's *Blood of a Poet* but the scene has its own fierce materiality. Percy infers that the presence haunting them is feeding off their fear. During another unsuccessful suicide attempt, this time by hanging, Polidori witnesses a figure resembling one of the four horsemen of the apocalypse, leaving the barn – this was a popular depiction at the time for death. Percy and Byron attempt to recreate the séance in order to banish their creation. Mary questions the metaphysical events and whether something can be destroyed after it has been created – it seems to her impossible. The men disagree and tell her that trough sheer force of will they can destroy the demon and return to normal. We see here Mary's mind already constructing the arguments used in *Frankenstein*.

In the basement they all discover Claire nude, covered in mud and looking as if she might have gone mad – she has suffered a miscarriage. They go ahead with the séance but in the middle of it Mary crushes the skull destroying it – she then attempts to kill Byron with a bone shard. Percy stops her and he proceeds to kiss Byron passionately on the lips – a retort of sorts to Byron's earlier kissing of Mary. Mary tries to flee the house weeping but suddenly finds herself in a maze of doors and rooms that look nothing like the house we have come to know. Russell at this point shifts to studio sets that are designed like a maze with no way out. She starts to hallucinate and in a series of flash-forwards sees her son, William, on his deathbed and then in a coffin; she looks on helplessly as Percy drowns in a lake; later his body is burned in a sacrificial bonfire. She attempts to kill herself by jumping from a balcony but is stopped by Percy. Mary awakens the next morning and everyone is refreshed and well, having breakfast in the garden by a beautiful tree, enjoying their tea and a glorious summer day.

In the midst of the breakfast Russell jump cuts to the contemporary era as tourists visit the Villa and take pictures – the picnic area is now empty but the tree is still there. A voiceover informs us that Mary's son William died three years after that night followed by Percy's drowning six years later – Byron would die two years after him in Greece, and Polidori shortly after - finally successfully committing suicide in London. Before his suicide Polidori published *The Vampyre* – a story based on his homosexuality, and fascination/repulsion with Byron and vampires. Mary Shelley published *Frankenstein* in January of 1818 two years after that fateful night. The film ends with a shot of the lake as Russell flash pans down and we see a dead baby, eyes closed, floating just under the water.

While the film indulges in some horror film mannerisms Russell sticks to the script and many of the visuals are incongruous but inspired. He uses elaborate, stunning, tableaus in still shots, and psychologically powerful panning shots of the enormous rooms – here Luchino Visconti meets Henry James but unlike these maestros Russell doesn't linger on his aesthetic prowess. Cinematographer Mike Southon also uses deep focus and vertical flash-pans throughout the film, taking full advantage of the many floors and balconies of the Palladian mansion. These vertical flash-pans are either used instead of cuts or, in more memorable moments they are used to create a new meaning. For example when the guests are running through the house terrified and the music is reaching a crescendo, Russell cuts to an outdoor fountain seen from above, empty of water but with a large fish incongruously flapping around dying; he then flash-pans up to the house with the guests running and screaming. Nature (the fish) in its death throes seems to have the house by the throat – and all Russell needed to create that moment was a 3 second shot. That single short take acts like a trigger mechanism - once he has it he can then use the house symbolically with dreams, nightmares, and waking life juxtaposed in rapid cuts that point toward Mary Shelley's interior life.

At first Mary is the only person seemingly not under the influence of laudanum but as the film proceeds we see only her hallucinations – a phantasmagoria that seemingly requires no drugs. Since the mansion houses a menagerie full of animals including goats and large snakes their presence is both natural and nightmarish – the two at a certain point meld into one – as it must have been for the writers involved that night. Most important of all Russell has great respect for these poets and he is up to the challenge of getting into the mind of Mary Shelley.

The screenplay gives prominence to the Shelley's as they are the outsiders who come to visit and so we see things, from the first, through their eyes. But it is clear from the start that Percy is already addicted to various drugs and off in his own world. During a thunderstorm when everyone runs for cover Percy gets naked and goes up to the roof to experience the electrical storm with rain and wind howling; in effect he is looking for an ecstatic experience, whatever the cost. Even Byron balks at the risk and forces Percy back into the house. Julian Sands manages to transform himself into Shelley giving an immersive performance, as one feels his desperation to make contact with natural forces that are beyond his reason, or his control. Gabrielle Byrne's Byron is by turns morose and predatory, self-loathing and monomaniacal, extroverted and withdrawn, laconic and ruthless – able to turn on anyone at anytime without rhyme or reason; this is exactly as he was portrayed in the writing of the time. People were fascinated and terrified of Byron and from Russell's depiction of him we can easily see why.

Russell and Volk wisely leave out much of the prosaic realities that befuddled the fabled Byron right up to the end when he died from fever due to Malaria and the bleeding from leeches that was then considered a cure, at the age of 36 in Greece. When Russell shows him terrified of leeches, seeing them in a pot of food that Polidori has prepared as a joke, he goes into hysterics with good reason. There are several moments where characters "see" the fate that awaits them and react instinctively as if someone were walking over their grave. So much of the film centers around death, the supernatural, and the creation of what is arguably one of the greatest novels ever written – moreover a work that gets more prescient with every passing year.

Russell seems to start out his film giving everyone equal time but in that group of people it was Byron and Percy who where the superstars, Polidori and Claire were friends/

lovers and Mary was, in real life, only the young mistress of Percy as the rash poet had married young and was still in the midst of a divorce so he could marry Mary. Her only claim to fame was that she was the daughter of Mary Wollstonecraft, the philosopher and feminist writer, and William Godwin the respected novelist and journalist.

Natasha Richardson gives a superb performance starting the film as a young, unsure debutante, barely audible in her speech; but very quickly Mary finds her footing, even challenging the great Lord Byron face to face, and shaking some sense into Percy as she locates the cradle of her own ideas about creation, destruction, and evil. By the end of the film she is unequivocally at the center of the storm - rock solid - with her terrors not necessarily conquered but acknowledged and accepted. Being an artist of course this is not where it ends but where it begins.

As shown by Russell and Volk Mary Shelley becomes the writer of *Frankenstein* that very evening, in that meeting of great minds, not only by bouncing around some ideas but by defending herself – when she says "once you've created it you can't get rid of it!" she knows she's right and that she's on to something. Being an artist she pursues that hunch to where it leads, which is *Frankenstein*. Russell and Volk also suggest – particularly in the film's final shot of a dead baby floating in the waters of a lake - that it was the death of her infant son that instigated the famous novel.

While we cannot know the origins of the initial spark for *Frankenstein* – it is possible that Mary herself did not know - what is certain is that, like many women of the 19th century she was very familiar with death. Death was a constant presence for her beginning with her own famous mother who died giving birth to Mary. The Shelley's were only able to finally marry after Percy's wife, Harriet, committed suicide by drowning herself in London's Serpentine Lake. There was also the death her two children, Clara and William, who died separately in Italy where the Shelley's had gone to see if the warm clean air could restore Percy's health – it didn't and he drowned in a storm while sailing in Northern Italy. One of the most painful deaths to bear was that of her older sister Fanny, who also inexplicably killed herself in a hotel room – Fanny may have harbored feelings for Percy as well and so the guilt must have been enormous from all fronts. When Mary has the monster say "I am alone and miserable. Only someone as ugly as I am could love me" she may very well have taken it from personal experience with her sister.

Something important that the film does not mention, and that even some biographers underplay, is that Mary Shelley was a political radical (like her mother) all of her life and that this quality was also crucially responsible for *Frankenstein*. Russell does show Mary's gutsy independent streak and as the film progresses we see her power as a woman come into its own. But the foundations for *Frankenstein* are to be found not only in that independent streak but the radical politics that were a part of it - let's see how.

Mary, like her mother, believed that cooperation, empathy and sympathy, particularly as practiced by women in the family unit, were the ways to reform civil society. She was a feminist in a different way from our more limited sexual/identity politics – what Mary Wollstonecraft wanted was not simply correct pronouns or even equal rights and equal pay under the law but a fundamental re-structuring of civil society itself. The primary problem was, as they saw it, that patriarchy was not only unsuited to human happiness (for men and women) but that it was doomed to self-destruction.

Both Mary Shelley and her mother saw patriarchal culture as geared toward competition, alienation, nihilism, egoism, and objectification (of everything including mankind itself) – a state of affairs that could only conclude with self-annihilation for the species as a whole. In essence this is the predicament of *Frankenstein*. The romantic individualists (such as Victor Frankenstein) that Mary saw in her own time were not only problematic (as companions) but self-destructive - in a sense they manage to anticipate Friedrich Nietzsche's Übermensch or "superman" who creates his own meaning and values outside of traditional morality, shared values or ethical principles –for Nietzsche once God is dead man himself becomes the only god. Mary Wollstonecraft on the other hand wanted to create a cohesive, feminist, social order based on care, altruism, love, and a sense of binding common human interests, based principally around child rearing and food/wealth distribution. It should go without saying that the ideas of both Mary Wollstonecraft and her daughter are as radical today as they were in the 19th century.

The philosophy of Mary Shelley also went completely against the Romantic ethos of the time (personified by Byron and her husband Shelley) promoting individuality, heroism, reason, and a hardened sense of will-to-power – ideas prized not only by her husband Percy but also her father William, and the great majority of Enlightenment thinkers. These Romantic ideas of having not only agency but also a will-to-power that is godlike were very seductive, then and now. When Ayn Rand in the early 20th century wrote: "Man – every man – is an end in himself" she might have beenquoting Lord Byron, Percy Shelley, or William Wollstonecraft.

Byron himself was perhaps the ultimate Romantic individualist of the group of poets, simultaneously scorning the common herd *and* refusing to submit to the code of his aristocratic class which he held in contempt – his great theme (in his masterpiece *Don Juan*) was *absolute* freedom, whatever the cost – that meant of course not only a personal cost to him but the damage done to others, such as women who found themselves emotionally devastated or pregnant – for Byron it was all collateral damage on the way to self-realization and the fulfillment of his genius. It should not surprise us that for young people of the period, not only in England but Europe, particularly France, Byron became something of a cult figure that was emulated in everything from his dress to his ethics to his playboy lifestyle. But Russell and Volk smartly see through the dark narcissism and desperate solipsism of Byron, making him and Mary antagonists early on – as if they sensed instinctively that they were enemies.

Frankenstein is, after all, about a scientist named Victor (as in victory) who is a "pure individualist," a "rational" man, a believer in science and progress, determined to find the truth of creation whatever the cost - he is confident that he can, eventually, achieve a mastery over nature, bending it to his will, or perhaps even supplanting it. He in fact does find the truth of creation and thus manages in the process to destroy not only himself but everyone he loves. When Mary has Victor Frankenstein say: "Once you've created it you can't get rid of it!" Mary here is talking about monsters from the Id as well as those created by scientists in a lab. In *Frankenstein* Victor, the ersatz Deus Invictus realizes at the end, as he searches for his creation on the frozen wastes of the North Pole, that the "sleep of reason produces monsters" – and that his life is shattered beyond hope - but too late. For Mary of course, the wasteland of ice where we leave Victor at the end of *Frankenstein* is emotional as well as literal – Victor will die alone frozen, preserved forever in his loneliness, an ironic monument of sorts to Nietzsche's superman.

Mary faced up to Byron and his age of Romantic heroism and had the courage of her convictions – she saw the weakness in their beautiful arguments for "individualism" and "freedom" and she stood up to them and created her own anti-Romantic fable that was at least every bit is as good as theirs. That famous evening as Byron's guest she found her voice as the writer of *Frankenstein*, a book that continues to haunt us to this day – and well it should for we still carry the baggage of Romanticism with us whether we care for their aesthetics or not. Russell's film is not only a wonderful tribute to those writers who came together one fateful summer night to write some scary stories but a work of art itself, borrowing from Fuseli and other painters but finding its own clear voice – not perfect but a *living* thing.

G

Hollywood Detour: Neo-Musicals, Neo-Noir, and Neo-Realism

THE BOY FRIEND (1971)

The Boy Friend started production ten days after Russell wrapped up his final cut of *The Devils*. This is Russell from a *Films and Filming* interview: "I never want to do a violent, disturbing film like *The Devils* again. That's why I did *The Boy Friend*. It's pure escapism and fun. And Twiggy became a kind of rejuvenating force for me."[84] The original musical production of *The Boy Friend* had been a project that had been gathering dust at MGM for years as no one could figure out how to turn the highly successful British stage musical of the same name (from 1953) by Sandy Wilson into a film without incurring production overruns; Wilson was doing a pastiche/parody of the Busby Berkley musicals of the 1920's that featured many dancers in costumes with elaborate and enormous sets. The original musical had run for just over five years in London and had made a star of the lead Julie Andrews.

MGM and EMI finally proposed a budget of 1/2 million Pounds with Russell to helm the film, to be shot in London based studios, using unknown actors in the leads that would bring down costs. Russell had used novice actors in his tenure at the BBC – most spectacularly James Lloyd, the painter, playing Henri Rousseau in *Always on Sunday*. Russell and his wife Shirley were friends of the model Twiggy and they had been searching for something they could work on together for years - *The Boy Friend* seemed to hold out some promise. NJ Stevenson:

> "Twiggy was already friends with Ken and Shirley Russell, to whom she had been introduced by Paul McCartney in 1967 when discussing an earlier shelved film deal – an adaptation of William Faulkner's 1927 fairy story *The Wishing Tree* – and she had mischievously been an extra in a scene in *The Devils* disguised by Shirley as a male courtier. She visited the family regularly for cinema nights... to watch Busby Berkeley movies and films by Mamoulian and Fred and Ginger movies."[85]

In her autobiography Twiggy explained that the "dancing nearly killed me" and while they had problems during production she and the Russell's remained friends.[86] The male lead went to Christopher Gable who found the "relentlessly cheery" aspect of the piece difficult.[87]

Susan Sontag in her *Notes on Camp* (1964) describes camp as a sensibility that emphasizes or revels in artifice, stylization, irony, playfulness, theatricalization and exaggeration rather than content, which is either relegated to secondary status or used ironically. Camp by definition (Sontag's definition) is a-political and a-historical since it views everything, even the earth itself, in purely aesthetic terms. By that definition *The Boy Friend* is camp.

To bring the film into the present moment Russell introduces British class tensions to create drama, hints of lesbianism to bring out a more modern sensibility, and bawdy physical comedy to alleviate the anachronistic plot. Russell significantly develops the character of the film producer from Hollywood who is there to see (and imagine) what *The Boy Friend* might look like as a film – this leads to some sharp comparisons of film and stage craft in which theater is seen as hopelessly bound by the rules of gravity and physical limitations while cinema is free of gravitational forces and the all encompassing arrow of time. The contrasts between the actual regional production of the musical and the producer's overblown imagination of the same work allow Russell a certain self-reflexivity that is also very contemporary.

Russell uses the iconography and style of Hollywood from *Flying Down to Rio* (1933) to *Footlight Parade* (1933) and from *42nd Street* (1933) to *Broadway Melody of 1940* (1940). He also took a page from the class divisions within a love story typical of the Astaire Rogers couplings throughout their heyday in the 1930's. Rediscovering old cinema was already by 1971 part of the lexicon of retro and *The Boy Friend* fits easily within the scope of that category – be it avant-garde such as Kenneth Anger's *Puce Moment* (1949) or based in Hollywood such as *Harlow* (1965) – two films that, despite the vast gulf that separates them, share a fascination with the aesthetic cues of the 1920's. But Russell's film did something new – in contrast to earlier work it put the whole of its content into quotation marks so the film exists as a post-modern contemporary work that is both critical and adulatory at the same time. The past, specifically the 1920's, is seen through the filters of camp, artifice, exaggeration and nostalgia that becomes an immersive experience with a wealth of references for cognoscenti. The "slippage" (Pam Cook) between time periods allows the imagination to wander freely from the period to the present moment and back with ease. "Authenticity" itself is placed in quotation marks.

As Sontag recognized in her famous essay, there is but a short step between camp and aestheticism, kitsch, and works that are artificial, affected and arch. Russell, with 30 great dancers at his disposal, and a top team of production and costume designers nevertheless becomes mired in a self-consciously hackneyed plot that might have made even Cecil B. De Mille squeamish. The plot becomes the line on which to hang all of the beautiful clothes and sets – and Twiggy's extraordinary debut as an actress - but ultimately it is also a line than entangles the film and throttles it. The film, as the lead actor Christopher Gable explained, is relentlessly cheerful to the point that the actors' faces seem forced into a painful rictus.

But the work is also a beautiful articulation of set design and wardrobe, which is where we may locate the real interest here, along with the acting of the leads. N.J. Stevenson articulates the undertow of the film's peculiar visual power:

> "Ken Russell's film is a defining moment in the historical dialogue between nostalgia, film and fashion that became ubiquitous by the mid-1960's: a style which looked backwards to move forwards. This 'nostalgia mode' began as an anti-fashion in the 1960's, becoming prevalent in popular culture by the mid-1970's."[88]

When Shirley Russell designed the look of the film in storyboards she used a mixture of original vintage pieces from her own extensive collection of clothes and costumes specifically made for the film. Often costumes would be made to order and be ready (from a London costumier) the following day.[89] This retro aspect of the sets and costumes is important if we are to understand the use of irony in *The Boy Friend*.

Stevenson explains the birth of the antique shop and its meaning:

> "At a time when second-hand goods were still very much tainted with the stigma of poverty, a small number of radicals instigated new systems of exchange of original clothing in the 1960's. In London, these numbered among them... the Chelsea boutique Hung on You and Sheila Cohen, who layered her finds with psychedelia at the Kings Road boutique Granny Takes a Trip; and Cleo Butterfield, now the owner of the C25 Vintage fashion archive, who opened her second-hand clothing ship, Sunset Boulevard, on Portobello Road in 1971...(retro-chic and anti-fashion) originated in the Portobello area in London, although the terms were imported from Parisian flea markets. Inspired in part by exhibitions of decorative art of the late nineteenth century, 1960's counterculture appropriated and modified into retro-chic, a self-consciously minority taste where ephemera from past times are collected and used as everyday objects to the point where contemporary life borrows from history...when it borrows it puts its loans, metaphorically speaking, in quotation marks."[90]

This retro-chic mode of life was, at least initially, a fundamentally anti-consumerist alternative practice done by a minority of artists, musicians, bohemians, and hangers-on – one of the most obvious and famous examples is Jimi Hendrix's collaged wardrobe of the late sixties that included 19th century military jackets, suggesting a radical individuality that would find its own way, in music and in clothes.

And so it is with Russell's film. MGM predictably billed *The Boy Friend* as a nostalgia fest where we might forget the present moment (wars, street protests, growing divisions between classes, cultures and sexes, etc.) and immerse ourselves in the fun of the "roaring twenties" – forgetting of course that this is the decade that produced the Great Depression. In spite of the nostalgia element Russell's film has (like Hendrix's retro-costume) an element of radical subversion as it plays with the idea of glamour, identity, authority, and role-playing. Adrian Garvey described camp in a different way from Sontag writing about Russell's film: "The thing about camp is that it is a very confusing, over-under-sideways-down way of looking at the world, which takes as basic the notion that nothing is quite what it seems...*The Boy Friend* is an 'anti-musical,' that is, a double edged sword that simultaneously mocks and celebrates the classic Hollywood musical."[91]

The Boy Friend is most certainly a multi-layered work both nostalgic and conformist, but also longing to escape nostalgia and conformity toward some reinvention of the self that is much like the playacting of children where as Garvey says, "nothing is quite what it seems." Russell himself saw the problems with a clear eye, many years after the fact in his autobiography, *An English Picture*, where he summed up the film himself:

> "I'd always wanted to do a musical but it's like trying to rebuild the pyramids when everyone's forgotten how they did it...the simplest thing confounded us... despite the big Busby Berkeley routines, the novelty value of the stage show, the great singing and dancing by the cast...plus the brilliant designs of Shirley Kingdom and Tony Walton, the film was a flop. The acting was too broad, the gags too labored, and the pacing too slow. I should have cut it during the script stage, but, determined to be faithful to the original show, I kept in everything!"[92]

Russell has the last word here.

LISZTOMANIA (1975)

Lisztomania was a project put together by Goodtimes Enterprises based in London and Ken Russell – they had worked the previous year on *Mahler* that had been a success critically and financially, and they sought to repeat that experience with the life of Franz Liszt (1811-1886). *Lisztomania* stars Roger Daltrey, playing the 19th century romantic composer who secured fame, romance, and fortune as a young touring pianist throughout European cities. Russell wrote and directed the film and he seems to have one single idea that he reiterates throughout: that Liszt was a proto-rock star and saw all of the benefits and the pitfalls of that world one hundred years before The Who played The Royal

Albert Hall. The film shows the influence of Fellini's *Toby Dammit* (1968) and *Roma* (1972), works that used theatricalized, episodic tableaus, and Tinto Brass's *Deadly Sweet* (1967), a film that used storyboards from cartoonist Guido Crepax in a literal way, often turning the set into a cartoon with live actors, very much in the spirit of the then contemporary Pop art movement. Russell took these elements and gave them a British comic touch that constantly sough to shock, transgress and/or titillate – depending on one's sensibilities. Certainly a film where Ringo Starr plays the Pope, with an almost straight face, has buttons it wants to push.

As in *Tommy*, *Lisztomania* is composed of theatrical sets with no pretension to realism – no attempt is made to create a realistic version of Liszt's 19th century Vienna, nor is there a single element of documentary that tells us anything about the life of Liszt. Let's first take a look at Russell's overall narrative strategy that sets the foundation for *Lisztomania* (made explicit in the title): was Franz Liszt the first rock star?

The term "Lisztomania" was coined by Heinrich Heine, the troubled romantic poet, in 1844 to describe the hysteria associated with Liszt's tours where "women fought over his cigar stubs and coffee dregs." His silk handkerchiefs and velvet gloves (Liszt was a dandy) were especially prized. It is estimated that Liszt gave over one thousand performances on the road between 1841 and 1849. He gave away much of his wealth to charities related to Christian organizations.

During a tour of the Ukraine in 1847 Liszt played in Kiev where he met the Polish Princess Carolyne zu Sayn-Wittgenstein who became a lifelong love. Carolyne was, unfortunately, already married to a military man and the Church, unwilling to anger the Polish military, refused to sanction Sayn-Wittgenstein's plea for an annulment - a decision that destroyed the religious Carolyne who devoted the rest of her life to seclusion and long written rants against the church. Liszt had profited from his early exposure to the violin virtuoso Paganini and he sought to, in effect, become the Paganini of the piano, which he succeeded in doing. As well as being a virtuoso violinist Paganini was known to be something of an amoral, narcissistic, rake who sought out the companionship of women on the road, indulging himself in every manner possible. He also developed a fan base that was robust in their sexual enthusiasm and musical adoration – something that Liszt surely picked up on. Can we then at least say that Paganini and Liszt were proto-rock stars? While it is tempting because of certain superficial similarities ultimately the answer is no – let's explore further.

The connection between sexual euphoria and music was already a well established one in the 19th century with troubadours in the middle ages and onward having a strong reputation not only for licentiousness and ribaldry, but also for seducing young people of both sexes (to the despair of their parents) – so much so that earnest religious leaders and puritanical philosophers, such as Rousseau in the 18th century, mitigated against traveling players (musical or theatrical) and sought to ban them legally. Rousseau was, of course, puritanical only in his philosophy, as in his life he enjoyed orgies and the companionship of many women over the years – and when he had a child at one point he put her up for adoption not wanting to have anything to do with her, so he could maintain the lifestyle to which he was accustomed. Surely an odd trait for a man who wrote not one but two books about rearing children so they could go on to become fully rounded adults - but as one would expect much of this biographical material was left out of his autobiography.[93]

What Paganini and Liszt did was not create this sexual euphoria, but rather they were the first to market it and then go on tour with it over the whole of Europe, creating not only a much larger fan base, that was previously regional, but unaccountable wealth from subscription concerts and private recitals. Mozart the child prodigy on tour was certainly a role model here but Paganini and Liszt went much further in organization, and strategic bookings before even starting their tour. While the Mozart's (being the first) were dependent on trial and error with occasional handouts from the ultra-rich Paganini and Liszt *managed* their fame. Nevertheless the adoration was different from what we see in 20th century audiences because the music was different and, just as importantly, they way it was heard was different – but how?

What Paganini brought to the table in his compositions was speed and virtuosity – no composition by him is equal to the violin sonatas of Beethoven, Mozart or Mendelsohn, but this hardly matters since that was not the point – it was all about the virtuosity, speed, and enthusiasm of the performance, not the content. In this sense Paganini sought to bring a rush of adrenalin to his performances and to his audience (akin to rock 'n' roll) but the music was still tied to a strict classical order that was, musically speaking, conservative. Liszt sought to distance himself from that classical order by the use of programmatic music not tied to conventional movements and by harmonic experimentation, including atonal passages, that anticipated 20th century music – in short Liszt was a radical musically. But Liszt's programmatic music such as his ambitious *Années de*

Pélerinage was a highly complex work that has no equivalent in rock (or blues) music – it has much more in common with the work of his friends Hector Berlioz, Frederic Chopin, and Richard Wagner, as one would expect. The audience appreciated this complexity, full of emotional nuances and ideas about pushing tonality to the breaking point (derived mostly from Beethoven's late work), and a great part of the excitement generated by Liszt (and his friends) was based on this complexity.

But there is one area - Liszt's harmonic playfulness, exploring the outer edges of tonality, that does have something in common with certain kinds of rock 'n' roll, that also ventured beyond the conventional 12 tone scale. Both are pushing boundaries. The Beatles' *A Day in the Life*, Jimi Hendrix's *If 6 Was 9*, and Frank Zappa's *Lumpy Gravy* are examples of rock music that danced on the precipice of tonality/atonality for the sheer pleasure of it. Tonality would only be shattered into fragments by Arnold Schoenberg and the second Viennese school in the early 20th century as they sought to open a new chapter in the history of classical music, and by inference close out another one.

No attempt is made by Russell to understand Liszt's music and how it might be different from earlier or later works – his concern is merely to depict Liszt with various groupies and to show him trying to compose music despite the demands of adoring fans – all shown in typical cartoon or burlesque style, even having Liszt play with an enormous circus tent size penis. *Lisztomania* also fails to take into account that before recordings the way people listened to music was completely different, and to a very large extent incomprehensible to us, and so the audience was different. When an audience member went to hear a symphony by Mozart or Schubert they understood that this would undoubtedly be the last time they would ever hear it. All performances were live, one of a kind, and once only – they would rarely be repeated unless one were wealthy and could afford private performances. The intensity of the listening experience for this audience was powerful, unique, and unrepeatable. Once recordings enter the picture the act of listening itself changes dramatically since one has access to nearly endless repetition. In short, the rock audience of the postwar era is a fundamentally different creature than the classical music audience of the 19th century.

Russell ends *Lisztomania* with the harried composer on a rocket ship (clearly made of cardboard), presumably bound to the present moment (1970's arena concerts), but what about the real Franz Liszt, who ended his days reading and meditating in a monastery, and was known as Abbé Liszt? *Lisztomania's* energies are all directed at a concept – Liszt=Rock Star – and so Franz, in a sense, need not be present. This is an important point because *Lisztomania* was, in many ways, a harbinger of things to come – Russell was again ahead of his time but this time not in a very positive sense.

The insistence on Liszt being a rock star is more than simply a flattening out of experience, an erasure of differences. *Lisztomania* denies Liszt his individuality, his eccentricities and contradictions, his lusts and his hatreds, his bad habits and his generosity, his regrets and his secrets - they all vanish in the smoke and mirrors of the all-encompassing present – not his present but ours. Liszt under the conditions of *Lisztomania* can only be someone who was too early to the game and/or someone who set the mold for our time. This point of view is fundamentally narcissistic as all the arrows point to our own time, the present moment. As Christopher Lasch put it in his classic study of narcissism:

> *"To live for the moment is the prevailing passion- to live for yourself, not for your predecessors or posterity. We are fast losing the sense of historical continuity, the sense of belonging to a succession of generations originating in the past and stretching into the future...The usual defenses against the ravages of age – identification with ethical or artistic values beyond one's immediate interests, intellectual curiosity, the consoling emotional warmth derived from happy relationships in the past, can do nothing for the narcissist."*[94]

Lisztomania inaugurates a "narcissistic cinema:" *Moulin Rouge* (2001) *Marie Antoinette* (2006), *The Great Gatsby* (2013) *The Decameron* (2024) – works that are sometimes referred to as jukebox films because they are influenced by music videos and have contemporary pop music hits (not written originally for the film) regardless of the time period being covered, be it Paris during the French Revolution, early 20th Century New York, or Medieval Italy. It doesn't really matter because it's not about those times or the people who lived in them – it's about "us."

Certainly there are connections that can be made between Liszt and a contemporary rock star or the audiences for the music – screaming kids are screaming kids after all – but Russell takes no account of the all important differences. For example, it's clear that the women in *Lisztomania*, even dressed in 19th century costumes, are contemporary women and the music, despite its frenzy and speed, is classical – what we have is merely a pastiche of both classical and rock modes of composition (and lifestyle) that never manage to come together even when they are in the same room screaming at each other. While pastiche might work for a short film (Pasolini's *La Ricotta*) or skit (SNL's *Star Trek* parody" "The Last Voyage of the Starship *Enterprise*" with John Belushi as Captain Kirk) it can rarely withstand the length of a feature film (two examples of that might be Rob Reiner's *Spinal Tap* and Monty Python's *The Life of Brian*). But ultimately *Lisztomania* falls under the weight of its own artifice – its own narcissism – and not even Russell's sense of humor can save it.

VALENTINO (1977)

Despite the fact that Russell in his autobiography mentions that he would rather forget *Valentino* it was a return to form. Before Russell even stepped on the set there was already a solid working screenplay that had been put together by Mardik Martin and Brad Steiger. Martin had previously written *Mean Streets* for Martin Scorsese and was known for writing dialogue that was true to life, specializing in the Italian American immigrant experience. He invaluably brought *Valentino* down to earth whenever it was wont to become a pastiche of 20's Hollywood melodramas. Brad Steiger had co-written the book *Valentino, an Intimate Exposé of the Sheik* on which the screenplay was based. But the genesis of *Valentino* belongs neither to the writers nor to Russell but to Irwin Winkler and Robert Chartoff, producers – a normal situation in Hollywood productions – who commissioned the writers to develop a screenplay and then, when satisfied, set about to find a director. They both liked Russell's work and sought him out – the three met in London and Russell agreed to direct.

Russell was again taking a chance on non-actors and they come through for him with Rudolf Nureyev (a ballet star) and Michelle Phillips (a singer with the famous pop group *The Mamas and the Papas*) delivering nuanced, complex, performances that also had an aspect of tongue in cheek – by now a Russell trademark - that he easily riffs on in the mise en scéne. Using Nureyev also had an aspect of the self-referential about it that appealed to him. Russell: "the casting was a case of a myth playing a myth...Nureyev is a myth, people don't know a great deal about him. He's before the public every day of his life and no one has heard him speak – and so, he's a living legend whom nobody knows."[95] The same might be said of Michelle Phillips, playing Natacha Rambova; Phillips was a star in a famous pop group also known for her flamboyant love life but her actual identity was also a complete mystery. Rambova similarly had a certain fame in the twenties predicated on scandal sheets and rumors in the industry that had little to do with her actual life. What Russell seems to have sought here is a *slippage* between identity and roleplaying, reality and fiction that would create sparks. Secondary players Felicity Kendal, Seymour Cassel, Linda Thorson, and Carol Kane deliver shaded performances of great depth, allowing Leslie Caron (a veteran of Hollywood's turf wars in its golden age) to deliver an outrageous, over-the-top performance as the larger than life Alla Nazimova – a fixture of Hollywoods silent period.

With *Valentino* Russell was back to doing a biography of someone that profoundly interested him, not only Rudy per se but the exploration of the gap between myth and real life; it also allowed him to re-create Hollywood in its infancy when the narrative strategies and the genres were just starting to congeal into place but were still moldable and fluid. Just being allowed to do a pastiche of Hollywood silent cinema must have pleased Russell to no end and he takes full advantage of the opportunity shooting mostly in England and Spain as the Los Angeles of the 1920's had, by 1977, disappeared. Even Valentino's Hollywood house was shot in Southhampton, Hamspshire, a short distance from where Russell was born. He wisely used the illusion making machinery of the dream factory – where a stretch of sand north east of Los Angeles could be "Morocco" in Josef von Sternberg's *Morocco* (1930) – and recreated "Hollywood" in S'Agaró, Girona, Catalonia, Spain and Elstree Studios near London – and it worked.

The screenplay by the team again takes up the maze structure of *Citizen Kane* and the rondo structure of *Mahler*, with the film beginning with Valentino's sudden death at age 31 from a ruptured ulcer. Russell uses actual footage of the funeral and also mimics the black & white footage of Valentino's hysterical funeral procession during the opening credits. We hear the song *There's a New Star in Heaven Tonight* written in tribute to Valentino following his death throughout the opening sequence. Using black and white film Russell mimicked the original footage so it is impossible to tell where one starts and the other begins. The way he did it was via analog technology, also used by Woody Allen in *Zelig*: The black and white film strips were laid on the floor and then stepped on and dragged scratching the emulsion from the top to the bottom of the frames, as happens when a film is projected too many times. The celluloid also picked up dust, hair and lint and these were then fixed on to the film, from which a new master was printed. This was the very technique that Huw Wheldon had warned Russell about and strictly prohibited him from doing during the filming of *Prokofiev: Portrait of a Soviet Composer* but now he was free to pursue his own way and it works beautifully for him. Not only is it a stunning opening but it also scrambles reality and fiction immediately as the credits roll, so we are, from the beginning, on shaky ground: How do you tell what is real and what is fake? Russell's answer clearly is: you don't.

Various reporters (rather than one as in *Kane*) cynically and aggressively ask some very personal questions at the funeral that lead to a variety of flashbacks from different points of view that recount Valentino's life more or less in sequential order, but Russell avoids changing the style of the film to suit various memories, dreams, and fantasies as he had done previously with *Mahler* and *The Music Lovers*. *Valentino* is a simpler film that is straightforward in its narrative line. Russell concentrates on the vast gap between the sheik personae created by Hollywood, the mass media of the time, and the actual person, the Italian immigrant who went through various small jobs (until he landed the biggest job) but only wanted to earn enough money to bring his mother to California where he might one day make a living by owning his own orange grove.

The idea is not as far fetched as it seems when we remember that Valentino had an agricultural degree from Italy, but it was not to be as he, among a few others denizens of Los Angeles in the 1920's, created (often unknowingly and unwillingly) not only the star system of the first studio era, but the idea – first theorized by the historian Parker Tyler in 1947 – that film stars are fundamentally Gods. Or, at least, our version of Greek/Roman Gods made flesh, not with painted marble but celluloid projected onto a screen. The idea had been kicking around since the very beginning of film - there was even a beautiful poem written in 1914 by Vachel Lindsay about Blanche Sweet the silent film actress that acknowledged her as a Goddess – and Lindsay even had the foresight to compare film reels to the "Papyrus rolls of Egypt's day." But it was Tyler who explained logically and in detail how that fusion of film star and God worked, but even Gods must sooner or later die and turn into museum relics. "I never wanted to be a God!" proclaims Valentino in Russell's film but, of course, it's too late – his friend and agent George Ullman (Seymour Cassel) can only offer a bemused smile and shrug his shoulders.

The God tag is more complex than merely a euphemism for "adoration" or "love." The 20's saw a plethora of alternative churches, religions and cults due to a crisis in faith. The world, as Virginia Woolf pointed out, changed fundamentally "sometime around 1910." The acceleration of technology was certainly a part of it – when we look at photographs of 1900 and compare them to the 1920's we see a different planet; and if we examine films from the same period it is even stranger as the way people moved was different – as if the space around them had been radically altered because, of course, it had. When Russell shows acolytes (mostly women) gathered outside of Valentino's house to chant their love in unison as if they were at a prayer meeting in a congregation it is not a conceit of the writers – such groups did meet and worshiped together. Clearly Valentino provided them with something they badly needed – it was more than a sexual charge, it was a fundamental spiritual need – they saw something that was larger than themselves, larger than the present moment. Clearly Valentino did not create this "aura" – neither did the crew of pre-programmed entertainments such as *The Sainted Devil* (1924) or *The Sheik* (1921) that Valentino starred in. The question goes begging – who created this "aura?" Russell posits the question but, while he leaves it unanswered, he does provide certain clues to what might have happened to Valentino as he unknowingly stepped into the middle of a whirlwind.

The questions being tossed out by journalists at the funeral are delivered with little regard to Rudy himself lying in an open casket with full makeup, as was the convention of the time. Since one of the central themes of the film is Valentino's sexual orientation the makeup matters. Being a homosexual or bisexual in Hollywood was taboo well into the 1950's so one can see the point of Valentino's paranoia. The first of these memories comes from Bianca de Saulles (Emily Bolton) who knew Valentino when he was a young taxi dancer and gigolo in New York City – it's to her that he explains his dream of one day owning an orange grove. It is also Bianca who remembers seeing Valentino dance with Vaslav Nijinsky (Anthony Dowell), teaching him how to do the tango. Nureyev the master ballet dancer does a wonderful job of teaching Dowell and then watching him outperform all comers in a spectacular display while wearing a suit. Russell originally had the idea of beginning his film with this exceptional scene, which is beautifully shot, as Anthony Dowell does a great job of simulating Nijinsky's high-octane dance moves. After getting into trouble with mobsters Valentino moves to California (as did the film industry itself) and June Mathis (Felicity Kendal), a movie executive, picks up the story as it shifts from New York to Los Angeles.

Mathis has a quiet, unrequited love for Valentino and pushes him onto Jesse Lasky (Hunt Hall), a studio head (of what would become Paramount) – a businessman more used to dealing with mobsters and crooked cops than artists or dancers. The irony here is that

Mathis succeeds beyond her wildest dreams, making Valentino truly out of her (or perhaps anyone's) reach. Mathis remembers an out of control party with infamous comic star Fatty Arbuckle. Valentino was to perform at the party doing the "Apache Dance" (also known as the "Bowery Waltz") a dramatic French dance for two where the man throws the woman around in a ballet of violence and feigned sadomasochism ending in a sex/death embrace reminiscent more of Edvard Munch's paintings than any sort of romantic pas de deux from Astaire/Rogers – the dance was popular in cabarets and "supper clubs" well into the early 1960's, after which it was considered politically incorrect.

Arbuckle, as he was known to do, obnoxiously takes over the party and challenges Valentino, who seems to be stealing some of his light. Lorna Sinclair (Penelope Milford) is Valentino's dance partner who just can't bring herself to do one more "Apache" and Arbuckle dismisses her brutally. Milford must be singled out as providing arguably the best performance in the film as Valentino's traumatized, exhausted, alcoholic dance partner in their cabaret act. Milford plays Sinclair like a veteran performer who has seen it all and has had her glory days, but now realizes that the game is up and she has nowhere to turn – it's a harrowing performance that one rarely sees in Hollywood films, and very different from the other actors, who seem to be playing more to the facetious, humorous aspect of the film. Horrified by Arbuckle's mistreatment of his partner, he takes Arbuckle's girlfriend (Carol Kane) and does the "Apache" with her, driving Arbuckle into an apoplectic fit, where he appears to be on the verge of a heart attack. The party is also where Valentino meets Hollywood's A-List and begins to see the outrageous amounts of money to be made, and also where he meets his first wife, the ex waitress now film star, Jane Acker. Valentino's entry into Hollywood is set via a dance ("The Apache") of love and death, and so it proves to be.

While *Valentino* was a success in Europe it was not in the US and some attributed an anti-American bias to Russell's work as partly to blame. One scene was especially singled out: Valentino courts Mathis – to try to secure a Hollywood contract – and he puts on the "collegiate, all American boy" outfit from the period trying his best to look, sound, and act "American" which comes off as ridiculous. Rudy even accentuates his bad American accent to make the point - but Nureyev is not merely satirizing Valentino's mismatch with American male archetypes, he is also satirizing the hopeless naïveté of that American model. Along with the obvious vulgarity of the journalists, with their exaggerated tough-guy cynicism; the ridiculous "product placement tours" that Valentino had to do to make a living, and are clearly mocking American consumer culture; and the moneygrubbing crassness of Jesse Lasky – it all might have been too much for American audiences. Russell defended himself in the press explaining that Lasky had been brutal with Valentino, as he was with all of his staff, and the yellow journalism of the time was, in fact, vulgar – but to little avail – the film did badly in the US and was quickly withdrawn from distribution. Fortunately for Russell the film was a hit in Europe, particularly England, and it put the director back on the map.

When Valentino shows up wearing his "all-American" costume Mathis explains to Rudy that he need not put on any American airs as it was the sultry "other," the Latin Lover who would seduce the public – there were already lots of boy-next-door types. This "other" was the man that women (and men) both feared and were intrigued by – certainly not the man most women wanted to marry but the one that stepped in at night when the lights went out. But neither Valentino nor Paramount invented the Sheik persona. In the early 20th century "eastern" or "Persian" looking males and females could be overtly sexualized – as was the case with Pola Negri and other "exotics" in the Hollywood of the twenties – in ways not available to westerners in the popular arts. Theirs was a mythical personae that was presumably free, sensual, and given fully to the taking and the giving of pleasure without guilt. This puritan fantasy was a powerful sexual stimulus not only to the American imagination but seen throughout western history, from Delacroix's imaginative "Persia"- created in a dingy Paris studio - to D.W. Griffith's "Babylon" – created in the hills of Hollywood.

Next up is Alla Nazimova (Leslie Caron), who makes an outrageously flamboyant entrance at Valentino's funeral. She proceeds to make a scene of grief so intense she feints, and when photographers ask her to repeat the scene for cameras, she obliges them – another event that is incredulous but historically accurate. In that sense Caron's performance is not a caricature but a credible performance of Nazimova who might have been a proto-performance artist as much as an actress, writer and director; but despite the outrageousness she had talent, co-directing (with Charles Bryant) one of the best films of the silent period, *Salome* (1922) from Oscar Wilde's play. Interestingly Russell would also tackle Wilde's difficult work twice, in *Dance of the Seven Veils* (1970) and *Salome's Last Dance* (1988) so there was a connection there. Nazimova's version seems like a photographed avant-garde staging that has some things in common with Sergei Diaghilev's productions of the same period with design help from avant-garde artists of the time like Picasso, but *Salome* has it's own strange dreamlike movements and modernist hair and make-up – nothing like it would be seen again until much later in the century with the work of people such as Julie Taymor and Derek Jarman.

Nazimova remembers working on *Camille* (1921) with Valentino as she was both producer and co-star – an atypical role for a woman of the time but not at all surprising for Nazimova. She also introduces Natacha Rambova (Michelle Phillips) to Valentino, who is seduced by the ambitious Rambova with her famous "dance of the seven veils." As depicted by Russell Rambova uses Valentino's infatuation to help her social climb and gain a foothold in the film industry. While Valentino is in the midst of a divorce he marries the scheming Rambova in Mexico and is then arrested for bigamy as he re-enters the US. Lasky refuses bail and Valentino spends a night in a Mexican jail where he is taunted and humiliated as the down-and-out prisoners and guards finally have an American figure of authority, power, and wealth that they can lash out at.

The facts of Valentino's life are certainly as melodramatic as his films but there is a sense of the tragic wrapped in comically absurd dress not to be found in either Valentino's or Nazimova's oeuvre – in fact it is not to be found in Hollywood at all. This tragic/absurd element would have to wait for the postwar era and the rise of auteur directors such as Ingmar Bergman (with *Sawdust and Tinsel*), Michelangelo Antonioni (with *The Lady Without Camelias*) and Jean-Luc Godard (with *Le Mepris*) to do it justice, and finally, Rainer Fassbinder pays lasting tribute in his late masterpiece *Veronika Voss*, but that's another story.

Once Rambova gets some power she predictably starts to make outrageous demands in all of Valentino's productions until they are both fired. The couple find themselves broke despite having run through several fortunes and so seek the help of an agent, George Ullman to sort out their business problems. Ullman helps them book personal appearances in a dance tour promoting *Mineralava*, a "miracle" beauty treatment, which is a success in the US – in effect the dancing becomes part of a promotional tour.

It is here that Russell delivers one of his most astute critiques of Hollywood and American media. While the success of the *Mineralava* tour takes everyone by surprise – including Valentino – it makes a great deal of sense once one understands that the society of the 1920's had entered into zone where all of media was being reduced to Spectacle (with a capital S) - something that Orson Welles picked up early on and viciously satirized in his *War of the Worlds* (1938) broadcast – a theme that would constantly recur in his work up until the last film completed in his lifetime *F is For Fake* (1973).

Spectacle was the fundamental condition of daily life under a capitalist/consumer society wherein direct experience is short-circuited, drained out from passive consumers, and then sold back to them as enervating products and imagistic entertainment. Under the umbrella of Spectacle *everything* is a commodity, every conversation is a pitch, and every relationship is a deal – and as we see in *Valentino* every dance is merely an entry point to public relations. But in the 1920's there was as yet no understanding of what Spectacle was (except of course in the broad sense) or how it worked – that would not happen until the 1960's where it was theorized most famously by Guy Debord in his short book *Society of the Spectacle* wherein he described Spectacle as: "...the sun that never sets over the empire of modern passivity. The Spectacle is not a collection of images, but a social relation among people, mediated by images that serve to alienate us from a genuinely lived life. This society eliminates geographical distance only to produce a new internal separation."[96] It is as if Debord had written Valentino's dream diary.

After Valentino reads an article challenging his manhood – a norm of the yellow press of the period that only the most uneducated public took seriously – he challenges the writer first to a duel, then to a boxing match. Rory O'Neil (Peter Vaughan), an Irish amateur boxer and journalist, seems ready to bring Rudy down but Russell shoots the match as if it were a ballet that has homoerotic overtones – something that would no doubt have sent the homophobic O'Neil into a rage. After loosing to Valentino O'Neil challenges him to a drinking bout that is also accepted. Although real enough historically the back-to-back fights drag on and the film looses its thread: the relationship of Valentino to the women in his life, his relationship to his job as a star, and his place in the emerging, all encompassing Spectacle – this lost thread happens at the worst possible moment as the film builds to its climax. The hapless O'Neil looses the drinking bout as well and Valentino goes home the winner, only to die of a ruptured ulcer from the massive intake of alcohol. As to be expected Nureyev and Russell stage the death as a pas de deux between Valentino and Death, as he staggers around, beautifully miming the melodramas of ham actors "dying," but also as a very serious dance with Death that ends with Valentino reaching for an orange on the floor, just beyond reach.

For all of the references to *Kane* in *Valentino* the simple orange is no match for "Rosebud," the sled that goes up in flames at the end of Welles' masterpiece where that sled, that Kane loved as a boy, is set afire along with all of his other possessions that were considered "worthless" by the executors after his death and the valuable things – some still sitting unopened in their boxes – were sold off. Welles smartly cuts from the sled in flames to the black smoke passing over fabled *Xanadu* and then pulls his camera back to the "No Trespassing" signs, creating a loop to the beginning of his film maze. The smoke might be Kane himself and his history receding into History and ultimately into oblivion. Russell can't inject the weight of those metaphors into the simple orange on the floor and his finale lacks the weight it so desperately wants to deliver. Nevertheless the film is a beautifully articulated telling of Valentino's life and death - the story of a simple Italian man who wanted to be a farmer, go to America and get rich, and he got what he wanted beyond his dreams - and he also lost everything that ever mattered to him – that is what we call tragedy - and Russell doesn't explain it, or theorize it, he shows it.

ALTERED STATES (1980)

Altered States was a return to Hollywood, in the literal sense, as the film was shot at Sunset Gower Studios and Burbank Studios in Los Angeles, initially for Columbia, but eventually the film was released via Warner Brothers. It was Russell's first film shot in the dream factory but locations ranged from Harvard Medical School to Chihuahua, Mexico. As with *The Boy Friend* and *Valentino* the project had been under development at the studio long before Russell stepped in as director. With *Altered States* it is worth recapitulating the pre-production drama as it is difficult to get a good idea of what the film is trying to do unless one gets some of the background, before Russell got the call to come to Hollywood.

The genesis of the film was a meeting between Paddy Chayefsky, the highly esteemed screenwriter, with friends Bob Fosse, the director of *Cabaret*, and fellow screenwriter Herb Gardner in 1975 – a project they agreed to work on together was an adaptation of Robert Louis Stevenson's classic book *Strange Case of Dr. Jekyll and Mr. Hyde*. Chayefsky wrote a three-page treatment that took place in the present and revolved around the American scientific community and their search for the original "archetypal" man, or man's "true self." Now devoid of God or a Christian narrative they asked, where does man come from? What does the first man look like? Chayefsky also based his treatment partially on John C. Lilly's sensory deprivation research conducted in isolation tanks using mescaline, ketamine (a psychoactive drug), and LSD to induce "trips" to parts of the mind hitherto unexplored. Lilly had written his own book *The Scientist* (1978) based on his research.

Columbia Pictures liked the treatment but suggested that Chayefsky turn it into a novel first that would have a chance to generate exposure and interest – a relatively common strategy in high-end film production. Chayefsky agreed and in 1978 turned in a finished novel. That same year production started and Arthur Penn was brought in to direct - he cast William Hurt (in his first film) and Blair Brown as the scientists who head into uncharted waters. A dispute between Chayefsky and Penn resulted in the director being fired. Stanley Kubrick and Orson Welles were successively asked to come on board and both turned down the project. Columbia started to backtrack sensing trouble and passed the project on to Warner Bros. – another common strategy in the industry. New contracts were signed and Russell (director number 27 on the list according to his agent) got the job.

Rehearsals started in March of 1979 during which Chayefsky and Russell fought for control of the film but this time Russell was given the green light and the writer had to back off. The problems between them were not that Russell had changed any of Chayefsky's verbose script – according to Blair Brown the script that Russell shot was exactly the one that Chayefsky brought in the first day and not a word was altered or removed. Even if Russell had wanted to change it his contract made that impossible. What Chayefsky objected to was the fast staccato pace of the acting, with actors often delivering lines while eating, getting drunk, or walking away from the camera, making it difficult to understand what they were saying. After seeing a rough cut Chayefsky withdrew his name from the project. This is Russell: "Paddy's (Chayefsky's) hallucinations were impossible to film, he'd write a direction like 'interstellar gas shot through 5 million miles of universe like a puff of cigarette smoke.' But I realized that the picture would only succeed to the extent that it dramatized a certain experience common to all men – and that experience isn't gas going through the universe."[97]

What "experience common to all men" did Russell find and bring to the forefront from Chayefsky's script? In 1967, during the fabled "Summer of Love" Edward Jessup (Hurt) is a Columbia University psychopathologist studying schizophrenia but, like R.D. Laing, he begins to think that there are other states of consciousness that are as real as our waking states, and that "normalcy" is a subjective state rather than a clinical reality. He begins to experiment with sensory deprivation and flotation tanks aided by two likeminded researchers, Arthur Rosenberg (Bob Balaban) and Mason Parrish (Charles Haid) – the former is willing to go along with the idea and the latter his highly skeptical. At a faculty party he meets a young genius whiz kid, his future wife, Emily (Brown). Chayefsky's script manages to get the university milieu succinctly so when the script shifts to "ten years later" when Edward is a tenured professor at Harvard Medical School we accept it. By then he and Emily have two daughters and are on the verge of divorce – they reunite for the first time in seven years with the couple who first introduced them.

When Edwards hears of the Hinchi tribe in Mexico that grow a mushroom, along with various other plants, that they use in their ceremonies to induce hallucinations Edwards is intrigued. The Hinchi call the final drink produced the "first/primordial flower" in recognition of the deep memory states that it can induce. Edwards travels to Mexico to experience this himself – he encounters bizarre hallucinations that Russell renders in an over-tonal/associational montage sequence that suggests he is inhabiting a primordial state of consciousness. Edwards leaves Mexico under a cloud, having come to the conclusion that it was a simple hallucinogenic drug, not an actual return to a primitive state, and the whole thing was a farce, but he brings a sample of the liquid mixture for testing in the lab and to see if he can push the drug and increase its potency.

Edwards decides to experiment on himself along with the help of his friends as he also tries to rebuild the relationship with Emily and his daughters. He concludes that combining the powerful drug with a sensory deprivation tank would increase its potential exponentially. He then experiences a series of increasingly drastic experiences, including one as an early Hominidae. Monitored by his colleagues just outside the tank Edward insists that his visions have "externalized" as when he comes out of the tank he is unable to use language – he insists on being X-rayed directly after coming out of one experiment and a veteran radiologist says the X-rays belong to a gorilla. At one point Edward emerges from the tank as a feral small-statured caveman – he proceeds to go on a rampage through the town, eventually breaking into the zoo before returning to his natural form.

Despite his colleagues' concern Edward stubbornly continues his experiments – exactly as Dr. Jekyll in the Stevenson story. As he continues regressing with each new experiment he experiences a more profound regression transforming into an amorphous mass of conscious primordial matter. An energy wave released from the tank stuns Edward's colleagues and destroys the tank. Emily comes and discovers a swirling maelstrom of energy where the tank had been and searches in the vortex for Edward, risking her own life. She finds him but is on the brink of becoming a non-corporeal energy and vanishing from reality altogether. The transformations no longer need either the tank or the drug and as Edward teeters on the brink of dissolution Emily reaches out to him – the result being that she begins to die, consumed by pure energy. As Edward sees Emily being consumed it stirs a sense of consciousness and he fights the transformation, returning to human form. Edward and Emily embrace as they both return to normal.

Chayefsky's script takes Stevenson's *Strange Case of Dr. Jekyll and Mr. Hyde* and transports it into a mélange of then current ideas about finding the "true" origin of man. These ideas in the sixties became a part of the cultural currency of that revolutionary period. Carlos Castañeda's bestselling books, particularly *The Teachings of Don Juan*, popularized mushrooms as a "natural" way to experience alternative realities that were presumably more primordial, honest and profound than mere everyday, surface reality which was denigrated to secondary status as merely a thin surface, much like the outer layer of an onion. Don Juan was not the famous European playboy of myth but an indigenous Yaqui magician in Mexico who helped Castañeda through his peyote and drug intake to achieve these higher states of consciousness.

Isolation tanks and "scream therapy" were also popular within a certain section of the economy that had disposable incomes and wanted to try new methods of psychotherapy that were still in the experimental stages. The most famous subject of "scream therapy" and isolation tanks – where one would presumably regress to early childhood and perhaps pre-birth, was John Lennon who not only openly talked about his experience but used it (his primal screams) in his vocals for his first solo album *John Lennon/Plastic Ono Band*. With both isolation tank therapy and psychotropic drugs ever present in the popular imagination of the period the film caught the Zeitgeist at the right moment, being also a love story with a happy ending – something always prized within the industry.

The special effects of the film, where we see inside Edward's mind would be something that would appeal to Russell as getting inside his character's heads was always a priority – the problem in this case would be how to generate "psychedelic" effects that were not cliché's, as we see in previous attempts such as Roger Corman's *The Trip* (1967). Certainly the net effect was meant to blow your mind but Russell's fabulist splitting and swirling montage, its Escher loops that are meant to be surrealist and irrational are, like Escher works themselves, bound to the gravity of rationalism by their very rebellion against it.

The effects and the montage of landscapes using neon filters, infrared film effects, and other procedures evoke *2001: a Space Odyssey* but go beyond it in terms of the quantity of different techniques and in duration. What it does not do – that *2001: a Space Odyssey* does perhaps better than any other feature film ever made - is venture out into the narrative redlines established by the Hollywood industry. Clarke and Kubrick obliterated that redline and reset it for a new generation creating a much more radical work where the narrative arc keeps breaking apart, not once but four separate times in the course of the work, but we follow the underlying themes of the film as they develop as the story arc repeatedly disintegrates. The images at the end of Kubrick's film do not belong to a single point of view as complexity and ambiguity are built into the structure of the film and by that point the fracturing of narrative *is* the narrative. The fact that it is possible to take that fragmentation even further is evidenced in the work of David Lynch, Peter Greenaway, Don Levy, Pasolini, and Godard who all made that lonely journey to outlying narrative territory – the ruins of genre – turning it into a home for their body of work.

The images in *Altered States* are all presumably from Edward's point of view so they can all, regardless of their "craziness," be subsumed under one category: Edward's trip seen from his point-of-view. More importantly once Edward is rescued by his wife he returns to "normal." In effect Chayefsky and Russell reject Edward's initial idea that "normal" is a subjective state since he proves at the end that there is, in fact, such an objective state and he wants to be a part of it – so much so that he fights for it as if his life depended on it – showing that "there's no place like home." Chayefsky and Russell step back from the abyss of genre narrative breakdown - the film ends as a love story with the man who realizes the error of his ways – in effect he is just another guy who works too hard and comes to realize what is really important: love. As Russell said "the picture would only succeed to the extent that it dramatized a certain experience common to all men" and on those terms he succeeds as the film is, in a sense, about a man who finally manages to see the light of day, gets his head together, and comes home to his family.

Robert Louis Stevenson's *Strange Case of Dr. Jekyll and Mr. Hyde* does not end well – more to the point Stevenson has the courage to end it ambiguously, almost in medias res – in the novel the good Doctor Jekyll realizes that he no longer has enough energy or elixir to return to his "normal" self and that the "evil" Mr. Hyde will soon win out – what will he do? As Jekyll's consciousness is fading fast he writes his account and accepts that whatever happens now will be Hyde's problem. By imposing a love story with a happy ending on a tragedy Chayefsky/Russell find only a bathetic solution, and by placing it within modern scientific studies of evolution and psychology they only gloss upon fashionable ideas then current without examining them critically - only illustrating those ideas with clever and beautiful images that, over the course of the film manage to tie themselves into a knot that at the very end, when all looks lost, magically transforms itself, like a fairy tale, into a lovely bow.

CRIMES OF PASSION (1984)

Crimes of Passion was conceived as an original screenplay by Barry Sandler centering on Joanna Crane (Kathleen Turner) who is a successful fashion designer by day but moonlights as a prostitute named China Blue by night. Around Joanna circle two very different men, Bobby Grady (John Laughlin), the owner of an electronics store who does surveillance as a sideline, and the reverend Peter Shayne (Anthony Perkins) a sexually repressed preacher who wants to "save" China Blue from herself, and maybe save himself in the process. Grady is the personification of the "normal" male and Shayne of a psychotic, delusional personality gone off the rails.

The script was passed around eventually landing at *Zoetrope Studios* in San Francisco where there were meetings with several possible directors, including John Frankenheimer and Bob Rafelson. Despite the popularity at the time of the erotic thriller and neo-noir genres – bolstered by the enormous critical and financial success of Brian de Palma's *Dressed to Kill* (1980), nothing came of it because of the sexually explicit content that might (and did) incur an initial "X" rating making the film difficult to distribute. Finally Russell got the call and he accepted explaining:

> *"The script offered something new in dealing with sex and family life and the masks we accept. It's a powerful subject, and I was quite taken with it, especially when I saw it dealt with these religious hucksters on TV. I know that I was obsessed with these terrible preachers. It's a film about the exploitation of women, especially at the hands of the macho American male...Americans are asked to live in a world of tcomplete fantasy which they can never live up to."*[98]

As Russell said it is a powerful subject – sex and family life – but is that the subject of *Crimes of Passion*? Surely in most people's version of "sex and family life" crime of any sort hardly plays a role at all. What the film does is, rather, re-invent stereotypes, in the manner of the classic film-noirs, and push them to their limits within a very narrow social world created in the studio – a parallel universe of sorts that acts as a metaphor for our everyday world – and then placing (again) a "normal" man in a "normal" family at the center of the storm.

Boby Grady is an ordinary middle-class electronics store owner who moonlights doing surveillance work since he has access to the basic electronic and video equipment that's needed. He attends a group therapy session where he complains about his wife who has lost interest in sex and he fears the marriage is in trouble. We see him at home and his wife Amy (Annie Potts) seems consumed by her depression, seeking solace by constantly watching television. Grady is approached by the owner of a fashion design house who thinks one of his designers, Joanna Crane, is selling clothing patters to his competitors and wants Grady to do surveillance work. Grady follows Crane and sees that the accusations are unfounded but also discovers that Joanna moonlights as a prostitute named China Blue, changing into a platinum wig. He proceeds to have a sexual encounter with her as China Blue and begins to see her on a regular basis, first professionally then romantically.

One of China Blue's regular clients is the reverend Peter Shayne who spends his days delivering sermons on the street, visiting peep shows on Times Square while sniffing amyl nitrite, and seeing prostitutes. He declares a need to "save" China Blue and shows her a cache of sex toys that he carries with him in a doctor's bag along with a Bible – one of the sex toys is an enormous vibrator in the shape of a sling blade that Shayne has named "Superman."

A difficult sex session with a dying man, whose wife wants China Blue to give him sexual gratification one last time, inspires Joanna to reveal her real name, and she reaches out to the dying man, compelling her to begin facing the truth about her double life. The reverend starts stalking Joanna, even moving into a seedy motel next door to hers, and he watches her activities through a peephole – in effect both the reverend and Grady are voyeuristically invested in the fantasy character China Blue created by Crane.The reverend also sets up a shrine with candles and photos dedicated to her as one might for the Virgin Mary. Sensing that he is mentally unhinged Joanna no longer wishes to see him as a client but Shayne follows her to her daytime apartment – once there he begs her to kill him.

Grady arrives to tell Joanna that he has left his wife but when he hears shouting from her apartment he breaks down the door, finding someone he assumes is Joanna cowering in terror not realizing it is actually the reverend dressed as China Blue, who tries to kill Grady with a pair of scissors. Joanna, now wearing Shayne's clothing leaps from the shadows and stabs the reverend with the "Superman" vibrator before he can kill Grady. Shayne dies convinced that his sacrifice has "saved" them both – and so, in a sense, he feels he is redeemed. In the final scene Grady is again in front of his group therapy session, explaining the end of his marriage and his new relationship with Joanna.

It is clear both Sandler and Russell place their focus on Joanna and Shayne who are both role playing, as a prostitute and as a reverend, respectively – and at the end they exchange clothes carrying this doubling to its logical conclusion in a Hitchcockian manner. Both characters are unable to integrate their sexuality into their everyday life while Grady can, eventually winning Joanna/China Blue over.

One of tenants of a Puritan culture, such as the one found in the US, is not that people are repressed or are afraid of sex, but rather that they compartmentalize sex from everyday life. The best example of this is the city of Las Vegas. This city is inconceivable in France or Peru – countries that are not Puritan - because sex is simply part of everyday life there (for better and for worse) as a matter of course. In the US it is a separate entity that can cross over into "everyday life" when permitted to do so – in effect the Puritan mindset is one of *control*. This why many people, men in particular, have double lives outside of their "normal" marriage that would be considered extreme, deviant, or illegal – it is simply compartmentalized so they never meet (until they meet – and problems arise). As the advertising that promotes the city in the desert explains: "What happens in Vegas stays in Vegas."

This social split is, of course, not a universal attitude spread evenly amongst all Americans equally – but it is a foundational part of the culture. This is a split that Joanna/China Blue is suffering in her body – and one that the reverend/sex maniac is suffering in his soul. That the two would meet and destroy each other (in a manner of speaking) is a Blakean touch that makes a great deal of sense. Joanna kills the reverend and the reverend destroys China Blue, leaving Joanna to find some sexual/emotional equilibrium with Grady.

The primary problem for the script is that its metaphors get congealed and fall flat in their garish studio surroundings before they are brought to life. Much of the problem is in the screenplay that relies on smutty, double-entendres and snappy puns suitable for an adolescent but not for a middle aged preacher like Shayne, walking a high wire act between good and evil, or an adult female like Joanna/China Blue who has seen it all – the facades, the masks, and the toys are surely, for her, passé. The weighty ironies sink the film because there is nothing to hang them on to – everything looks fake except for Amy's bored, suburban housewife, with only a television to keep her company – her brain looks like it might flat-line at any moment due to overexposure to the cathode ray tube.

As predicted by many in the industry the film received an "X" rating and the distributors demanded cuts before they would release the film. Sandler said: "by the fifth round of cuts I think they (Russell and the editor) were so beaten down from looking at the thing and from pressure from the press and elsewhere that they finally went with an "R." Russell complained that Joanna/China Blue's motivation was lost in the cutting room floor but it was too late. The film received generally bad/mixed reviews but did relatively well at the box office - Turner's and Perkin's excellent go for broke performances undoubtedly helped.

While there are precedents for the characters of the reverend/psycho (*Night of the Hunter*) and Joanna/China Blue (*Klute*) in the history of Hollywood both of those films managed to transcend their literary metaphors and ironies becoming stories about lost people that are, despite the odds, believable as human beings. *Crimes of Passion* wants to paint its kinky, sensationalist, "sex as commodity" story in a negative, even execrable light but Russell manages to both sensationalize and trivialize the subject at the same time – the film seems to exist in a studio set netherworld of sordid silliness, exhausted boredom, and mind-boggling perversity. In that sense the work has more in common with the horror movies of Roger Corman from the same period than the psychological films of Bergman or Polanski. The therapy sessions that bookend the film, like Alfred Hitchcock's reminders of the rational "normal" world, (seen, for example, at the end of *Psycho*) feels like an add-on to justify the programmatic traumas on display, and their dissipation into apologue and the ruins of genre fiction.

NESSUN DORMA (AND NONE SHALL SLEEP) (Short/1987)

Nessun Dorma is an aria from Puccini's unfinished opera *Turandot* from 1924, the year Puccini died – it was posthumously completed by Franco Alfano and premiered in 1926. Russell's sixteen minute film was part of an anthology film titled *Aria* that consisted of ten films by different directors, each showing the director's choice of visual accompaniment to an operatic aria of their choosing. As to be expected the results are mixed but, aside from Russell's piece, works by Charles Sturridge (*La Vergine Degli Angeli* from Verdi's *La Forza del Destino*), Jean-Luc Godard (*Armide* by Jean-Baptiste Lully) and Derek Jarman (*Depuis le Jour* from Gustave Charpetier's *Louise*) are superbly done. Coincidentally two of the films include a car on fire, Sturridge's film and Russell's.

The reason "none shall sleep" in *Turandot* is that that a passionate prince has fallen in love with the cold hearted Chinese Princess Turandot – she will not only *not* marry anyone who cannot answer three difficult riddles but have them publicly beheaded. A nice, handsome, Persian Prince (who won the love of the townspeople) has only recently lost his head (literally) when out of nowhere a new nameless Prince (improbably) announces his love for Turandot and his intentions for marriage – to top it off he answers the riddles correctly. Turandot is horrified and refuses to marry anyway – the Prince tells her that if she guesses his name he will submit to death, but if she is unable to guess it she must marry him – Turandot accepts the gamble. She then tells the entourage of the Prince and everyone in the palace that "none shall sleep" until she has that name. In the end Turandot realizes the name is "love" and she falls in love with the Prince, sparing him, and all is set right.

By the 1920's when Puccini wrote *Turandot* opera had entered into its late mannerist phase with outrageously bathetic and unrealistic scenarios, saccharine music, and melodramatic plot twists so extreme they might make Hollywood producers queasy – but Russell was hardly adverse to melodrama and he knew his opera. He was also a Puccini fan staging *Madame Butterfly* in the brief period in the 1980's when he was staging operas in Europe between films. His opera work was always modern, like Peter Sellars' work, but without Sellars' hard political edge.

Turandot opens Russell's film dressed as the "Princess" of some foreign land that likes gold and diamonds with Turandot in close-up with the rings of Saturn encircling her neck as if she were a planet in the firmament. But all is not right - Turandot seems out of sorts. People dressed in faux Egyptian clothing dance in a circle – a ritual is being performed in a bare stage where men stretch out their arms as if to receive something. People place diamonds on hands and feet. A lean young African male seems to be in charge of the proceedings as Turandot, despite being a Princess, seems a bit lost. Suddenly a contemporary looking handsome young man – the Prince - enters and he speaks to her but no words come out.

Russell then jump cuts to a night scene: a car is on fire on its side and Turandot, in contemporary clothes, is seriously bleeding by the side of a road as emergency personnel are trying to save her. The upturned car has as a large Phoenix painted on its hood – the bird of rebirth. The handsome young Prince from before is there in contemporary clothes and he again says something we can't hear. Later in an operating room the lean black male is a surgeon and he stretches out his arms ritualistically to receive the surgical gloves. Russell does a great job of crosscutting between the close-ups of the doctors, nurses and attendants. At a certain point Turandot flat-lines but is resuscitated by electrical shock. From the faces of the medical personnel it is clear that Turandot has survived the operation and we see her in close-up again at the end, smiling, as she realizes that she will live.

Russell manages to turn an overwrought and under-cooked two-hour opera into a condensed 16 minute film and bring it into the modern age with Puccini's intentions intact – a superb achievement - of the ten films in the anthology Russell's is the only one that can make that claim. The shorts by Sturridge, Godard and Jarman are superbly realized films but they use the idea of the opera (rather than the opera itself) to stage their own, often eccentric, conceptual work. Meanwhile Russell, perhaps because he already had experience with operas, modernizes and compresses Puccini's work but never looses the thread of the original opera.

The first half of the film is clearly Turandot's dream as she lay dying on the street and in her later recovery the same people make an appearance but as medical personnel in a modern hospital. The film addresses Puccini's theme – a woman murders a man that loves her (the Persian Prince) but is ultimately redeemed by love. That he would focus on redemption makes sense since the subject had preoccupied him since his early short film *Amelia and the Angel*. Here the angel might be the second lucky Prince who finally makes Turandot say his name – "love" – so she can begin to live. He is also the man we see by her side in front of the car – and finally he is also probably the man that called for the ambulance. He is speaking to her (to the camera) but we don't hear anything – perhaps he's saying it will be alright - and so it is at the hospital as the aria finishes and Turandot gets a second chance.

SALOME'S LAST DANCE (1988)

Salome's Last Dance was the second time that Russell had dealt with the story of John the Baptist, Herod and Salome – 18 years earlier he had made a biography of Richard Strauss, *Dance of the Seven Veils* for the BBC that imagined parts of Strauss' opera *Salomé*. Wilde had been inspired by various readings, including Flaubert, Jules Laforgue, Stephane Mallarmé and in particular Joris-Karl Huysman's *Against Nature* where Gustave Moureau's Symbolist paintings of Salome are described in detail. Wilde was something of a Symbolist himself, that is, someone who sought to represent Truth (with a capital T) symbolically through language and metaphorical images rather than realism. In literature the style originates with the 1857 publication of Baudelaire's *Flowers of Evil* and the short stories of Edgar Allan Poe – the style is often self-consciously decadent, gothic, morose and pathologically sexual, existing in a haunted mansion or a palace rather than outdoors or in a conventional bedroom – the work in many ways anticipated the work of Sigmund Freud and Surrealism. True to form the first printed edition of Wilde's play used illustrations by Aubrey Beardsley.

Russell is true to Wilde's text but adds a brilliant framing narrative wherein Oscar Wilde (Nickolas Grace) and his lover Lord Alfred "Bosie" Douglas (Douglas Hodge) are going out for an evening at a friend's brothel where they are surprising Wilde with a private performance of his banned play *Salomé* where all the roles are to be played by prostitutes and staff. Russell opens his film with a beautiful night shot of horse drawn carriages arriving at the expensive Victorian mansion housing the brothel while children and adults run with sparklers - one of Russell's favorite visual motifs - as Wilde and Bosie, dressed for a night out, exit a cab and enter the whorehouse. Immediately we see that they are bickering and on a downward spiral. Wilde notices that Bosie is "venturing below stairs" and the jealous author assumes his much younger paramour is meeting a boy they both have their eyes on, but he learns that he is preparing as an actor in a surprise performance of *Salomé*.

Despite the heavy atmosphere Wilde delivers one of his famous quips as he enters: "There is only one thing worse that being talked about and that is *not* being talked about."

Douglas Hodge is painfully brittle and shallow as Bosie, which fits the character perfectly, and Nickolas Grace is competent as Wilde delivering his famous repartee with sardonic nonchalance, but he lacks the overpowering intelligence and the sheer disgust with society and people at large (including himself) that permeated every work that Wilde ever wrote. By placing Wilde's *Salomé* within the context of the author's own life Russell is able to comment on the themes of love, corruption and deceit that are interwoven throughout the play and also reflected in Wilde's life. When we see the goings on in the brothel echo those of *Salomé* we are reminded that Wilde would end up in prison, a shattered man – but for the moment he sits down in a Victorian couch – an audience of one – and leafs through coffee table book that is the credit sequence that we see in close-up, using Aubrey Beardsley's beautiful pen and ink drawings, set to melancholic music – the stage is set for *Salomé*.

Wilde's play had been adapted to film before by Alla Nazimova (co-director and star) and Natacha Rambova (adaptation and costumes) in 1922 in one of the great silent films of Hollywood's first golden age. With outrageously futuristic costumes and original sets the film seems to anticipate the work of Derek Jarman, Julie Taymor *and* Ken Russell. With Nazimova's/Rambova's film looking over his shoulder Russell had a lot to live up to but he was up to the task. Once again he was fortunate in having a great cast to help him realize his vision, particularly Imogen Millais-Scott as Salome, who gives an overwhelming, idiosyncratic, nuanced performance as the troubled, doomed princess.

In previous incarnations, from Caravaggio, Titian, Gustave Moreau and Franz von Stuck among others, Salome is always pictured as a dark haired, exotically beautiful femme fatale. Millais-Scott is not by any stretch the iconic Salome and that precisely is the point – she is, in the "real life" framing narrative that brackets the film, Rose, a newly acquired working-class, British chambermaid at the brothel. The other actors take their lead from Millais-Scott and follow her highly theatrical, almost dance-like, incantatory performance that over-enunciates the words on purpose as in an amateur play, which is what this production is supposed to be – she seems to channel Sarah Bernhardt (who was set to play in the original production before it was banned) as well as Nazimova herself. Millais-Scott's performance is so intense one thinks that maybe she imagines she's doing the lead in *Lulu*, Alban Berg's opera – but of course there's a connection between Lulu and Salome, both being sisters in Dionysian despair and self-destruction.

Since the amateur actors in the production are working in the brothel Salome/Rose, is in fact an underfed, underpaid chambermaid who speaks softly and shyly in a strong Cockney accent when she isn't coughing from the probable effects of tuberculosis - as Rose she is more reminiscent of Mimi in *La Boheme* than Salome but clearly that is Russell's intention. Rose/Salome are, as chambermaid/queen, in effect, both at the very bottom and at the very top of the social hierarchy – a dangerous place to be and Russell has every intention of using his framing narrative to comment on Wilde's time as well as his own.

Salome's Last Dance takes place on Guy Fawkes Night, 1892 – a British celebration usually with fireworks (hence the sparklers at the beginning) of the failed attempt 400 years earlier to blow up the Houses of Parliament and kill the King. If this day is a celebration of a failure by overzealous Catholics *Salomé* the play celebrates the Catholic faith via the failure of Salome to seduce the Christian Saint John the Baptist thereby sealing her doom as well as his. Certainly from a post-Freudian age one can see *Salomé* as the triumph of faith over sex or the mind over the body – a theme that would seem to haunt Wilde as it reappears in his most popular work *The Portrait of Dorian Gray* (1891). John will not succumb to Salome's charms, regardless of how tempting and beautiful she is - but Wilde and Russell have some thoughts about that.

"They say that sex is the theater of the poor" quips Wilde to Alfred Taylor (Stratford Johns) the brothel's portly boss - Taylor transforms easily into the play's debauched Herod, looking like Trimalchio, the overfed oligarch in Fellini's *Satyricon*. Bosie plays a caged John the Baptist with some emotional force, as if the martyred saint role somehow suited him – tormented by semi-naked spear carrying courtesans, he is attacked through the bars in his cage by a large phallus. The event itself is blurred by the flash from a camera as the official photographer – played by Russell himself in another transformation, wearing false white bushy eyebrows, beard, and a beret – tells Wilde that he expects to capture many more pictures before the night is out.

The most incredible metamorphosis on view is the pale, tubercular chambermaid who can barely talk, into Salome. From her simple black and white uniform she suddenly seems to be horizontal in the princess' beaded garment, transformed wordlessly into a self-possessed icon of feminine power. It is as if a long suppressed and dormant part of her personality had found release and Rose's body were suddenly overwhelmed by a scourge of passionate lust and raging hate that finally – thanks to Wilde – can come out into the open. But once this force is unleashed all bets are off. Violence comes up as a theme early – Wilde can't believe that someone that shy, skinny and undernourished can do a dance of the seven veils. "She better" replies Taylor, "or I'll kill the little bitch."

As in the Bible King Herod begs his young stepdaughter Salome to dance for him, promising to give her absolutely anything she desires, much to the irritation of her mother, Herodias (Glenda Jackson) who realizes that Herod no longer loves or desires her but lusts after her daughter. The guards make fun of Jews for only worshipping what they can't see while Russell as the photographer – looking like a mad Moses impersonator – tells the guards that he went into the hills (in the Lake District?) for three days looking for gods: "I even called them by name! But I didn't find any. I think they are dead!" says Russell overacting in the manner of a Valentino movie. He holds his large wooden box camera as if it were a piece of video equipment, occasionally firing off some flashes that resemble sparklers.

Salome is not interested in her stepfather Herod, the Roman king of Judea, but becomes fascinated by John the Baptist, Herod's prisoner, when she hears that he has been saying terrible things about her mother. This is typical teenager's response and Salome was approximately 14 when she was queen of Galilee, a minor principality in the Roman Empire. John responds to Salome's seductions by condemning her: "Daughter of Babylon – it is through woman that evil enters the world!" On that line Russell cuts to a double take as Bosie/John and Wilde exchange a look of sly, bemused acknowledgement, subtly pointing out not only the Bible's consistent misogyny but that of Wilde's decadent circle in London.

Salome goes underground to the dungeon prison area where they are keeping the future saint - she and John the Baptist then perform a call and response duet in which she exclaims a love for some part of his body, while John insults her, and she moves on to another part. Millais-Scott takes obvious delight in Wilde's purple prose – where romanticism falls into the shallow ravine of decadence, narcissism and irony. She also takes delight in the lashes that her soldiers inflict on John until she raises her finger, like a queen, so they can stop long enough for her to speak. Finally she makes John a promise that will doom them both: "I *will* kiss your mouth, John the Baptist." Bosie/John sees Wilde flirting with a pageboy painted in gold and utters his curses as much to him as to anyone.

Salome returns to court as a petulant teenager who didn't get what she wanted and Russell interjects body humor as Herod says he notices a wind "like the beating of wings" as someone on stage farts – a stage direction not found in Wilde. Herodias is tired of the whole business and suggests John the Baptist be given over to the Jews who also want to imprison him for being a Catholic. Russell immediately cuts to three midget Hassidic Jews eating Porridge (a comfort food) who concur exclaiming that it is impossible that John the Baptist has seen God since no one has seen him since the prophet Elijha (800B.C.). As the three midgets engage in a heated debate on the possibility of seeing God, Herodias and Herod, who are bored by the discussion, move the proceedings along by having naked servants carry the Hassidic midgets away. Herod asks Salome to eat some fruit in front of him and she obliges him by suggestively eating a banana – a shot that provides the poster for the film. Herod tries to cheer himself up despite hearing John the Baptist's denunciations by starting a dance with his half naked female slaves on the theme of "I'm happy" that Russell shoots parodying Hollywood musicals. A spurned Salome then agrees to dance for Herod – the dance of the seven veils that ends with Salome naked – on condition that she be given anything she asks for.

Everyone watches Salome dance, including John the Baptist who seems to join the party onstage via a dumbwaiter – the only one not interested is her mother Herodias who slips into a large basket with two burly male guards for some fun. Even Wilde seems aroused by the dance and starts to seriously flirt with the young golden pageboy. The moment Salome's last veil drops it is Russell, as the photographer, who gets the close-up as he takes a picture with his flash box camera. John is beheaded and his head is given to Salome on a platter. She kisses the mouth of John just as she promised - and talks about her continuing love for him as Russell shows us Wilde in tears.

Herod realizes that Salome is insane and capable of anything – including having him assassinated on a whim - and he cannot allow her to return to being a queen and orders his guard to put her to death. Unfortunately for Rose - the humble staff worker - Alfred Taylor who runs the brothel also realizes it is too dangerous to allow Rose to return to being a chambermaid after she has felt her power as a queen – and so Rose must also die, but in the world of "reality." Taylor's/Herod's only directive is: "Kill that woman" as he exits. Wilde applauds the production and goes up on stage to congratulate Bosie/John the Baptist and repeats Salome's line: "Let me kiss your lips." When the police burst in to arrest Wilde for the performance he quips "I didn't know this was a double bill with Gilbert and Sullivan!" Outside as they are all being taken away the police explain that aside from the illegal staging "a chambermaid has been murdered." "Murdered? Nonsense!" quips Heroidas, as she enters the police van. "It was death by misadventure! She slipped on a banana peel!" On this last line Wilde, Taylor and the police all laugh as they drive off. The chambermaid (the working class) is the butt of jokes even in death. For his final shot Russell suggests *Citizen Kane* as the camera pans down to the dangerous looking iron spikes from a Victorian fence as the credits roll.

Russell's framing narrative follows suit with Wilde and acts as a mirror to our own time, as during the play the homoerotic tensions between Bosie/John and Wilde reach a boiling point and Wilde has a tryst with a gold-face brothel denizen portraying a pageboy in Herod's court. Bosie sees them and it is he who betrays his lover to the police blurring the personal and the theatrical. The parallels between Salome's obsession with John the Baptist and Wilde's ill-fated affair with the young Bosie are clear enough. At the end Wilde is led away, arrested for homosexuality – something that actually happened but three years later after a scandalous trial that destroyed him.

As is typical of Russell in his later work he can interject the most blatantly obnoxious adolescent humor (Salome eating a banana suggestively) alongside very moving images and line readings such as Millais-Scotts confrontation as Salome/Rose with John the Baptist/Bosie, that has to be one of the acting highlights in all of Russell's work. What makes it so riveting is that the actors are able to deliver as both characters that they are playing – in the brothel and in Wilde's 1st Century court - shifting ever so slightly from one to the other, in a dance of death. Bosie and Rose are basically teenagers who seem to have the capacity to become Salome or John the Baptist, in effect, they rise to the occasion - catching even themselves by surprise.

Millais-Scott's waif like appearance put on an extra layer of pressure dictating that her transformation into a seductive princess from chambermaid would have to come entirely from within. On top of that was the pressure that a few weeks before shooting began the actress came down with a serious virus, from a lifelong diabetes-related kidney problem that she was born with; the virus left her nearly completely blind, and she was told the only cure would be a kidney transplant. She had to call Russell to tell him but he stuck by her and made the film around the problem by using stationary camera set-ups – typical of him he used the difficulty to his advantage by coming up with some of his most beautiful tableaus. Millais-Scott never worked as an actress again but she clearly put everything she had into Russell's film realizing that that might be the case. The genius of the performance turns not just around Salome but on a disempowered and invisible woman – a chambermaid in a brothel – who gets one shot to be a queen. This is a character that suddenly finds her power, charisma, and even her entitlement to the point that she *becomes* Salome – and then pays dearly for it. Russell keeps the political aspect as a subtext but it is present: Taylor, the capitalist running the brothel but maintaining ties to elite London society, including Wilde's decadent entourage, is the mirror image of Herod the King of a small outpost of civilization finding ever new ways of amusing himself – neither man can allow a woman to wield power. It's a tour-de-force counterpoint between the framing narrative of a ham amateur performance and Wilde's Symbolist play into one of Russell's most ingenious, melancholic, visually stunning, and moving films.

LAIR OF THE WHITE WORM (1988)

Lair of the White Worm, based on Bram Stoker's unfinished novel, was a project cooked up by the US studio Vestron Pictures, who had released *Gothic*. Russell wrote the script based on the source novel but incorporated elements of *The Lambton Worm*, a British folktale version of the Loch Ness Monster, but taking his cues from his early love of Fritz Lang's silent adventure films such as *Die Nibelungen*. In effect, with *Lair of the White Worm* he finally got to make a film where a dashing knight with a sword slays a dragon and saves a fair damsel from death – more or less – although there is a surprise ending in store for this knight that is more *Caligari* than anything found in Lang's cardboard heroics. Vestron promised Russell that if he directed they would finance D.H. Lawrence's *The Rainbow* – a longstanding dream project. Russell was an admirer of Bram Stoker and Gothic horror so accepted the deal, despite having a screenplay for *Dracula* that had been pitched around the various studios for over a decade without success. As he put it himself he went from trying to adapt Stoker's best book to adapting his worst.[99]

Russell changed the setting from Australia to the British countryside of Derbyshire, located next to a snake-like river and *Thor's Cave* – a mammoth cave structure on the side of a mountain near a national park full of caves and severe rocky hills that look prehistoric – an excellent location for such a tale as the landscape conjures irrational pre-historic fears that always lie just under the surface. Russell insisted that the film he wrote was a comedy and certainly the 1970's and 1980's were rife with comedy/horror films, the most conspicuous being *The Rocky Horror Picture Show* (1975) and *Beetlejuice*, made the same year as Russell's film

The novel by Stoker certainly had no intentional humor in it – the story, like *Frankenstein* by Mary Shelley, is obsessed with the idea that electricity from the sky in the form of lightning storms can be harnessed for good/evil. This aspect of the story is ignored and Russell shifts the story to a more straightforward fusion of vampires and an enormous worm-monster that must be appeased with sacrificial victims. The novel has a more sinister and realistic worm that simply devours any living thing that comes near it.

Angus Flint (Peter Capaldi), a Scottish archeology student is excavating the site of an ancient convent at a local farm. There he uncovers an unusual elongated skull that looks like it might some kind of dinosaur. The farm/convent is owned by the Trent sisters, Eve (Catherine Oxenberg) and Mary (Sammi Davis), who have converted the old convent into a contemporary bed-and-breakfast where they both work. Angus believes that the bones must be connected to the local legend of the Lampton Worm, a mythical snake creature said to have ben slain, in medieval times, in a local cavern by the ancestor of the current lord of the Manor, James d'Ampton (Hugh Grant). When Flint discovers the skull he lets out an enormous primeval scream of victory that suggests that no matter how educated we may be, as the archeologist Flint surely is, we are all cavemen at some level.

The two couples go off to the local pub where a folk/rock band is playing a song about the Lambton legend and we see a silly 20 foot long carnival snake come out as people dance around it – James helpfully takes a nearby sword and cuts it in half with almost a straight face. Once vanquished Eve, the appropriately named damsel in distress, is free to dance with her victorious knight.

Russell's best effect in the film happens when the dig uncovers a perfectly preserved Roman mosaic under the farm – what looks to be the floor of a mansion or temple depicting a snake. Seeing this beautiful, sophisticated mosaic floor under the wet, primeval earth in the middle of a contemporary bed-and-breakfast gives us a creepy Sebaldian sense of history, or even pre-history, always lying literally just under our feet, waiting for an excavation to bring it up to the present time – also going in some sense from subconscious to consciousness.

There is a long tradition of this sort of horror in British cinema most memorably executed by *Qutermass and the Pit* (1959) where workmen digging in a new subway connection in contemporary London uncover an unusual skull in an area that had, since medieval days, been a magnet for strange, unexplained occurrences. One of the excavators discovers the old medieval street under the current one with the name of Hob's Lane – Hob being an old English term for devil. In this classic film, of course, the rational and reasonable excavation crew, and the archeologists that they bring on board, find more than they bargained for lying just under the surface of a normal London street. What makes *Quatermass and the Pit* such a great film is the writing by Nigel Kneale as he uses the horror and science fiction genres to investigate ideas about human evolution and identity. Russell's script in this sense is sorely lacking as it is shackled to its genre rules and willingly sees them through to the bitter end, but, as he said, he does provide comedy.

When a watch belonging to the father of the Trent sisters, who disappeared a year earlier, is discovered in the local caves James comes to believe that the worm myth may have something to it after and needs to investigate. The father was last seen at the estate of the sexy and enigmatic Lady Sylvia Marsh (Amanda Donohoe) who happens to be a priestess to the ancient snake god and something of a vampire who occasionally shows her fangs. Sylvia goes to the bread-and-breakfast to steal the skull but before leaving leaves a little memento as she spews green venom on a crucifix hanging on a wall – she is angry that in the medieval period the Christians built a convent over her pagan snake sanctuary. Eve comes later and touches the venom to see what it is and experiences repressed memories of nuns being savagely raped and killed by Roman soldiers, impaled on spikes. The rapes are shot on video and rendered with psychedelic colors. We even see Jesus (Lloyd Peters) on the cross being torment by a giant snake as Eve suffers an emotional collapse.

Lady Sylvia picks up a young naïve Boy Scout hitchhiker named Kevin (Chris Pitt) and she brings him to Temple House, her luxurious home where she seductively gives Kevin the use of her indoor pool. Unfortunately for Kevin she bites his sex, paralyzing him with her snake venom, then she pushes him under with her boot to answer the door. She explains that she's doing him a favor as it could have a gone a lot worse for Kevin, although it is difficult to see how. It is James calling and he and Lady Sylvia get along very nicely and enjoy some wine by the fireplace, kissing and promising to meet later. Hugh Grant plays all of his scenes with a droll, ironic sense of the absurd – something that he would turn into a successful template for all of his early work as a romantic lead – he is the perfect match for Donohue's over-the-top performance as the snake priestess. Russell has a lot of fun playing off their hijinks to Capaldi's and Davis' more earnest and realistic renditions of Angus, the stalwart Scotsman and Mary the down-to-earth survivor.

In another comic interlude James falls asleep and has a dream in which he imagines himself inhabiting the painting in his bedroom of an ancestor knight beheading Dionin the pagan snake god. As he enters the cave in the painting – achieved through video superimposition – he suddenly finds himself in a large hangar with a jet plane. Lady Sylvia welcomes him aboard but all of the women in his life are suddenly stewardesses in this dream plane and he is the only passenger – the two principal women in his life Eve and Lady Sylvia begin to physically fight for him and he gets aroused – something that Russell depicts by having Grant raise the pen he's holding in the form of an erection. While amusing, the adolescent visual pun seems to lack the right context that might make it work, although what that context might be is hard to fathom. As a saving grace the actresses appear to have a great, and infectious, time imitating stewardesses in James'/Hugh Grant's dream and thereby save the scene from becoming puerile.

In the morning James investigates the mountainous cavern near Temple House, with Agnus, Eve and Mary. When Eve returns to Mercy Farm on her own she is abducted by Lady Sylvia, who is casually perched on a tree, wearing chic sunglasses. She intends to sacrifice Eve to her snake-god while James correctly theorizes that a giant snake roams the caves that connect to Temple House (which is actually a temple) through underground caverns. James cranks up his stereo to play some Turkish flute music from his residence at full volume in an attempt to charm the serpent from her lair – it works like a charm as Lady Sylvia comes out of her basket and slithers and bends toward the music. Amanda Donahue gives a hilarious performance that actually has some depth as well, shifting from bemused immortal who has seen it all to angry priestess, and from sexy independent woman to viper with fangs so large they put those of Bela Lugosi's in the original *Dracula* to shame. As Lady Sylvia lays out the situation for Eve, we get some exposition and explanations, the most absurd being that the sacrificial victim must be a virgin and "they are so hard to find now" - shades of Andy Warhol's *Dracula* (1974) – another vampire comedy where virgins were in short supply.

At dawn police officer Ernie (Paul Brooke) arrives at the farm and Mary innocently accompanies him to the police station, but Ernie soon reveals that they are driving to Temple House. Mary discovers Ernie has been bitten and is now a vampire under the serpents' spell. Angus follows in pursuit and is bitten and paralyzed by Lady Sylvia, now naked but covered in blue paint, ready for Eve's sacrifice as the giant white worm has come out of its hiding hole ready to receive the new victim.

Angus uses an anti-venom serum he had acquired earlier from the local hospital to prevent Lady Sylvia's bite from afflicting him and is able to thwart the sacrifice by pushing Lady Sylvia into the hole as the worm devours her. He then drops a handy grenade he happens to have with him and destroys the beast. All the while James leads a hapless crew to investigate the local caverns and their link to Temple House – when they regroup they realize that the nightmare is over, Lady Sylvia and the worm are history.

After Eve and Mary are taken to the hospital Angus visits James in his roadster but James receives a sudden phone call from the hospital explaining that the serum they sent him was the wrong one – it's actually used to treat arthritis. Horrified Angus checks himself in the mirror for any signs of a change. Russell then very smartly shifts to an exterior shot as Angus comes out looking at ease and unworried – clearly he is now a vampire. He gets into James' car and they drive off for a lunch celebration. In the car Angus sinisterly smiles before James shifts gears on his roadster exposing the deadly looking vampire bite on Angus' leg as the men exchange a look that signifies that Angus knows that James knows.

The film ends in a strangely similar way to Roman Polanski's brilliant *Fearless Vampire Killers* made two decades earlier, where in the last moment of the film you realize the vampires have won. Unfortunately *Lair of the White Worm* is caught in a limbo between far better films about monsters and vampires from the same period: (*Lost Boys, Vampire's Kiss, An American Werewolf in London, Vampire in Venice*) and far better B-Movies about beautiful women being sacrificed in pagan rituals: (*She, Prehistoric Women, The People That Time Forgot*). Certainly the film is not ambitious enough to chart new territory for the genre as did F.W. Murnau's *Nosferatu* (1922), Mario Mava's *Planet of the Vampires* (1965), or Francis Ford Coppola's *Dracula* (1992).

Moreover the film seems unsure about what it wants to do which is odd as Russell was always so insistent on the direction of his material. Originally Eve was meant to be nude during the ritual, like Ursula Andress in *She*, but Catherine Oxenberg refused to do a nude scene so Russell had her in her underwear. When Oxenberg agreed to use a negligee Russell told her that the budget could only afford Marks & Spencer, a British retail store for working people – showing that he treated the material as something of a joke. Eve's incongruous white underwear guarantees that the film will not have the erotic charge of adolescent drive-in films that featured the naked sacrifices of beautiful women to fiends, monsters and devils: (*The Devil's Lover, Massacre in Dinosaur Valley, Nude for Satan*) but the film still developed a cult following in its second life in streaming.

One of the great pleasures of the film is Sammi Davis and Peter Capaldi who are wonderful natural actors and they shine here, as their counterparts Hugh Grant and Amanda Donahue are at the opposite end of the acting spectrum: theatrical, playful, outrageous, tearing the scenery to shreds. There are many small pleasures in *Lair of the White Worm* – at least enough to make it worth the time. But as Russell himself said to his critics, who bashed him (particularly in England): "How on earth can you take seriously the vision of Catherine Oxenberg, dressed in Marks & Spencer underwear, being sacrificed to a fake, phallic worm two hundred feet long?"[100] Russell has the last word here.

WHORE (1991)
Whore was based on an original play titled *Bondage* by David Hines who wrote his work based on conversations that he had with prostitutes while he worked as a taxi driver in London. Russell was approached by Hines to see about helping get the play made into a film. He liked *Bondage* and brought in Deborah Dalton to write a viable screenplay. Unable to secure financing in England due to the sexual subject matter, Russell got Trimark Studios, in California to agree to do it but the setting was changed from London to Los Angeles. Due to budget restrictions the film was shot over a period of two weeks in September of 1990, an unusually short time frame in which to make a feature film but Russell was experienced by now with low budgets, last minute shifts in location, and compressed schedules.

Despite Russell's unfamiliarity with Los Angeles he does a good job of capturing the city's downtown area at one of its many moments of transition – in this case from a moribund concrete jungle of offices that shut down after 5 PM, leaving the downtown area a depopulated no-man's land, to a more viable city center with artists moving into empty loft spaces enjoying the cheap rents in the Skid Row area, and clubs and bars opening in the shadow of city hall, making the place something of an oasis on weekends for club-goers, night-owls, and young people on the lookout for something new. The fact that the city was made for cars rather than human beings is something Russell picks up on and italicizes with his framing that puts Liz (Theresa Russell) in the midst of multi-level traffic coming in all directions with seemingly no one on the street but her.

Liz addresses the audience directly on her life and problems on the street throughout the film, a technique used for the first time in a feature film in Lewis Gilbert's *Alfie* (1966) where Michael Caine explains himself, at length, directly to the camera – a narrative form that would be brought to its nadir in Phoebe Waller-Bridge's *Fleabag* (2016-2019). A more subtle and aestheticized version of treating the handheld documentary camera as a style was seen two years after *Whore* in Woody Allen's *Husbands and Wives* (1992) with Carlo Di Palma faking the movements of cinema verité while keeping his lighting and color scheme under perfect control. Unfortunately *Whore's* cinematographer Amir Mokri didn't have the luxury of time to set up his shots so the film tends to have the flatness and gray skies associated with Los Angeles forcing him to shoot on the run and get his shots as they drove through the city. In that sense Russell reinvents Italian Neo-Realism for a new era but the results are mixed. *Whore* stretches for authenticity and always seems to fall short of the mark, but Russell had not lost his incredible eye, and his short take of a wedding dress shop, over-lit from within, is one of his best shots. It also makes narrative sense since the shop offers merchandise that for Liz is out of reach, not financially but because of her circumstances and life choices - Russell and Deborah Dalton elaborate on Hine's play, and on how those two things came together and exploded in Liz's face, more in the spirit of social realism than on any sort of moralizing superciliousness.

We meet Liz trying to flag down customers on a busy downtown street near the famous 2nd Street Tunnel under Bunker Hill. One man stops and demands anal sex and she crassly declines him. When a van stops she also brushes off the driver, recalling the last time she went along for the ride it turned out there were several men inside the van and they gang-raped her, beat her, and left her for dead. Russell shows the flashback not from her point of view but as if a documentary camera were present. She is rescued, in a manner, by an elderly man passing by who gives her his handkerchief and offers to take her to the hospital and give her some money – later she sends the man his money back with a thank-you-note and a new handkerchief – clearly Liz has got her own set of morals while trying to survive on the mean streets of LA.

Disgusted with her life as a prostitute Liz is attempting to escape from her pimp, Blake, a very businesslike, controlling man – she stops at a strip club for a drink and explains her situation to us as in Albert Camus' *The Fall* but now it is a penitent prostitute instead of a penitent judge. Liz explains that she was a regular small town girl who married a violent drunk named Bill – they had a son together but Liz could not cope with his abuse and alcoholism so she escaped with the infant child. She ended up working the night shift at a diner and lived in poverty until one night a customer offered to pay her for sex. Liz agreed and began prostituting herself independently until she met Blake who took her to Los Angeles where one could hope to make much more money. Unfortunately for Liz Blake is as cruel, vicious and controlling as her husband.

While working in downtown LA Liz finds a fellow prostitute has been stabbed in the stomach and brings the woman into a movie theater bathroom to help stop the bleeding - Liz is helped by Katie, an intellectual with whom she befriends. Katie gives Liz a copy of *Animal Farm*, which becomes the first book she ever finishes reading but Blake is threatened by their friendship and threatens to kill them unless they break it off. Liz next meets Rasta a homeless man/street performer whose act is to walk barefoot on broken glass for money. Despite Liz's misgivings she goes with Rasta to the movies.

As Russell shows it the movie they are watching is Blake explaining his life to the audience, giving the impression that Liz and Rasta are watching Blake deliver a long soliloquy about himself. This scene is an homage of sorts to Delmore Schwartz's *In Dreams Begin Responsibilities* (1938) but it lacks the powerful emotional edge – alternating with hard turns between rage, nostalgia, and hopelessness – that permeates Schwartz's story. Clearly Russell doesn't want Blake to be a one-dimensional "bad guy" so he gets a chance to explain himself in the film within the film but the explanations seem contrived and generic.

In the following scene Liz addresses the audience, in a sense trying to win the audience back. She talks about her son, whom she clearly loves, though he is now in foster care. Later that night she secures a wealthy older client who brings her to a parking garage in his vintage car. While the two are having sex the man has a heart attack and dies. Liz panics and tries to save him without success – she calls Blake who takes Liz's money and tries to rob the dead man. Liz tries to stop him and he then tries to strangle her, threatening that he will find her son and force him into gay prostitution. Liz replies that before that happens she would kill him. Blake decides to kill Liz but is saved by Rasta who comes to the rescue, killing Blake by slitting his throat, but Liz is clearly, once again, traumatized, and free only to go back to the streets.

Much was made at the time that *Pretty Woman* (1990) directed by Garry Marshall and written by J.F. Lawton, shared a similar plot line and came out at the same time as *Whore*, but while Marshall's film turned out to be one of the most successful films of the decade *Whore* languished and did not do well at the box office, effectively ending Russell's Hollywood sojourn. While Russell and his team insisted that *Whore* was the real thing and *Pretty Woman* was basically a male fantasy, there are problems with that position. Despite its realism one of the words most used in the negative reviews of *Whore* was "inauthentic" – a word not used for *Pretty Woman* since it would be absurd – much like calling *The Red Shoes* an inauthentic portrayal of the world of contemporary dance. One review was scathing but closer to the mark, from Mark Caro of the Chicago Tribune: "*Whore* purports to be a truthful, uncompromised view of a prostitute's life, but it takes only a minute to establish that these "realities" have more to do with the British director's loony-bin worldview that America's gritty streets."[101] This brings us closer to the problem. *Whore* purports to be a harsh, realistic document – in the style of Free Cinema – of prostitution in Los Angeles. *Pretty Woman* purports to be a romantic comedy that borrows freely from *Cinderella* and *Pygmalion* but takes that mixture and places it in a contemporary context as a man and a woman negotiate the first steps of a relationship with a mixture of cold economic transaction, caution, sexual desire, and sentiment. Fair enough, *Pretty Woman* fulfills the *Cinderella*/*Pygmalion* myths - the fundamentally nice but poor girl from the streets becomes a wealthy lady who remains nice, that is, she keeps her sense of self. From that perspective the film is as much a fantasy for women as it is for men and it operates in a consistent form, keeping that balance in play to the end of the film when all of the parts tie up in a bow.

While dealing with class issues was a staple of the classic Hollywood era – one need only think of Frank Capra's or Preston Sturgess' films – the Hollywood of the 80's and after shied away from class issues or kept them as "local color," By the late 1980's the days of *Blue Collar* (1978) and *Cutter's Way* (1981) were history. In *Pretty Woman* class comes forward and announces itself operatically – literally so when the sophisticated and wealthy man takes the pretty woman to her first opera where they bond emotionally during the production. As in the classic Hollywood films of the past the work recreates for a modern audience the American myth par excellence, that is, that no matter who you are or where you come from, no matter what your station in life or your handicap, you can rise above it all if your love, your bravery, and your desire are strong enough. *Pretty Woman* flat-out delivers the myth in modern dress – it doesn't matter that the film is all frosting without even a cake for support – the cake is unnecessary.

Whore's problem is twofold – first, while the scenes of Liz are realistically shot they are not real. Whores in Los Angeles do not wait outside the 2nd Street Tunnel for clients as they would quickly be picked up by police, or they would be hit on by street people who live in the area, or they would be run over by bad drivers that are endemic to the city. If Russell really wanted to make a film about prostitutes he needed to immerse himself in that world – in the manner of Free Cinema – and have Theresa Russell intermix with real prostitutes and then see what happens. This would have required more time and more energy and perhaps even at some point a jettisoning of the original script, which was British, for an examination of life in Los Angeles in 1990 for working women who happen to be prostitutes.

The other problem is that Liz's direct address to the camera feels forced and is not enlightening except for the traditional expository conventions that follow the genre but add nothing to it. In that sense *Pretty Woman* knows what it is – *Whore* does not – it is not a brutal exposé, (as was Godard's savage *Sauve Qui Peut La Vie*), it is not a fantasy (as was *Catherine and Co.*), it is not realism (as was Fellini's *Nights of Cabiria*), it is not an erotic cartoon of prostitution hiding under a counterfeit "realism" (as was *Leaving Las Vegas* made five years later). *Whore* seems to be full of strident angst, contempt, and fury but signifying nothing – not knowing what it is or what it wants to do – lost in LA.

HD

British Television Redux & Home Video

CLOUDS OF GLORY (1978)

Part 1: *WILLIAM AND DOROTHY*
Part 2: *THE RIME OF THE ANCIENT MARINER*

Clouds of Glory was made as a two-part film for ITV British Television. The title comes from Wordsworth's poem *Trailing Clouds of Glory* – a hymn to childhood and its closeness to the sense of wonder and the natural world – it also comes from Russell's observation, in his autobiography *A British Picture*, that he was fed up with Catholic liturgical incense and its dubious "clouds of glory" (an eternal afterlife) and was now committed to the Lake Poets and their pantheistic worship of Nature. The first section, *William and Dorothy*, is about the close emotional relationship between William Wordsworth and his sister and muse Dorothy; the second *The Rime of the Ancient Mariner*, is about the relationship of William and Dorothy to Samuel Taylor Coleridge, a fellow Romantic poet who had a troubled emotional life and a lifelong dependency on pain killing drugs. *The Rime of the Ancient Mariner* is still probably Coleridge's most famous poem, with well known scenes from it that have found their way into many novels and films often without people being aware of their origin. Wordsworth and Coleridge are sometimes referred to as "The Lake Poets." This is a reference to the Lake District where they lived for a time – an area that is in North West England and includes the Cumbrian Mountains. Its literary associations are not only with the Lake Poets but, sometime later, John Ruskin and the Pre-Raphaelite Brotherhood – which Russell fictionalized in *Dante's Inferno*. The Lake District is also where Russell owned a house and shot many of his films so it is safe to say that the area is visited now as much to see film locations as where Wordsworth and Coleridge went hiking.

After his ventures in Hollywood the film is also a full return to form and he takes advantage of being able to shoot his beloved Lake District in saturated color. For the first time the credits to the film simply read "A Film by Melvyn Bragg and Ken Russell" (in part 2 the names are reversed). Bragg and Russell had known each other since they both started to work at the BBC under Huw Wheldon. Bragg wrote *The Debussy Film* and *Always on Sunday* for Russell, and later after they both left the BBC, he wrote the ambitious and complex *The Music Lovers*. Bragg had, in the intervening years, become a powerful producer eventually getting his own program *The South Bank Show* (1978-2010), modeled on *Monitor*, that became the most popular and long running arts program in British broadcasting history.

Both sections deal with a major crisis and the poetry echoes those relationships in a way that feels unforced. Russell very smartly chooses his actors and they again come through for him delivering spellbinding portraits of the two early Romantic English poets and their wives. David Warner plays William Wordsworth and he is able to embody the radical, revolutionary aspect of the poet – something that is difficult for us to see from our perspective. For us, having read Rimbaud, Apollinaire and Allen Ginsberg in school, Wordsworth seems like a poet wallowing in sentimental and romantic clichés about "Nature" – too bland even to be off-putting - but Wordsworth was the first poet to turn away from mythological and grand historical subjects shifting towards a more descriptive format where he portrayed the nature around him, and even at times his immediate loved ones, using everyday language and colloquial terms.

Both Wordsworth and Coleridge were heterosexual but their relationship was not simply one of collaborating on some poetry for fun – they met in 1795 and created an emotional bond that had the intensity of people in their early 20's who fall in love. They were, like many others of their generation in England, disappointed by the French Revolution and by their own constitutional monarchy under George III. They sough to find a third way by going back to nature, back to the elemental. They were very different people: Coleridge was a perpetual adolescent, excitable, voluble, deeply insecure and prone to manic depression; Wordsworth was more reserved, methodical, logical and even-keeled. Wordsworth grounded Coleridge and the latter's unbounded enthusiasm energized Wordsworth. What they shared was a radical ambition to remake the world through poetry. Unlike today where poetry books are considered the venue of specialists, aficionados, and professors of literature, poetry then was a social practice that included the general population, in a similar way to pop music today; in our world people are involved with pop music and have strong opinions, they fall in love with certain songs, learn the lyrics by heart, and it becomes "their song" – so it was with poetry when Wordsworth and Coleridge were young.

David Warner who plays Wordsworth was a genuine force of nature as an actor throughout the sixties and seventies - he made the most "60's" Hamlet at the Royal Shakespeare Company's iconic Peter Hall production – a Hamlet up to his neck in self-doubt, full of sarcastic fury directed toward society at large, and a hopelessly ironic vision of the universe that he himself found unsatisfying, in short, a modern Hamlet. Warner encapsulated sixties rage in virtually every performance he did regardless of the script and *William and Dorothy* is no exception. Felicity Kendal who plays Dorothy regularly did adaptations of Shakespeare and classic novels, such as *The Tenant of Wildfell Hall* for British television - Russell had used her previously in *Valentino* and liked her work. David Hemmings, forever known as the photographer in Antonioni's *Blow-Up*, is Samuel Coleridge and Kika Mirkham, fresh from Truffaut's brilliant *Two English Girls*, is Sara Coleridge the put upon wife that must deal with her husband's long-standing addiction to laudanum – a pain killer and tranquilizer in liquid form that was mixed with water and that was widely used all through Europe at the time as a recreational drug.

In 1798 Coleridge and Wordsworth published a joint volume of poetry, *Lyrical Ballads*, which is now considered the starting point for the English Romantic age. The star of this collection was Coleridge's *The Rime of the Ancient Mariner*. In 1800 Coleridge and his wife stayed with the Wordsworth's for 18 months and this is the period covered in *Clouds of Glory*. Aside from his obvious genius Coleridge was a difficult man – he had what today we would probably call bipolar disorder – he also had bouts of anxiety and depression that were physically debilitating. He was treated for rheumatic fever with laudanum, which probably started him on the road to being a lifelong addict. His marital problems, due to his emotional absence from his family and eccentric dietary restrictions, made him a difficult partner. In those 18 months there were tensions between the two poets that were sometimes harsh, due to a clash between Coleridge's Kantian idealism and Wordsworth's materialist pantheism – it all led to Coleridge becoming addicted to opium, an addiction that further distanced him from his family. Despite the heavy drug use Coleridge was an avid and brilliant essayist who transformed Shakespeare studies with his essay on *Hamlet*, which is still in print, and sometimes found as a supplement to the text.

Bragg's/Russel's version of these two poets is, as one would expect critical but respectful to a fault – both men were romantics themselves and identified closely with the Lake Poets, but when it comes to family matters the women, in many ways, have the last word. When Wordsworth is shown reading out loud from his notebooks to a visiting acolyte from the USA the visitor is astounded that a mere notebook entry could be as good as his best work – William explains that his sister wrote the poem. Later in part two when he is stuck and can't finish a poem it's his sister who finds just the right words to finish the work. This is historically accurate but Dorothy, like the wives and girlfriends of many writers, artists, (and later pop songwriters) never got credit for their contributions. Coleridge is shown as someone completely unable to deal with the day-to-day *management* of a relationship and a family. Like many Kantian idealists he could deal very well with Life and Love in the abstract but not life and love in the practical everyday sense of the term; in short, Coleridge could write a poem about Love but could not be bothered to change diapers, make a meal, or talk about his emotions in a forthright manner. Similarly when Wordsworth tells his sister that he is about to wed she is all for it in the abstract, but when the time comes to be a bridesmaid in her brother's wedding she can't handle it, falls apart, and eventually collapses from the nervous strain.

This gap between the abstract and the real is something that is brilliantly navigated by Bragg/Russell as they show people falling madly in love with one another, overcome with emotion, but then finding themselves unable to deal with day-to-day matters leading to the inevitable disillusionment, estrangement and anger. The "hangover" after the giddiness of the love was gone was often brutal and the sensitive poets were the worst at being able to deal with it.

Russell shoots his beloved Lake District with Wordsworth in voiceover reading his poetry, and while David Warner's reading is heartfelt and well done the shots that Russell chooses tend to be cliché and generic – flowers in bloom, water rippling in the wind, etc. - more reminiscent of stock photography seen in calendars and greeting cards – he doesn't seem to have worked to find the shots that would go with such poetry and simply assumed that if Wordsworth was talking about pansies he must show pansies. Russell, as in his film illustrating Holst's *Planets* seems to take these shots at face value without taking into consideration their condition - the emotional account for such images is maxed out, overextended and in bankruptcy due to saturation – their worth as images is zero in the wider social context in which images live and work. Once the state of an image reaches zero it is, in the strict sense, meaningless except for its function within a social system. For example we might see such images (of pansies) in bank lobbies, insurance company headquarters, or care facilities, to signify certain emotions such as "peace" or "harmony" but the images themselves are empty, they are there to illustrate an idea, in effect, the images are put to work.

They end the two part film with Coleridge, emotionally wrought, at the end of his tether, wandering in a drug induced haze, bumping into walls and raging against his wife, as he imagines murdering her violently by driving a harpoon into her chest; meanwhile on the soundtrack we hear Coleridge's poems of love – the two make perfect sense emotionally together as a fusion of what we have been seeing separately for two hours. This push/pull or dialectic tension between two opposing emotional idioms happening at the same time was unusual in cinema where, for obvious reasons, the music or voiceover tends to reinforce the images, but as we saw in Russell's earlier work with the painter Dante Rossetti where he deliberately creates a tension between music/voiceover and image, he was after something else. Like Godard with his work of the 1960's or Welles from the 1970's image and sound/music were at times in harmony but at others in opposition or in tension, each going its own separate way. Where does this formal idea come from and what was the point?

This strain between idioms occurring simultaneously in a work comes from orchestral music itself and may be where Russell, a lifelong music fanatic, first became aware of it. In 1785/86 Mozart wrote some piano concertos that were completely revolutionary, in that the piano separated itself from the orchestra and even contradicted it, going its own way. For example the Piano Concerto no. 20 starts off briskly, "allegro" and ready for a good trip with the orchestra – but when the solo starts the piano is slow, melancholic, solitary – as if the piano had changed its mind and had its own ideas. Before Mozart the piano had always responded "appropriately" to the orchestra, literally and figuratively playing along – but no longer. Now the soloist and the orchestra would be separate and sometimes even in tension, antagonists, mimicking and taunting, sometimes even stepping on each other's lines – by the 20th century it is no great exaggeration to say they were no longer on speaking terms. Russell takes that idea and adapts it to cinema.

At the very end of *Clouds of Glory* Russell ups the ante by cutting from Coleridge's vicious dreams of murder and mayhem, to Coleridge as a young man joyfully taking his marriage vows, his wife looking on in wonderment and love – both looking toward the future. The memory of that initial love and the poetry survive Russell seems to say – the rest flows away. As Russell pans over the lush countryside we see the smallness of the cares and the worries, the dramas and the traumas – people are all seen in situ, in the context of the grandeur of Nature, a presence that is within and without us, and perhaps, as Wordsworth and Coleridge suggested, ultimately unknowable.

THE PLANETS (Short/1983)

The Planets was broadcast in 1983 as part of *The South Bank Show* (1978-2010) presented by Melvyn Bragg. *The Planets* is a seven movement orchestral suite written by the British composer Gustav Holst between 1914-1917, that is, exactly during WWI. Holst was more interested in astrology than in astrophysics and his suite takes the idea of a series of mood pictures based on astrological symbols being set to music creating an episodic symphonic work. Russell was always a fan of the work and this is his personal interpretation of the fifty-minute piece.

Russell's film uses found footage in black and white and color from a variety of sources, much like avant-garde films such as Bruce Conner's *A Movie* (1958). Unfortunately problems arise almost immediately. The found footage that Russell uses is, on the one hand, too obvious and literal, and on the other, the thematic categories that he is using are culturally determined in a way that Russell seems oblivious to. For example during the Mars section, that Holst predictably relates to war and violence, has footage of wars but they are wars that are already historicized cinematically – the footage has been seen many times in many different contexts, such as Marcel Ophuls' film *The Sorrow and the Pity* (1969), and so this new context, illustrating Holst's music seems rather trite and perhaps even offensive.

When Russell brings in Jupiter, which Holst associates with "jollity," Russell uses found footage from European pagan rituals where people are forcibly sprayed with water; Germans are drinking beer in festivals; Bolivians and Peruvians in native costumes are dancing; Europeans are alpine climbing; Americans are wearing Indian feather hats in patriotic parades, etc. While these things might very well be associated for him with "jollity" we can safely say that is not the case for everyone. The film seems to swing wildly from cliché images that are too overused (areal shots of "majestic mountains") to found footage showing things that are by no means as universal as Russell seems to assume. For example seeing a lot of Germans drinking beer, or Peruvians forced to perform "native" dances in costume for tourists, might not be associated for everyone with "jollity."

Caught between a rock and a hard place *The Planets* cannot go anywhere – it is stuck in a limbo of photography more appropriate for a calendar showing the seasons than a work of music presumably giving us the orchestral version of "the music of the spheres." *The Planets* seems desperate to please, shock and/or amuse and Holst's popular work seems more banal than the film offers. Russell's film suggests, more than anything else, the photography exhibition *The Family of Man* put on by Edward Steichen at MoMA in 1955. While this exhibition was enormously popular – it is still today the most widely attended photography exhibition in history – there were problems that apply equally to Russell's film.

While the exhibition received exaggerated praise from critics in the US both at the time and even later, Roland Barthes caught the gist of the problem with his succinct French elegance in a review at the time of the exhibit's premiere in Paris:

> "...the difference in human morphologies is affirmed, exoticism is stressed, the many variations of the species are manifested, the diversity of skins, skulls and customs and notions of Babel are extended over the image of the world. And then, from this pluralism, magically enough, a unity is derived: man is born, works, laughs, and dies in the same fashion everywhere...this evidently comes down to postulating a human essence, whereupon God is reintroduced into our Exhibition: the diversity of mankind proclaims his will... Everything here, the content and appeal of the pictures, the discourse justifying them, aims at suppressing the determining weight of History: we are kept at the surface of an identity, prevented by sentimentality itself from penetrating in that further zone of human conduct..."[102]

For Barthes, of course, "Nature" was itself historical and went through many phases and faces – the latest incarnation being influenced by global warming and ways to "manage" nature. Russell's film erases differences by trying to find the commonality between dancing Bolivians in costume and dancing Americans – and as Barthes makes clear what gets lost in the cutting room floor are their respective specific identities, their (often brutal) historical realities – replaced by ceremony and sentimentality.

Of course, Holt's *The Planets* was based on yet another myth – astrology – but the abstractions of music let Holst slide as we might imagine or dream anything listening to his music, but Russell's "family of man" grounds the work in particular realities, and whether he acknowledges it or not, those realities are loaded with a History that he cannot escape; yet strangely even in two or three second clips they slip out here and there – History suddenly shows its strange face. For example we might notice the horrifying rictus of performing Bolivians, forced to smile for the boss as they dance – the jolt is intense - but before we can grasp it the film has moved on to more banal, cliché images of Nature suggesting an earthly Paradise that never was, except, of course, in the movies. For example a beautiful waterfall in Hawaii is, indeed, an illustration of the wonders of Nature, but what is left out is the history of Hawaii: Its local culture and language were systematically destroyed by American imperial power in 1898 during America's first gilded age, and eventually turned into a resort. It seems that after all this time we still can't see ourselves, or the planet we inhabit, with any sense of reality – like Holst we prefer the myth of "natives" in costume to the real history and astrology to cosmology.

RALPH VAUGHAN WILLIAMS: A SYMPHONIC PORTRAIT (Short/1984)

Ralph Vaughan Williams: A Symphonic Portrait is Russell's fifty-five minute film, made for British television's *The South Bank Show* about the British composer (1872-1958) who had a very long life and went through various phases in his career. As one would expect of a film about a composer that Russell loved he put everything he had into it and it is one of his best late works. Russell begins his film with one of his own children on his lap in an interior shot as he sits between a bookcase and a fireplace, as he is showing his daughter a photo book on the life of Ralph Vaughan Williams (henceforth RVW), explaining the details as he turns the pages. In effect, his film will offer a more adult version of this modus using Williams' nine symphonies, as counterpoint as Russell recounts the life for his daughter and for us.

It makes a great deal of sense that someone who was enamored by the work of Elgar and Delius, as was Russell, would also love the music of RVW– all three were influenced by Tudor music and British folk songs but Williams went further, producing a vast output of compositions in every genre composing music to the very end. Like Elgar and Delius he was influenced by Debussy and Ravel, and like them he stayed away from German Romantic music preferring his art down to earth and home grown taking freely from native folk music. This links him to Béla Bartók, Bohuslav Martinu, and Aaron Copland – all composers who were unabashedly impassioned by their national music.

Over Russell's shoulder we see a sample of RVW's house as a boy, already composing music at age 5 - a work called *Robin's Nest*. He was described in his early years as "that extremely British product, the natural nonconformist with a conservative regard for the best tradition." The same could be said of his music. He was allowed to go to the Royal College of Music but expected to attend Cambridge, which he eventually did, meeting Bertrand Russell, the great philosopher who was teaching there then. Ken explains to his daughter that RVW and his first wife Adeline were married in 1897, and she played the cello very beautifully but with great difficulty due to her chronic arthritis – they honeymooned in Berlin and when they returned to England settled in London – there were no children. We see the pictures that Russell is pointing to in close-up as in his BBC work but the context is a more familial one.

Ralph Vaughan Williams: a Symphonic Portrait is one of the best and most charming of his later films. This is due in no small measure to Ursula Vaughan Williams his co-host (and official co-writer of the film) and the composers' younger second wife – they were married in 1953. Fortunately for Russell and for us, she is articulate, remembers everything, and is sensitive to a fault, providing Russell with some great moments that you can only get when you have a collaborator like her willing to give you the gift of themselves, their time, and their memories. Using her and his own daughter is a stroke of genius on Russell's part for another reason – it puts him in the position of being a teacher (with his daughter) and a student (with Ursula) so he is not at any point the all-knowing narrator, as in the BBC films but a tactful teacher and a curious student willing to learn – it makes Russell more human and we can identify with him here in ways not possible in earlier work.

At first he's showing his daughter (and us) the basics of the composer's life and a moment later he is asking Ursula for more details about RVW and the times they shared together. He knows that he has something special in that mix – it's as if someone had made a documentary about Mozart and were interviewing Constanze Mozart about what Wolfgang was thinking about when he composed certain concertos – it would be a priceless treasure and so it proves to be here. He also borrows a page from *The Debussy Film* so we see his film crew going to the various parts of England that motivated the composer with Ursula along, setting up his shots mostly along the coast, in London, and finally in Stonehenge. It's an inspired take on his own past work and he makes the most of it, even managing it with his usual humor.

As he is explaining to his daughter the musical world at the time that RVW came along he tells her that all the young composers of the early century were influenced by Wagner and Brahms, "and it's very nice music, listen!" On the word listen Russell cuts to the interior of a massive cave –shades of *Lair of the White Worm* – with what appears to be a very tall, imposing, figure in a cape seen in silhouette walking toward the light – we hear the dramatic crescendo from Brahms 4th symphony. "Very nice and very German" says Russell "but not something you want to listen to every day, and by the turn of the century people were beginning to say: 'where's our own music?' That's enough of old Brahms! Give us something fresh!" Russell's introduction to Ursula is a masterly feat of pulling the rug out from genre expectations as on that final word "fresh" Russell cuts to the caped figure from the opposite side as she comes out of the cave and we see what looks to be a very small, nice, pleasant, old English lady wearing a scarf for a windy day. Russell here subverts the prospects of Wagnerian mythos – the silhouetted figure, the cave, etc. - and gives us a British grandmother, but not any grandmother, it's Ursula Vaughan Williams and she's at the seashore in Southampton to talk about RVG's first symphony, also called *The Sea Symphony*.

Ursula explains that a huge influence on RVW and his generation was the work of Walt Whitman. They were looking to find something at the opposite end of the spectrum from the pompous German music of Wagner and the harmonically conservative music of Brahms – and Whitman was the antidote. It's easy to see why they all found that work liberating as Whitman didn't do mythic epics in the European style, with fire and brimstone; on the contrary, he very consciously set out to do the opposite, finding value in the everyday, the corporeal, even the mundane and the very small – his great poem is called *Leaves of Grass* for a reason – in short Whitman was a self-deprecating radical, something that would be very appealing to a British sensibility. What British composers discovered was that they could take subjects literally under their feet, such as the London of the turn of the century, or the seashore in a little provincial town on the coast, and turn it into art, in effect it gave them permission, it opened that door that they could not find on their own.

When Ursula finishes speaking Russell yells "cut!" and we see him in an orange mac and his crew of six shooting with the usual lights and mike boom. As is normal for such shoots Russell is standing next to the director of photography. He then cuts to himself introducing Ursula properly as RVW's wife and biographer: "Shakespeare said that there were seven ages to man and we are going to explore the nine symphonies – or the nine ages - of Ralph Vaughn Williams." We notice that he pronounces the English name properly, not as Ralph but "Raef." As the film crew is disbanding Ursula approaches Jane, the script/continuity person, and asks her if she remembered everything she was supposed to say – Jane says she forgot to say "it was his first symphony and that he conducted the premiere on his 38th birthday." Russell here has some fun introducing information not directly from Ursula but from someone reminding her of everything she forgot to say.

His cinematographer wants to know the meaning of the cave and Russell hurries off saying: "I'll tell you later." Another joke about film scholarship, a subject that Russell, like Orson Welles and Federico Fellini, loved to skewer – of course there is no "later." As we see Ursula ceremoniously returning to the cave (whatever it may mean!) Russell explains in voiceover that: "the *Sea Symphony* put RVW on the map, breathing new life to a dying Victorian tradition and although an agnostic he also started airing out the churches." From the interior of a British cathedral we see Ursula enter and talk about the *Fantasia for Strings on a Theme of Thomas Tallis* based on the 16th century British composer of sacred music and one of RVW's most well known compositions. We hear it as Russell cuts to various parts of the cathedral from very low to the floor so we get the full expanse of the medieval architecture – we even see part of a mass looking down the main aisle toward the pulpit, emphasizing Russell's faith as choir boys parade double file.

From Big Ben's Clock in London we pan down to Russell and Ursula in the back of Rolls Royce convertible in the streets of the city talking about RVW's 2nd or *London Symphony* that he wanted to call "Symphony by a Londoner" –"all noise and scurry" claims Russell giggling as we hear the work over the streets of the city, which are reminiscent of his *Monitor* film *London Moods* but now in color. He goes to many of the same places as his early film that still look much the same but shoots from a different angle as if determined to make it better this time around. For example in the earlier work he had filmed the unusual statue dedicated to the fallen soldiers of WWI – unusual because it is one of the few statues which is horizontal as the soldier is lying dead on a long plinth. In the earlier film he shot from the side with everything symmetrical to the frame, but here he shoots from one end with the heavy boots in the extreme foreground, reminiscent of Andrea Mantegna's painting of the dead Christ using extreme foreshortening, and the bustling traffic of London in the background, full of life. It's a much more dramatic perspective and Russell takes advantage of the beautiful light.

In one of the lovely British parks surrounded by traffic Ursula and Russell debate as to whether a certain sound in the symphony refers to coins in a beggars hat or horse bells but come to no conclusion. "In either case it's a beautiful sound," says Russell, clearly wary of academic debates. We then see them in a medium long-shot sitting in a park bench with an alley like path leading away behind them towards a mysterious deep space but we don't hear them talking - only the 2nd symphony – the still shot is beautifully done as it suggests RVW is there with them having a three way conversation but with music instead of words.

It would not be a Ken Russell film if he didn't take some extreme chances and he does so for the next scene scored to the "nocturne" sequence from the *London Symphony* suggesting a Saturday night out on the town. We see Ursula and Russell at a local disco dancing under the multi colored ball that throws its lights on the floor typical then for discos. Young punks and rockers are also in the mix looking over the situation but our two leads seem to not mind the looks and they find their groove – and have some fun in the process. As to be expected Ursula is a graceful dancer and Russell is outrageous – part Jerry Lewis and part Rudolph Nureyev on acid – but then we remember that when he was very young he aspired to be a professional ballet dancer so he had a feel for it. It's also typical of Russell to find the modern version of London, not one from the 30's that RVW knew when he was writing the symphony. In any case, that London is long gone, and while he could have easily provided period photos from the 30's, as in his BBC days, he chose a more dangerous route – the danger being that he would make a fool of himself but he manages to pull it off and Ursula very graciously went along showing how the *London Symphony* is, in effect, timeless.

Typically Russell cuts from the high spirits of the disco scene to a shot of London Bridge at dusk seen from a boat going down the Thames as Ursula recalls that the final movement of the symphony was based on H.G. Welles' novel *Tono-Bungay* at the end of which a destroyer is going down that same Thames but the ship, and London sink into the waters, and eventually England and even the river itself all disappear. Clearly Ursula, like RVW, (and H.G. Welles) saw London in geological time as well as with the normal clock of a human lifespan – the scene becomes a curious and haunting farewell to the city, as well as a celebration – all of it is in the music and Russell is intent on showing it to us. For all-encompassing, and all-embracing artists like RVW, or Russell, the bumps in the road – and even the end of the road itself – are all a part of the experience and they want to put it into their work.

Russell cuts smartly from the statues of soldiers throughout London, with traffic blazing around, to an open, barren field with Ursula being the only person, or living thing, for miles – suddenly a modern tank comes up and over a short hill as Russell explains in voiceover: "The third symphony (done directly after WWI) shuns all heroics and patriotism. There's no pomp and circumstance anywhere in it. He hated the establishment, turned down a knighthood and refused to become the Master of the Queen's Music. The 3rd or *Pastoral Symphony* seems like an elegy for all of his friends killed during the war." As the tank rolls along Ursula goes in the opposite direction, crossing the enormous tracks that the tank has made on the soft ground. But it isn't all doom and gloom - during the fast moving scherzo from the same symphony the film crew, Ursula and Russell break open a case of red wine outdoors in a picnic area and toast to RVW drinking from white plastic cups as they film each other enjoying the beautiful day.

The following scene of friends sitting around a dinner table listing to RVW's music is one of the few instances where we see people who love music, and in some cases make their living from it, actually listening to music. While watching the funny penguin scene from *Scott of the Antarctic* (1948) in a theater Ursula and Russell talk about his work producing soundtracks, most famously this one that became his 7th symphony. Prokofiev and Shostakovich, the other great composers of symphonies in the 20th century also worked on films but despite the success of *Scott of the Antarctic* RVW never went back to it. He was also 80 years old at the time and finally married Ursula his second wife.

For the 9th symphony she and Russell go to Stonehenge to talk about the final work. Russell finds it a summation saying: "It's all there isn't it? His love of folk songs, poets and composers, our history, architecture, the landscape and its people, the sea, and the unknown, past, present and future. All incredibly concentrated in this last great visionary work." Ursula adds that "the 9th has no finality – it seems more like the beginning of a new exploration – and perhaps that is how all journeys should end." On that note Russell wisely lets the music speak as he recapitulates images from the film in a beautiful montage, ending back where we began with Ursula and the crew at Stonehenge. Using the film trick pioneered by Georges Méliès suddenly the crew disappears and then Ursula disappears leaving only the stones.

An appropriate ending no doubt but Russell very wisely adds a coda – a bookend to the beginning where he is reading from a picture book. Now he is outdoors in London on a bench with his daughter just outside the Festival Hall where the music had its premiere in April 1958 just before RVW died – and even though he was deaf toward the end like Beethoven he attended. "It's his swan song" explains Russell. His daughter wants to know what a "swan song" is. As he explains the two walk off down the embankment overlooking the Thames and the Houses of Parliament at dusk, the lights are already on as the camera stays behind - a similar ending to his early short film *Peepshow* but now it's Russell going down the road with his daughter. It is, as Ursula said of the 9th, the beginning of a new exploration on which we fade out on arguably Russell's best late work. Ursula and Russell really bond in this film and you can sense it as the film progresses – as they swing from meditative explorations of death, to having a ball at discos, and from the questions that arise when setting war and its tragic aftermath to music, to whimsical picnics with a film crew, we catch the real meaning of the music as well.

RICK WAKEMAN: IT'S A LOVELY LIFE (Music Video/1984)
This three minute music video, made for Rick Wakeman's song *It's a Lovely Life* uses images from Russell's *Crimes of Passion* but reedited in a more abstracted style normally found in avant-garde films with shots running backward or shots repeated with jump cuts that show a suburban un-loveliness that works well to illustrate Wakeman's lyrics but does not transcend it. Wakeman did the music to Russell's feature film and this song is part of the official soundtrack and is based on Antonin Dvorak's *From the New World Symphony*, a favorite of Russell's, that might also be seen as a nod to the film being Russell's own take on "the new world."

ELTON JOHN: NIKITA (Music Video/1985)
This music video was written and shot by Russell to coincide with Elton John and Bernie Taupin's song *Nikita*, one of the biggest pop hits of its day. It is arguably Elton John's best video and one of the best in the genre, managing to tell a story coherently, with

some complexity, in just under five minutes. Bernie Taupin's lyrics are a basic love story between a wealthy Englishman and a poor East German security guard who only get to meet at the famed Check Point Charlie, the crossing point between East and West Berlin as Elton (coming from the capitalist West) is driving a Rolls Royce and Nikita (an East German guard coming from the Communist East) is stationed at the border. The Berlin wall would feature in many photo shoots, videos and films throughout the 1980's just before it came down in 1989 – perhaps most spectacularly in Wim Wenders' *Wings of Desire* (1987). Russell illustrates the story but in a dreamlike, highly theatrical way, making use of his "compression" to give the love story some breathing space even within the 4:40 minute time frame – something of an achievement.

The film begins with Elton John dressed in contemporary 80's sunglasses, but a boater straw hat with a red sash from the 20's, and a red varsity jacket from the 50's rocker days, sitting casually in the back of a convertible Rolls Royce taking pictures and singing. With German guards incongruously goose-stepping around in the snow we see that Elton's interest is voyeuristically focused around a young woman, Nikita (Anya Major), who seems to be in charge of the post. The chauffeur drives the car through with Elton and Nikita meeting for the first time as he continues singing. In a comic turn Elton's passport photo shows he is wearing the same clothes and has the same expression on his face of unrequited longing that he exhibits in the car. Clearly she is intrigued but Russell cuts to a nighttime shot with Nikita posted in a lonely looking tower over some barbed wire – a traditional shot from WWII films. Elton has painted a large heart on the frozen ground and looks up at the guard tower continuing his song. She sees him finish his heart painting on the tower security monitor and seems to find it beautiful.

On another day Elton again comes up to the checkpoint but in different clothes signifying a new day as Nikita seems more warm, charming and friendly – a relationship is just beginning to form it seems. Elton photographs her in close-up as another more menacing security guard comes up (Andreas Wisniewski) and takes Elton's passport and gives him a suspicious glance, looking for a reason to deny entry. Elton and Nikita exchange a pas de deux from afar as he continues his song. The security guard refuses to give Elton permission to enter and the chauffeur has to back up and leave. Later that night – perhaps in a dream - Nikita and Elton are in a disco dancing to the song while looking deeply into each other's eyes; a moment later they are at a soccer match and rooting for Elton's team; then we see them playing chess but Elton only has eyes for Nikita; then we see them having fun in a bowling alley with Nikita dressed completely in red and bowling badly but laughing.

Back in the world of reality Elton is at home looking at slides of Nikita that he's taken. On the lyric "Nikita you'll never know" we see a close-up of her as she suffers through another day without love, surrounded only by goose-stepping guards in the snow, fading to black. The film goes beyond the basic pop lyrics to give some sense of the tension as Russell equates East/West, male/female relations. But Elton John's odd choice of clothing and his faux seriousness and one-note "longing" get to be heavy handed and long winded even at under five minutes. Russell manages to save the film through ingenuity, good cinematography, editing, and excellent acting from Major as Nikita and Wisniewski as the security guard who save the day and bring a dose of much needed humor, realism and balance to the video.

CLIFF RICHARD: SHE'S SO BEAUTIFUL (Music Video/1985)

Cliff Richard is a British singer who started his career in the fifties as a "rebellious" rocker in the style of Elvis and Eddie Cochran – his 1958 hit *Move It*, as *Cliff Richard and the Shadows*, is widely regarded as the first British Rock n' Roll record. Unlike other rockers Richard managed to adapt to every new decade and every passing trend with aplomb becoming successful many times in his long career. In the 1980's Richard had again reinvented himself and the "she" in *She's So Beautiful* is planet earth, as the new environmental awareness, that started in the 1960's, was finally coming into its own, even becoming something of a trend, and many pop artists jumped on board. Andrew Lloyd Weber's work heavily influenced the song, written by Hans Sven Poulsen, that has major elements of light opera, and the video, as was typical for Russell, follows the thematic line of the content.

Russell consistently cuts to various kinds watches and clocks – the first with a small illustration of planet earth – so we make the connection to time running out as Richard emotes in the light opera style in front of a spectacular waterfall in Russell's Lake District. He then intercuts birds and jet fighters in the style of *Koyaanisqatsi* (1982) but without the consistency of tone and seriousness. Richard then takes a basketball with the earth painted on its surface and starts to play with it rather awkwardly. We then see the basketball/globe pass over shots of babies and children. The kids start to play with the earth ball until it suddenly seems to catch fire but the children put it out with some handy nearby water from a lake and they continue on with their joyous play, hitting a ram on the head but it doesn't seem to mind at all. Various adults start to play ball with the earth in different sorts of games, from rugby to tennis, all dressed in colorful outfits such as kilts and bright colored blouses as we see in children's films. Finally the ball comes back to Richard who gives it a good spin to a fade out.

Poulson's song and Richard's interpretation has a sing-along quality perfect for a commercial and lacks any sort of melody or lyric of interest. Likewise much of the imagery is banal and more reminiscent of commercial photography than any sort of ecstatic immersion in nature, which is clearly what Russell was after. Just as damagingly Richard, like Elton John, is not able to do much except display one emotion (in this case profound compassion) for the duration of the video, which is annoying. Only the children, who are clearly having a ball (in every sense) making a movie and playing outdoors, save the film from becoming unbearable kitsch.

FAUST (1985)

Faust (1859) is an opera by Charles Gounod with a libretto by Jules Barbier and Michel Carré from Carré's play *Faust et Marguerite*, which is, in turn, loosely based on Goethe's *Faust, Part One*. Russell directed several operas in the 1980's as he was offered jobs by opera entrepreneurs who liked his film work and saw him – as well as Fellini- as a natural opera directors. Fellini never took up the challenge but Russell, aside from Gounod's work, directed Stravinsky's *A Rake's Progress*, Arrigo Boito's Wagnerian opera *Il Mefistofele*, and two Puccini operas, *La Boheme* and *Madame Butterfly*. While Gounod's *Faust* was distributed by Deutsche Grammophon Russell' other operas have never been officially released in any form.

Faust was an opera production that captured a live performance at the Teatro Margherita in Geneva in 1985, with an orchestra conducted by Edoardo Müller. It is not a film, in the sense that Ingmar Bergman's *Magic Flute* (1975) or Joseph Losey's *Don Giovanni* (1979) were operas that were shot as films – they also had the budget to shoot on 35mm film and in the case of *Don Giovanni* even use actual palatial locations in France and Italy giving the filmmaker great freedom in camera set-ups and staging. Russell's three hour *Faust* uses video and the basic single camera set up in front of a stage, in effect recording Russell's production for posterity.

Russell uses modern staging like Peter Sellars but without the hard-edged political allegories found in the American's opera work. Russell also uses clothing and sets that come from different periods often mimicking classic films from Fritz Lang's *Metropolis* to F.W. Murnau's *Faust*. The duel between good and evil in *Faust* is very clear in all of its versions, and Russell only highlights it by making Marguerite a nun who, momentarily, looses her way, finding it again just before she dies and ascends to heaven. In that sense Russell's version of the opera has an even clearer Christian message that Gounod's original. His staging, using the colors red for Faust, black for Méphistophélès and white for Marguerite emphasize that dichotomy.

In one sense *Faust* is a Christian fantasy, nevertheless, the opera's power comes not strictly from faith in Biblical mythology – anymore than *Antinoge's* power as a play finds it necessary for someone to believe in Greek burial rituals or the divine right of kings – in fact one can find these things ridiculous and still find Antigone's search for justice on earth, whatever the price, very moving. Similarly, Faust's story (Goethe's and Gounod's) moves us because of Faust's cruel, cynical treachery and Marguerite's betrayed innocence – by the time Faust finally realizes that power has gone to his head and that he has destroyed the one person that actually loved him it is too late. These are universal themes that need no religious foundation.

ELTON JOHN: CRY TO HEAVEN (Music Video/1986)
Cry to Heaven is a 3:45 minute song written by Elton John and Bernie Taupin from their album *Ice on Fire*. Russell made the film specifically to fit Taupin's lyrics that deal with the death of a young man in the British army and the reaction of his working class wife and child. This is a theme that had long preoccupied Russell, perhaps due to his experience in the two branches of the service when he was young. An early film for *Monitor*, *London Moods*, deals obliquely with the theme by using statues through London erected to fallen soldiers. Due to budget the film had only a three-day shooting schedule –unusual even for the notoriously limited time frame for music videos – and Russell delivered.

The opening shot is a beautiful but horrifying still life of broken glass covered in blood with a mans beret lying nearby as inspectors wearing rubber gloves clean and sort through the rubble. Elton John appears in a small concrete courtyard in a council estate wearing motorcycle gear singing: "I found a black beret on the street today. There's a white flag flying" plays as we see a white handkerchief fall from one of the windows of a tall council flat. We see another window in close-up with kids pressed up against the glass looking glum. As the handkerchief falls by Elton's boot a dog comes and takes it away to: "There's a mad dog barking in a burned out subway where the sniper sleeps at night." For the subway Russell uses an all-concrete modernist tunnel that Kubrick also used in *A Clockwork Orange* - the underpass under Wandsworth Road in London - where Alex beats up an old man. It works well for Russell too who lights it differently from the front instead of using Kubrick's dramatic backlighting.

"No birthday song to sing again." The lyric gives us a close-up of the soldier's wife with candles all around as she gets up – we realize she has been kneeling in a church but there is an incongruous red light shining as she departs to: "Wrap them up in your father's flags." Russell them pans upward to a golden Christian cross on the far side with light streaming from it – he then does a beautiful overlapping dissolve from the cross to a portrait of the soldier with his family and their dog – the same dog we saw earlier retrieving the white flag – as we hear: "There are many graves by a cold lake."

Russell then cuts to a very chancy shot of a baby on a sofa looking at a television with Elton in white clown makeup performing his song. The room with the TV is obviously staged with merely an old beat up lamp from the post-war era signifying "working class family." "But the kids just watch the storm" continues with John in full make-up. "I saw a black cat tease a white mouse" brings in a new sub-theme: the innate violence of nature as animals kill for sport or pleasure and how people and even countries behave in a similar fashion. Russell shows two porcelain sculptures of a cat and a mouse – and suddenly the white mouse is broken to bits. The toddler goes off and out of the apartment down to the small patch of garden separating the flats and he suddenly finds himself in a war zone with bulldozers, flames and jackhammers – the dividing line between war's destruction and construction seem to dissipate as in a dream. "No birthday songs to sing again." There is then a repeat motif with now clearly a woman's arm throwing out the handkerchief out the window as Elton is back in the courtyard of flats. Quick cuts of previous footage take us to the wife sitting by herself on the large couch, in tears, looking off into space, repeating the motif/title: "And let them cry to heaven." In the final moments the toddler is seen wearing a small beret similar to his dads and Elton back at the courtyard exits the frame as Russell holds the concrete and fades to black.

Cry to Heaven is arguably the most successful music video that Russell made. Certainly the three to five minute video format was made for him since he specialized in a cinema of "compression." Many people at the time —from Susan Sontag to Norman Mailer - recognized that the format in essence brought back the imaginative lyrical cinema of the silent period but with pop music added. Unlike most feature films that were "prose" pop videos were "poetry" – by design or by default - edited to music cues and Russell clearly feels at home here. The film takes many risks, not least the Pierrot costume and white face that Elton John wears for the video within the video section.

Although the film suggests "war" in a general sense the Falklands war between Argentina and England had happened only four years before and the images of soldiers coming back maimed or dead was still fresh on people's minds. The video also hints at a futurist dystopia, in the manner of J.G. Ballard or Anthony Burgess where there is constant civil or terrorist war in London itself and the soldier was another working class victim. Bernie Taupin's lyrics lay out the cat/mouse analogy in a very literal way, suggesting that such wars are eternal – or at least they will last as long as human beings are on earth. The song's despair is matched here by Russell's heart-on-sleeve take on the soldier's lot and he delivers an imaginative, superb short film.

CLIFF RICHARD & SARAH BRIGHTMAN: ALL I ASK OF YOU (Music Video/1986)
Phantom of the Opera is a musical from 1986 by Andrew Lloyd Webber, with lyrics by Charles Hart and Richard Stilgoe based on the novel of the same name by Gaston Leroux. It tells the story of a beautiful soprano, Christine Daaé, who becomes the obsession of a mysterious, disfigured musical genius living in the subterranean labyrinth beneath the Paris Opéra House. *The Phantom of the Opera* was the longest running show in Broadway history as well as the most financially successful entertainment event in history until it was surpassed by *The Lion King* in 2014 – after much infighting it was finally turned into a successful film nearly 20 years after the initial production in 2004 by Joel Schumacher but using a different cast from the original production.

The video by Russell was shot especially for the song from the musical with the director using a blue-screen, and so all of the background images were added later in a video studio. The two leads, Cliff Richard (who was not in the original production), dressed in a white suit, and Sarah Brightman (who premiered the role of Daeé in London), dressed in white evening gown and necklace, sing in the traditional musical format, that is, facing the camera rather than each other, but looking just above the lens toward some unspecified space "beyond." Russell uses what looks to be stock footage of sunsets, birds over the ocean, white clouds moving swiftly in a blue sky, waves crashing, and so forth to create a presumably romantic mood.

The two lovers finally turn to each other and sing into each other's eyes for the remainder of the song with Brightman running on a beach - superimposed on video – and leaping into the arms of Richard as the two perform a nice pas de deux – at the finale the two kiss as Russell's camera encircles them with "nature" now not only in the background but also superimposed transparently over them so the couple is sandwiched, in a manner of speaking, with natural grandeurs.

Russell's work here, as always, is bound to the content and he illustrates Lloyd Webber's romantic song with panache – Richard and Brightman work well together. Brightman is a specialist in the music of the composer having originated the female lead in *Phantom of the Opera*, a piece that was written specially for her. The use of a video blue screen, where the background is added later in the studio, is one that has dated badly, at least for serious or romantic material. There are other artists who used it at the time, such as Elvis Costello, but his videos from the 1980's have a particular brand of absurdist humor that lends itself to the clunky and obvious fakery of the blue screen. Russell's use of it here is perfunctory and lacks individuality, imagination, or emotion – a strange thing to happen in a song that is meant to be about a love that lasts forever. Nevertheless the song, and the video, were enormously popular at the time and enjoy repeated viewings to this day on *YouTube* as Andrew Lloyd Webber remains a force in the musical world.

SARAH BRIGHTMAN & STEVE HARLEY: THE PHANTOM OF THE OPERA
(Music Video/1986)

Rather than making a condensed version of the complex narrative of *Phantom of the Opera* Russell only uses one song but gives us an idea of the whole through inference. The character of The Phantom, Steve Harley, who was in the original production in London, is consistent throughout the work, that is, he is obsessively possessive and in love, while the character of Christine (Sarah Brightman) changes dramatically in the piece from a fresh, young ingénue to a more serious woman, aware of herself, her strength, her sexuality, and the complicated world of love. Brightman became a major star because of the role and she shines in Russell's film. Since the official feature was made in 2004 using different actors Russell's film is also a document of Brightman's and Harley's performances the same year that the work premiered in England.

The opening shot shows a 19th century poster for *Cleopatra*, an opera production with Christine Daaé as the lead. From the bottom of some grandiose stairs we see Christine open two Art Deco doors and run frantically down the stairs like a teenager wearing what appears to be a white wedding dress. Russell cuts to two twin women laughing, that for a second look like a mirror image as they make way for Christine – clearly late for a performance as she makes her way to her dressing room where she finds a gift box. Inside is the veil for a wedding dress as she sings her first song, *Angel of Music*, the code name for The Phantom. Wearing the veil Christine turns toward the mirror from which strange white light is emanating – reminding of us the twins that at first looked like a mirror – but Christine does not seem afraid, rather, she steps confidently into the mirror passing through it to another dimension or reality.

In this alternate reality underneath the Paris Opera House is, of course, the sanctuary of the Phantom – Russell shoots him dressed as Dracula in a flowing red cape, with a red light signifying that Christine might have gone into one of the circles of hell. At the bottom of some stairs she rides a gondola with a skull at its head, surrounded by massive gothic sculptures of nymphs and a labyrinth of passageways. A snake entwines a headstone as she descends into a nether world of death. From the point of view of Christine the approach to the Phantom looks a bit like a ride in a Disneyland version of a gothic romance. But of course Russell does not shoot from an "objective" point-of-view, but, as we have seen, from inside the characters in the piece. Harley plays The Phantom beautifully as a hardened, obsessive, menacing control freak, with little love in the bargain – living in the depths of darkness like a rat disguised as a count.

Brightman lives up to the star billing playing Christine as if she here under a hypnotic spell, all wide eyed teenage fascination, so the innocence of the gothic elements make a lot of sense. It is also in the book, as The Phantom has learned to hypnotize with his voice. The fact that Christine is so passionately honest and pure also makes for a more balanced meeting, that is, between irrepressible innocence and obsessive corruption. In a Blakean sense such a meeting can only end in the death of one or both participants.

As Brightman sings "You give your love to me, for love is blind" we see The Phantom envelop Christine in his cape from which she emerges in the costume of Cleopatra. As Christine sings she is suddenly no longer in the basement of the opera house but on stage as Cleopatra, with a 19th century audience dressed for the night out, admiring her, including a hopeful paramour in the form of a young, blonde man of means. He blows her a kiss from the audience seen by Christine but also by The Phantom who, in a jealous rage, concentrates on the enormous chandelier dangling above the audience. As Christine sings we see her from above, The Phantom's point of view, looking like an Egyptian Queen. The Phantom cuts the ropes, seen in silhouette, as in Murnau's *Nosferatu*. On a high note the chandelier comes down on the young man and suddenly Christine's high note becomes a scream as Russell fades to red.

Russell here beautifully executes a gothic sensibility throughout as, from the beginning, we see Christine descend stairs to another world – his Freudian leanings were always operational and they manifest themselves here in various guises – the watery graves, the doubling, the mirror that becomes a passageway. While the film's technical specs have dated it to the 1980's the aesthetics remain rooted in gothic horror to which Russell was always attracted from his very first short films, finding their culmination in *Gothic*, made the same year as *Phantom of the Opera*.

SARAH BRIGHTMAN - WISHING YOU WERE SOMHOW HERE AGAIN
(Music Video/1987)

Another song from the *Phantom of the Opera* with Brightman, wearing a 19th dress and cloak as in the musical, walking through an actual British cemetery with very old headstones sinking into the ground askew and covered by overgrown weeds. She stops to put some flowers by a grave and Russell superimposes a young man's face over it using a video dissolve that dates it badly – the effect would have been bad even its day as there is too much unearned emotional weight placed on it turning it into kitsch. Brightman's rather hypnotized rendering, that worked in *The Phantom of the Opera*, does not work here and turns the video into a one dimensional soap opera in gothic costume. When Brightman closes the cemetery gates behind her at the very end one feels she's glad that's done – for Russell too.

KEN RUSSELL'S ABC OF BRITISH MUSIC (1988)

Ken Russell's ABC of British Music, made for the *South Bank Show* is, as one would think, a whimsical tour of British music with Russell as host, guide, explorer, and pundit as he takes us on a kid's journey – with adults invited - from A to Z. The 75 minute film starts with Russell himself appearing atop the Albert Hall taking the lid off the building (literally) – thanks to animation heavily influenced by Terry Gilliam's work with *Monty Python's Flying Circus* using photos, cut and paste, and imaginative editing to create a surreal topsy-turvy world on a modest budget. "Here we are at last night's Proms" says Russell – to found footage of a crowd singing the British national anthem at the closing night of the Proms – a classical music festival held every year in London that features a phantasmagoria of greatest hits of the best and the brightest – and we are now going to encounters Russell's version of the Proms in an ideal world. Before we get our bearings Russell is ready to move to "B" with the Beatles and Benjamin Britten, whom we see suddenly as the fifth Beatle in a promotional poster – an unlikely event as Britten preferred his opera seria, but Russell has great fun intercutting screaming kids in the ecstasies of Beatlemania to Britten's work as if the youngsters were screaming for one of Britten's overly serious operas.

"C" is for conductors and composers and Russell gives us his top ten list using variety music as in a game show which is incongruous and whimsical but one supposes that it is Ken Russell's ABC so makes no pretense to objectivity. With Delius he uses fragments from his own film of Delius, *Song of Summer*, to great effect. For "Disco" he offers a strange series of variety acts closer to a Eurovision song contest montage than to any disco but it's funny nonetheless. Elgar of course receives a heartfelt welcome, and Russell again uses his own film on the composer as well as documentary footage, ending his piece by reprimanding the indifferent British public for not having bothered to save Elgar's house from destruction. "F" is for film music and Russell devotes a long passage to the film *Things to Come*, written by H.G. Welles with music by Arthur Bliss – clearly a touchstone for him. He then cuts to a contemporary composer, Thomas Dolby, in his small recording studio, working on *Gothic*, Russell's just then completed feature film so we see how comparatively easy it is for Dolby to gather together a full orchestra from a computer.

"G" is, oddly, for girls and he gives us a sampling of the composer Dame Ethel Smyth's modernist work – she conducted one of her works from a prison cell, where she had been put for her suffragette work and Russell, as in his BBC work has an actress dressed in the clothes of a suffragette conducting, with a toothbrush, from behind bars – again the most surrealistic touch (the tooth brush) is historically accurate. Russell nicely intercuts her music with suffragette marches in London from the early century, and on to Kate Bush doing a modern variation. Not wanting Dame Ethel to be the only classical woman on the program he moves on to Liz McConkey's *Proud Thames* a fully romantic orchestral piece that was bound to please Russell's tastes. He superimposes McConkey's profile over the Thames. Superimpositions were something he rarely used before but with the use of video editing it became much simpler to do and Russell seems to have taken well to it creating very painterly effects.

"H" is for Holst which Russell reminds us is the most popular work of classical British music in the 20th century. We are treated to "Mercury" from Holst's *Planets*, but Russel, as in his interpretation of the whole piece by Holst, uses random stock film from the vast encyclopedia of available images. Russell even includes jet fighters doing fancy maneuvers seemingly not aware of the multiple meanings that such images can have – simply going for "dramatic images" regardless of their content and references.

At that point it's time for "Heavy Metal" and we get to see Russell dressed up as if he were an overly enthusiastic fan going to an Iron Maiden concert – not something you see every day surely. In "J is for Jazz" he presents an all female jazz band playing 40's swing music but none of the greats from the British school of jazz such as George Shearing, Winifred Atwell, Ronnie Scott, or John Dankworth make an appearance. The scene with the women dressed in 40's gowns dancing to a swing band feels more like a fever dream Russell might have had when he was in the service during the 1940's still on the lookout for Dorothy Lamour.

"K" is, of course, for kitsch – and Albert Ketélbey, who wrote short incidental music for films and television, and "light orchestral music" as Russell rides a magic carpet over a generic desert dressed as a genie who may have had too much to drink. Oblivious to political correctness Russell then dresses up as a Chinese guard, more Fu Man Chu than anything we might find in China (it is kitsch after all) using Ketélby's music to score various scenes of everything from Chinese parades in Beijing to the Queen Mother herself on parade – Russell here edits to body movement rather than to create metaphors.

Russell gets a phone call (on a Mickey Mouse phone) and moves on to "L" for Lloyd Weber, one of Russell's favorite contemporary composers. In "M" for modern Russell slams an enormous fan over a pillow to display some of the atonal and concrete sounds in the music of Cornelius Cardew – but Russell astutely reminds his audience that there always has been a "modern" music, one just has to tune in – and he shows us Stonehenge – from his own footage taken during his film on Ralph Vaughan Williams. He then shifts easily from Brian Eno's *Music for Airports* to the populist Peter Maxwell Davies.

"N" is for neglect, for the "unsung heroes" whose music did not coincide with the taste of the public or critics, but who made their own work their own way regardless. Russell then gives some names and samplings of their music, such as Arnold Banks, Alan Rawsthorne, Frank Bridge, George Butterworth, and E.J. Moeran, and others. The lucky composers got work writing for films and television and those not so fortunate ended up teaching or working day jobs and Russell gives a brief sample of each composer in case one of them piques our interest.

"O" is for opera and as to be expected Russell does not pass up the opportunity to dress up in a cape and top hat but he gives British opera bad marks overall, even putting down Benjamin Britten, the most well known British opera composer, by saying that while he was well regarded at home those abroad seemed unimpressed by child abuse and aging pederasts as subjects – a reference to Britten's *Death in Venice* – his version of Thomas Mann's novel that follows along the lines of Luchino Visconti's film version a half century later – a film Russell satirized in *Mahler*. Russell gives the nod of approval (from a box seat at the opera while drinking white wine) to William Walton's *Troilus and Cressida*, an opera that the critics savaged, driving Walton into exile. He gives us a sampling of "what we lost" using footage from an onstage production and intercutting shots of nature that he has used in previous films, at times superimposing them.

"P" is for punk and Henry Purcell – Russell smartly cuts between Purcell's opera and punks making themselves up as there is a connection there of extreme theatricality and good tunes. Russell has a lot of fun intercutting the Queen Mother with Freddie Mercury dressed as an English monarch stepping onto the stage to wild applause. Thanks to video superimposition Russell is able to step into the scene as the Queen is on a balcony and he gives her a nice elbow poke in the ribs. "U" is for ugh! – for the critics – as Russell shows a funeral procession in fast motion – as in Rene Clair's silent films, with a voiceover of various critics lambasting his own favorites, starting with Elgar. Their voices have been put through a synthesizer so they all sound like Minnie Mouse when they pronounce Elgar to be a provincial bourgeois.

"V" is for video and Russell does a reprise of his own video *Nikita* that he made for Elton John and before we know it Russell gives a farewell by tipping his clown hat as he then delivers a long tracking shot from inside a car as it drives through the contemporary British countryside – surely for him the foundation and the backbone of British music as it was for Ralph Vaughan Williams, Elgar and Delius.

A BRITISH PICTURE (Short/1989)
In 1989 Melvyn Bragg, a good friend of Russell's and the creator and host of *The South Bank Show*, asked him to make an autobiography on film and gave him carte blanche to do anything he liked within the allotted low budget and 55 minute time frame. *A British Picture* had been the name of his autobiography published the same year so it was time to look back but Russell definitely did it his way, with tongue firmly planted in cheek.

The opening shot of a film was always supremely important to him and Russell starts his film with a powerful and controversial image: a picture of "Jesus" on a kitsch gold frame sitting in an artist's easel on a beach – as we move closer the "Jesus" image changes to one of Dorothy Lamour – a black and white glamour shot from the 30's. This is no doubt an image of adolescent fervor for Russell but Lamour, orchid in her hair, makes for an odd version of Mary. The third image is another black and white photo of his parents on their wedding day and then a flower in full color – nature's bounty and sexuality. Shifting to the result of this marriage, a pram rocking in front of a cathedral, Russell in voiceover explains his early days, after being christened Henry Kenneth Alfred Russell in 1927 shortly after he was born.

He explains that his first memory is of his mother and her sister having discussions on the available films to see that week from the newspaper. Russell cuts to *Old Mother Riley* (1937) a British comedy about a "normal" British family that takes in a loud, eccentric and gregarious Irish washerwoman, Old Mother Riley, who turns the house upside down but all for the better in the end. We see the two sisters dressed in the clothes of the 1930's do a critical take on *Old Mother Riley* as they both intone simultaneously: "What do you expect? It's a British Picture!"

"Like me the talkies were still in their infancy" explains Russell, linking up his own move to language as a youngster with the medium itself. Russell shows a little boy using a hand-cranked projector to show Betty Boop and Charlie Chaplin films. Using extensions on his projector he was able to finally show feature films explaining that Fritz Lang's *Metropolis* was "at the top of the bill, and still is." Very soon he learns to combine music, using his parent's gramophone, with silent films and from then on Russell was on his way. We see various films with Dorothy Lamour from her "sarong series" as Russell explains why he joined the Navy. We then see the little boy who stands in for Russell waving some nautical flags and a contemporary female Navy officer flirtatiously answering back with her own flags and a wink. In an inspired bit of casting Russell himself plays his commanding officer in the navy – dressed in a 19th century officer's costume circa the Napoleonic wars – as he berates Russell the little boy (in a bathtub). Invalided out of the Navy Russell discovers classical music, including the work of Tchaikovsky and Mahler. He cuts nicely from Russell as a little boy in a French sailor's uniform to his own scene from *Mahler* where he satirizes Luchino Visconti's *Death in Venice* as a little boy likewise plays in a train station.

Russell again casts himself as an Air Force officer interviewing the little boy in typical Monty Python style telling him "you're nothing but a bloody wanker – what are you?" The boy gives the correct answer, which is, of course: "a bloody wanker SIR!" Such is Russell's time in the British armed forces. We invariably notice that as Russell grows up his stand-in remains about five years old, which is clearly telling us something important, but it wears thin after one hour despite the boy's charm and enthusiasm. We see excerpts from his early short films as he explains that the female star of *Peepshow*, his first film, was his future wife Shirley. One of his friends on that shoot was a Catholic who managed to convert Russell by telling him there was "a great spaceman in the sky who created the universe and made man in his image" – while we see little Ken in a spaceman suit looking up to the heavens. He then cuts to a point-of-view shot of the little boy to a beautiful young nun holding a rosary explaining things while looking down – it seems wherever Russell is ready to join an enterprise, be it the Navy or the Catholic Church, his heterosexual impulses are never far off. In this respect at least Russell was an everyman and no doubt this accounts for his ability to look at "ordinary" lives with some insight, honesty, and respect.

Proceeding to his BBC work for *Monitor* he first mentions the "inspired" work of Huw Wheldon that set him on the right course, mentioning that in the ten years they worked together their most popular film with the public is still *Elgar*. In another inspired bit of casting his daughter Victoria Russell plays a newswoman asking him typical questions such as "why do you deliberately set out to shock the audience?" The little boy answers (via Russell's adult voice) "because I believe in mass therapy!" "Why the preoccupation, one could say reverence for art? What does art mean for you?" Little Ken babbles like a monkey which strangely seems to satisfy his interlocutor. "You've virtually invented the biographical drama and the jar is exhausted – what next?" Russell's one word reply is: "Satire." No doubt this is the right answer but why is the "jar exhausted?" is left unanswered. On the word satire Russell cuts to scenes from his biography of Strauss, *Dance of the Seven Veils* that inaugurated his second satirical phase as a filmmaker.

We next see Russell wearing a simple fake plastic mustache, nose and glasses from a costume shop asking himself if he is a sex maniac. "No" replies the little boy, "but Strauss was." After 34 films for the BBC, explains Russell, there was a goodbye and no "golden handshake – in fact no handshake at all." The feature film world would prove to have it's own difficult barriers as "when you mention the word art they think you mean Art Garfunkel."

Russell explains how no one would finance *Savage Messiah*, the biography of Henri Gaudier-Brzeska, and so he financed the film himself by mortgaging his house. He explains: "I was glad to as I owed a debt to its hero – a person who was an artisan as well as an artist. Often on the verge of starvation he turned his hand at anything to earn a crust for himself and his beloved girlfriend – his only love. Although his genius was never appreciated in his own lifetime he was always aware of his own talent and that was enough to keep him going." The connections with Russell here are clear enough – especially that part about being an artisan and an artist – Russell was very proud of that. He moves on to his more controversial films – "especially the religious ones" – with scenes from *Tommy* and other works from the 1970's that fuse iconoclasm, sexual symbolism, Catholic imagery, along with rock n' roll to create a combustible narrative.

Russell then takes us through his conversion from Catholicism to his newfound religion in the Lake District and the resident poet who will be forever associated with that landscape (aside from Russell himself) William Wordsworth. Russell made a film about Wordsworth that put those feelings into his film but also, true to form, didn't leave out the harsh realities and contradictions that Wordsworth and his friend and collaborator Coleridge experienced while fighting their way in the literary worlds of early 19th century England. Russell explains that he wanted to stay in the Lake District continuing to make films but Hollywood called and he and his girlfriend Vivian moved to Los Angeles where they realized they hated the city and the smog. Russell absurdly recreates Los Angeles with a children's plastic pool, an umbrella, and a lounge chair – all incongruously sitting in a misty British lawn.

Before leaving tinsel-town he and Vivian were married by actor turned preacher Tony Perkins (after *Crimes of Passion*) aboard the *Queen Mary* – then a minor tourist attraction in Los Angeles. A little girl reads some bad reviews over a fireplace as the little boy listens with apprehension. Hearing the little girl say the lines "erratic and erotic spasms of ugliness - ideas as pretentious as they are bizarre full of hatred, contempt, rage, disgust, despair and mockery...should be banned on the grounds of indecency" is sobering but little Ken explains that at least his many awards were of some comfort – Russell cuts to a row of stuffed toys on the mantle – presumably his "awards." As little Ken can no longer withstand the bad reviews he is set to throw them into the fire but the little girl explains that they are reviews of his favorite composers, Elgar, Debussy, Prokofiev, Bartók and Delius.

Regardless of the way that artists have been misunderstood in their own time it galled Russell that no one wanted him anymore, either in Hollywood or British television despite the fact that he had enjoyed great successes in both venues. He and his wife set down to work and wrote a series of screenplays but they were considered "un-commercial." Finally we see Melvyn Bragg call and little Ken answers as he asks Russell to do a film on Ralph Vaughan Williams. His return to British television thanks to *The South Bank Show* was set as the composer was another Russell favorite. This and regular work making music videos kept him busy again.

Russell was sued for walking off the set of *Moll Flanders* based on Daniel Defoe's novel from 1722 - a film he was set to direct but problems of who was in charge led to Russell walking away. It's unfortunate as the story of the "fortunes and misfortunes" of the eponymous Moll were made for Russell. Incredibly he found a lawyer who was willing to work for him for free if Russell agreed to make a music video as his second job, after lawyer, was as a rock n' roll singer. Russell agreed and we see shots of one of the more absurd videos of the 1980's (which is saying something) with Russell himself playing a dancing priest visiting a maximum security prison – shades of *Jailhouse Rock* but without the great music by Jerry Leiber or the fantastic moves by Elvis - although Russell dances well in the film. The jail video was something of a hit – perhaps it was all of those sweaty young men dancing in striped pajamas with abandon. His good luck continued on with *Salome's Last Dance* and *The Rainbow* – two strong showings with Russell in top form. We finally see Russell playing himself with his crew in the Lake District, but wearing a clown wig yelling: "cut - job well done. A quick pint and then back to work!"

His drink is interrupted by a phone call and he rushes to get it – it's his old friend Melvin Bragg with a new suggestion: a documentary about himself! Russell agrees and then, still wearing his clown wig, tells Bragg: "Of course it's going to a straight documentary!" On that note we cue the credits with charming off-stage pictures from the shoot of the film we've seen. While one wishes at times for a more thoughtful, reflective Russell *A British Picture* is a wonderful autobiography on film from a filmmaker who could not look back without also looking at the all-important here and now and its uncertainties, contingencies, absurdities, and urgencies, all wanting space to breathe and live – Russell could not do it any other way.

PANDORA'S BOX: IT'S ALL COMING BACK TO ME NOW (Music Video/1989)

Pandora's Box was a short-lived all-female pop band that made one album called *Original Sin* released in 1989 from which the song *It's All Coming Back to Me Now* was the hit single. Pandora's Box was influenced by heavy metal rock, Gothic and Catholic imagery and iconography, and theater musicals such as *Phantom of the Opera* – in many ways Russell was the perfect director to make a video for them. The six and a half minute film begins with Gothic imagery as we see and old graveyard full of fog, as in a Hammer film, as the ominous music starts in. In one of Russell's most beautiful and baroque shots we see what looks to be a car and a motorcycle entwined like a sculpture and on fire sitting precariously over the side of a neoclassical building, perhaps part of the cemetery. It's a great shot – like a nightmare that David Lynch might have had after a bad night of watching too many old horror films. Over the word Pandora etched into a tombstone a woman falls unconscious on top of the text dressed like a biker. At that moment the image shifts to negative black and white film so everything is reversed – the darks are light and the lights are black.

Russell then cuts to stock footage of horses running through fire – for some reason this was footage that was extensively used in the 70's and 80's, often in slow motion, in clubs and music videos with varying degrees of success. The footage is usually taken in the coastal towns of Spain where some towns still harbor a pagan "festival" that was eventually transformed into a Catholic one to honor St. Anthony the Abbot, the patron saint of animals. The festival is called *Las Luminarias* (*The Bonfires*) and takes place January 16th. Why a saint who loved animals would want to see horses on fire has never been explained but the "festival" continues to this day. The footage, unfortunately, does nothing for Russell's video except to push it toward cliché.

Russell cuts to a close-up of an ambulance rotating red light and we get the first glimpse into the fact that an accident has occurred and we are seeing the unconscious images of the victim, perhaps a dying flash. Russell smartly returns to his first great shot of the motorcycle on fire on the side of the building, now populated by the band members dressed like Heavy Metal gargoyles on top of the building exulting in the collision of a car and a motorcycle on fire as in some strange, unknown ritual. The same "Queen of the Night" (as we might call her), still unconscious, is then set upon by bikers straight out of Kenneth Anger's *Scorpio Rising*, they begin to make love to the unconscious queen.

Russell then indulges his love of *Metropolis* and has the queen laid out in a Heavy Metal bed but wearing a crown, looking like Maria the robot in Frits Lang's *Metropolis* – again Russell shifts to black and white negative film confirming that the queen/robot will now perhaps be brought to life through electricity. This interest in *Metropolis* was in the air in the 1980's – the era of Reagan and Thatcher - as the idea of "control" via a "deep state" or plutocracy was taking center stage in various forms, from cartoons in newspapers to art cinema and from fine art to music videos – one example is Madonna's video *Express Yourself* (1989) directed by a young David Fincher in which Madonna dresses up like Fritz Lang (with monocle) on a set that resembles the fabled film. *Metropolis* itself was given a facelift of sorts in 1984 with hand made colorization and a new soundtrack provided by music producer Giorgio Moroder utilizing Freddie Mercury and other pop stars of the period.

Under the clouds of a ceremony in formal dress a black man and woman enter the picture wearing robes and a ritual of fire begins as the group dances around the queen in a liturgy with Eastern overtones. The man carries a large Egyptian symbol of eternal life and the woman seems to understand and dance around it while the troupe introduce a large gold metal sculpture that symbolizes the planets around the sun – the music of the spheres - a piece of sculpture that was favored around the time of Newton who theorized (incorrectly it turned out) the motions of the planets and stars. The black woman pours some ointments on the queen and another on her hands.

As the African man kisses her on the mouth Russell cuts to the same man giving mouth to mouth resuscitation – while she is dressed the same the man is now dressed as a doctor. Back in the biker dream a beautiful woman places a Heavy Metal mask on our queen as Russell cuts to an oxygen mask being placed over her face, as the woman who was pouring the ointments comes back as a nurse administering fluids intravenously into her arm. At the apex of the song the queen is given an electrical shock or "cardioversion" as a final attempt to resuscitate – linking the queen definitively to Maria, the robot but in this case the electrical shock does not bring life. Other attendants – who were previously in the dancing ritual – are now nurses who take the queen into the ambulance to the hospital. A return to the horses on fire motif dissolves into the first shot of the bike/car on fire on the side of the building with the Heavy Metal crew on the roof as the lead singer intones one last time, slowly as if fading away: "It's all coming back to me now" as the image fades to black.

Russell's work here owes much to his earlier short film *Nessun Dorma* (*And None Shall Sleep*) from 1987. In this short film that stages a section from Giacomo Puccini's opera *Turandot* there is the same basic narrative thread, as we first see Turandot's dream with bright theatrical lights as she appears to be a princess surrounded by actors in elaborate costumes - then the same actors are seen later as doctors and nurses in the midst of a car crash as Turandot, the victim/princess has been dreaming. In *Turandot's* case the woman survives, but in *It's All Coming Back to Me Now* she doesn't, although the respective endings were not Russell's inventions but were prescribed by their authors: Giacomo Puccini for *Turandot* and Jim Steinman who wrote *It's All Coming Back to Me Now* especially for the group.

DUSK BEFORE FIREWORKS (Short/1990)

Russell's 34 minute short was part of an omnibus film wherein each of the three films, titled collectively *Women & Men: Stories of Seduction,* is taken from a classic American short story that deals with heterosexual seduction; the other two films are based on Mary McCarthy's *The Man in the Brooks Brother's Shirt* and Ernest Hemingway's *Hills Like White Elephants*. Strangely the other two directors, like Russell, were British (Frederic Raphael and Tony Richardson respectively) and the films are programmatically illustrative with no sense of poetics or personality. From looking at *Hills Like White Elephants* one would never know that the brilliant short story by Hemingway is one of the landmark works of the 20th century, influencing writers as different as Joan Didion and Martin Amis, while *The Man in The Brooks Brother's Shirt* lacks McCarthy's sarcastic feminist take on the war of the sexes. The story *Dusk Before Fireworks* was written by Dorothy Parker in 1932 while she was living at the Lowell Hotel in the upper east side of New York City – a place for the well to do - the story was first published in Harper's Bazaar that same year.

Parker is far better known today for her quips and quotes than for her books which she would have hated as, despite her legendary quick wit and mastery of the sarcastic put-down she didn't have any use for it. Her summation of the famous "Algonquin Round Table" (that included herself) was: "There were no giants. Just a bunch of loudmouths showing off, saving their gags for days, waiting for a chance to spring them. It wasn't all that good – there was no truth in anything they said. It was the terrible day of the wisecrack, so there didn't have to be any truth."[103]

What she would have made of our day, where everyone is working very hard to unload their wisecracks on social media on a nonstop basis 24 hours a day, is not hard to imagine. She might very well have written a short story about it – a form in which she was a master. What Parker brought to the table was a caustic, bitter, brutality and she spared no one, not even herself - that she could do this and be funny at the same time was her art. Like Hemingway (see *A Clean, Well-Lighted Place*) Parker was an existentialist writer before the term existed and like him she earned a good living by writing for magazines like Harper's – they were professionals. *Fireworks Before Dusk*, despite the great title – something she excelled at - is not one of her better stories and falls under the "advice to young women in search of Mr. Perfect" stories.

The plot is, to put it kindly, simple – almost like a skit or a one-act play for actors. Russell shoots from a stationary camera and he does a reasonably professional job, taking his usual crew with him including master DP Billy Williams who does a great job lighting the luxury penthouse that is the single set for the film. In New York City Hobie (Peter Weller) a suave, rich, handsome bachelor has invited a young woman, Kit (Molly Ringwald) to his apartment for some fun. They flirt and she wants some sort of commitment from him and he promises to comply as soon as he gets his life in order. As he tries to take her clothes off she balks every time the phone rings which it does constantly with women calling him. Hobie is exasperated – or pretends to be but is actually bemused - by the constant interruptions but what can he do? Just as it looks like they might make a go of it the phone rings again and Kit leaves in a huff, at which point the phone rings yet again and Hobie asks the woman on the line to come over – he's not busy tonight after all - that's the story and the film.

Parker's best bit of dialogue – that has a strong feminist bent to it - is strangely left out:

Hobie (angry): *"What's the matter with WOMEN anyway?"*
Kit: *"Please don't call me "WOMEN."*
Hobie: *"I'm sorry, darling, I didn't mean to use bad words."*

The dialogue has Parker's typical sarcasm where we realize Hobie is a misogynist early on but Kit is oblivious, or pretends to be oblivious, since Hobie is so incredibly handsome and wealthy. That bachelors in New York (and even elsewhere) are sometimes cold hearted, one-track, and out to score is hardly news to anyone. Parker's warning about eligible bachelors in Manhattan to young ladies is certainly dated, in every sense, as today, in an updated version of the story, Kit would be a part time escort getting her degree in psychology at Columbia, and Hobie would be a psychotic killer in the manner of Patrick Bateman in Brett Easton Ellis' novel *American Psycho* – or a more feminist take might be Mimi Cave's film *Fresh* where the suave, handsome, eligible, bachelor is a cannibal. In any case neither Russell nor the scriptwriter Valerie Curtin, does anything to make the story relevant for the present moment – they simply transpose it to become a coherent one-act play and then film it very professionally.

There is one aspect of Parker's story that we must mention that rings true and has some relevance for our time – the use of the phone as an instrument for infinitely delaying sexual intercourse. If Ms. Parker could see the modern smartphone and its dating apps one assumes that after she stopped laughing she would immediately seize upon it as the idea for a story – something that might not be said of her contemporaries who would be more befuddled by the whole thing. When Parker wrote the story telephones in homes were still something unique – only rich people, like Hobie, had them and most apartments, if they had a phone at all, had only one phone for everyone in the building. The phone did not become ubiquitous until the 1950's.

The telephone's strangely disquieting, magnetic presence was immediately felt by sensitive people right from the start, as when Edgar Degas (who could afford a phone in the early 20th century) when he was asked, by his friend Ludovic Halévy, why he refused to get one, had a very interesting reply. Degas asked Halévy what he did when the phone rang. Halévy replied that he went right away and answered it, of course. Degas then said, "so when the bell rings you stop what you are doing and immediately go to it – therefore the phone is the master and you are the servant – in my house I am the master."[104] Never have wiser words been used with regard to that small instrument of communication. Unfortunately Russell's film only does a credible job illustrating Parker's story but does nothing with it. It lays flat like an illustration or advertising from the 1920's, like those of J.C. Leyendecker, that is perfectly generic, handsome, serviceable, and managing all the while to say absolutely nothing at all – but beautifully.

THE STRANGE AFFLICTION OF ANTON BRUCKNER (Short/1990)

Russell's 42 minute film on Austrian composer and master organist Anton Bruckner (1824-1896) concentrates on a brief and little known episode in the composer's life: His stay, during middle age, in a sanatorium because of what was then known as "numeronamia" and would now be called an obsessive-compulsive disorder. Bruckner needed to count whatever was around him and then try to develop correspondences and meanings from the numbers. While not a serious life debilitating illness, his "numeromania" inhibited his writing music and made him difficult, and at times impossible, to communicate with. His sister placed him in a sanatorium to see if they could cure him – at that time the prescribed cure was rest and daily baths in freezing cold water where the subject was forcibly immersed underwater for periods of time to shock the body back to "normal" – something akin to a softened version of waterboarding.

Bruckner was considered something of an oddball – a half-genius half simpleton who was always falling in love with teenage girls and asking them to convert to Catholicism so he could marry them. Not surprisingly none ever did and his lifelong bachelorhood left him – like Rousseau, another subject of a Russell biography – cranky, miserable, and irritable – a man whose only consolation was his music, which he was always rewriting. Retrospectively Bruckner now is seen in many ways to be like his younger contemporary Gustav Mahler as the last of the great romantic 19th century composers who used polyphonic dissonances and roving harmonies in their work. The difference was that Mahler was cosmopolitan and had a sense of humor and indulged himself in his work with parodies and ironic quotations while Bruckner was all heart on his sleeve romantic. Mahler who befriended Bruckner admired his work while Brahms, who never met him, found it lacking. Strangely Russell chooses to pinpoint Bruckner's brief stay in a sanatorium to, in effect, act as a synecdoche for his whole life but the film does, by the end, give us a fully rounded personal portrait of the man – a superb achievement.

Anton Bruckner (Peter Mackriel) arrives by horse and buggy to the sanatorium while counting the revolutions of the wheels. When he arrives at the stately chateau he counts the spokes on the wheel and then tries to devise some commonality between the two numbers, which of course are random. The female nurse Grete (Catherine Neilson) and the male nurse Hans (Carsten Norgaard) - shades of Hansel and Gretel - welcome Bruckner and are not at all surprised when he asks them to please memorize the important numbers in case he forgets them. They seem to know exactly what he needs and escort him, with knowing smiles, inside the beautiful sanatorium.

Russell shoots the immersion in freezing water inside a white room with a white tub and attendants dressed in white, as if reality were slowly dissipating into a white blankness. Bruckner accepts the strange waterboarding like a child presuming that the grownups know what they are doing. Mackriel shines as Bruckner, a naïf in sheep's clothing who is lost in the world but somehow, with a little help from family and friends, finds his way – or at least he gets to compose the music he hears in his head and he gets it played. We see him in a vast field of rocks picking them up and counting them while the nurses look on stiffly as in a Magritte painting. A beautiful long shot of Bruckner picking daisies with his guards close by, is accompanied by his 7th symphony - Russell holds the shot for longer than usual and then cuts abruptly to a close-up of more waterboarding for full effect so we experience the shock of the sudden shift from warm spring day to immersion into freezing water – for Russell it was always about the corporeal element getting its due. As Grete finishes spoon feeding him soup Bruckner asks her if she knows how many spoonful's he's eaten – when she guesses incorrectly he tells her: "17."

In one of the funnier scenes in the film we then see Bruckner at a Catholic confession with a bored priest barely able to stay awake as Bruckner, very seriously, talks about his recent sin of masturbation, referring to it, with some mortification, as "self-abuse" – a common 19th century term. When Bruckner mentions dreaming about his nurse turning the pages to his 7th symphony the priest realizes that he is listening to Bruckner and absolves him immediately telling him he must play Bach on the organ as penance, after which he goes back to sleep. Bruckner takes the priest literally and goes immediately to the organ and starts to play as an assistant with a hand crank creates the airflow for the organ. Bruckner was an accomplished organist and highly sought after in that world and we see a fine example of it here. The only time we see Bruckner happy and smiling without a care is when he is playing Bach in the church.

In one of the most extraordinary scenes of creative thought in action – one of the few successful ones in any case – Bruckner suddenly gets up from his organ playing and goes rushing out to the nearby forest and Russell shoots him with long, lovingly detailed tracking shots, similar to those in *Elgar*, past the beautiful trees of the Lake District. The two nurses follow in hot pursuit as they assume Bruckner is trying to escape but find him hugging a tree and singing out his *Te Deum* (1883), one of his Catholic compositions written for choir and orchestra. That the idea for the piece would have come to him while playing Bach makes sense as the piece quotes from Bach and from Renaissance polyphony. It's a wonderful moment as Grete looks at him with a sense of pity and wonderment and it is she that gets the close-up as we hear Bruckner's *Te Deum* fill the soundtrack as Bruckner rattles off numbers and notes that would make no sense to anyone but him. The fact that this scene is very emotionally involving makes a lot of sense as Russell by 1989 had rediscovered his Catholicism and would have found the *Te Deum* (literally *You God*) one of Bruckner's most moving works. The close-up of Grete also gives her suddenly greater prominence forcing us to pay attention – at first she seems like a distant but friendly nurse but as the film progresses she develops into something else altogether, becoming Bruckner's friend, confidant and psychiatrist.

During a post waterboarding massage from Hans Bruckner mentions that he loves teaching and then gets very melancholic, saying: "but not women" as he begins weeping. This is, as with so much of Russell's work, historically accurate. Bruckner was a teacher to both sexes but could not keep his mind or his hands off the young women and after complaints was sent to teach men only. While hardly unique in this aspect it affected Bruckner emotionally and he never got over it.

The next time that the composer is being spoon fed soup like a baby Bruckner asks Grete the number of times he was fed and she gives him the correct number, now well aware of "Herr Bruckner's" obsession – the scene is comical as it shows that not only is Bruckner being helped (presumably) to get better but the nursing staff is also adapting to his numbers game, playing along with him. This is a very smart observation about institutions where the changes that are supposed to be happening only to the patient get more complicated. For human beings, being social animals, it would be inevitable that the influences and effects would happen in multiple directions, not one - Grete has started to count, even if only as a game.

When Grete comes to take Bruckner's pulse he gets animated telling her that she needn't bother as it is exactly the same as Wagner's *Ride of the Valkyries* and he proceeds to start singing it enthusiastically, even ecstatically, as Russell cuts to Anton running through fire, which turns to be a field of cows as Hansel and Gretel his nurses look on. Bruckner counts the flowers in the field, spouting poetry and talking animatedly about Wagner, which again is very true to form as Bruckner was an avowed Wagnerite – Wagner returned the complement calling Bruckner the only Symphonist post-Beethoven that was worth anything. Bruckner explains himself to his two nurses as they play cards: "Brahms' music comes from his brain, and Wagner's music comes from his balls, and mine comes from God! He's rather unfashionable these days." He continues counting flowers as his nurses escort him back to the sanitarium as Bruckner counts their steps – by the time they reach the sanitarium all three are counting and laughing.

After another soup count-off Bruckner talks about his past giving his working class background that would have counted against him in the musical world of his time. His father had been a church organist and played in clubs as well and taught Bruckner everything so he could land a good job, which he did. Bruckner has retrieved a picture of his beloved sister who died young and suddenly after what seemed to be only a minor cold – of course for Bruckner, who wants to make sense of the world through numbers, religion, or music such a meaningless death coming from nowhere is simply not accountable. One is also reminded of Russell's own cousin Marian who died young while playing alone on the beach after stepping on a buried landmine. "Shall we pray for her?" asks Grete. Bruckner gets his rosary and they kneel bedside looking at her picture to Bruckner's 9th symphony. Bruckner is next seen counting headstones in an old graveyard where the crosses and statues are all slanted as they slowly sink into the earth – a favorite place for Russell to shoot from his BBC days.

A picnic lunch in the grass with his nurses gives Russell a chance to do a neo-Impressionist "luncheon on the grass" scene and he takes full advantage, arranging his group around a beautiful still-life of food as in Manet but without the nude, as Bruckner says he loves being in the sanitarium: "I've been here for three months now and still no doctor! But I don't mind. It's like being on holiday, except for the cold baths." He's reminded of his first love who turned him down – "they all turned me down, the blue ladies." Anton asks Grete to dance with him in the garden while Hans plays a country accordion. Russell shoots the dance beautifully in medium long shot with the fields in full bloom acting as a chorus.

In their next waterboarding session Bruckner drags Grete into the tub with him and laughs like a little boy as the male nurse also laughs – Grete and Anton are framed by Russell like a couple in a love scene while both are laughing at the situation but Bruckner still wants to know when he is going to finally see the doctor but no answer is forthcoming from Grete. In the following scene Anton and Grete are both in bed with Bruckner in pajamas and Grete sitting fully clothed in the stiff 19th century style. She asks him if he has ever seen a woman naked. Bruckner thinks for a long time and says no but qualifies his answer by explaining that he had visited a morgue after a fire in a school to identify the bodies and women were there naked, looking as if they were simply sleeping and he begins to weep.

As he moves to hug Grete Russell cuts from close-up to medium shot as we see Grete suddenly completely naked holding Anton and comforting him as he continues speaking about his teaching days and his work with the Choral Society and their guilds, the naked Grete with him in bed seemingly a dream as she strokes his head. The British actress Catherine Nielsen as Greta really shines here as she exposes bits of her character and her emotional situation slowly throughout the film, often without dialogue, merely through facial expressions and body language so by the time we see her naked we know her – she is no longer the stiff and formal nurse we met at the beginning but a fully rounded character so her nudity makes narrative sense. Anton recounts how his coworkers set up a meeting with a woman, perhaps a prostitute, and he was embarrassed and horrified by it all so he had to run away. He quit the Society after that experience as he couldn't face his colleagues anymore. He explains that he then went immediately to a bridge by the river to commit suicide but found himself counting his steps to get there and then the boats on the river and he didn't stop counting.

In one of Russell's most inspired and beautiful scenes Grete, still naked, asks him how many hairs she has on her head. Bruckner says he has no idea, "only God knows." Grete lowers her head in close-up putting her head right up to Anton's face and asks him to count. As he starts to count they both laugh and then start to count the stars outside the window but give up – there are too many. Bruckner realizes his folly and says aloud, to himself as much as to Grete: "To count would be to diminish His glory" as we hear again his 9th Symphony. Russell cuts to the stars at night – he then dissolves to a stained glass window image of Christ on the cross swirling in a circle as if the window were a constellation – he then cuts to a generic shot of a magnificent sunrise which is too much like stock photography to have the full symbolic meaning that he is looking for. Still, a true Catholic believer at this point, Russell shows the music of the spheres and Bruckner's music as one. Anton explores Grete's body with his eyes and hands as she looks off to the distance seemingly entranced by the music.

We see Bruckner climbing down off an enormous tree – shades of *The Baron in the Trees* by Italo Calvino – but now Bruckner seems finally alive and in tune with his surroundings, no longer counting the branches. In a beautiful meadow of flowers, where the characters walk with flowers waist high, reminiscent of *The Music Lovers* and other films where he has used fields in a similar way, Bruckner wonders if the universe is egg shaped as the image of God "laying the egg of the universe" appeals to him. Grete tells him its time for him to go home as he is cured. "So soon?" asks Anton. On the way back we see Grete walking in medium-close up not Bruckner or his male nurse – we are fully immersed in Bruckner's mind, in love with her as he hears his 9th symphony, still to be written. Later, seemingly alone in the sanitarium Bruckner hears his String Quintet, that has never been played publicly and follows the music - Grete and Hans have asked for a quintet formed by Bruckner's ex students to come and play his work and the composer sits in a chair prepared especially for him. Grete explains that these are his friends who love him and wanted to express their thanks as Bruckner, in tears, listens to them play.

In a beautiful coda that wraps up all of the narrative strands Russell gives one final twist to the narrative that is extremely satisfying and feminist – more so than many explicitly feminist works that proselytize and explain to no end but do little else. Grete and Hans show Bruckner to his carriage explaining that his sister is very happy that Anton is cured and ready to come back home. After they get the confused Bruckner on the carriage, somewhat perturbed that his stay in ending so quickly – not even a hug from Grete – but he waves goodbye as Russell holds on Grete and Hans who have the last word. After Anton is gone Hans calls Grete "fräulein doctor" and asks her if there was a satisfactory conclusion with her patient. Of course, Grete had been the doctor that Bruckner was waiting for all along, assuming she was only a nurse – as most male patients would have assumed at the time (or perhaps even now). "Yes" replies Grete "I should be glad to get out of this nurse uniform into something less constricting. He's a nice man – I quite liked him." Hans asks the obvious question: "May one ask fräulein doctor if anything…" "That would be unethical" replies Grete. "He might never have written another note of music – now he will die as he lived – a more or less happy celibate. But now we must prepare for our next patient…a banker who thinks that he's a rooster! You must find me that feather boa of mine." Russell's Freudian joke that ends the film is fitting as Bruckner's calamitous counting – that impaired his composing and communication – was finally brought under control.

The reason Russell is so successful with his feminist coda is that his interest is in the emotional content of the scene rather than the ideological ramifications of it – although this political sympathy for women is ever-present in his work, from his early portrait of Shelagh Delaney, through Isadora Duncan, Sophie Brzeska, and on to Lady Chatterley – all true to form feminist portraits where the political or ideological is submerged within the emotional core of the work. Here we get a full picture of Anton Bruckner from his three months in the sanitarium - not only his emotional interior world, but his family life, his day-jobs as teacher, organist and choral master, his austere sexual situation, his relationship with his doctor, and his music – it's a great accomplishment that Russell is able to compress all of that information and emotional nuance into 42 minutes in a heartfelt effort that works on every level.

PRISONER OF HONOR (1991)

Prisoner of Honor was a film project about the Dreyfus affair in France at the end of the 19th century. It was produced by Richard Dreyfuss the American film star, for whom it was a personal project, that he spent several years getting off the ground in the late 1980's. It was made for Warner Bros. Television and released by HBO, the American cable television company in 1991. Dreyfuss admitted that there was speculation as to whether he was related to the actual Alfred Dreyfus, around whom the plot pivots - true or not, when he was a young man he believed it, read books about the subject, and wanted to make a film someday about the event. Once his fame reached a point where such a project became possible he acted on his instincts. Since the actual Dreyfus spends most of his time during the proceedings in a jail in Devil's Island Dreyfuss chose to portray Coronel Picquart, the "man of honor."

The film was written by Ron Hutchinson who was known then primarily for his successful work in the theater but also wrote biographical feature films such as *The Josephine Baker Story* and *Marco Polo*. It was Dreyfuss who brought Russell on board saying: "We wanted a rude director who says to the audience: 'Watch this! Come over here! I know this isn't the way you usually see it, but come over and try it.'"[105] Dreyfuss was initially turned down by studios despite his star billing at the time of production: "When you go to a studio what they need for their agenda that year usually is not a film about the French Army in 1894,"[106] he said. Unfortunately Dreyfuss took his turn at the helm a little too seriously and took the project away from Russell once shooting was completed, re-editing the film so at some points it is too conventional and at others too jagged and unclear – mistakes not found in other films where Russell has been in control at the editing table. From *Delius* to *The Strange Affliction of Anton Bruckner* Russell was always a master editor using traditional match cuts, cross cuts, jump cuts, cutting on action, and Eisenstein's "montage of attractions" to full effect. Despite the falling out at the end with Dreyfuss and the money men Russell left his name on the film and whatever flaws it might have in the editing it has much to recommend it.

The film chronicles the real events that saw French Captain Alfred Dreyfus (Kenneth Colley), sent to prison at Devil's Island for espionage near the end of the 19th century. The French had only recently (1870-71) fought the Germans, and lost, being forced to cede Alsace-Lorraine, and so were virulently anti-German with accusations of being a spy a dangerous provocation that could get a person killed. Coronel Georges Picquart

(Richard Dryfus) is given the job of justifying Dreyfus' conviction as there are doubts that have been planted by the press. Instead, he discovers that Dreyfus, a Jew, was merely a convenient scapegoat for the actions of the true culprit, a ranking Christian member of the French General staff, Maj. Esterhazy (Patrick Ryecart) who sold state secrets to pay for his luxurious lifestyle. Picquart's attempt to right the wrong sees his military career temporarily destroyed and his long-term relationship with his mistress Eloise (Catherine Neilson) severed forever. Neilson was the doctor in Russell's *The Strange Affliction of Anton Bruckner* and she shines here as the only female in a film completely dominated by men and their world – despite being a minor role it's important because she provides a completely different, outsider, feminine point of view. The famous author Émile Zola (Martin Friend) gets involved and is also found guilty of libel and sentenced to prison but, having many friends with influence, escapes to England. Zola's *J'Accuse!* – a letter to the press that exonerates Dreyfus and names the true culprits - becomes the most famous letter by an author ever sent to press and is arguably the only letter to the editor from that time still read today.

Picquart was basically an intelligent, superbly organized, but naïve officer who loved the army and assumed they wanted him to actually solve the case, not simply provide a good cover-up and he took his officer's code of honor – that his loyalty was to the *idea* of the army, not to any one man - to its logical conclusion, preferring to destroy his life in the process rather than lie. Eventually Dreyfus was exonerated, rehabilitated and even reinstated in the French Army although at a lower rank. Incredibly he fought in WWI at Verdun and survived, dying in 1935 as the world readied itself for another world war.

Russell liked framing devices in narratives that have a built-in binocular vision that he found emotionally satisfying. Hutchinson and Russell add a sophisticated and beautifully articulated framing device here - a parenthetical prelude and coda to the film that takes place in the twenties in England, after the Great War is history. As the film opens in 1923 a young reporter arrives by car and meets an older man in a lavish, conservative, country estate – the sort of place that fox hunting might be done. The reporter explains that his editor has an idea for a story demonstrating how in a few years whole nations can become completely irrational, and consumed by hate – shades of *The Devils* here. The older man replies that he assumed his editor was an idiot but perhaps he was wrong, as there is merit to this idea. The editor wants the inside story of Dreyfus, Picquart, Zola, and Esterhazy – the main players in the famous Dreyfus case that convulsed France towards the end of the 19th century. The old man relates, with some authority, what he insists is "the real story" to the younger man and the bulk of the film is that story, brought to life. The older man describes the affair as a tragicomedy as Esterhazy, the true culprit in the story, just needed money because he married a woman who he assumed was rich but turned out to be poor, so to maintain the lifestyle to which he was accustomed – that was lavish and complicated - he sold state secrets, there was nothing more to it.

The writer has a theory – popular in France after the Great War – that the Dreyfus affair so weakened the French army's morale and authority that the Germans came to believe they would have an easy time in a war and launched into WWI thinking it would be over in a matter of a few months. So in effect, under this theory, WWI came about because a man named Esterhazy needed money because he married the wrong woman? The question is left unanswered but the absurdity of the human condition, even in its larger historical arcs, is left hanging over the narrative. Later at the film's coda we will find out who the older man was but as the film proper starts, in January of 1895, we see Dreyfus being traditionally dishonorably discharged from the French Army by having his sword ceremonially broken by his commanding officer.

Later in the halls of power General Boisdeffre (Oliver Reed) and Coronel Picquart talk over some inconsistencies in the case – why would a man deliver a long list of possible secrets for sale to a German officer in the middle of Paris where they were easily seen? Dreyfus was not an idiot and he had no lovers – his family life was "indecently moral" and he had no debts or expensive tastes. "Little boys?" asks Boisdeffre, "Dreyfus wouldn't have known what to do with them." There must be a missing piece in the puzzle. Picquart is hired to find it but keep it within military circles and not let it out to the press. Russell has a fine time showing the German officer that received the French state secrets, enjoying himself in a homosexual brothel, clearly not a person whose primary interest is espionage as everyone seems to know who he is and they don't take him seriously – the enigma becomes even more confounding. Picquart infiltrates the brothel and his confidant hands him another list for the sale of state secrets – Picquart examines the handwriting and it matches the first list - Esterhazy is their man not Dreyfus. Unfortunately for Picquart despite Esterhazy's flagrant womanizing, uncouth rudeness, loutish behavior in gambling dens, and pathological narcissism, he is part of the establishment so to bring him down would be nearly impossible; but Picquart, while not oblivious to the dangers, has only one way to proceed due to his code of honor – he will go after Esterhazy and prosecute him as a traitor, whatever the price.

In a scene that clearly Russell loved shooting in Boisdeffre's office the General is having an official portrait painted dressed as a Roman Emperor wearing a tunic and a garland crown made of gold – as the Caesar's of the Roman Empire once did. This is, again, historically accurate as many top brass not only in France but elsewhere in Europe, saw themselves as Caesar redux and made paintings that showed them as Greek or Roman emperors, or at least posing as if in the Pantheon among the greats. This is a tradition that continues to our day with oligarchs from Washington to Baghdad.

Russell smartly shoots Picquart standing in front of the painting, while he talks, offering two contrasting views of ethics – an idealization that people will see, and the mundane reality that no one wants to hear. With the aging war minister in the office, played with gravitas by Lindsay Anderson, the great British director, and Picquart they try to make sense of the new developments. The war minister suggests there are now two spies at hand, Dreyfus and Esterhazy, and the latter should now be prosecuted. Picquart rejects this idea, saying it is clear that Dreyfus was a fall guy, a patsy who happened to be at the wrong time/wrong place (and wrong religion) – their traitor is Esterhazy. When the latter is informed of the accusations afoot he demands a trial to clear his name, certain that the military top brass will back him up no matter how much evidence has piled up against him.

Eloise and Picquart meet in a large hotel restaurant that is one of the most beautiful depictions of the 19th century Belle-Époque ever committed to film – straight out of John Singer Sargent and his portraits of beautiful rich ladies in their salons – the production design by Ian Whittaker and set decoration by Jill Quertier are standouts here really giving us a sense of a time and a place that look lived in, the Belle Époque before it all came crashing down after WWI. Eloise tells him he's a fool to stick his neck out for the military – he will only wind up in prison like Dreyfus. She gives him an ultimatum to come away with her and he rejects her offer, needing to see the trial through to its conclusion because he is a "man of honor."

Eloise turns out to be right, and it is Picquart who ends up in prison for falsifying evidence. Major Henry (Peter Firth) is set up to find some way of indicting Picquart and he fabricates documents but does so with such ineptitude that the army is humiliated, and Henry winds up in prison alongside Picquart and Dreyfus. The Army appears to not know what they are doing, but as to be expected, what they are most worried about now is a public relations disaster that they need to fix. Henry is forced by his superiors to take the honorable way out — he is given a straight razor in prison and commits suicide.

After the verdict of the second trial, Emile Zola, the most infamous writer in France, writes *J'accuse!* the letter that indicts Esterhazy and the top brass of the Army in a cover-up based on anti-Semitic grudges within the military. The Army goes after Zola, suing him for libel, but quickly backtrack when the full story comes out. The army has no choice but to reinstate Dreyfus but Esterhazy is allowed to remain in the Army. Picquart is not only released from prison but becomes Minister of War. The voiceover from the beginning, belonging to the reporter, comes back explaining that Picquart got the job he always wanted but died shortly after so never got to participate in WWI.

Russell and the writer Hutchinson then close out their framing narrative, returning us to the chateau in England in 1923 where the older gentleman has been telling this story to the young reporter over some brandy. "You see — a comedy!" explains the older man who then reminds the reporter that there was supposed to be some financial remuneration for his time. This should tip us off that the older gentleman enjoying his brandy is Esterhazy, always in need of cash — the reporter gives him the agreed upon amount and Esterhazy's final comment is: "No doubt Picquart was the best of them. But he was a man of the past century." "Can we then say" asks the reporter "that Esterhazy is the only man of the group that belongs to the 20th century?" "The FIRST man of the 20th century!" says Esterhazy. The reporter asks him to sign the older man's book, titled *Prisoner of Honor*, and he signs "Esterhazy" on the title page, and closes the book as the credits roll.

No doubt the ethically compromised position of Esterhazy, always short of cash and morals, but loaded with charm and a pathological narcissism, make him the model for the 20th century man. Russell's film is not so much cynical as wizened and melancholic. We would see Esterhazy again in the 20th century playing many roles, in many countries through many wars, hot and cold, though gilded ages and bankruptcies, empires won and lost, but for the Dreyfuses' and the Picquart's it seems to never quite work out.

Russell and Hutchinson's brief coda doesn't only wrap up Picquart's story but places it within the larger historical arc – a Belle Époque that was certainly very belle for some but for most it was merely a brutal prelude to the 20th century, a time and a place that Picquart was clearly unsuited for and he had the graciousness, we might even say the good fortune, to bow out before the Great War announced its entrance onto the world stage, guns blazing; what he would have made of all the carnage, the blunders, the chaos, the stupidity and the double dealings – we can only guess.

THE ROAD TO MANDALAY (Short/1991)

The Road to Mandalay is a 35 minute film – really a home movie - with Russell and his family on board a van in Southhampton, England, his home town, looking for a restaurant called *Mandalay* and, as one would expect, everything that can go wrong, does. *On the Road to Mandalay* is also a song made famous by Frank Sinatra from his classic *Come Fly With Me* LP, a concept album with travel songs, but it is also the capital city of Myanmar (formerly Burma) and so was a part of the British Empire. In this case there is a restaurant called *Mandalay* in the center of Southampton that the family is eager to try, all being fans of curry and Eastern food, and Russell is the designated driver of a large family van with two aunts June and Muriel Codd, along with Rupert Russell, Ken's youngest son, who looks to be about seven.

Russell shoots his aunts from inside an old brick townhouse looking through a window as they spot Ken before he arrives – a traditional shot in narrative films but not usually seen in home movies. After a bit of arguing they get in the van in search of *Mandalay* but find the new street regulations make it impossible to turn in the right place and they soon get lost in a roundabout despite Ken's reassurances. To pass the time they sing songs, argue, laugh and talk about the family as families do.

While many artists over the years have disowned family life, preferring a bohemian or solitary lifestyle with a few like-minded artistic friends, others take up family life grudgingly or simply out of sheer indolence; but there are a few artists who do love and care for their families – at times even making the family the subject of their work, despite the fact that family members often don't understand what the artists are doing; the classic example is arguably James Joyce whose wife Nora didn't bother to read his complicated novels. From Rembrandt to Gerhard Richter, from Bach to Paul McCartney, and from Jean Renoir to Ken Russell there are a minority of family loving artists who invariably find room to put their families into their work, whether they like it of not. Such artists are usually finely attuned to the brevity of a human life and its attendant small moments, their place or link in a chain of being that stretches in a fragile timeline - their work reflects that understanding.

While they are searching first for a place to park they become hopelessly lost, but Russell finds time to stop by certain landmarks in Southampton, such as the monument dedicated to the crew who stayed behind as volunteers as the Titanic went down – Russell shoots the bronze relief head on as in his work with the monuments to WWI in *London Moods*. While he gives us a tour of his home town Russell gets so lost he ends up on the ferry to the Isle of Wight while the aunts go on about how hungry they are and Ken's son plays with a toy dinosaur. At the island there are "No U-Turn" signs everywhere and Ken is forced to go straight into the Isle of Wight where he runs out of gas.

Narrative kicks in as one would expect with the separation of the family as Ken goes off in search of petrol and immediately the family unit falls apart as Rupert runs away and June gives chase while Muriel, the eldest, who is hard of hearing, gets left behind with the van. Rupert soon finds an amusement park for children based on dinosaurs with small-scale models of typical British towns and rides for kids. June finally finds Rupert on the beach collecting sand near a strangely deserted modernist house that looks like something out of a dystopian film of the future. Back by the side of the van Muriel is doing an impromptu dance to keep herself company. June and Rupert take the time to take the ski lift to the top of the island – a scene scored to Sinatra's *Road to Mandalay*.

Ken returns with petrol to find the family in disarray and gets everyone together and back to Southampton where they take the ferry. Once back on the mainland they finally find the restaurant, or at least the neon sign, (still lit) in a pile of rubble – the place has been completely demolished to make way for a new building. "Just like the Blitz" mentions Muriel as Rupert lets off a high pitched scream directly in Ken's ear and Russell returns the favor screaming along with him as the credits roll.

Russell presents us with a portrait of his family and himself but well within the parameters of a made up world co-existing with the real Southampton – there are no boundaries here only passages. In that sense it is a film that will only get more interesting with time as the world that Russell depicts fades into history and its details, that now seem quotidian, will come to the foreground. The film is a portrait of England post-empire, post-industrial, and post-utopian – a world where signs no longer make sense, parking is impossible, and restaurants disappear overnight. A society in transition obviously but where are we all going asks Russell? No answer is forthcoming but as with most families the talk, the gossip, the laughter and the screaming are nonstop. Russell had formed a family before he ever set out to get a job at the BBC and he was first, a family man, and this is his loving tribute as we see the Russell clan in action, giving us a self-portrait warts and all, as they graciously show us their home town.

THE SECRET LIFE OF ARNOLD BAX (Short/1992)

The Secret Life of Arnold Bax is a one-hour film made for *The South Bank Show* with the director taking the lead role. While Russell acted in brief minor parts in many of his own films and the works of other directors these were mostly cameos often of a comical order, but here the lead part calls for a lot of complex dialog in a serious, difficult part that is not completely sympathetic. As Melvyn Bragg says at the opening introduction to the film, Russell felt very close to the material and to Bax's music and wanted to play the role, that is, to put himself fully into the film as the embodiment of Arnold Bax. While the film has comical elements, as does all of Russell's work, it is a contemplative piece with an elaborately written screenplay that at times mimics traditional British plays from the period covered, that is, the early 1950's, by which time Bax was well into his sixties and nearing the end of the road. In that respect it is somewhat reminiscent of Alain Resnais' work from the same period as Russell's film, such as *Mélo* (1986) and *La Vie Est Un Roman* (1983) in which Resnais also mimicked the traditional play in its use of verbose dialogue, mannered set-pieces, and spare settings, sometimes only suggesting reality with basic props or a painted backdrop. Russell, as he had learned from his film on Delius, concentrates on a brief moment in time, a few months, from which we may gleam the story of a life.

Russell does a magnificent job as Arnold Bax who was by the end of his life – he died at age 69 in 1953 – a contradictory figure. A successful composer in many ways, as the Master of the King's Music, with an honorary doctorate from Oxford, a composer of relatively well known romantic music that was heard regularly on the radio, and as creator of soundtracks to successful films – but he was also regarded by many critics and the avant-garde elite as a minor, conservative, composer of sentimental music, perhaps fit for cinema screens but surely nothing more serious. He knew exactly where he stood and it bothered him to no end, knowing that, despite his relative success and privilege he could do nothing about it. He hated the avant-garde as much as he loathed the classical music that used folk-idioms from their home countries such as those of his compatriot Ralph Vaughan Williams. In a sense he isolated himself but he also felt uncomfortable as a loner and outsider – the role never suited him as it did Satie or Bartok- and he never seems to have found his niche.

The cosmopolitan Bax had numerous affairs with women over the years in places far and wide from Moscow to Paris, and despite his marriage he had one long complicated affair with Harriet Cohen, that lasted over thirty years. The British born Cohen was a beautiful, talented pianist who was his muse, lover, confidant, and friend. Russell picks up the story when Harriet finds, thanks to a newspaper article, that Bax's wife had died a year previously and he never told her, despite the fact that he had been promising for years to marry her once she died. On this difficult moment Russell opens his intimate film on the complicated life of Mr. Bax when he was looking back not forward – as he himself put it in interviews at the time he had said all he wanted to say and didn't want to repeat himself – but repeat himself he does not in his music but in his life with three very different women as Russell charts his final days.

Russell opens his film on an appropriately subdued minor key as two old friends transitioning begrudgingly from middle to old age, Bax and the Canadian actor John Ireland (Kenneth Colley), who were friends, are in a movie theater having just finished watching David Lean's adaptation of *Oliver Twist* (1948) for which Bax wrote the original score. Ireland asks him: "How much did they pay you to write that lot?" "Not enough to pay for Harriet's flat" replies Bax, making it clear that he is under financial duress and he is also a man with responsibilities, a man with a history. They talk about what they might want to do after the screening. Ireland: "It's my treat, what do you fancy?" Bax looks at Annie (Hetty Baynes) the usherette selling candy with some interest but Ireland tells him: "You can't have her." Bax shoots back: "Neither can you old man, come on, I'll buy you a drink."

On this melancholic note Russell cues up a record player playing Bax's music and pulls his camera back to a traditional postwar living room with Harriet Cohen (Glenda Jackson), Bax's longtime mistress waiting for Bax to come home and confront him with the news. It's a pleasure to watch Glenda Jackson, in her final film for Russell, play on the same stage with him. Clearly they know each other well and that works for the characters and their longstanding relationship. The set is lit and laid out like a play. Bax duly enters and puts away his coat as if it were his apartment and Harriet informs him of the news. They have a discussion in which it becomes clear that Bax abandoned his wife over thirty years earlier when his two children were still babies and has been promising to marry Harriet ever since but something always seems to comes up. The argument remains inconclusive and Bax leaves clearly with no intention of every marrying.

In a train ride Bax is picked up by Sybil Chadwick (Melissa Docker), a young pianist who is enamored of his music and wants to meet him so badly she set up a whole scenario to get him on a date. While the meeting is unlikely an emotional or sexual affair starting in a train compartment features as a fantasy in many people's lives all through the War and the immediate postwar era – made into a memorable fantasy/romance film *Brief Encounter* (1945), one of few great studio films that the British managed to pull off that explores their own inner lives superbly well. Bax has his own brief encounter with Sybil – Russell shoots their first kiss in the forests of the Lake District at dusk in medium long shot as it would have been framed in the 1940's scored to Bax's romantic 1st symphony. Here we truly enter the mind of Bax as we can't be sure if this is fantasy, a memory, or contemporary reality – it doesn't matter as we inhabit Bax's worldview completely which is what Russell wants.

They make a date for a theater in London to see *Oliver Twist* and hear Bax's score but Sybil stands him up. He sneaks into the theater towards the end of the film to hear his own score but is thrown out by Annie but they manage a bit of flirtation before Bax is shown the door. He waits until the theater closes and stalks Annie as she leaves the theater following her to nearby late night gentleman's club where she has a second job as a performer. As Bax follows Annie through London Russell shoots on the street itself with modern cars and signage – it's as if we are now inside Russell's mind rather than Bax's and he is following not Annie but Hetty Baynes the actress who would become his third wife. In any case by this point Russell/Bax is one person, as Russell surely intended when he decided to take on the lead role.

At the club Annie does a spirited strip tease with feather-wings as she moves to the music with a hot pink light on her. This was actually a very typical kind of show for supper clubs that would usually be followed by a magician or some comedy, giving the evening more of a burlesque/vaudeville feel – the nudity was discreet and often covered by highly formal dance moves or props. Women who worked such places were often waitresses, candy girls in theaters, or bartenders in their day jobs.

Bax looks at his watch and remembers an appointment with Harriet. In her flat they rekindle their romance over Bax's music, written for her, during a tryst they fondly remember, but with some sadness too, knowing that those times are far in the past now and unlikely to return. On that note Bax exits to Harriet's response to hearing the story of the tryst on the train: "You're not going to marry her are you?" "Not thinking of marrying anyone" replies Bax, sounding like a line he's used too many times. Russell's acting here as the old bachelor, who has seen better days, is superb.

The words *Part Two* come up, as in a play as Russell cuts to Annie smoking cheerfully and being amused by Bax's sophisticated adoration, fascinated by his old world politeness, and charmed by his gifts. At the hotel Bax asks her to interpret one of his symphonic poems where he wants her to play a sea nymph, naked of course. Having women as nymphs or goddesses was one was one sure way of getting them naked with no eyebrows raised but Annie, being working-class, does not seem familiar with this convention and sees just another "old fart." On that note they retire.

Later at the beach Annie is wearing a bathing suit while Bax insists that "a nymph in a bathing costume just looks bloody daft!" She asks for ten quid extra for the "naked." Bax agrees and sets up his gramophone on the sand and, inspired, starts to dance by himself still wearing his overcoat to his own music. Russell does an inspired solo dance on the beach here, using his large body and gravity to do the work and the rocks as props to bounce around; the dance ends perfectly as Bax collapses next to the gramophone and pretends to have passed out from the effort. When he gets up Annie, still in her bathing suit, is doing the dance by the waters – channeling *The Birth of Venus* as Russell shoots her against the incoming waves. Annie gets cold and tired and decides she's had enough and comes in. "But you've missed the climax!" Exclaims Bax as the music is just building up to its climactic romantic end. "Story of my life" replies Annie. Bax listens to his music as it climaxes on an empty shore – sans nymph – perhaps the story of his life.

Later they have a hot toddy at the hotel, a traditional British drink for cold days as Annie tells the sulking Bax she will do the dance in their room. Annie does a sprightly modernist dance/strip tease to Bax's music that ends with some spirited lovemaking interrupted by a phone call from Harriet – Annie ends up on the floor and she breaks Bax's record as revenge. Harriet has accidentally cut her wrist or perhaps she tried to commit suicide and the couple return to London in silence. On the way out of the hotel room Bax notices the broken record and picks up the pieces of vinyl and throws them into the fire. Russell cuts to an agonizing close-up of Bax, his face lit up by the glow of the fire from his own music going up in flames. Bax realizes his compositions don't stand a chance in the contemporary musical world but there's nothing that can be done and he's resigned to it.

Back in London and Harriet's flat she lies in bed convalescing and listening to his symphony dedicated to her. They reminisce about their time together when they were young, as she was convalescing over another old injury. Harriet asks him to remove the bandage and he claims ignorance of how to do it. "You'll get used to it" replies Harriet as Bax carefully removes the bandages as we see a close-up of Bax looking defeated, gratified, and relieved as Russell fades to the credits.

Strangely when one hears the music of Bax and his contemporaries in England, such as Elgar, Delius or Hubert Perry, that all composed late Romantic music into the 20th century, what one hears now is not the rhapsodic, all-encompassing Romanticism they sought to create but the catastrophic failure of Romanticism itself – always nymphs and never flesh and blood humans always Love but never love expressed in everyday life on the fly. Bax's world seems to have gotten smaller as he went along, for a whole host of reasons, and by the end it's just him and his long suffering girlfriend listening to his music from a simple record player in a small flat – but that is *something* after all Bax seems to say, without a word spoken.

THE MYSTERY OF DR. MARTINU (Short/1993)
Bohuslav Martinu was not a doctor but a Czech composer (1890-1959) of modern classical music whose vast output, writing 6 symphonies, 15 operas, 14 ballet scores and a large body of chamber music, belies the fact that he lived always on the run in the chaotic center of the storm of Europe at mid-century. His "doctorate," as such, was in music, earned so he could teach and earn a living, as Martinu came from working class parents and needed a job straight out of school. As with his film on Bruckner Russell finds an incident in the composer's life that caused a trauma, and a stay in a hospital, using it as a window into the composers' inner world and a way into his biography as

a whole. The film is also something of a concept film as the one hour running time is split into two 30 minute sections – the first part is a recurring dream that Martinu experiences while convalescing in a hospital, the second section is that dream explained by Martinu's friend, music teacher, and armchair Freudian psychoanalyst, professor Mirisch (Martin Friend). Such an approach is so loaded and dangerous that it is surprising that it works as well as it does.

Russell was not new to using dream imagery, it being a present even in his BBC documentary days, despite the prohibitions by Huw Wheldon. For example *The Debussy Film* begins with a dream and *Isadora, The Biggest Dancer in the World* ends with one. As he went into features dreams took on a more prominent role, taking center stage in both his 16 minute film *Nessun Dorma* (*And None Shall Sleep*) from 1987 and in the music video for Pandora's Box *It's All Coming Back to Me Now* from 1989 both of which are mostly composed of dream images. But Russell, always with his feet firmly on the ground, kept a notion of the "brutality of factual reality" close at hand to act as a counterpoint – *The Mystery of Dr. Martinu* is no exception.

Dream imagery is best represented perhaps in painting and collage as once narrative enters the picture problems ensue. A good example is Alfred Hitchcock's *Spellbound* (1945) that used the talents of Salvador Dali, the doyen of dreams, at least in the art world. His backdrop and floor with multiple eyes are merely generic and cliché ridden, more analogous to kitsch illustration. Once inside the labyrinth of *Spellbound's* narrative, created by veteran screenwriter Ben Hecht, Dali's imagination seems suddenly affected, arch, and rather silly – it's simply trying too hard. Even when we use language to explain our real dreams they suddenly loose all mystery and fall flat; and any psychoanalytic take on dreams, which tends to be programmatic, are equally in danger of being boring and hackneyed. In any case Russell manages to keep all of the narrative balls he's juggling in the air for the full hour without a misstep and *The Mystery of Dr. Martinu* is one of his best late works.

Like many composers and artists of the 1920's Martinu moved to Paris where he came under the strong influence of Stravinsky's neoclassical style, creating dense polyphonic structures that were at once romantic and ironic, literal and abstract. The propulsive, angular style that Stravinsky mastered struck a chord with Martinu who also incorporated Czech folk forms and American jazz idioms as in his famous *Kitchen Revue*.

Martinu's stay in Paris was life changing and it was where he - a late bloomer - found is voice as an artist, but as the Germans marched into Paris at the beginning of the war Martinu and his wife, the French seamstress, Charlotte Quennehen, moved to the US in 1941. They finally settled in an apartment on 58th street near Central Park with the help of friends who got him teaching jobs. Charlotte never cared for the US and returned to France while Martinu, in 1946, accepted an offer to teach at the prestigious Berkshire Music School. In Great Barrington, Massachusetts he was lodged along with the students where he had an apartment. One night he took a walk on the terrace of his apartment, a section of which had no railing, and he fell off, landing on concrete. He was hospitalized with a fractured skull and concussion drifting in and out of a coma for several days but he survived. When Charlotte returned she found a different man: gaunt, irritable, loud and in constant pain. He was diagnosed with asperger syndrome and with autism but nothing was ever conclusively proved. He sought out a psychiatrist to help and he eventually started to compose music again, and some sense of his old self came back. Russell chooses that fall and his stay in the hospital, in the early months of 1948, where he has recurring dreams as his focal point.

Russell begins his film with the full title: *The Mystery of Dr. Martinu: A Revelation by Ken Russell*. Let's see what the revelation is. We begin with Martinu's dream, as he wakes up on a stretch of deserted beach – there is a radio playing popular music of the late 1940'S and he notices that his hand is covered with ants, as in Buñuel's film *An Andalusian Dog* (1929) in which Surrealists Salvador Dali and Luis Buñuel created what they thought was a symbol of fetish, masturbation, and the feeling of "avoir des fourmis"(literally to "have ants") that also means "feeling sexual" in French slang – but as with any ambiguous shot, the interpretations are greater than the sum of its parts. In Buñuel's film the shot is a point-of-view from a woman and the man's hand is trying to get through a door and she is blocking him. Russell pans from Martinu up to a couple on the beach, dancing to 40's swing music, the man in uniform and the woman in a floral summer dress. A miniature plane lands on the beach and some people strangely dressed for winter with umbrellas and overcoats run toward the plane – the crowd greet an aviator who is by the toy plane and hoist him up on their shoulders like a hero. A nearby reporter asks him how it feels to have crossed the Atlantic. We realize the aviator is Lindbergh who replies: "Great!" Martinu's 3rd Quartet was inspired by (and is dedicated to) Lindbergh's transatlantic flight. A reporter asks Martinu how he feels having composed the first piece of music dedicated to the famous event and Martinu also says "great" but, strangely, with little enthusiasm. Suddenly Martinu hears someone calling him from a lighthouse that's very far away but he reaches it in a matter of a few steps seeing a naked woman at the top railing calling him. He tries to go inside the lighthouse but a guard asks him for money and his passport. The French guard looks at his passport and asks him what he's doing "here." Martinu says he's looking for a job. "Couldn't you get a job in your own country?" "I played second fiddle with the Czech Philarmonic" replies Martinu "but Prague is a dead city, it has nothing to offer a young composer with new ideas. Paris is the home of the avant-garde." The guard lets him in exclaiming "and the Folies Bergére!"

As he climbs the lighthouse he stops half way up as there is a production of one of his modernist ballets, influenced by Erik Satie's *Parade*. Charlotte is there dancing in the style of a flapper from the twenties. She seems quite charmed by him and he asks her to marry him – she accepts and they dance as Martinu is suddenly wearing a top hat as out the window of the lighthouse we can see the Eiffel Tower. As wedding gifts Martinu receives a toy piano and she gets a Singer sewing machine. Charlotte Quennehen was a simple hearted seamstress from Picardy that Martinu married early on when he was young and finding his way between Prague and Paris. The couple seem to settle in with Martinu composing on his toy piano and Charlotte sewing with her new machine.

Suddenly we see a completely naked young woman in an open field dancing while carrying an enormous Czech flag to his *Fantasies Symphoniques No. 6* written while in the US – then the naked dancer is inside the small space where Martinu and his wife are working, still dancing but now covered with the flag, framed against the window facing the Eiffel Tower. The young dancer dramatically flings off the flag and runs off - Martinu catches it and frantically runs after her up the stairs to the lighthouse. Once he reaches the top they are separated by all of the glass and apparatus.

He seems to know her and calls her Slava. "We haven't much time Slava I have a gift for you." "You have?" intones Slava from behind some thick glass that distorts her features – an astonishing image that was used for the poster for the film. Slava was the nickname for Veteszlava Kaprálova, a fellow Czech composer who was studying in Paris in the 30's – she became Martinu's student and then lover. He fell madly in love with Slava and proposed divorcing his wife and moving to the US together but she returned to Prague.

Kaprálova was not simply a muse for Martinu but an accomplished composer who specialized in piano works and songs but she died at the age of 25 of typhoid fever before the war started. Her piano pieces *April Preludes* have entered the standard repertoire despite the small amount of work she was able to produce. Kaprálova and Martinu wrote some passionate letters but her bad health and their lives on the run from German occupations as the war heated up made a relationship impossible. Martinu wrote arguably his best known work for her, the *Double Concerto for Two String Orchestras, Piano and Timpani* (1938).

"I have a gift for you Slava – the headscarf I gave you in Polička." "Seems like another lifetime" says Slava. "Don't say that! It wasn't that long ago, it was just before we left France for America." "But I never went to America" explains Slava. "But this is America!" counters Martinu. Polička is the small town where Martinu was born in a tower overlooking the town and, as Martinu remembers it, where he and Kaprálova once vacationed when they were young visiting the old places he knew. Their shared memories don't seem to quite match up but they finally meet up and kiss but as Martinu turns he accidentally falls off the railing from the top of the lighthouse down to the rocks below. Russell shoots it using video superimposition that flattens the image but since it is a dream it works. The moment he hits the rocks he wakes up on the same beach and his hand is again covered in ants. The camera pans and there are some suitcases from the 1940's waiting for him along with his wife carrying her sewing machine already in its case. They carry their luggage along the rocky East Coast of the US and notice some American pilgrims from centuries ago are there and they help them navigate the terrain, even handing Martinu a little golden statuette of the Statue of Liberty. While enchanted by their hospitality Martinu hears Slava calling him from the lighthouse.

Martinu then encounters another checkpoint with another guard. "Since when do you need a passport to enter Coney Island?" asks Martinu. "This is Ellis Island buddy – passport." The guard not only lets them pass but gives them some popcorn and Coca-Cola, as if they were entering a movie theater. They explain that they don't like popcorn or cola. "That's a very un-American activity" explains the guard, adding: "Nobody said you had to like it – you want to belong dontcha?" Martinu and Charlotte take their popcorn and Coke and enter the US. On their way inside Martinu asks what movie is playing – it's "Donald and Donna go to New York"

Inside the movie theater everyone has the same popcorn and Coke and everyone is saying the word "quack-quack" like a duck – the couple decide they must join in and also start to quack like ducks. This is certainly the strongest criticism Russell ever depicted against American corporate cinema and its stranglehold on the befuddled, branwashed population. With such a scene it would be unlikely that his film would have gotten much distribution in the US but he knew that was unlikely anyway as Martinu was little known or appreciated in the US despite his long fruitful stay there. Martinu was not a master of self promotion in the style of Igor Stravinsky, Arthur Rubenstein, or Eugene Ormandy – all exiles that did very well in America – he was more in the mold of Béla Bartók, someone that didn't have a self-promotional bone in his body, and could easily have disappeared into the American scene without the help of friends.

In response to this homegrown American conformity Martinu writes some of the most complex music of his life with multilayered symphonies that were always sliding around the tonal scale, sometimes tragically and sometimes mischievously, and sometimes both – like Bartók he rebelled quietly and let the music do the talking. In their newfound home we see the same room as before, that was in the lighthouse, but now the window looks out to the Statue of Liberty and Martinu's piano is painted with the American flag as Charlotte continues to sew out American quarters that occasionally drop to the floor. Martinu uses the sound of the constantly running sewing machine to imagine a train with Slava on top dancing with the Czech flag. Suddenly she is inside his little apartment with his wife but now dressed in a traditional Czech costume, continuing her dance. Again she runs away and Martinu desperately follows her up the stairs to the top of the lighthouse.

At the top of the stairs Slava is playing table football with a man dressed as a Nazi. Slava wins and the Nazi pounds her pelvis with one of the playing poles. We see that the whole room is decorated with Nazi flags as Slava and the Nazi fight at the top of the lighthouse and he throws her off and Slava falls to the rocks below – Martinu tries to help but he is also thrown off and he falls to his death but just before he hits the rocks he wakes up on the same stretch of beach.

When he wakes up he runs to the lighthouse where Slava is, as always, calling out to him. There is a line of men waiting to get in and he is too late, the guard won't let him in. He tries to bribe him with Czech currency but the American guard dismisses it as worthless, telling him it's too late. Suddenly a P-47 fighter plane strafes the guard box with bullets and the guard is killed allowing Martinu inside. He can only peer into one of the rooms in the lighthouse where he sees Slava making love to a young man, one of the people waiting outside earlier, but as she proceeds she slowly starts to turn into a marble neoclassical statue – Martinu screams but cannot help her. Later she fellates the other man who was waiting while a background of enormous butterflies surround them. Suddenly the man being fellated finds himself in a wheelchair and is electrocuted as the chair becomes an electric chair used in state sanctioned executions. Martinu attempts to climb to the top of the lighthouse but finds a minotaur whom he slays with a handy nearby sword. Once he reaches the top of the lighthouse he finds Slava naked and reaches out to embrace her but he again falls off the railing to the rocks below.

But this time when we next see Martinu he is not on the beach but lying unconscious and bleeding on the ground floor of the dormitory in Great Barrington, Massachusetts as one of the students is trying to wake him. Martinu's dream is over. When his wife comes to visit while he is convalescing with good news about the premiere of his 5th symphony in Prague he berates her saying she knows nothing about music and is tone deaf therefore not capable of making a sound judgment – she runs out crying.

Professor Mirisch who is Martinu's friend and fellow music teacher, also plays armchair psychoanalyst. He starts off on a light foot telling him he doesn't need a degree in psychology to understand the meaning of the lighthouse, but the obnoxious guard must represent his experiences at the Prague conservatory of music where he was victimized and eventually expelled. "There is a tinge of guilt about deserting your homeland with the woman and the flag.

The influence of Surrealism is strong through especially the meeting with your wife." Yes, admits Martinu. "And Slava the unattainable dream girl, just always out of reach – yes Slava holds the key to the problem" exclaims Mirisch. "This Vietezslava Káprálova must have been some girl!" He asks if she has a picture of her and he produces one from his wallet - clearly Martinu is still in love with Slava and probably always will be. "Beautiful girl. In your dream you claim you went together to visit your home town with her, and then she brings about your own death..."

Martinu assesses that the audience imitating ducks in the movie theater must be related to the choir of the villages in Czechoslovakia imitating toy ducks but updated to Donald Duck and America. Slava represented Czech culture and the Nazis were trying to destroy her – something that they almost succeed in doing, and Martinu was helpless and could only watch. Martinu feels guilty that he didn't fight in the war but his friend tells him he did better by surviving and writing music, like his *Symphonic Poems* – an elegy to martyrs. The image of Slava as the ideal woman also recurs in Martinu's opera *Julietta* in which a man pursues a woman and then finds that she is merely a figment of his own imagination but it's too late for him to start over. Mirisch explains that "perhaps she is the image of "Julietta" which would explain the man ending up in the electric chair – chasing an idealized woman is very dangerous! But what about the image where Slava/Julietta herself changes into a piece of marble sculpture? Very puzzling."

As for the lighthouse Martinu was born in a tower of St Jakub Church in Ploička where he grew up - his father was the town fire watchman. As a boy he played in the great heights overlooking the whole town and countryside – Mirisch reasons that the tower is very much like a lighthouse and Martinu must have combined the images in his mind transferring them to France and to the US.

As Mirisch and Charlotte are seen walking in the Massachusetts countryside Charlotte explains how hard it's been for her to play second fiddle to a ghost, Slava. Mirisch asks her if she is sure Slava is dead. Charlotte explains that she is and that the last time she saw her was with Martinu in the tower. Mirisch asks what tower. "Why the tower in St Jakub Church in Ploička – we took a vacation all three of us." Mirisch realizes that Martinu has left out a crucial detail of his story – the vacation was with three people not two. Charlotte was there and had caught Martinu and Slava in bed together in the tower. "I'll never forget the look in his eyes when he saw me – the hatred."

When next Mirisch sees Martinu he tells him he's uncovered the mystery of his dream. Charlotte is there with him and he proceeds to explain. "You were both in the tower but it was not you who fell. Your desire to kill Charlotte when she discovered you with Slava in the tower was so strong that you repressed it and transferred it to your own fall." In a sudden shift in tone to the present post-war moment (1948) Mirisch informs Martinu that Russia has just invaded Czechoslovakia and he will not be able to return home as planned but must stay in the US. Martinu tells him that he will write music with Czech themes and that will be his homecoming. We then see Slava leading the children seen earlier at the beach — all dressed in traditional Czech clothing — dancing to Martinu's late *Orchestral Poems* — a similar scene in some ways to the ending sequence to *Isadora Duncan, the Biggest Dancer in the World*, scored to the final section of Beethoven's 9th symphony.

Russell wraps up his film with a beautiful coda, as Mirisch is driving Martinu and Charlotte away from the hospital and he looks back at them in the rear seat and tells them "And now I will tell you about my dream — it will make your hair curl!" Martinu and Charlotte look at each other as if saying — oh well, let's make the best of it, as the credits roll.

Russell's armchair psychoanalysis — mirroring Mirisch's — is well taken as he does not try to explain Martinu's dream, or why it keeps repeating, from an "objective" scientific point of view (as does Hitchcock in *Spellbound* and other films) but, rather, as the point of view of another character who does not take himself that seriously. Strangely this makes us feel that Mirisch is probably right whereas the cold "objective" doctors in Hitchcock's films always feel overbearing — as if they had merely scratched the surface but thought they had plumbed uncharted depths making their assessment of the facts problematic. Russell wisely keeps the explanations in quotation marks from the point of view of a character as eccentric as Martinu himself.

Russell clearly felt at home creating a dream world, like his contemporaries Bergman, Has, Tarkovsky and Fellini, he used it as an essential part of his work throughout his career, but Russell had a much more literal minded British way of handling the material — with a full knowledge of the hard historical realities always looking over his shoulder — as it surely must have been for Martinu as well.

DIANA (Music Video/1993)
Diana was a four minute video from a song by Bryan Adams about Princess' Diana's failed marriage to Prince Charles. Apparently Diana liked the song and found it funny and became friends with Adams. It used stock footage of the couple edited to the music, but it was retired from circulation and shelved by Adams himself in 1997 after Diana's tragic death.

KEN RUSSELL'S TREASURE ISLAND (Short/1995)

Ken Russell's Treasure Island is a one hour film for kids that has as its premise that the infamous pirate Long John Silver was actually a woman named Long Jane Silver (Hetty Baynes). The film is more akin to Kathy Acker than Robert Louis Stevenson but with a decidedly British sensibility. Stevenson's novel for young adults *Treasure Island* gave us the clichés of maps marked with "X" for treasure, one legged seamen, and nasty pirates with parrots perched on their shoulders – all standard fare that the Disney Corporation has turned into a real gold mine that is still in production. Finer fare such as *Time Bandits* have also plundered Stevenson's plot and also found gold.

Hetty Baynes plays Long Jane Silver like a combination of Betty Grable, Marilyn Monroe and Mae West adding her own British sense of absurdist humor – pretending to be a cook but always, calling people "land lubbers," smoking dark cigarettes, and with a (stuffed) parrot constantly on her shoulder – all sure giveaways that she's a pirate. Once the deal is made that she and her crew will come look for the treasure, she and her men break out into song about the importance of hygiene during pirate excursions using the tavern table as a stage where her crew turn out to look more like the seven dwarves with Long Jane Silver as Snow White. They continue singing as they march on board an actual replica of an 18th century ship that has been immaculately restored.

A title card in appropriate pirate typography reads "Three Months Later" as we see a toy model ship sailing in a cardboard ocean and a painted sky with stars. The little boy hears Long Jane Silver plotting with her men to take over the ship and steal the treasure once it's on board. The boy is taken captive and the pirates sing a jolly song as they take command of the situation. A mutiny amongst the mutineers leads to Long Jane Silver playing her "girl in distress" routine saving herself in the process.

Back in England everyone seems to have got island fever and in a final dance Long Jane Silver, pregnant, finds love amongst the wealthy socialites who financed the voyage. Even the remaining pirates, in leg irons, join in the festive song and dance that culminates, like any good comedy, with marriage and a party. While the film's verbose British wordplay makes the film somewhat out of reach for many children its one-note cartoonish narrative, sets, and acting style make it difficult for adults; in effect, *Ken Russell's Treasure Island* is caught between a rock and hard place, but the enthusiasm of the players just manages to carry the day.

THE INSATIABLE MRS. KIRSCH (Short/1995)

The Insatiable Mrs. Kirsch is part of an omnibus film titled *Tales of Erotica* put together by Regine Ziegler and Trimark Pictures based in Los Angeles. The other films are Susan Seidelman's *The Dutch Master*, Melvin Van Peebles' *Vroom, Vrooom, Vroooom*, and Bob Rafelson's *Wet*. Of the four films only Seidelman's work is up to the mark – creatively engaging with the contemporary world, via the sexual trials and tribulations of a dental hygienist in New York City and her erotic dreams that are triggered by a 400 year old painting in the Metropolitan Museum of Art.

Russell's 24 minute short is a take on the man and woman who meet in nondescript country hotel and by the end enter into some sort of relationship. The narrative path here is so well trodden that hotel films constitute a genre of their own – from *Grand Hotel* to *Grand Budapest Hotel*, from *Chelsea Girls* to *Four Rooms*, and from *The Shining* to *Fawlty Towers*, hotels seem to be a natural for cinema where the compartmentalization that happens in conventional narratives and the physical separation of rooms imposed on the architecture of hotels gracefully blend together and mysteriously fuse – this fusion is taken to its logical conclusion in the current melodrama/soap opera *The White Lotus* – a hit series for HBO. Since beds play a big role in the hotel world it would seem that erotica would not be far behind – but successes on this front are negligible – unfortunately Russell's film is no exception. Its clichés never develop or do anything interesting but are occasionally brought up to speed with some contemporary jokes.

A handsome young writer (Simon Shepherd) taking a rest in a country hotel notices a beautiful young woman (Hetty Baynes) and begins to stalk her. Russell's opening shot is of the woman seen from a distance on the top of a rocky cliff looking out to sea - shades of British landscape painting such as those by George Hull or Robert McIntyre who specialized in ocean scenes. Russell slowly pans over to the writer sitting on a grassy knoll looking at her dreamily – this corresponds to the closing shot - which is of the two characters walking down a country road together. To make it easier on himself the lovelorn writer acquires the room next to hers. Rather than engage her in conversation – which would seem to occur naturally to a professional writer – he vicariously observes the woman as she eats fruits and vegetables suggestively, in the manner of comedy porn - as might occur naturally to a film director. She also seems to have many Polaroids with her that she drops to the floor but we can't seem them as they all fall with the image side to the floor. Polaroids were then known, aside from making art or family pictures, for providing readily available erotic images of loved ones that one could carry around in a bag.

In one of her walks around the country, followed closely by her admirer, the woman hikes to a nearby "hill figure." These are enormous pre-historic visual representations created by cutting into a steep hill – a type of geoglyph usually designed to be seen from afar rather than from above, as are the figures in Nazca in Peru. These figures are usually animal or human forms – here we see the *Cerne Abbas Giant* chalk figure near the village of Cerne Abbas in Dorset, England. The figure shows a naked man wielding a club looking ready for a fight. The woman dances beautifully inside the figure and drops down directly onto the penis, spreading her legs playfully in some secret pagan ritual that she has invented. The man is, as the British say, gobsmacked.

Back at the hotel he listens on the adjoining wall using the traditional water glass to the ear and he hears what sounds to him like a woman using a vibrator on herself and we see just that. Russell shows the woman dressed suggestively pleasuring herself with a handy set of three vibrators. In effect, the image is now at the service of the man's imagination as he conjures all sorts of naughtiness, such as the woman kissing the dildo, etc. But the images fall into vapid platitudes on the spot and never recover - even as cliché they are stale and prosaic. The best part of the film is when the hapless writer follows the woman to the seashore and the rocky shore provides a nice repeat of the *Cerne Abbas Giant* theme as the caves suggests that man cannot escape his distant pre-historic past no matter how sophisticated and civilized he may become.

Of course there has to be a reveal and it comes when the writer finally confronts the woman face to face. The writer has sent the woman a bottle of champagne and an offer to meet in her room where he admits to being intrigued - she coyly offers room service to go with the champagne. It turns out the "vibrator" sounds the man was hearing, that were the trigger to his erotic fantasies, were in fact an electric breast pump – she has just had a baby and the Polaroids were of her prematurely born infant still in an incubator. They have a laugh and we see them walk along one of the country roads and there is an old ruined castle in the background suggesting perhaps a "romance in ruins." In voiceover the writer informs us that the woman is a choreographer which explains her expert dance by the *Cerne Abbas Giant* – she was happy because her infant was now healthy enough to come home. He adds: "unfortunately there is a Mr. Kirsch but we all became friends and I am godfather to the infant, now five years old, named Max."

In the final shot we see a color family photograph – and we also note that Mr. Kirsch is none other than Ken Russell himself and Hetty Baynes, who plays the woman, is in fact Russell's wife. The film should perhaps have been titled *The Insatiable Mr. Russell* but despite the charm of the actors and the extraordinary scenery of the British countryside the film cannot escape the grip of genre that binds it to conventions that feel already to belong to a distant past – pre *L'Avventura* pre *A Married Woman* pre *The Green Ray*, pre *The Silence* – all films that heavily feature hotels but are not simply "modern" – they are ahead of the game as films now are still playing a hopeless game of catch up. As for Russell's *The Insatiable Mrs. Kirsch* it must have been fun for him to make a film of his and his wife's fantasy life but we are left out in the cold – in the graveyard of genre with nowhere to turn.

MINDBENDER (1996)
Mindbender is a feature length film written by Russell and Yael Stern-O'Dwyer. It concerns Uri Geller, the world famous psychic and magician who rose to fame in the Middle-East in the 1950's/1960's to become a wealthy headliner in Las Vegas in the 1970's. His most famous trick was bending metal spoons with his mind. Russell disowned the film that was released and it appears to be a completely conventional biography with nothing to recommend it except the acting, which is strong throughout.

The original concept of the film, that Geller might somehow be a misunderstood artist of sorts due to his strange powers that no one understands, and many doubt are even real, is problematic. Geller used his "power" – or his bag of magician tricks- to go to Las Vegas and make a fortune. This is an unlikely scenario for a starving artist or misunderstood poet. If Geller is remembered at all now it is via his various appearances on late night American television performing tricks – an odd subject that wastes the talents of good actors and technical people who, as usual, all come through for Russell.

IN SEARCH OF THE ENGLISH FOLK SONG (Short/1997)
Like *Ken Russell's ABC of British Music* made nine years earlier *In Search of the English Folk Song* is a personal look at contemporary British folk songs and the history that has informed them in their current configuration – in that sense the 50 minute film is more

of a time capsule of folk music in England in 1997 than a history per se. While he interviews well-known personal favorites, such as Donovan, the film ignores the more obvious groups like Fairport Convention, Pentangle, and the Incredible String Band as well as recognized geniuses of the English folk song such as Linda and Richard Thompson or Nick Drake, in favor of unsung guitar heroes playing in local bars.

Russell always liked strong opening shots and he delivers here with his usual absurdist humor. We see Russell himself, aged 70, lying back in a reclining chair inside a greenhouse, wearing dark glasses with the word "FALLING" imprinted on the top and side of the glasses. He hears music and in seemingly a trancelike state goes outside. We see that he's in an immaculate garden with a female singer crossing a little bridge as they sometimes have in British parks. Russell then wakes up in his chair and tells us that he's "had the strangest dream!" He goes to his record collection of old 78RPM records to find the singer. Hi finds it: "*Died of Love and Brigg Fair* by Joseph Taylor, recorded by Percy Granger." Granger recorded music as well as composed and played it – he was something a musical ethnographer and performed a similar function as Harry Smith in the US some years later with his *Anthology of American Folk Music*. Russell explains the music to his dog who looks at him quizzically as Russell shows us charming footage of British musical enthusiasts dancing in the early part of the 20th century, all wearing suits and long dresses. Since he lives in the country Russell says, "what better place to find "country music? So let's go to the local pub The Turfcutter's Arms."

We see Russell with a small video camera shooting in the pub and occasionally helping himself to a pint. He interviews the young man who explains that his father, Barry, is a real folk singer from the old days and so they walk over the Village Green, as the British call it, to meet up with this original. It turns out Barry is an aficionado of American Indian culture – so much so he was given an Indian name by one of the tribes and writes folk music influenced by Indian culture and history. Russell is amazed that a local man, born and living in the south of England should have identified so closely with American Indian culture. Barry himself can't explain it as it is purely an emotional response. Russell then makes a video to go along with one of his folk songs. Russell here beautifully shows the permeability and adaptability of human culture – its libidinous promiscuity - always changing and always moving around, appropriated and sometimes transplanted to the most remote places that one can imagine.

Apparently one of the things that happens in the transplanting process is that signals get crossed or buried, or new hybrids spring up – strange mutations that are hard to imagine take shape. For example the singer, transfixed by American Indian culture, seems to have an American muscle car in his yard with the Rebel flag as a license plate – perhaps unaware that racists in the American south often use the flag as a symbol for white supremacy – but somehow in the new setting it all works together, signifying "USA" – in their new home the old codes fall away to make way for new codes or new ideas. In the American tradition Barry cooks up an outdoor barbecue and does some dad dancing along with Russell to his own music.

Russell follows a woman's voice singing a traditional English folk song from the 17th century and peers into a window, as we see what appears to be an old woman singing and weaving with an old loom. Suddenly she takes off her top and wig and she is a sexy young blonde woman. "I wish I didn't have such a vivid imagination" intones Russell – no doubt many audience members feel the same but it is Ken Russell after all. We next see her naked but covered by the bottom part of door in a stable as, with top hat and cane, and nothing else, she continues singing. Ken's imagination seems very one-track but clearly the singer relishes singing the bawdy song, from England's deep history. Ken's producer, Maureen Murray, arrives in a van to ask Russell how his film is going. In answer Russell sings her another bawdy song about a "skipper's penis" and they go off, laughing, to find the English folk song.

Maureen and Ken pick up a local hitchhiker who happens to be a "protest" folk singer and they go to the Greenham Common where they find an old factory where women worked during the war. The place eventually housed nuclear missiles in the sixties and so women protested and some had concrete poured on them as they were building bunkers. Russell asks the women to sing one of these protest songs and they do, settling in the overgrown fields that once was an air force base, mentioning Ronald Reagan and Castro among other "strong arm men" of the period, using humor, bawdy and otherwise, to ridicule the cold war politics of assured mutual destruction.

The next stop is provided by a handy postcard received by Russell as an invitation by June Tabor, a classically trained folk singer, who gives a standout a cappella rendition of *The King of Rome* (the name of a local British pigeon). Her combination of earnestness and humor, affected emotiveness and directness, is folk music made flesh seen in one long close-up. June then analyzes the song for Russell explaining how it works and why it is particularly "British" and also "universal" at the same time.

Russell and Maureen then go to the Fairport summer folk music festival and get the traditional shots common to festivals as we hear a full rendition of Eliza Carthy playing the violin and singing "Good Morning Mr. Walker," a song she wrote about an overly ardent suitor. He then interviews Ashley Hutchings, one of the founders of Fairport Convention and an expert in the history of English folk music who is at the festival. His idea is that folk music died before the advent of radio, movies and television when people had to make their own entertainment by reading aloud or playing an instrument or singing – it was a world where everyone was a participant not one where some played "traditional" music and others listened passively.

As they leave the festival they find Donovan, improbably hitchhiking back to the city, or Rjkvara (Nirvana), as he has written on the sign he's carrying as his destination. Russell and Donovan stop and chat about what the word Nirvana means to Donovan and where he first heard it. He then plays a song named *Nirvana* that explains, in a folk song, the meaning of the word. Russell very nicely segues from Donovan singing to shots of the road as Maureen and Russell head for Glastonbury and the "mystic vale of Avalon." We then see parts of the famous and highly theatrical Glastonbury summer festival with a black reggae band called Edward II. Russell shoots the various props and costumes – from faux African tribesmen to sixties mods and from ape suits to Las Vegas showgirls – with the flash cuts that he used as early as *Pop Goes the Easel*. Back at home Russell ponders reggae music, explaining that "we (the British) have always plundered other people's cultures so maybe there is, in fact, no such thing as truly "authentic" English folk music – there are all sorts of other possibilities - the Beatles, why there's folk music everywhere!" He starts to sing a song to his dog who yawns.

He then hears some orchestral folk music coming from the nearby lake and he goes out to investigate – sure enough it's the Percy Granger Chamber Orchestra let by Joe Conway. "*Country Gardens* my favorite folk song!" exclaims Russell. Maureen explains that it's a dance tune not a folk song. Russell retorts by singing to *Country Gardens*: "Ken Russell in search of the English folk song... but he quickly realizes he is not a very good singer: "Well, maybe it is a better song without words" muses Russell as the credits roll.

Russell's humorous take on just what constitutes folk music, or if it even exists, is in many ways an inspired bit of Free Cinema updated to the 1990's but with Russell himself as the actor who improvises with the locals. While some of the material is a bit stale and dotty Russell gives a spirited tour, with his producer, of the local talent there in 1997; as such the film will only get more interesting and undoubtedly also more strange as time passes. In the late 90's there was to be a folk revival of sorts with Belle and Sebastian in Scotland among many others but that was to be another story – Russell stays close to home and makes an irreverent portrait of himself as an aging enfant terrible trying to make a film about folk music even if by the end no one knows what it is, although The Percy Granger Orchestra seem to have the answer, and the last word, as the young players continue playing with unabashed joy past the credits.

DOGBOYS (1998)

Dogboys (a.k.a. *Tracked*) was a film produced by Showtime Networks, the American based production and distribution company, about a prison in the US where guards take to the sport of hunting criminals and then pretending that they died trying to escape – this was one of many loose adaptations of *The Most Dangerous Game*, the short story by Richard Connell first published in 1924 that has inspired many films from Italian Giallos to French sex thrillers. Russell was brought on board and the film was re-edited after his work was finished – standard practice in the Hollywood industry. As Russell put it himself it: "it paid the rent."[107] By 1998 Russell had two ex wives and several children so there was some urgency to making money on a regular basis. His own screenplays, ranging in adaptations from Bram Stoker's *Dracula* to Lewis Carroll's *Alice in Wonderland* never found financing so he took on work wherever his agent could find it.

LIONS MOUTH (Short/2000)

Lion's Mouth was a 27 minute film about a journalist Josephine Heatherington (Diane Laurie) who investigates the story of a Reverend H. Davidson, a vicar who was defrocked after taking in prostitutes; after his defrocking he preached on the streets, primarily Brighton Pier, reenacting scenes from the Bible, but when he reenacted "Daniel in the Lion's Den" he was eaten by a real lion. The reporter treats is as an event that actually occurred and is herself won over by the vicar's faith. Ken Russell is listed as one of the actors playing "Ken the clown" so it is intriguing what he would have made of a story ready-made for someone falling in and out of his religious convictions over the years – clearly an issue for Russell from his first conversion to Catholicism while making *Peepshow* in 1956. *Lion's Mouth* never found distribution and remains unavailable.

THE FALL OF THE LOUSE OF USHER: A GOTHIC TALE FOR THE 21ST CENTURY (2002)

The Fall of the Louse of Usher: A Gothic Tale for the 21st Century is an 80 minute film loosely based on Edgar Allan Poe's *The Fall of the House of Usher* but taking cues mostly from his own watershed film from 1970 *Dance of the Seven Veils*, that used cartoonish imagery, radically disjointed episodic fragments, and absurdist narratives that refuse to develop or resolve themselves in a traditional manner. It is, very much in its own way, a punk aesthetic where the anger and the destructive forces ("let it all come down") are transposed to cinematic conventions rather than musical (The Sex Pistols) or literary (Kathy Acker).

Poe's original tale is told in the first person: A man who comes to stay at the estate of his friend Roderick Usher, only to find that his host has just suffered the death of his twin sister who is to be buried in the family crypt near the house. The friend notices that this dead sister looks very much alive in her casket – almost as if she was in one of her cataleptic fits that she suffered from walking around the house in a trance when she was alive. As the days roll on Roderick goes mad – realizing he has buried his twin alive – something witnessed by the reasonable and normal friend who is narrating. At the end the sister returns to get her revenge, destroying Roderick and the house itself, that was, we are told, built on shaky ground near a lake. The friend leaves just in the nick of time witnessing the complete destruction of the Usher family and home.

Russell foregoes first person narration from an outsider perspective and we get instead Roderick Usher himself, in voice over, explaining why he had to rip the eye off his wife and eat it – which we see in close-up – thereby landing him in an insane asylum. Roderick (James Johnston) is something of a post-punk rock star and his antics and bizarre behavior – looking somewhat like a cross between Nick Cave and Sid Vicious – along with his constant narcissistic need to explain himself is made to seem plausibly like those of a rock star gone off the rails. Russell plays Dr. Calahari in the lunatic asylum with a fake German accent although he seems more interested in his sexy nurses than in curing the mad Roderick, and true to his namesake he is clearly as mad as a hatter.

From out of nowhere we see a young naked woman kneeling on a dining room table, covered in blood, with hands tied to the overhead lamp being attacked by a crazed group of women, some wearing Halloween devil outfits, and another dressed as a mini-skirted nun playing the violin - a nod to *The Devils* perhaps - but it doesn't play well in any sense of the term. What it does do is provide some memorable, badly needed, B-Movie "tasteless excess" that gives the film a jolt - a sense of heading into the murky waters of the subconscious – whether Roderick's, or Russell's, or both we cannot be sure. When we see a flashback of Roderick at a sound studio singing with affectations that might make Johnny Rotten squeamish we are presumably meant to see that he has some talent but this epiphany is not forthcoming, not even when he plays a sensitive part on a violin – Roderick's music is a washout and his poseur rock god ticks are annoying.

There are some genuinely funny parts to the film, as when a nurse – whose panties are clearly visible in the shot – is taking Dr. Calahari's pulse while he's looking at a porno magazine. A song by Roderick about "Annabel Lee," the title of the last poem that Poe wrote, exploring the theme of death, is illustrated with images of Roderick and his girlfriend taking drugs by one of the beautiful lakes near Russell's home but, again, this seems like a bad rock-video from the 1980's when those sorts of romantic shots were already cliché's, sometimes self-consciously so to get a laugh (Elvis Costello) and at others heart-on-sleeve to bring a tear (Celine Dion).

Russell's mad doctor antics slowly take over as the film progresses – although he seems more like a mad director than a mad doctor as he views rushes of music videos of Roderick on an IMac with his assistant nurse. As if Poe's story were not enough Russell adds a Frankenstein sub-theme, referencing Lang's *Metropolis*, which is perhaps not the smartest thing to be doing when one has entered into schlock and shock as a modus operandi. Finally we see the mad Dr. Calahari with a home video camera and the game's up – Dr. Calahari is Ken Russell – as he films a man and a woman in Halloween outfits doing some horrendous and embarrassing "dance/fucking" in his garden – fortunately they are wearing masks so their expressions are not seen. In one of Russell's funniest shots the mad Dr. Calahari /Russell watches more videos on the glass front of his microwave oven! This self-evident "fuck-you" gesture is the most "punk" shot in the film and shows that Russell (at age 76) was still very much alive and kicking.

The ending of the film appropriately foregoes all logic as the narrative of mad rock-star Roderick evaporates. Some "real" doctors come to the asylum with shotguns and Dr. Calahari makes a run for it. Two children (Russell's grandkids) dressed normally but with Halloween devil hats make room at the dining room table for man dressed in an ape costume who begins to cry, but the children console him and the ape whips out a large radio/tape player to play Roderick's song about Annabel Lee.

A woman dressed in robes wanders incoherently in the forest but Russell has changed the color of the video so it looks like infrared film as the forest turns a beautiful red with patches of purple and blue – it's his best shot in years and one wishes he had used this infrared effect more throughout the film and abandoned the more conventional video colors – automatically color corrected in most consumer video equipment - seen throughout the film. The woman in the forest joins Roderick on an inflatable water-slide but when they kiss the water-slide deflates and the two come tumbling down to earth.

Russell's eccentric take on Poe's legendary story is far too slight for a feature length work but might have made a funny short film. Randy doctors, crazy violin playing nuns, sexy nurses, narcissistic rock stars, and bizarre ritual sacrifices of beautiful women on a kitchen table, are all certainly the possible ingredients for a good drive-in B-Movie but *The Fall of the Louse of Lusher* is not that film. The work wanders about Russell's own house and garden without any wonder or poetry to keep us grounded – a waste of Poe's haunting story of a family's will-to-self-destruction overwhelming all limits and all reason to achieve it's horrifying end: oblivion. Like the water slide the film deflates at the end bringing the whole enterprise crashing to earth.

ELGAR: FANTASY OF A COMPOSER ON A BICYCLE (Short/2002)
Forty years after *Elgar* (1962) Russell was invited by *The South Bank Show* to make a film celebrating the anniversary of a film many critics consider the best film every made about a British composer and some think of as the best cultural program ever produced by the BBC. In celebration Russell made a beautiful 50 minute color short that he titled *Elgar: Fantasy of a Composer on a Bicycle* (2002).

It is Russell's final great work where he, in a sense, bids Elgar and cinema a fond farewell. Russell's opening sequence, of Elgar on his bicycle riding through the Malvern hills is shot from a stationary camera at a distance, more elegiac, stately, and pastoral than his original opening of *Elgar* where he put his camera on a car and used high speed tracking shots and quick cutting to follow Elgar riding a horse through the same countryside. Although there were no longer any restrictions on him imposed by *The South Bank Show* (they didn't dare) he chose to follow Huw Wheldon's rules at the BBC: a 50 minute maximum time slot and only the use a voice over narrator and Elgar's music to make his points – the actors never speak a word – it was an homage of sorts to Wheldon's influence and his days at *Monitor* and Russell gets some of his fire back to make one final great film.

Russell in voiceover tells us a bit of background history and he decides to illustrate one of Elgar's pieces, *Fairies and Giants*, to us by having a British marching band dressed in full uniform, parading around a miniature British village, turning them into giants – he then shoots some young women dressed as fairies, with angel wings as in his early short *Amelia and the Angel* (1958). Male and female principles are set up as distinct opposites: giant vs. miniature, solid vs. ephemeral, comical vs. touching.

These opposites seem to reconcile in Elgar's own relationship with his wife as we see them honeymoon in the Isle of Wight wearing the traditional bathing suits of the early 20th century and riding a bicycle for two. Russell was married four times in his life and seems, like many of the men he made films about, to have needed female companionship - its tenderness and sexual component as well as its domestic arrangements - as a constant; to the end of his life he saw this arrangement of men and women not only in a positive light, but as a fundamental bridge where opposites may meet, reconcile and come to understand and love each other so there was a spiritual component as well. Russell pays homage to Elgar's marriage with an extended take of the couple framed by a window in winter light shot from the outside, with pouring rain, as we hear one of Elgar's songs with the words composed by his wife, one of their many collaborations. In the following shot it is spring and the couple is pushing a baby pram as Russell explains the composer's precarious financial situation – akin to his own before Huw Wheldon and the BBC came to the rescue.

In one of Russell's most moving sequences he shoots Elgar flying a kite in the Malvern hills, with a string and a tin can attached, with his 7 year old daughter so she can hear the wind up close directly from the kite itself, acting as an enormous microphone to the heavens – with both of them laughing it is certainly one of the great images of family bliss made by a man who, with five children himself, knew something about it.

One of the things that Russell wanted to do with this sequel was to cover an aspect of his life that he had not been able to touch on, that is, the fact that Elgar enjoyed the companionship of several women over his long life, some of them muses, friends, lovers and fans. In some cases he wrote music specifically for them as was the case with Dorabella, one of the engaging portraits in his *Enigma Variations*. Dorabella was a young fan who eventually became a lover and muse. She had a "charming stammer" according to Elgar that he captured in his musical portrait of her. Russell plays the piece as we see Dorabella cycle (for 40 miles!) to visit her lover and friend and then play badminton with him in his backyard, as his wife looked on and made tea.

Variaton number 13 has been identified as Helen Weaver, a woman that rejected his early proposal of marriage but kept in touch with him – Russell shows the couple walking in an old graveyard, flowers in hand, one of his favorite shots with many variations over the years. We then see Weaver fully dressed and holding a bouquet of flowers in a pool of water – a modern pool – posing as the famous Pre-Raphaelite painting by John Everett Millais – Weaver as Lizzie Siddal as Ophelia - seen from a different angle in Russell's film *Dante's Inferno*.

Rosa Burleigh was another friend who eventually wrote a book on Elgar and had hopes of marriage if he ever decided to finally divorce his wife, which he never did. Russell does another wonderful take on the bicycling scene from *Jules and Jim* with Rosa and Elgar in bikes as they stop when she falls off due to a sudden tractor and he stops to mend her – all scored to the *Enigma Variations* - they decide to picnic where they are and enjoy the day. Russell makes sure we understand that these moments didn't simply just happen, but rather, that people then took the time to create them and enjoy their time together, and if we have lost that ability – so characteristic of the Belle Époque – we are the sorrier for it.

Elgar's favorite instrument was the violin and his extraordinary violin concerto – arguably the best of the 20th century - was dedicated to "Wind Flower" and many musical detectives have since then tried to figure out who she was – like Beethoven's "Immortal Beloved" she remains an enigma even though some writers are sure they have uncovered the secret. Russell has a beautiful young dancer perform a modern dance, with shades of Isadora Duncan, to the music and asks us to "judge for yourselves."

Elgar's wife Alice is the number one Variation of his *Enigma Variations* – proof for Russell that he recognized her contribution and importance to his work and his emotional life despite his many friends and lovers. It is safe to say that without Alice we would not know who Elgar was – she was tireless in pursuit of recognition for his work as much as he was inept at self-promotion – they made a great team and he knew it. She finally succeeded in making Elgar famous in their own lifetimes, even getting a knighthood, honorary doctorates, and many offers to write music. The final variation in his *Enigma Variations* is a self portrait, full of pomp and glory as if Elgar were hiding behind his trophies and his knighthood – an odd self portrait to say the least but it doesn't detract from the beauty of the work as a whole. *The Enigma Variations* was full of parodies, quotes and musical asides, full of grandiosity and whimsy seemingly playing with each other just for the fun of it – it was a marvelous response to the German "total work of art" espoused by Wagner and the closed circle of the classical style espoused by Brahms – more importantly it opened the stage out to let in much needed oxygen and the musical revolutions of the 20th century.

When war was declared in 1914 Elgar was horrified to see that his *Pomp and Circumstance* was being used as a recruiting song and as a march for young soldiers going off to fight in France – he hated the war and the powers that be that brought it on. The leaders and oligarchs who gambled on war were hardly "sleepwalkers" as some historians have reasoned much after the fact, but predatory vultures waiting to see who would get the Austrian Hungarian Empire, teetering on self-destruction, as well as other prizes up for whoever took the risk and the initiative – it was the opposite of sleepwalking, but rather a situation where no one wanted to blink lest they miss their chance and someone else gets the prize. Elgar saw the war in economic turns, and being from the working classes – his father had been a piano tuner – he had no sympathy for the predators in power. When he was asked to write music by royals or statesmen he politely declined. The fact that his "Land of Hope and Glory" lured thousands "to the gates of Armageddon" caused a deep depression – he withdrew from social life to a remote country cottage to write string quartets of lamentation for his dead friends. Russell shows a string quartet composed of doctors, nurses and injured servicemen playing his music.

After the war his wife Alice died and he buried all of his honors, his medals, and his honorary doctorates with her as they had meant so much to her. He did not write much music after that except for a cello concerto, that was Alice's requiem of sorts – and has since become his best known work after *The Enigma Variations*, with all of the great cellists having taking turns doing their version of it, including the justly famous, luminous recording by Jacqueline du Pre from 1965.

In the final sequence we see Elgar as a young man riding his bicycle through the contemporary town of Worcestershire, full of small cars looking for parking. Elgar passes the Elgar Museum and has a quick look inside, finding his old piano. He doesn't linger and seems not nostalgic at all. Quite the contrary he seems young, carefree, and eager to get on with it. He rides by other landmarks of the town including the cathedral that the Catholic Elgar would have known well.

Russell can't help but add some absurd humor as he places himself next to the life size bronze sculpture of Elgar in the middle of the town square and Russell shakes hands with the bronze replica of Elgar as if posing for the official portrait, but he also doesn't linger as the camera pans quickly to the young Elgar as he rides his bike directly into the Cathedral and up one of the isles toward the nave coming out the other side. For a finale, as one would expect, he rides up to the Malvern hills for a final look around as the sun sets, resting his bike on the topmost hill overlooking the town – a perfect bookend to the first *Elgar* film from 1962.

In *Elgar: Fantasy of a Composer on a Bicycle* we see actors playing his wife, and his many friends, picnic, play games, have dinners, mourn their dead loved ones, go to work, flirt, get married, and play with their pets and their kids – all the themes found in *The Enigma Variations*. But Russell this time around is older and is more aware of time passing – when a young Elgar and his wife get up from a picnic spread Russell holds the shot italicizing it and we feel the evanescent presence of those people and the "eternity" suggested by the landscape all around. The present moment, always in flux – the enigma of everyday life - was something Russell, like Elgar, emotionally and instinctively understood, it rightly fascinated them and their work stands in awe of it. Russell's two films on Elgar are a testament not only to Elgar but to Russell's body of work as a whole; the "reality" of Elgar in 1962 and the "fantasy" in 2002 are really one – an appropriate masterwork on which to close the book.

THE GIRL WITH THE GOLDEN BREASTS (Short/2006)

The Girl With the Golden Breasts was part of an omnibus film titled *Trapped Ashes* created and written by Dennis Bartok consisting of four 20 minute episodes with four very different directors - the other three were: Sean Cunningham, John Gaeta, and Monte Hellman. Veteran director Joe Dante (*Gremlins*) was brought on board to helm the linking scenes that take place in a "haunted house" located inside a film studio. The basic plot is that a movie studio tour goes wrong when the tour guide (Henry Gibson) and his group, by accident or by design become stranded in a haunted house – the guide explains the only way out is for each of the members of the group to tell a horror story. Finding all of the exits locked they proceed to do so and Russell gets the opening film as a young woman Phoebe Kane (Rachel Veltri) tells her improbable story of a breast implant operation gone wrong.

Phoebe is an aspiring actress who has trouble getting parts that should be obviously going to her, being a young, spunky, beautiful woman – she concludes after some scrutiny using a mirror that the fault lies with her small breasts and decides on implants. She goes to a doctor Larry (Winston Rekert) who tells her there is a newer method for implants than silicone that consists of using actual breasts from women who have recently died. The doctor suggests this is not much different than getting a new set of eyes or a kidney from a donor.

She agrees and as the operation is underway in a hospital room we notice that doctor Larry is smoking a cigar as he preps for the operation – a sure sign that Larry is insane and things are not going to go well for Phoebe. In the middle of the operation the doctor asks for a drink and the nurse gives him one – a hilarious take on doctors and hospitals reminiscent of *Candy* (1968) where James Coburn, playing a brain surgeon, takes the term "operating theater" far too literally.

Russell – following Bartok's script – uses extreme close-ups of the operation as we see Phoebe's breasts cut open and new breasts placed inside in extended close-ups. All of the four segments have one scene that was meant to gross out audiences and make them squeamish in the manner of torture porn or the films of Hershel Gordon Lewis (*Blood Feast*, 1963) but the scenes lack the openly sadistic frisson of torture porn or the absurdist charms of Gordon Lewis who specialized in politically incorrect horror/

comedy/soft-core films – a strange hybrid genre where realistic "medical operations" were often performed with much blood, on beautiful young women.

In Russell's film the implants seem to work and suddenly Phoebe is in much demand. In a new film she is making one of her love scenes with a costar Zack (Scott Heidl) goes awry as her breasts start to suck the blood from his body leaving a scar on his chest. She claims she got carried away in the love scene but later – as Zack and Phoebe become actual lovers - he gets his tongue caught on her nipple as it sucks his blood. He's forced to use some scissors to separate himself and he immediately dumps her, terrified of her "vampire breasts." Phoebe returns to the clinic where she had the operation but Larry is missing and she is told that he is in another facility in San Pedro – a working class area south of Los Angeles with a harbor and many warehouses and old storage facilities.

Phoebe enters a warehouse that looks like a meat market with human parts – including Larry who is hanging by a meat hook. Terrified she nevertheless moves forward looking for answers. Three male "doctors" dressed as women and wearing makeup tell her that Larry conducted experiments on himself and died, donating his body to science. They explain that her operation is irreversible and her breasts will always suck the blood of victims but will also keep Phoebe young forever. They then remove their shirts to reveal female breasts – presumably also with vampire qualities as the film cuts back to the framing narrative in the haunted house where the participants are listening, incredulously, to Phoebe's story.

Russell's slight film illustrates Bartok's basic plot and theme – but its one-note take on breast implants is hardly worth the effort. While there have been great – at times brutal - satires of Hollywood by Hollywood – from *Sunset Boulevard* to *Inland Empire* – this film lacks the gravitas of Billy Wilder or the psychological depth of David Lynch. It even falls flat as hospital satire – not up to standards set by films such as *The National Health* (1973) by Jack Gold or *Britannia Hospital* (1982) by Lindsay Anderson – two films made by British directors who found just the right note between horror (of a more realistic sort) and comedy - and without the need to use torture porn as an element to keep audience attention from flagging. Russell's satiric phase was certainly in full operational mode by the time he made *The Girl With the Golden Breasts*, but it is a hollow and shallow film - its take on the horror genre is paint-by-numbers – it spins its narrative wheels for nothing.

EIN KITTEN FÜR HITLER (A KITTEN FOR HITLER) (Short/2007)

A Kitten for Hitler is an 8 minute black and white film parody of sentimental Christmas and family films that Russell abhorred. Despite having 5 kids and 4 wives the genre always rubbed him the wrong way as the sentiments were never earned, they were expected – if one understood the mechanics of film one could see the obvious mechanism for sentiment coming a mile off. He decided to compress all of these clichés into eight minutes making a faux trailer for a film with a German title – although the actual genesis of *A Kitten for Hitler* appears to be a bet that Russell made with his old friend Melvyn Bragg. Bragg, as one would expect of a man who ran the longest arts program in British history, was adamantly against censorship of any kind, even material that he himself found abhorrent. Russell bet him he could make a film that even Bragg would want to ban.

The story concerns a young Jewish boy from Brooklyn, in 1941, Lenny (Rusty Goffe), who is so taken aback by Hitler's anger that he decides to send him a kitten – a cute furry toy – as a Christmas present, thereby softening his heart. Goffe was then a 59 year old actor who was very short and so often played children's roles, including a famous turn in *Willy Wonka & the Chocolate Factory*. Russell's opening scene is of Santa Claus, played by Russell himself, superimposed on a background of New York in the 30's, giving us an illustration of the time and place. The usual male voice that accompanied *News on the March* films from the period is used ironically here to explain the action and the typography for the film's credits mimics the "heroic" typefaces used in WWII propaganda films.

Lenny doesn't just ship the kitten to Germany but takes it to Adolf Hitler (Phil Pritchard) and Eva Braun (Rosie Thewlis) himself. At first Hitler is taken with the toy kitten and, incredibly, seems to be won over by the animal's cuteness even repenting how mean he has been recently. He offers Lenny a bagel in return for his gift and Lenny then shows the couple a swastika tattoo on his stomach that he has put there in honor of the Fuhrer. Russell, in a nod to Hannah Arendt, turns Eva and Hitler into a boring and banal suburban couple who also happen to wield enormous power over millions of people. Eva notices the Star of David on Lenny's chain around his neck and informs Adolf that Lenny is a Jew. Suddenly the smiles disappear and Hitler throws the kitten away as Lenny is led off to a concentration camp. Lenny's mom Rachel (Elize Tribble Russell) tries to get him back but too late.

Russell uses actual documentary footage of WWII – focusing on Germans marching - the same footage used by Leni Riefenstahl for *Triumph of the Will* (1935) - intercutting with his own de-saturated video. These shots do not match in the editing but clearly the mismatching here is done on purpose as later when the mother walks up the steps to the White House her steps and the superimposed steps (of the Capitol) do not match, creating a sense of dislocation and unreality.

Lenny is killed in one of the camps and part of his skin is used to make a lamp – we recognize him via the tattoo. After the war is won by the allies the lamp is given to Rachel, his mom, as she takes the lamp to the White House where president Truman is going to ceremoniously offer a posthumous medal to Lenny. When he does so the lamp lights up magically without being plugged in and the Swastika becomes a Star of David – pronounced a miracle via text and triumphant orchestral music. Russell cuts to the lamp as he superimposes Lenny smiling at the ultimate victory of the allies against Germany, as in a patriotic film, but one where the air has been removed and the "victory" has turned to ashes.

Russell's use of actual war footage here is brutal and morally questionable – as he meant it to be – although it must have been fun for him to use Reifenstahl's footage for a black comedy about the banality and absurdity of Nazism. But while he had used the character of Hitler before, in *Dance of the Seven Veils*, here the irony falls flat and seems disconnected to anything except a need to shock at all costs. This strangely connects *A Kitten for Hitler* to contemporary avant-garde "practice" where "épater la bourgeoisie" has been the rallying cry since the Dadaists of the early 20th century, that is, to make something as offensive or as "difficult" as possible (Viennese Action, Performance Art, etc.). While such works tend to reinforce a sense of moral righteousness among already converted cognoscenti they invariably fail badly as propaganda and as art.

A Kitten for Hitler certainly qualifies as black humor, and to some extent as a fine art video, but more realistically it is a piece of self-conscious kitsch with an underlying cautionary tale about hate being far stronger than love in the real world – what we call History. In that sense the film has the moral foundation of an Aesop fable, such as *The Frog and the Scorpion* – also used by Orson Welles in *Mr. Arkadin*. No doubt that Russell won his bet with Bragg but he lost something more precious: time. By 2007 Russell was 80 years old and suffering many serious medical conditions including heart problems

– he must have known he didn't have a lot of time ahead of him, in fact he died three years later. *A Kitten for Hitler* seems, despite its potent black humor, and its excoriating take on "good taste," like a waste on so many levels.

BOUDICA BITES BACK (Short/2009)

Russell's final film was, appropriately, a biography: *Boudica Bites Back*, a 16 minute "cine-opera" film (according to Russell) made two years before he died. The film was self-financed, shot on video, and features many of his friends and family. Boudica was a Celtic/British Queen who led a series of uprisings against the Roman Empire around 60 AD. Boudica did not speak English but an older form of Welsh – she had two daughters by the King of the British Iceni tribe. When he died he left his kingdom to his wife and daughters but the Romans had other plans. They decided to annex the kingdom and confiscate the King's property, seeking out the iron, tin, copper and excellent wool that the area was known for – despite the dangers and the great distance (then) to Rome the extensive mineral wealth made it enticing but the powers that be in Rome were undecided if it was worth the effort.

The British were then composed of separate ruling states and tribes and they left no record of their struggles so what little we know of them, and Boudica, comes from the historian Tacitus based in Rome. Despite early successes against the Romans – defeating a whole Legion, killing approximately 80,000 Romans and Britons who were fighting alongside the Roman Empire – Boudica was eventually defeated and, as was customary then, brought to Rome where she was publicly flogged and her two daughters were raped. She never met Caesar but was aware of him and his war against the British a generation earlier. The emperor in her time was Nero who felt, along with a section of the ruling class, that Britain was not worth the expense but Suetonius's eventual victory over the region, and a large part of the Roman Senate hungry for new territory, made him reconsider. Britain was made the westernmost colony of the Roman Empire that they ruled for approximately 400 years until their own empire slowly collapsed and the last Roman legion in charge of keeping order in Britain was eventually called home in 410AD, to "secure a final line of defense."

Boudica over the years became something of a saint/martyr for the British — a normally secular society. The resurrection of Boudica as a British heroine began in the English Renaissance with poems (Edmund Spenser) and music (Purcell) using her story; in the 18th century she was revived again with paintings by John Opie as she became a heroine fighting foreign powers such as the dreaded French and Spanish; in the Victorian era the Suffragette movement used her as a symbol of female empowerment; and finally in WWII she was again used as an example of heroism and sacrifice against overwhelming odds. By the time Russell made his film Boudica was something of a British cultural icon. Ken Russell's *Boudica Bites Back* never received distribution and is not available at the time of writing.

George Porcari

George Porcari was born in Lima, Peru in 1952. He attended Catholic school, becoming an altar boy, which he very much disliked. He and his parents lived in San Isidro, which was then a well-to-do neighborhood between Miraflores and central Lima. His favorite activities were going to the nearby beaches, making art and watching television. In 1962 the family emigrated to Gardena, a working class suburb in the South Bay section of Los Angeles. The family arrived at the same moment as the Cuban missile crisis that Porcari watched on television without much interest, preferring *The Rifleman*, *Lost In Space*, *Dobie Gillis and The Twilight Zone*.

Porcari attended Gardena High School, which was then a Vo-Tech (vocational-technical) school where one could major in various trades – Porcari's major was auto repair. After graduating in 1970 Porcari got various jobs, unloading trucks – where he joined the teamsters union – in factories or in garages. His worst job was picking up dead birds from the no-man's-land area just beyond the runways at LAX. In this time he was taking pictures, in the style of Garry Winnogrand and Robert Frank but in color, using slide film. He also made a short Super-8mm film, *Greetings From LA, 1978!* before moving to New York City the following year.

In New York Porcari first lived at the Empire Hotel for a few months, which was then a youth hostel, but he eventually found an apartment on Delancey Street near the Williamsburg Bridge. He worked briefly as a waiter, a guy Friday, a clerk for a firm that imported chandeliers, and a telephone operator for a jewelry company. His first real job was working for the Strand Bookstore on Broadway, eventually helping the book buyer. In 1984 Porcari returned to Los Angeles to attend the Art Center College of Design in Pasadena where he received his MFA and also got a job as the book-buyer for the library – he retired as Acquisitions Librarian after 29 years at the age of 65.

Porcari has been exhibiting his photography and collage work since his first exhibit at the Laurie Rubin Gallery in New York City in 1988. The most recent exhibit of his art in 2024 was at the *As Is* Gallery in Los Angeles: *Still Lifes with Books*. In 2021 the Tif Sigfrids Gallery exhibited color photographs of Los Angeles taken in the seventies. In 2016 the Haphazard Gallery in Los Angeles published a catalog for an exhibit of his photo work and collages titled *Greetings From LA: 24 Frames and Fifty Years*. Porcari published his first essay – on the photography of Richard Prince - in *Arts* magazine in 1987. Over the years he consistently published essays on films and photography in various small journals while working as a librarian. In 1999 he started writing regularly for *CineAction* magazine, based in Canada, and in 2018 he published a book on the work of Michelangelo Antonioni titled *The Antonioni Adventure*. The following year he published a book, in collaboration with the poet Bruna Mori, titled *Beige*, that incorporated photographs of suburbia with poetry and memoirs. In 2024 he published a collection of essays on film and photography titled *One Second to Live: Photography, Film and the Corporeal in an Age of Extremes* – these two books, like the one on Russell, were designed by Jessica D'Elena-Tweed.

In January of 2024 Porcari moved back to Lima, Peru with his 96 year old mother. He lives in the same San Isidro neighborhood that he grew up with (now very changed) with his girlfriend Erika and her son Alejandro. In 2025 CineAction magazine published his essay on Godard: *The Odyssey at Cinecitta: Alberto Moravia's Desprezzo and Jean-Luc Godard's Le Mepris*. The same year *VuelaPluma*, an academic journal based in Lima, published (in Spanish) his essay: *Under a Real Sky: Photographic Adventures With Edgar Degas*. He is currently at work on a book on the photography of Edward Weston and Tina Modotti.

Footnotes

Introduction

1. **Ken Russell**, *Altered States, The Biography*, Bantam, 1991
2. **Ken Russell**, *Altered States, The Biography*
3. **Elize Russell**, *Ken Russell: The Boy Behind the Man*, ReFocus, the Films of Ken Russell, Edinburgh University 2023
4. **Elize Russell**, *Ken Russell: The Boy Behind the Man*
5. **Peter Blake & Ken Russell**, *Living the Life*, Season 1, Sky Arts, January 15, 2012
6. **Ken Russell**, *Altered States, The Biography*
7. **Elize Russell**, *Ken Russell: The Boy Behind the Man*
8. **Matin Harrison**, *Young Meteors: British Photojournalism 1957-1965*, Jonathan Cape London, 1998
9. **Ken Russell**, *Altered States, The Biography*
10. **Ken Russell**, *Altered States, The Biography*
11. **Mathew Melia** In conversation with Roger Crittenden, *Ken Russell at the BBC*, The Delius Society, YouTube, 2023
12. **Ken Russell**, *The Lion Roars Ken Russell on Film*, Faber and Faber, 1993
13. **Ken Russell**, *The Lion Roars*
14. **Michelle Mercer**, *Footprints, The Life and Work of Wayne Shorter*, Tarcher Perigree, 2007
15. **Ken Russell**, Interview, *Oui Magazine*, June, 1973
16. **Francoise Truffaut**, *A Certain Tendency in French Cinema, The French New Wave: Critical Landmarks*, ed. Peter Graham, Palgrave, 2009
17. **Ken Russell**, *Altered States, The Biography*
18. **Ken Russell**, *The Lion Roars*
19. **Davis Serritt**, *Jean-Luc Godard Interviews*, University of Mississippi, 1998
20. **Ken Russell**, Interview, *Oui Magazine*, June, 1973
21. **Ken Russell**, *Altered States, The Biography*
22. **Ken Russell**, *Altered States, The Biography*
23. **André Bazin**, *Chris Marker's Letters From Siberia (1957), Essays on the Essay Film (Film and Culture Series)*, Columbia University Press, 2017
24. **Al Sentor**, *Interview with Ken Russell*, YouTube, 2008

Monitor and Omnibus

1. **Ken Russell**, *Altered States: The Autobiography*, Bantam, 1991
2. **Ken Russell**, *Altered States: The Autobiography*, Bantam, 1991
3. **Ken Russell**, *Altered States: The Autobiography*
4. **Ken Russell**, *Altered States: The Autobiography*
5. **Felix Nadar**, *When I was a Photographer*, MIT Press, 2015
6. **Miles J. Unger**, *Picasso and the Painting That Shocked the World*, Simon & Schuster, 2018

Pop Goes the Easel

1. **Ali Smith**, *Autumn: a Novel*, Pantheon, 2016
2. **Todd Gitlin**, *The Sixties: Years of Hope, Days of Rage*, Bantam, 1993
3. **Sue Watling**, David Alan Mellor, *Pauline Boty The Only Blonde in the World*, Whitford Fine Art, 1998
4. **Thomas Crow**, *The Hidden Mod in Modern Art: London 1957-1969*, Paul Mellon Center, 2020
5. **Sue Tate**, *Pauline Boty: Pop Artist and Woman*, Wolverhampton Art Gallery, 2013
6. **Sue Watling** David Alan Mellor, *Pauline Boty The Only Blonde in the World*
7. **Sally Yard**, *Willem de Kooking: Works, Writings, Interviews*, Poligrafa, 2007
8. **Marc Kristal**, *Pauline Boty: British Pop Art's Sole Sister*, Frances Lincoln, 2024
9. **Herbert Marcuse**, *One Dimensional Man*, Beacon Press, 1964
10. **Tony Scherman & David Dalton**, *The Genius of Andy Warhol*, Harper Collins, 2009
11. **Joan Didion**, *The White Album*, Farrar, Strauss, Giroux, 1979
12. **Sue Watling**, David Alan Mellor, *Pauline Boty The Only Blonde in the World*

Dante's Inferno

1. **Lucinda Hawksley**, *Lizzie Siddal: The Tragedy of a Pre-Raphaelite Supermodel*, Seven Oaks Press, 2016

Song of Summer

1. **Roger Crittenden**, Ken Russell's *Song of Summer: The Virtue of Restraint*, ReFocus: The Films of Ken Russell, U Edinburgh, 2023
2. **Roger Crittenden**, Ken Russell's *Song of Summer: The Virtue of Restraint*

Diary of a Nobody

1. **Evelyn Waugh**, *The Essays, Articles and Reviews*, Little Brown & Co., 1984
2. **Gilles Deleuze**, *Gilles Deleuze From A to Z*, Semiotext(e) DVD, 2011
3. **Ken Russell**, *Altered States: The Autobiography*, Bantam, 1991
4. **Brian Hoyle**, *No Better Director to Learn From: The Collaboration and Parallel Careers of Ken Russell and Derek Jarman*, Mathew Melia ed. ReFocus: The Films of Ken Russell, U Edinburgh, 2023
5. **Edward Norman**, *Religious Symbolism in British Film: Derek Jarman*, York Minister, 2004
6. **Ken Russell**, *The Lion Roars*, Faber & Faber, 1994

Ken Russell and D.H. Lawrence

1. **Mateja Dedović**, *An Extraordinary Parallel: Ken Russell and Dennis Potter Side by Side*, ReFocus: The Films of Ken Russell, U Edinburgh, 2023
2. **Stephen Walsch**, *Stravinsky: The Second Exile, France & America*, University of California, 2008
3. **Caroline Langhorst**, *Performed Masculinities: Oliver Reed in Ken Russell's Films of the 'Long 1960's'*, ReFocus The Films of Ken Russell, University of Edinburgh, 2023
4. **Virginia Woolf**, *Character in Fiction*, from *Selected Essays*, Oxford, 2009
5. **Virginia Woolf**, *Character in Fiction*, from *Selected Essays*
6. **John Richardson**, *A Life of Picasso Volume 3 1917-1932*, Knopf, 2007

The Devils

1. **Ken Russell**, *The Lion Roars*, Faber & Faber, 1994
2. **Aldous Huxley**, *The Devils of Loudun*, Harper Perennial, 2009
3. **Ken Russell**, *The Lion Roars*, Faber & Faber, 1994
4. **John Baxter**, *Ken Russell: An Appalling Talent*, Michael Joseph, 1973
5. **Aldous Huxley**, *The Devils of Loudun*
6. **Francis Bacon and David Sylvester**, *The Brutality of Fact: Interviews with Francis Bacon*, Thames & Hudson, 1987
7. **Brian Hoyle**, *No Better Director to Lean From: The Collaboration and Parallel Careers of Ken Russell and Derek Jarman*, ReFocus: The Films of Ken Russell, University of Edinburgh, 2023
8. **Ken Russell**, *The Lion Roars*, Faber & Faber, 1994
9. **Michel Foucault**, *Discipline and Punish: The Birth of the Prison*, Vintage Books, 1965
10. **Ken Russell**, *The Lion Roars*, Faber & Faber, 1994
11. **Mark Kermode**, *Director Ken Russell, The King of Cult Classics Who was so Much More than a Sensationalist*
12. **Adam Powell**, *Nicolas Winding Refn and the Ken Russell Style*, ReFocus: the Films of Ken Russell, U Edinburgh, 2023
13. **Albert Camus**, *The Rebel, an Essay on Man in Revolt*, Vintage Books, 1992
14. **Caroline Langhorst**, *Performed Masculinities: Oliver Reed in Ken Russell's Films of the "Long 1960's,"* ReFocus: the Films of Ken Russell, Edinburgh University, 2023
15. **Ingmar Bergman**, *Interview: Religion and God*, 1962, YouTube
16. **Oliver Sacks**, *The Possessed*, from *The Man Who Mistook His Wife for a Hat*, Everyman's Library, 2023

Mahler

1. **Ken Russell**, Altered States, the Autobiography, Bantam, 1991
2. **Virginia Woolf**, Mr. Bennett and Mrs. Brown, Selected Essays, Oxford, 2009
3. **Ken Russell**, The Lion Roars: Ken Russell on Film, Faber & Faber, 1994
4. **Ken Russell**, Interview, ClassicFM.com
5. **Leo Carey**, The Meaning of Mahler, New York Review of Books, December 17, 2015
6. **Ken Russell**, Interview, ClassicFM.com

Tommy

1. **Bruce Fink**, Rock Musical Tommy Has Resonance in Real Life Psychoanalysis: The Work of French Doctor Jacques Lacan Supports the Play's Basic Story Line, Los Angeles Times, October 4, 1992
2. **Greil Marcus**, Lipstick Traces: A Secret History of the 20th Century, Harvard, 1988

Gothic

1. **Dorothy & Thomas Hoobler**, Little,Brown The Monsters: Mary Shelley & the Curse of Frankenstein, Little,Brown 2005
2. The Monsters: Mary Shelley & the Curse of Frankenstein

Hollywood Detour

1. **Ken Russell Films**, The Boy Friend, Films and Filming vol. 18, 1 October, 1971
2. **NJ Stevenson**, Shirley Russell and the Role of The Boy Friend in 1970's Retro, ReFocus: The Films of Ken Russell, University of Edinburgh, 2023
3. **Twiggy**, Twiggy, Granada Publishing, 1975
4. **Twiggy**, Twiggy
5. **NJ Stevenson**, Shirley Russell and the Role of The Boy Friend in 1970's Retro
6. **NJ Stevenson**, Shirley Russell and the Role of The Boy Friend in 1970's Retro
7. **NJ Stevenson**, Shirley Russell and the Role of The Boy Friend in 1970's Retro
8. **Adrian Garvey**, The Boy Friend: Ken Russell's 'Anti-Musical', in Laurel Forster and Sue Harper (eds), British Culture and Society in the 1970's: The Lost Decade, Cambridge Scholars Publishing, 2010
9. **Ken Russell**, The Lion Roars: Ken Russell on Film, Faber & Faber, 1994

10. **Leo Damrosch**, Jean-Jacques Rousseau: Restless Genius, Houghton Mifflin, 2005
11. **Christopher Lasch**, The Culture of Narcissism, Norton, 2018
12. **Jade Evans**, Mythologizing Valentino: Stardom, Biography and Performance Ken Russell's Valentino, ReFocus: The Films of Ken Russell, U Edinburgh, 2023
13. **Guy Debord**, Society of the Spectacle, Zone Books, 1989
14. Altered States, Wikipedia, 2025
15. Crimes of Passion, Wikipedia, 2025
16. **Ken Russell**, A British Picture, William Heinemann Ltd, 1989
17. Lair of the White Worm, Wikipedia, 2025
18. **Marc Caro**, Whore, Wikipedia, 2025

British Television Redux

1. **Roland Barthes**, The Great Family of Man, Mythologies, Hill & Wang, 2012
2. **Dorothy Parker**, Quotes, Goodreads Website, 2025
3. **Roy McMullen**, Degas: His Life, Times and Work, Houghton Mifflin, 1984
4. **Richard Dreyfuss**, Man of Honor, Wikipedia, 2025
5. **Richard Dreyfuss**, Man of Honor, Wikipedia, 2025
6. **Ken Russell**, Altered States, The Autobiography, Bantam, 1991

Filmography

Knights on Bikes (Short/1956)
Peepshow (Short/1956)
Amelia and the Angel (Short/1958)
Lourdes (Short/1958)
John Betjeman: A Poet in London (Short/BBC/1959)
Gordon Jacob (Short/BBC/1959)
Fritz Kotner (Short/BBC/1959)
Spain to Streatham: The Guitar Craze (Short/BBC/1959)
Variations on a Mechanical Theme (Short/BBC/1959)
Scottish Painters (Short/BBC/1959)
Portrait of a Goon (Short/BBC/1959)
Marie Rambert Remembers (Short/BBC/1960)
Journey Into a Lost World of Mary McCarthy (Short/BBC/1960)
Cranko at Work (Short/BBC/1960)
The Strange World of Hieronymus Bosch (Short/BBC/1960)
The Miner's Picnic (Short/BBC/1960)
Picasso (Short/BBC/1960)
Architecture of Entertainment (Short/BBC/1960)
A House in Bayswater (Short/BBC/1960)
Shelagh Delaney's Salford (Short/BBC/1960)

The Light Fantastic (Short/BBC/1960)
Lotte Lenya Sings Kurt Weill (Short/BBC/1960)
London Moods (Short/BBC/1961)
Jack Yeats (Short/BBC-1961)
Old Battersea House (Short/BBC/1961)
Prokofiev: Portrait of a Soviet Composer (Short/BBC/1961)
Daumier: A Double Life (Short/BBC/1961)
Antonio Gaudi (Short/BBC/1961)
Preservation Man (Short/BBC/1962)
Lonely Shore (Short/BBC/1962)
Elgar: Portrait of a Composer (Short/BBC/1962)
Pop Goes the Easel (Short/BBC/1962)
Mr. Chescher's Traction Engines (Short/BBC/1962)
Watch the Birdie (Short/BBC/1963)
French Dressing (1964)
The Diary of a Nobody: The Domestic Jottings of a City Clerk (Short/BBC/1964)
Bela Bartok (Short/BBC/1964)
Alfred Hitchcock (Short/BBC/1964)
The Dotty World of James Lloyd (Short/BBC/1964)
The Debussy Film (BBC/1965)
Always on Sunday (Short/BBC/1965)
Don't Shoot the Composer (Short/Sunday Night-ITV/1966)
Isadora Duncan, The Biggest Dancer in the World (Short/BBC/1966)
Billion Dollar Brain (1967)
Dante's Inferno: The Private Life of Dante Gabriel Rossetti, Poet and Painter (BBC/1967)
Song of Summer (BBC/1968)
Women In Love (1969)
Dance of the Seven Veils (Short/BBC/1970)
The Music Lovers (1971)
The Devils (1971)
The Boy Friend (1971)
Savage Messiah (1972)
Mahler (1974)
Tommy (1975)
Lisztomania (1975)
Valentino (1977)
Clouds of Glory Part 1: William and Dorothy Part 2: The Rime of the Ancient Mariner (The South Bank Show/1978)
Altered States (1980)
Crimes of Passion (1984)
Rick Wakeman: It's a Lovely Life (Music Video/1984)
Elton John: Nikita (Music Video/1985)
Cliff Richard: She's so Beautiful (Music Video/1985)
Faust (Opera/1985)
Elton John: Cry to Heaven (Music Video/1986)

Cliff Richard & Sarah Brightman: All I Ask of You (Music Video/1986)
Gothic (1986)
Sarah Brightman & Steve Harley: The Phantom of the Opera (Music Video/1986)
Nessun Dorma (Short/ Omnibus Film: Aria/1987)
The Planets (Short/The South Bank Show/1983)
Vaughan Williams: A Symphonic Portrait (Short/The South Bank Show/1984)
Ken Russell's ABC of British Music (Short/The South Bank Show/1988)
Salome's Last Dance (1988)
The Lair of the White Worm (1988)
A British Picture (Short/The South Bank Show/1989)
The Rainbow (1989)
Pandora's Box: It's All Coming Back to Me Now (Music Video/1989)
Dusk Before Fireworks (Short/Omnibus Film: Women and Men: Stories of Seduction/1990)
The Strange Affliction of Anton Bruckner (Short/1990)
Whore (1991)
Prisoner of Honor (1991)
Road to Mandalay (Short/1991)
The Secret Life of Arnold Bax (Short/The South Bank Show/1992)
Lady Chatterley (Mini Series/BBC/1993)
The Mystery of Dr. Martinu (Short/1993)
Bryan Adams: Diana (Music Video/1993)
Treasure Island (Short/1995)
Four Windows: William Walton, Bernard George Stevens, Benjamin Frankel & Humphrey Searle (Short/South Bank Show/1995)
Alice In Russialand (Short/1995)
Mindbender (1996)
The Insatiable Mrs. Kirsch (Short/Omnibus Film: Tales of Erotica/1996)
Ken Russell: In Search of the English Folk Song (Short/Channel Four Films/1997)
Dogboys (1998)
Lion's Mouth (Short/2000)
The Fall of the Louse of Usher: A Gothic Tale for the 21st Century (2002)
Elgar: Fantasy of a Composer on a Bicycle (Short/South Bank Show/2002)
Revenge of the Elephant Man (Short/2004)
The Girl With the Golden Breasts (Short/ Omnibus Film: Trapped Ashes/2006)
Charlotte Brontë Enters the Big Brother's House (Short/2006)
Ein Kitten für Hitler (A Kitten for Hitler) (Short/2007)
Boudica Bites Back (Short/2009)

Index of films

Alfred Hitchcock (Short/BBC/1964) 148, 298, 373

Altered States (1980) 290, 294

Always on Sunday (Short/BBC/1965) 62, 64, 67, 117, 157, 274, 320

Amelia and the Angel (Short/1958) 14, 40, 41, 150, 167, 300, 392

Bela Bartok (Short/BBC/1964) 33, 109

Billion Dollar Brain (1967) 154, 156, 157, 177

Boudica Bites Back (Short/2009) 400, 401

The Boy Friend (1971) 30, 244, 273–277, 290

A British Picture (Short/The South Bank Show/1989) 17, 319, 345, 349

Bryan Adams: Diana (Music Video/1993) 380

Cliff Richard & Sarah Brightman: All I Ask of You (Music Video/1986) 338

Cliff Richard: She's so Beautiful (Music Video/1985) 334

Clouds of Glory Part 1: William and Dorothy Part 2: The Rime of the Ancient Mariner (The South Bank Show/1978) 319, 321, 323

Crimes of Passion (1984) 31, 295, 296, 298, 332, 348

Dance of the Seven Veils (Short/BBC/1970) 30, 64, 80–82, 88, 117, 236, 287, 288, 301, 347, 389, 399

Dante's Inferno: The Private Life of Dante Gabriel Rossetti, Poet and Painter (BBC/1967) 18, 34, 35, 64, 82, 113–135, 181, 245, 319, 393

Daumier: A Double Life (Short/BBC/1961) 15

The Debussy Film (BBC/1965) 59, 61, 64, 65, 109, 117, 127, 157, 245, 320, 327, 373

The Devils (1971) 166, 167, 169, 201–21, 273, 274, 362, 390

The Diary of a Nobody: The Domestic Jottings of a City Clerk (Short/BBC/1964) 151

Dogboys (1998) 388

Don't Shoot the Composer (Short/Sunday Night-ITV/1966) 16, 75, 78, 109, 177

The Dotty World of James Lloyd (Short/BBC/1964) 15

Dusk Before Fireworks (Short/Omnibus Film: Women and Men Stories of Seduction/1990) 352

Ein Kitten für Hitler (A Kitten for Hitler) (Short/2007) 398–400

Elgar: Fantasy of a Composer on a Bicycle (Short/South Bank Show/2002) 391, 395

Elgar: Portrait of a Composer (Short/BBC/1962) 16, 19, 21, 28, 29, 52–59

Elton John: Cry to Heaven (Music Video/1986) 336, 338

Elton John: Nikita (Music Video/1985) 332, 345

The Fall of the Louse of Usher: A Gothic Tale for the 21st Century (2002) 31, 389

Faust (Opera/1985) 237, 335, 336

French Dressing (1964) 59, 76, 152–154

The Girl With the Golden Breasts (Short/ Omnibus Film: "Trapped Ashes"/2006) 396, 397

Gordon Jacob (Short/BBC/1959) 16

Gothic (1986) 35, 261–71, 307, 341, 342

A House in Bayswater (Short/BBC/1960) 19, 47, 51

The Insatiable Mrs. Kirsch (Short/Omnibus Film: "Tales of Erotica"/1996) 382–384

Isadora Duncan, the Biggest Dancer in the World (Short/BBC/1966) 64, 69, 117, 166, 224, 373, 380

John Betjeman: A Poet in London (Short/BBC/1959) 16, 43

Journey Into a Lost World of Mary McCarthy (Short/BBC/1960) 15

Ken Russell: In Search of the English Folk Song (Short Channel Four Films/1997) 384–388

Ken Russell's ABC of British Music (Short/The South Bank Show/1988) 342, 384

Knights on Bikes (Short/1956) 37

Lady Chatterley (Mini Series/BBC/1993) 35, 177, 189–199

The Lair of the White Worm (1988) 307–312

The Light Fantastic (Short/BBC/1960) 19

Lion's Mouth (Short/2000) 388

Lisztomania (1975) 30, 277–282

London Moods (Short/BBC/1961) **51, 155, 329, 336, 367**

Lonely Shore (Short/BBC/1962) **19, 41**

Lotte Lenya Sings Kurt Weill (Short/BBC/1960) **15**

Mahler (1974) **48, 223-39, 277, 283, 284, 344, 346**

Mindbender (1996) **384**

The Music Lovers (1971) **127, 157-60, 164, 254, 284, 320, 359**

The Mystery of Dr. Martinu (Short/1993) **372, 373, 374-380**

Nessun Dorma (Short/ Omnibus Film: Aria/1987) **299, 351, 373**

Padora's Box: It's All Coming Back to Me Now (Music Video/1989) **349, 373**

Peepshow (Short/1956) **38**

The Planets (Short/The South Bank Show/1983) **324-326**

Pop Goes the Easel (Short/BBC/1962) **35, 91-111, 120, 248, 251, 387**

Prisoner of Honor (1991) **361-366**

Prokofiev: Portrait of a Soviet Composer (Short/BBC/1961) **15, 16, 27, 28, 139, 283**

The Rainbow (1989) **35, 177, 187-89, 307, 349**

Rick Wakeman: It's a Lovely Life (Music Video/1984) **332**

Road to Mandalay (Short/1991) **12, 366-368**

The Secret Life of Arnold Bax (Short/The South Bank Show/1992) **368-372**

Salome's Last Dance (1988) **387, 301-307, 349**

Sarah Brightman & Steve Harley: The Phantom of the Opera (Music Video/1986) **339**

Savage Messiah (1972) **151, 166-172, 224, 347**

Scottish Painters (Short/BBC/1959) **15, 19**

Shelagh Delaney's Salford (Short/BBC/1960) **15, 21, 45-47**

Song of Summer (BBC/1968) **34, 64, 81, 117, 137-149, 342**

Spain to Streatham: The Guitar Craze (Short/BBC/1959) **19**

The Strange Affliction of Anton Bruckner (Short/1990) **354-362**

15, 19

Tommy (1975) **240-259, 278, 347**

Treasure Island (Short/1995) **381**

Valentino (1977) **224, 282-290, 321**

Ralph Vaughan Williams: A Symphonic Portrait (Short/The South Bank Show/1984) **326-332**

Watch the Birdie (Short/BBC/1963) **48**

Whore (1991) **312-316**

Women In Love (1969) **35, 101, 175-187, 191, 192, 195, 197, 254**

412

www.ingramcontent.com/pod-product-compliance
Lightning Source LLC
Chambersburg PA
CBHW042100290426
44113CB00005B/113